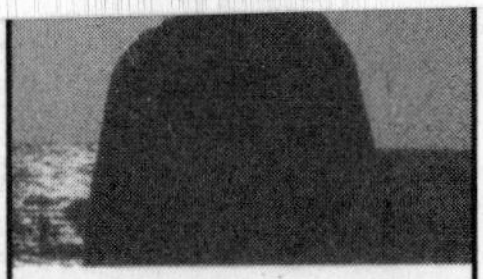

武井宏之

I want to have a bigger perspective on things.
I want to broaden my mind.
—Hiroyuki Takei

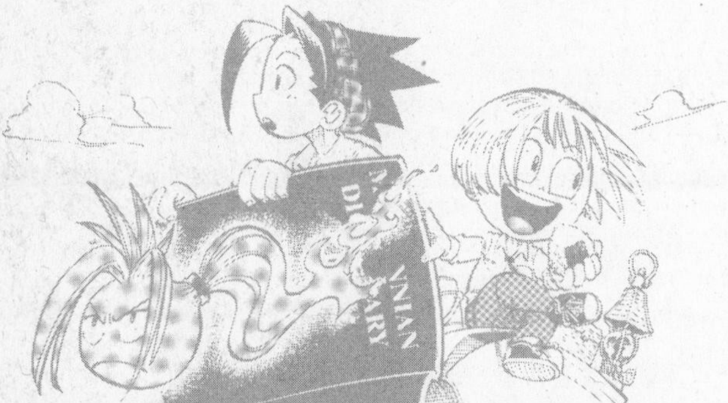
MANTANNIAN

Unconventional author/artist Hiroyuki Takei began his career by winning the coveted Hop Step Award (for new manga artists) and the Osamu Tezuka Award (named after the famous artist of the same name). After working as an assistant to famed artist Nobuhiro Watsuki, Takei debuted in **Weekly Shonen Jump** in 1997 with **Butsu Zone**, an action series based on Buddhist mythology. His multicultural adventure manga **Shaman King**, which debuted in 1998, became a hit and was adapted into an anime TV series. Takei lists Osamu Tezuka, American comics and robot anime among his many influences.

SHAMAN KING VOL.7
The SHONEN JUMP Manga Edition

This graphic novel contains material that was originally published in
English in **SHONEN JUMP** #27-31.

STORY AND ART BY
HIROYUKI TAKEI

English Adaptation/Lance Caselman
Translation/Lillian Olsen
Touch-up Art & Lettering/Kathryn Renta
Additional Touch-up/Josh Simpson
Design/Sean Lee
Editor/Pancha Diaz

Editor in Chief, Books/Alvin Lu
Editor in Chief, Magazines/Marc Weidenbaum
VP of Publishing Licensing/Rika Inouye
VP of Sales/Gonzalo Ferreyra
Sr. VP of Marketing/Liza Coppola
Publisher/Hyoe Narita

Printed in the U.S.A.

Published by VIZ Media, LLC
P.O. Box 77010
San Francisco, CA 94107

SHONEN JUMP Manga Edition
10 9 8 7 6 5 4 3 2
First printing, August 2005
Second printing, November 2007

THE WORLD'S
MOST POPULAR MANGA

www.viz.com

www.shonenjump.com

SHONEN JUMP MANGA

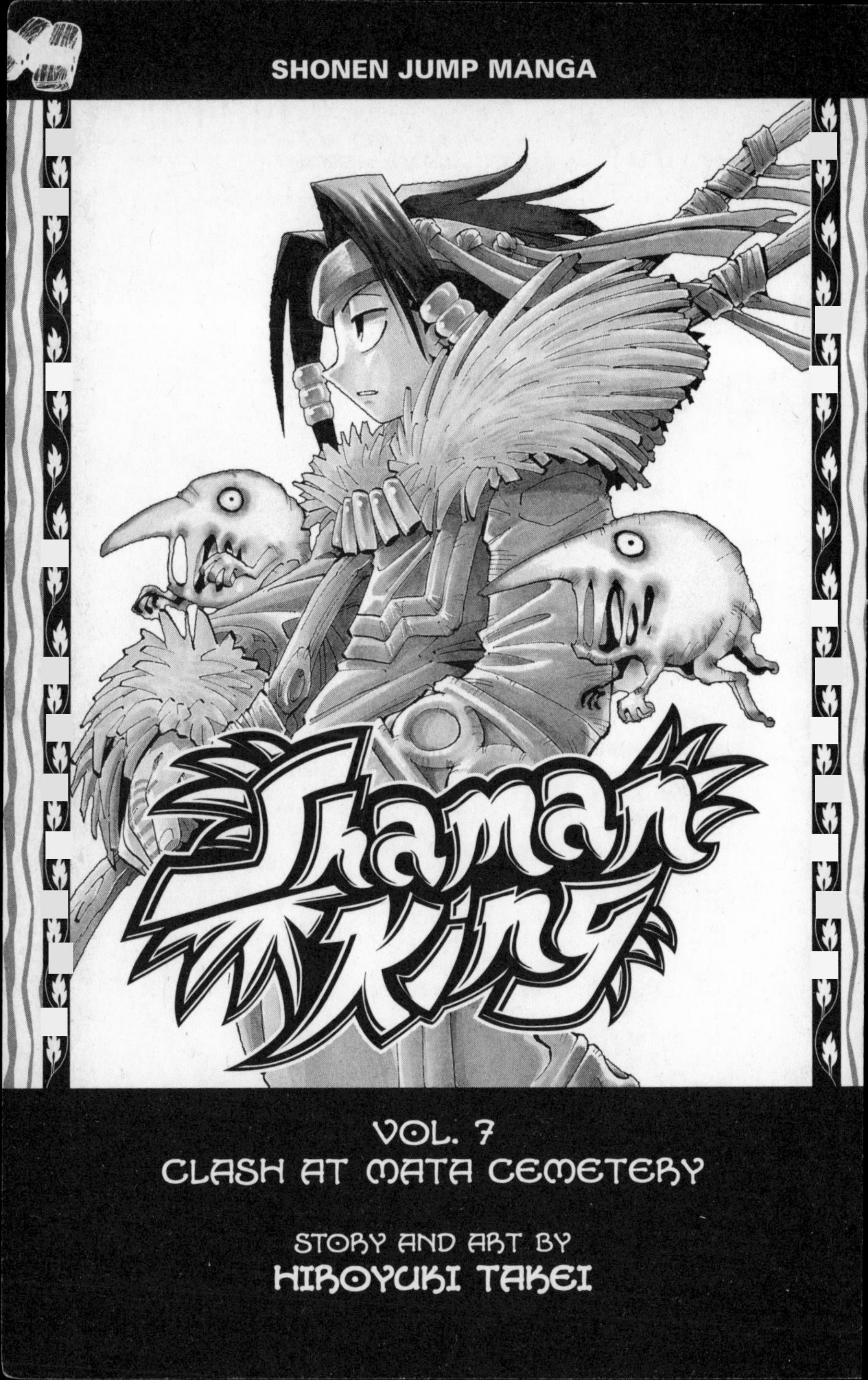
Shaman King

VOL. 7
CLASH AT MATA CEMETERY

STORY AND ART BY
HIROYUKI TAKEI

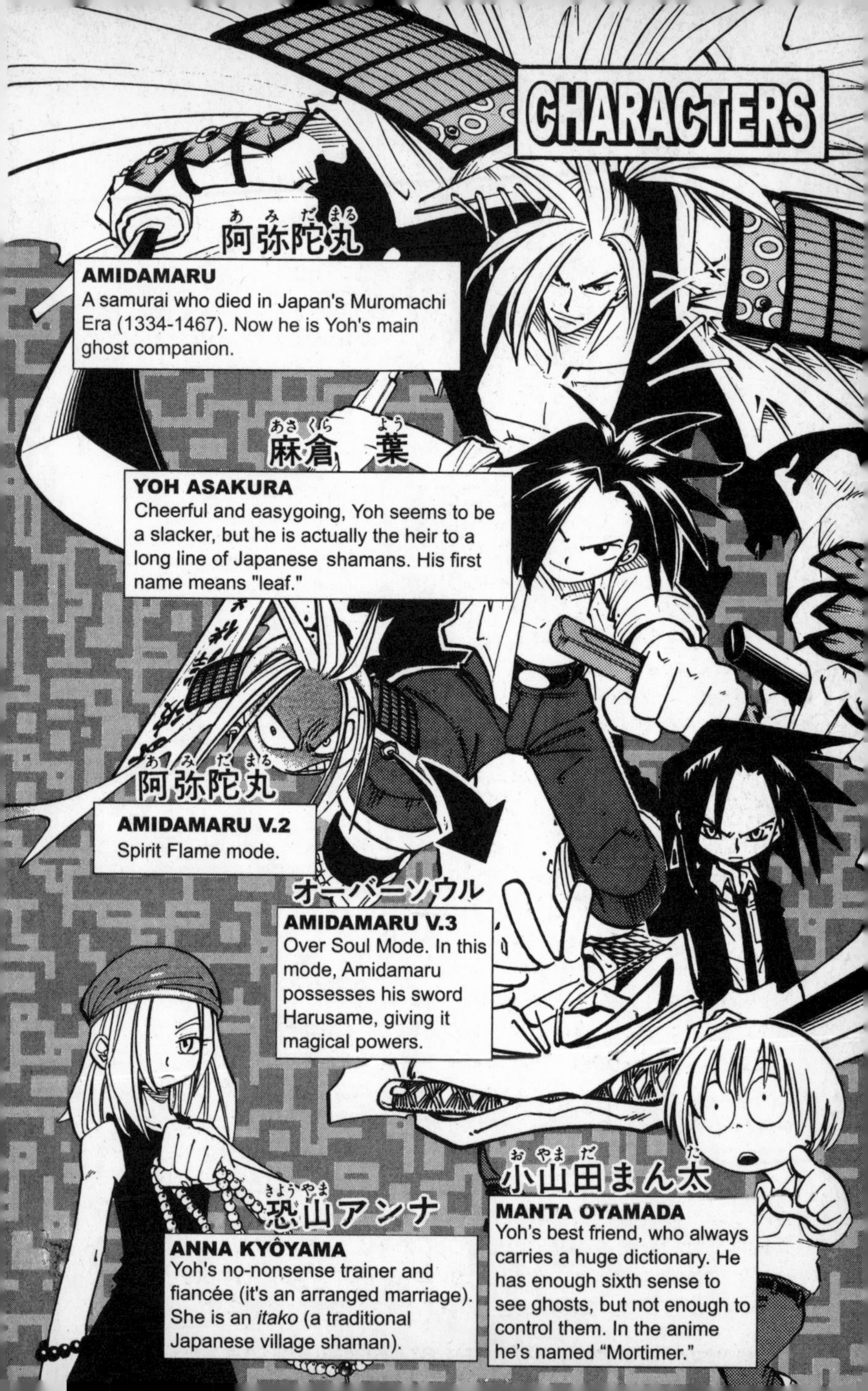
CHARACTERS
あみだまる
阿弥陀丸
AMIDAMARU
A samurai who died in Japan's Muromachi Era (1334-1467). Now he is Yoh's main ghost companion.
あさくら よう
麻倉 葉
YOH ASAKURA
Cheerful and easygoing, Yoh seems to be a slacker, but he is actually the heir to a long line of Japanese shamans. His first name means "leaf."
あみだまる
阿弥陀丸
AMIDAMARU V.2
Spirit Flame mode.
オーバーソウル
AMIDAMARU V.3
Over Soul Mode. In this mode, Amidamaru possesses his sword Harusame, giving it magical powers.
きょうやま
恐山アンナ
ANNA KYÔYAMA
Yoh's no-nonsense trainer and fiancée (it's an arranged marriage). She is an *itako* (a traditional Japanese village shaman).
おやまだ た
小山田まん太
MANTA OYAMADA
Yoh's best friend, who always carries a huge dictionary. He has enough sixth sense to see ghosts, but not enough to control them. In the anime he's named "Mortimer."

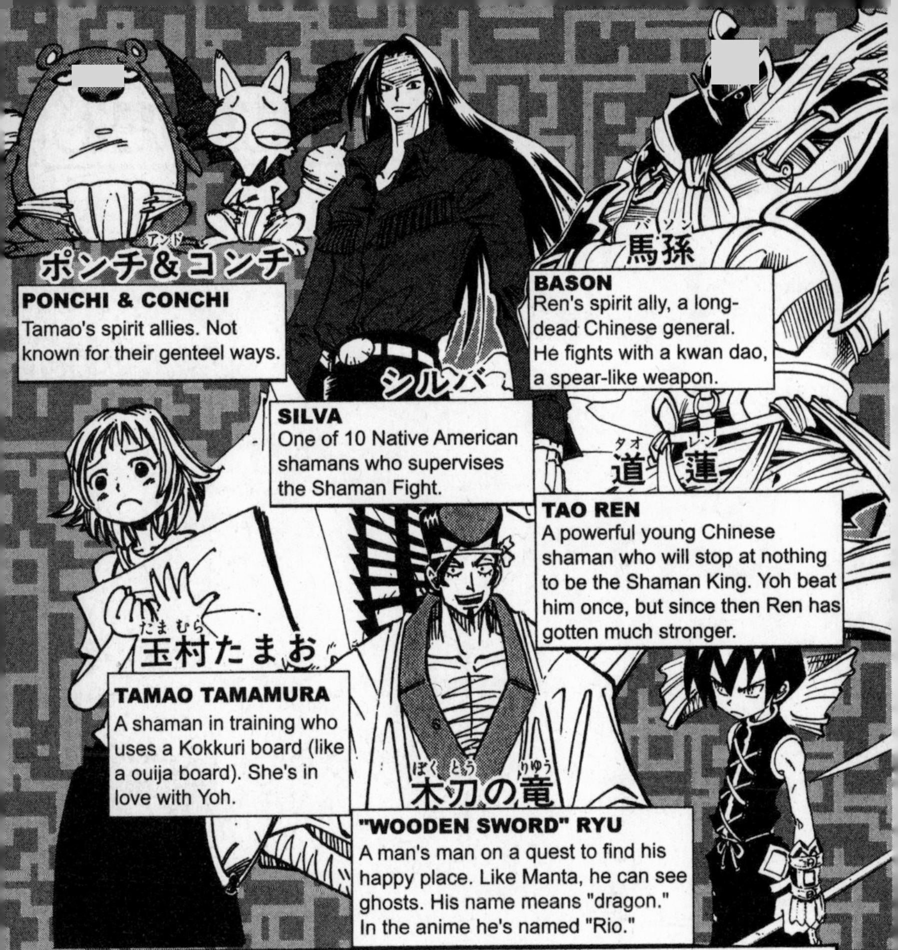

馬孫
BASON
Ren's spirit ally, a long-dead Chinese general. He fights with a kwan dao, a spear-like weapon.
ポンチ&コンチ
PONCHI & CONCHI
Tamao's spirit allies. Not known for their genteel ways.
シルバ
SILVA
One of 10 Native American shamans who supervises the Shaman Fight.
道蓮
TAO REN
A powerful young Chinese shaman who will stop at nothing to be the Shaman King. Yoh beat him once, but since then Ren has gotten much stronger.
玉村たまお
TAMAO TAMAMURA
A shaman in training who uses a Kokkuri board (like a ouija board). She's in love with Yoh.
木刀の竜
"WOODEN SWORD" RYU
A man's man on a quest to find his happy place. Like Manta, he can see ghosts. His name means "dragon." In the anime he's named "Rio."

THE STORY SO FAR...

Yoh Asakura is a shaman — one of the gifted few who, thanks to training or natural talent, can channel spirits that most people can't even see. His goal: to win the "Shaman Fight in Tokyo," the once-every-500-years tournament to see who can shape humanity's future and become the Shaman King. Already, Yoh has won one match and lost one match...and his next match is against the powerful shaman Tao Ren! To prepare for the fight, Yoh went home to Izumo, Japan's land of the gods, to learn how to develop a stronger spirit. But will Yoh's new and improved Over Soul be enough?

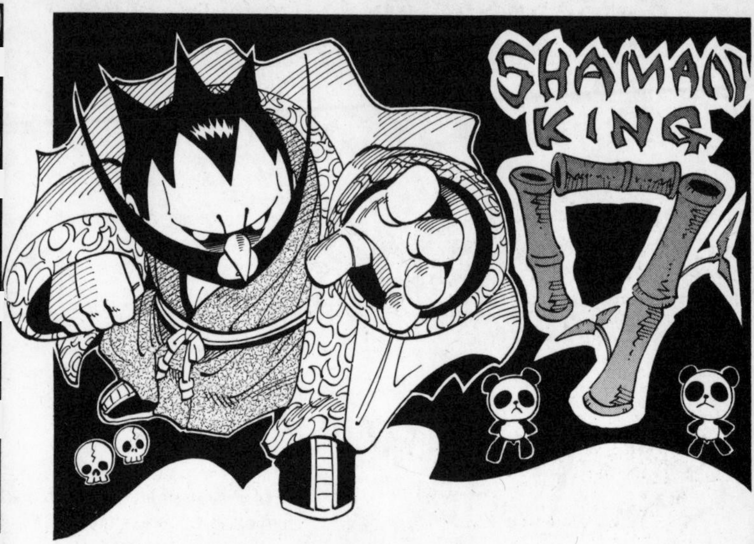
SHAMAN KING

VOL. 7: CLASH AT MATA CEMETERY

CONTENTS

Reincarnation 54: Slogan

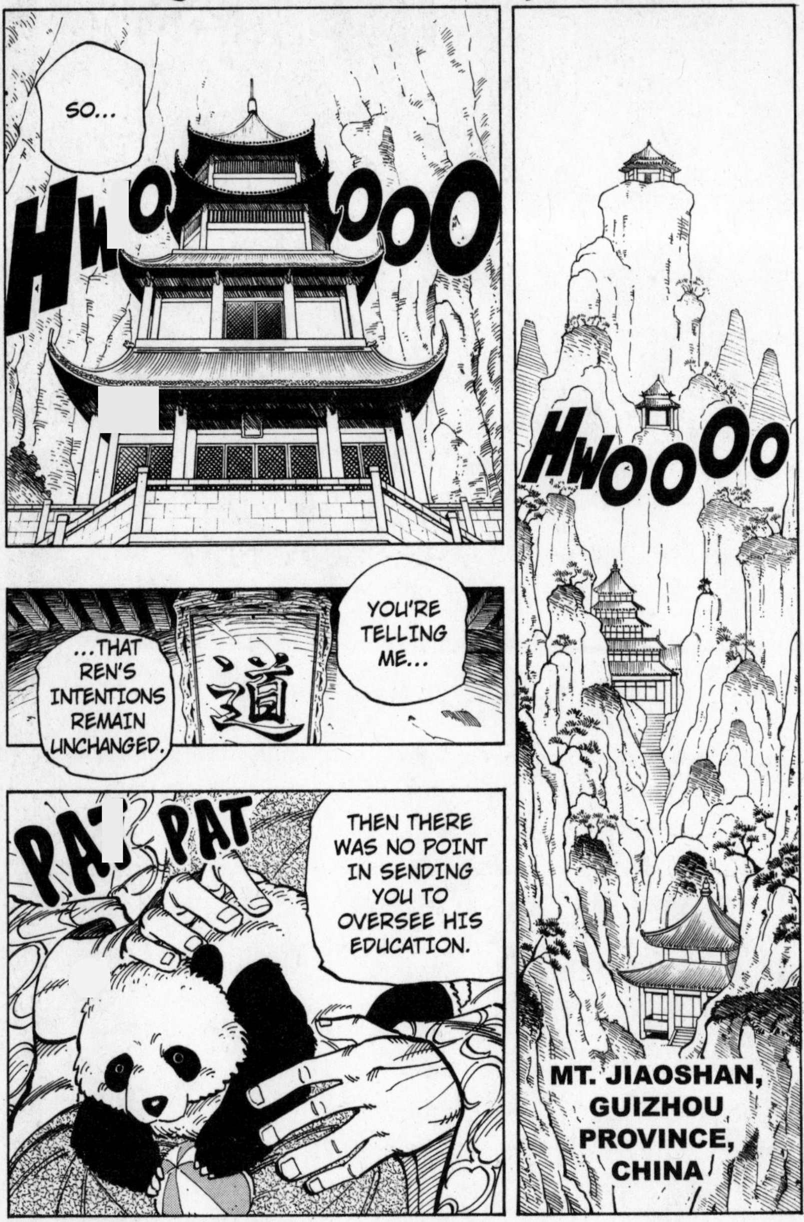
HWOOOO
MT. JIAOSHAN, GUIZHOU PROVINCE, CHINA
SO...
HWOOOOO
YOU'RE TELLING ME...
...THAT REN'S INTENTIONS REMAIN UNCHANGED.
THEN THERE WAS NO POINT IN SENDING YOU TO OVERSEE HIS EDUCATION.
PAT PAT

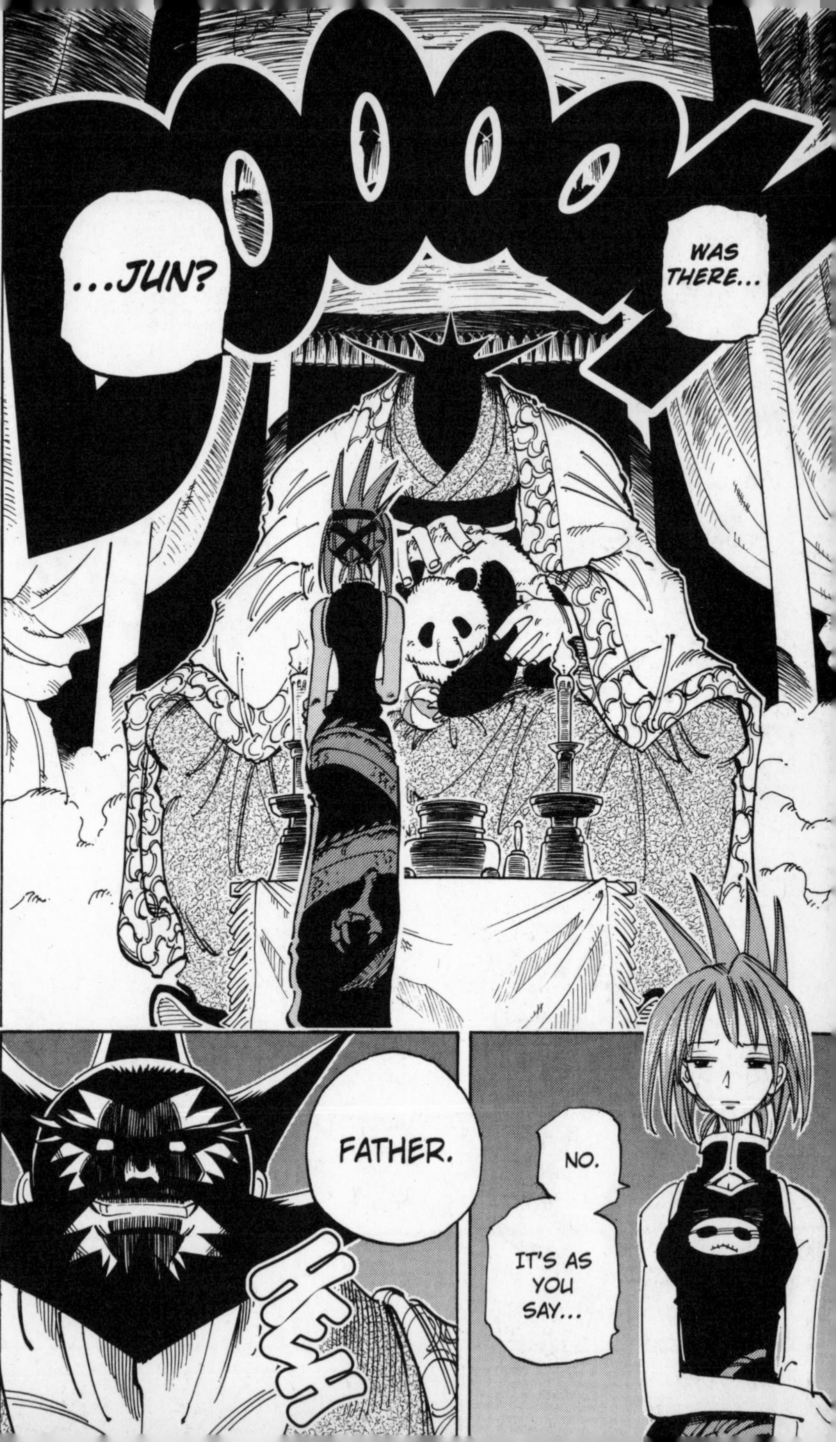
WAS THERE...
...JUN?
NO.
IT'S AS YOU SAY...
FATHER.
HEH

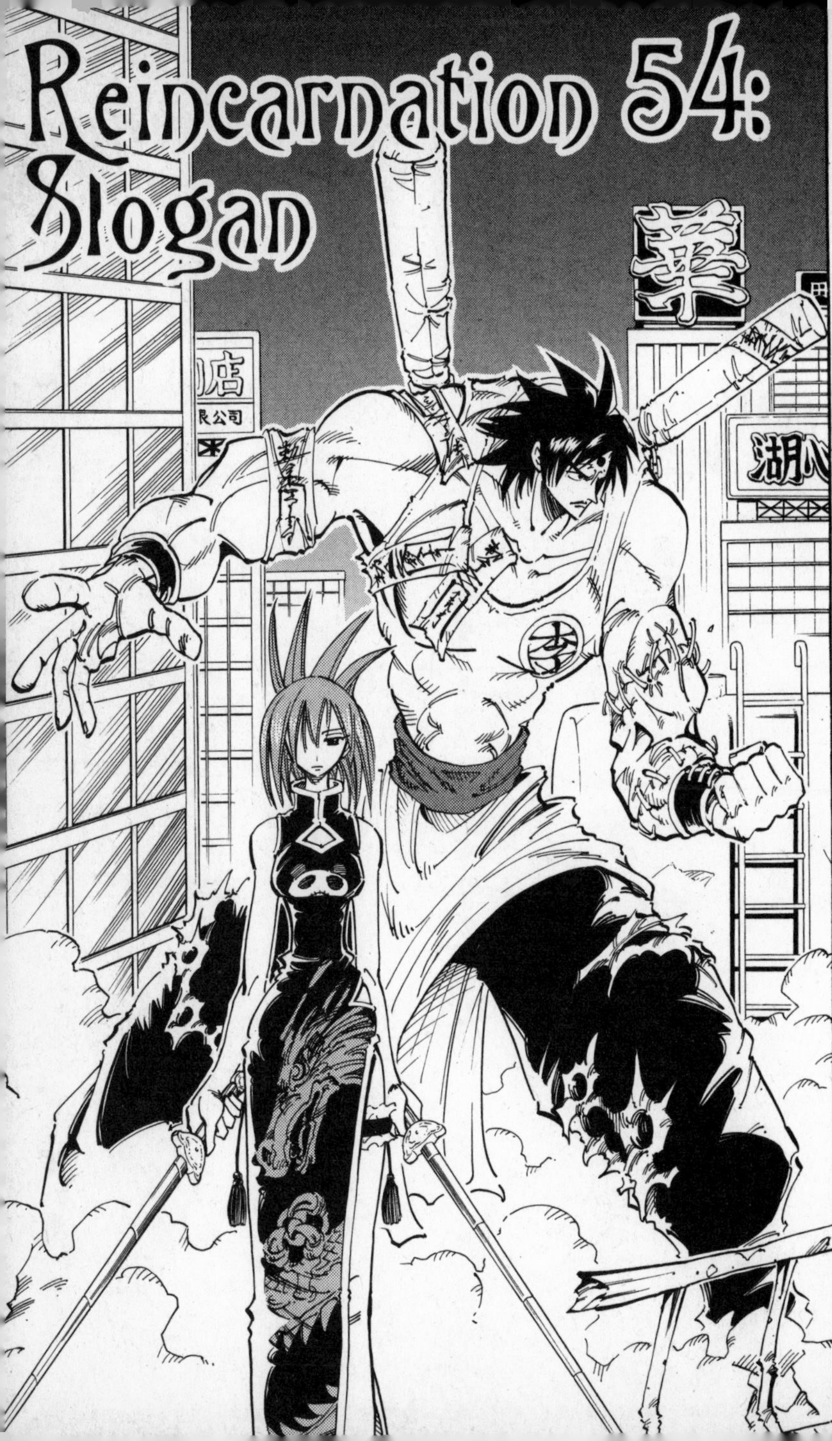
Reincarnation 54:
Slogan
華

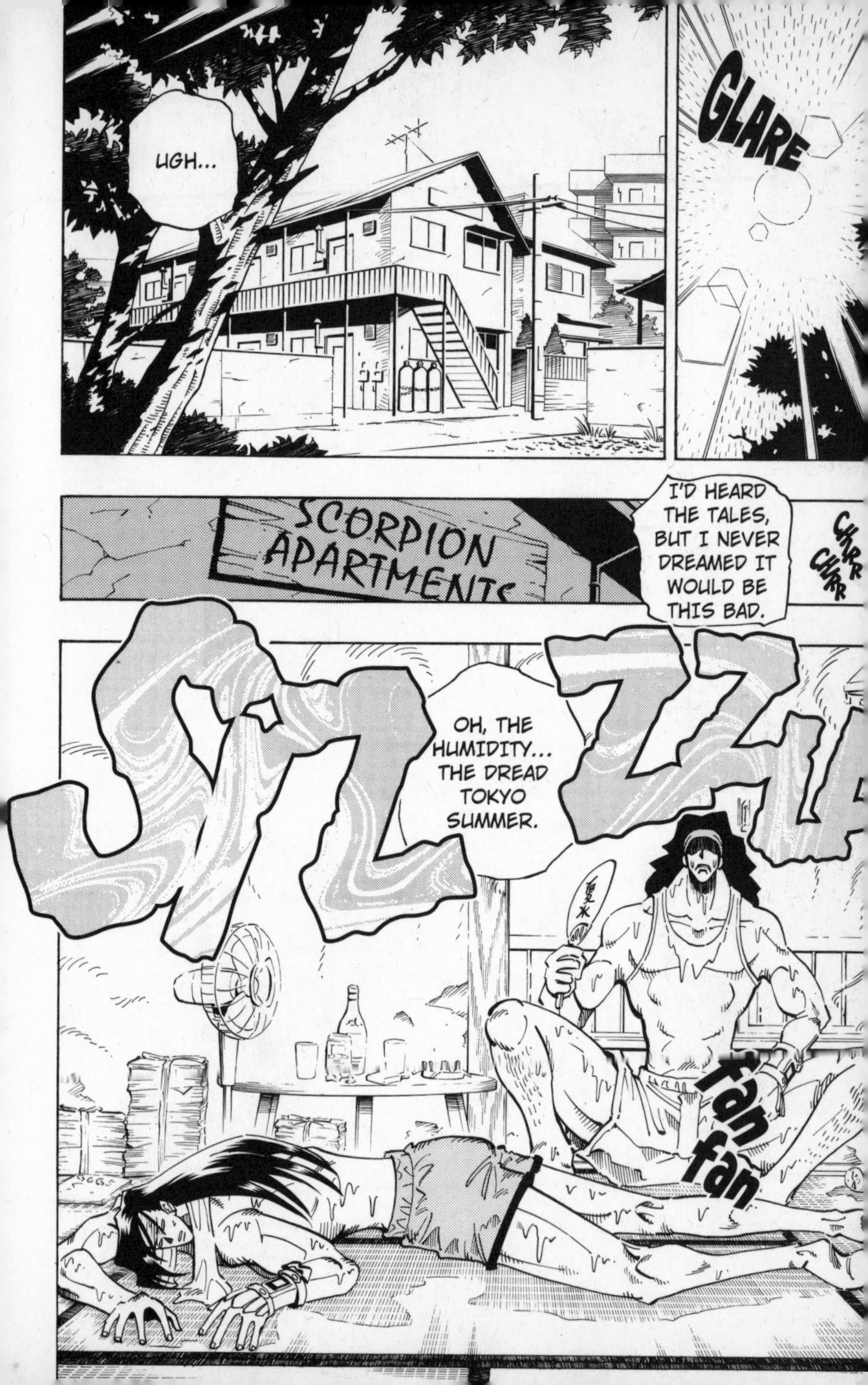
GLARE
UGH...
SCORPION APARTMENTS
I'D HEARD THE TALES, BUT I NEVER DREAMED IT WOULD BE THIS BAD.
CHIRR CHIRR
OH, THE HUMIDITY... THE DREAD TOKYO SUMMER.
fan fan

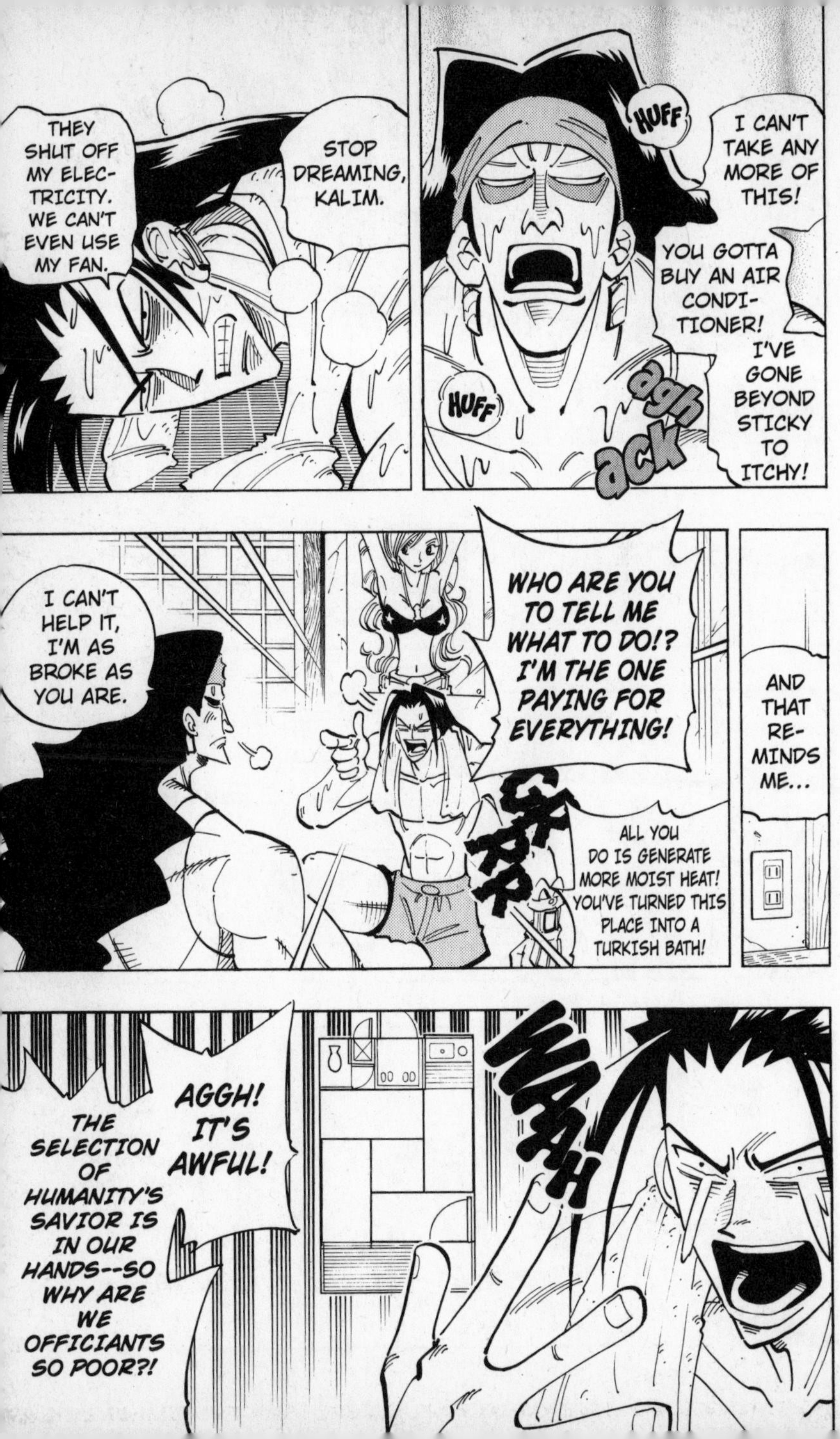
HUFF
I CAN'T TAKE ANY MORE OF THIS!
YOU GOTTA BUY AN AIR CONDITIONER!
I'VE GONE BEYOND STICKY TO ITCHY!
agh
ack
HUFF
STOP DREAMING, KALIM.
THEY SHUT OFF MY ELECTRICITY. WE CAN'T EVEN USE MY FAN.
AND THAT REMINDS ME...
ALL YOU DO IS GENERATE MORE MOIST HEAT! YOU'VE TURNED THIS PLACE INTO A TURKISH BATH!
I CAN'T HELP IT, I'M AS BROKE AS YOU ARE.
WHO ARE YOU TO TELL ME WHAT TO DO!? I'M THE ONE PAYING FOR EVERYTHING!
WAAAH
AGGH! IT'S AWFUL!
THE SELECTION OF HUMANITY'S SAVIOR IS IN OUR HANDS--SO WHY ARE WE OFFICIANTS SO POOR?!

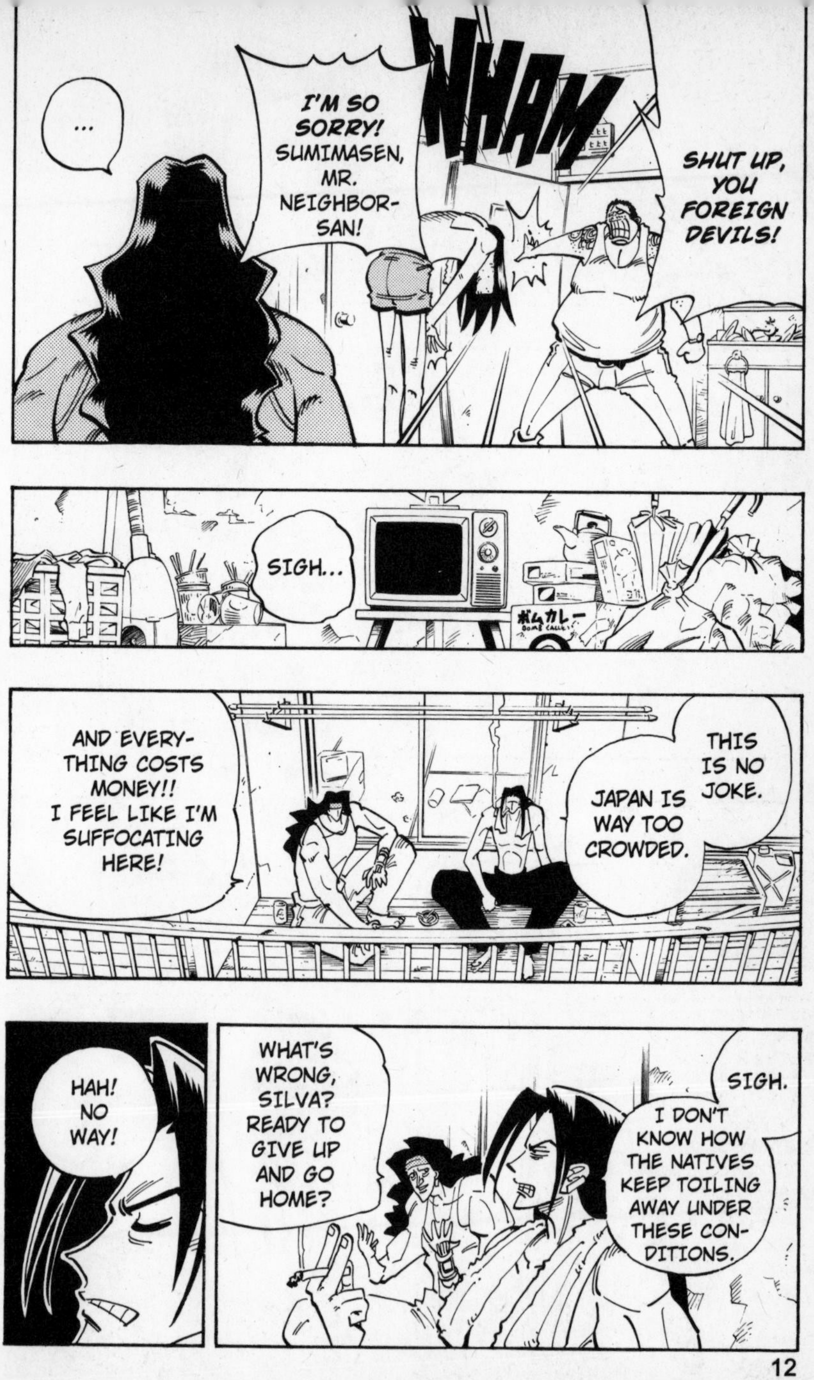
SHUT UP, YOU FOREIGN DEVILS!
WHAM
I'M SO SORRY! SUMIMASEN, MR. NEIGHBOR-SAN!
...
SIGH...
ボムカレー
THIS IS NO JOKE.
JAPAN IS WAY TOO CROWDED.
AND EVERYTHING COSTS MONEY!! I FEEL LIKE I'M SUFFOCATING HERE!
SIGH.
I DON'T KNOW HOW THE NATIVES KEEP TOILING AWAY UNDER THESE CONDITIONS.
WHAT'S WRONG, SILVA? READY TO GIVE UP AND GO HOME?
HAH! NO WAY!

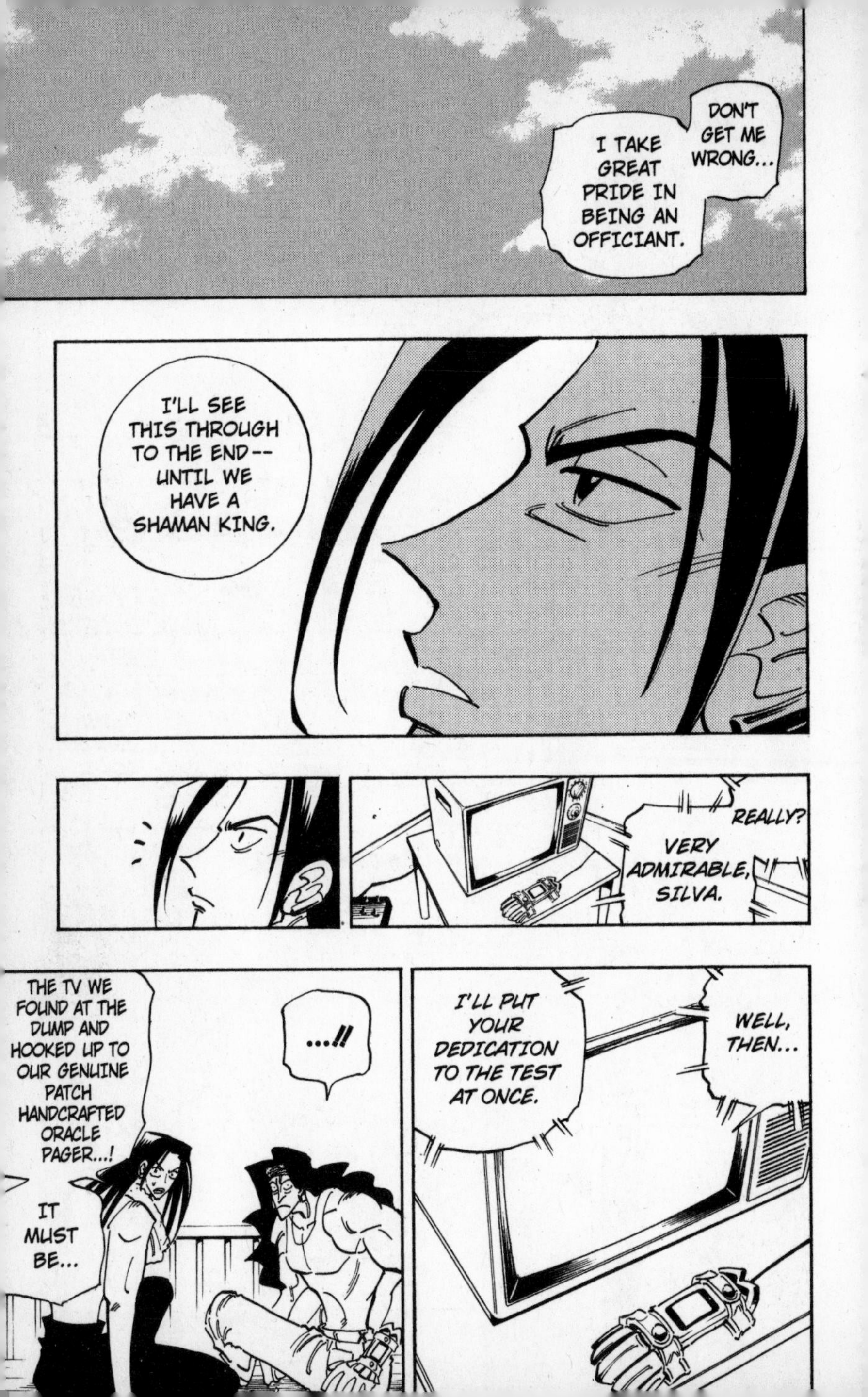
DON'T GET ME WRONG...
I TAKE GREAT PRIDE IN BEING AN OFFICIANT.
I'LL SEE THIS THROUGH TO THE END-- UNTIL WE HAVE A SHAMAN KING.
REALLY?
VERY ADMIRABLE, SILVA.
WELL, THEN...
I'LL PUT YOUR DEDICATION TO THE TEST AT ONCE.
...!!
THE TV WE FOUND AT THE DUMP AND HOOKED UP TO OUR GENUINE PATCH HANDCRAFTED ORACLE PAGER...!
IT MUST BE...

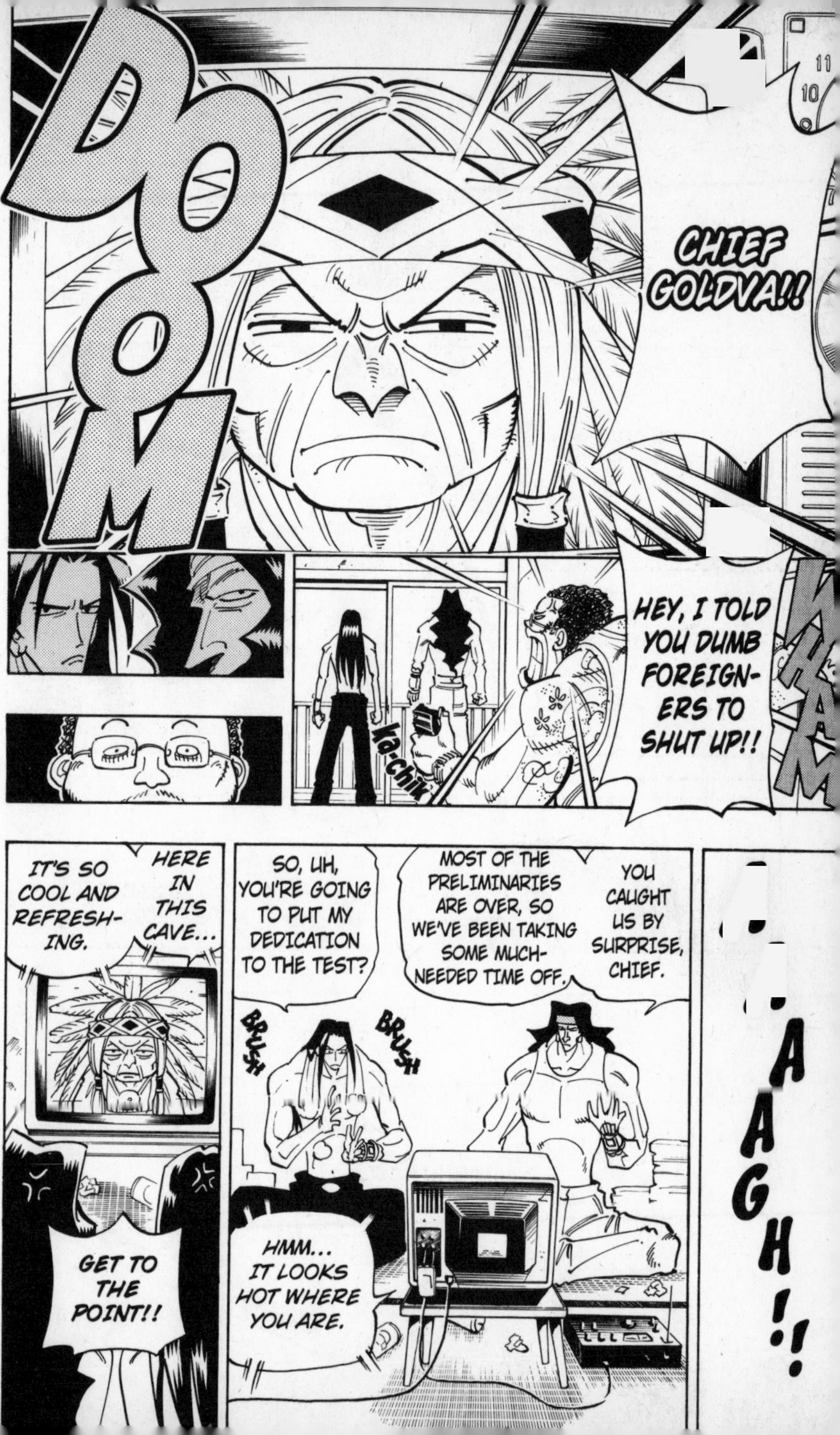
DOOM
CHIEF GOLDVA!!
HEY, I TOLD YOU DUMB FOREIGNERS TO SHUT UP!!
ka-chik
AAGH!!
YOU CAUGHT US BY SURPRISE, CHIEF.
MOST OF THE PRELIMINARIES ARE OVER, SO WE'VE BEEN TAKING SOME MUCH-NEEDED TIME OFF.
SO, UH, YOU'RE GOING TO PUT MY DEDICATION TO THE TEST?
BRUSH
BRUSH
HMM... IT LOOKS HOT WHERE YOU ARE.
HERE IN THIS CAVE...
IT'S SO COOL AND REFRESHING.
GET TO THE POINT!!

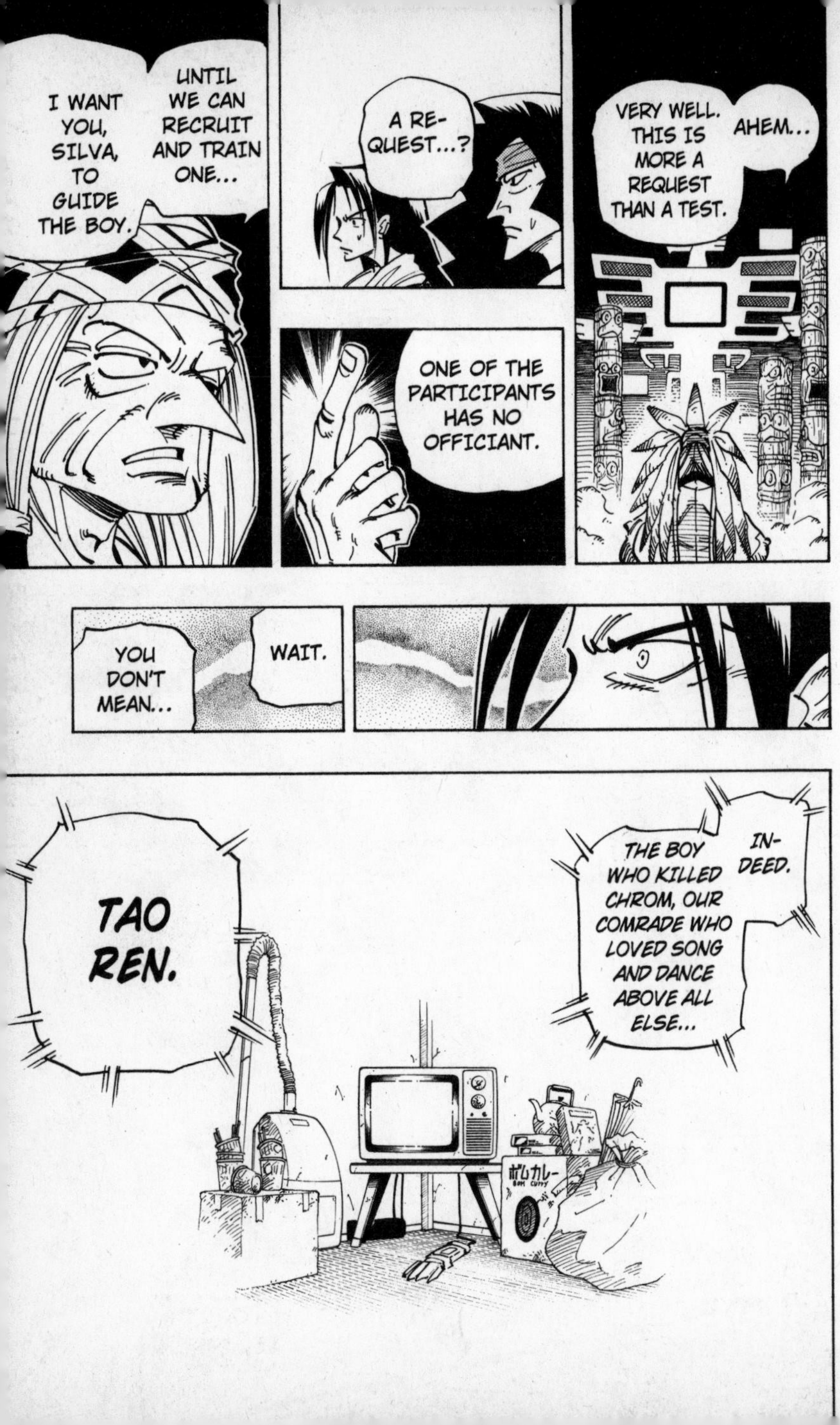
AHEM...
VERY WELL. THIS IS MORE A REQUEST THAN A TEST.
A RE-QUEST...?
ONE OF THE PARTICIPANTS HAS NO OFFICIANT.
UNTIL WE CAN RECRUIT AND TRAIN ONE...
I WANT YOU, SILVA, TO GUIDE THE BOY.
WAIT.
YOU DON'T MEAN...
IN-DEED.
THE BOY WHO KILLED CHROM, OUR COMRADE WHO LOVED SONG AND DANCE ABOVE ALL ELSE...
TAO REN.
ボムカレー
BOM CURRY

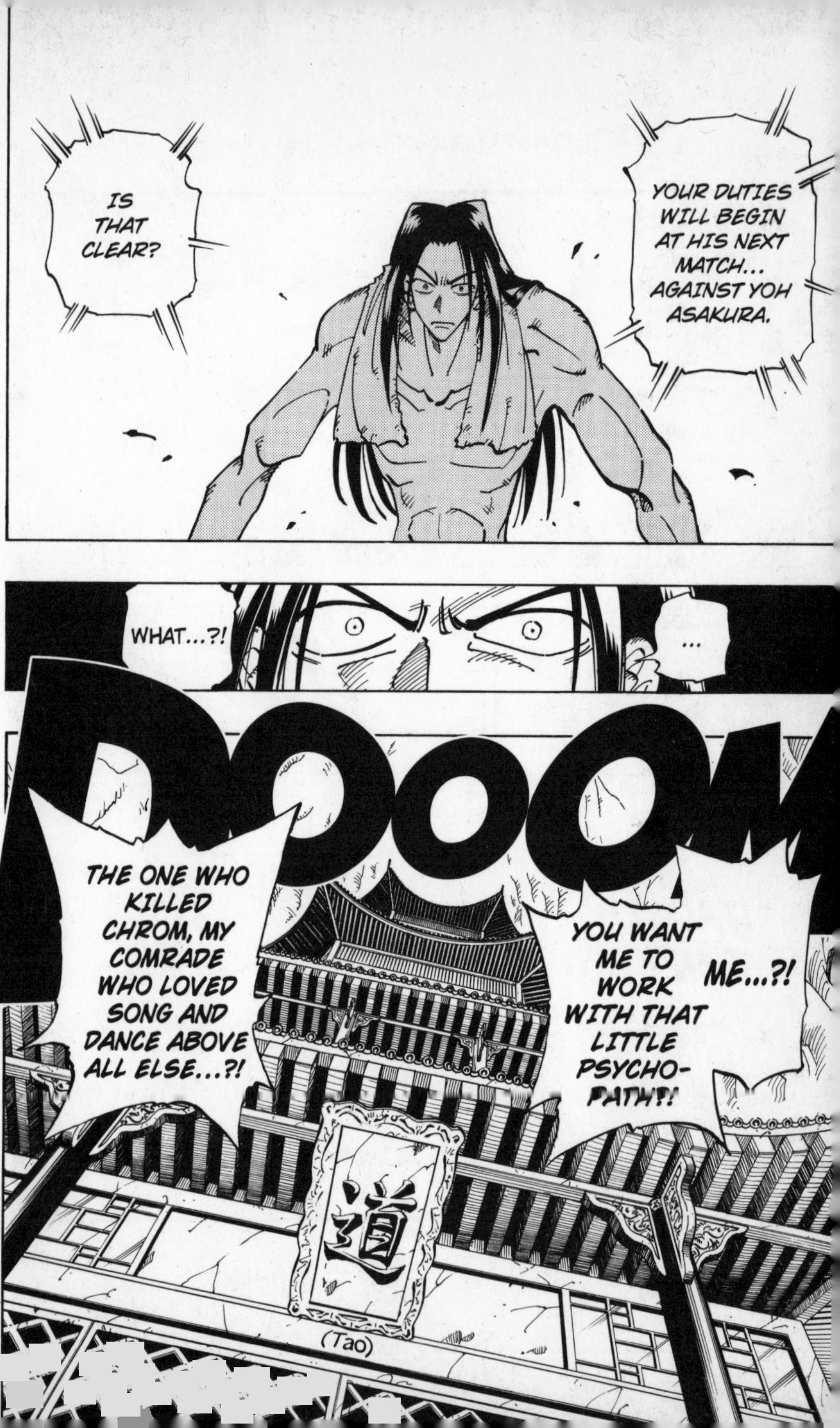
YOUR DUTIES WILL BEGIN AT HIS NEXT MATCH... AGAINST YOH ASAKURA.
IS THAT CLEAR?
...
WHAT...?!
DOOOM
ME...?!
YOU WANT ME TO WORK WITH THAT LITTLE PSYCHO-PATH?!
THE ONE WHO KILLED CHROM, MY COMRADE WHO LOVED SONG AND DANCE ABOVE ALL ELSE...?!
道
(Tao)

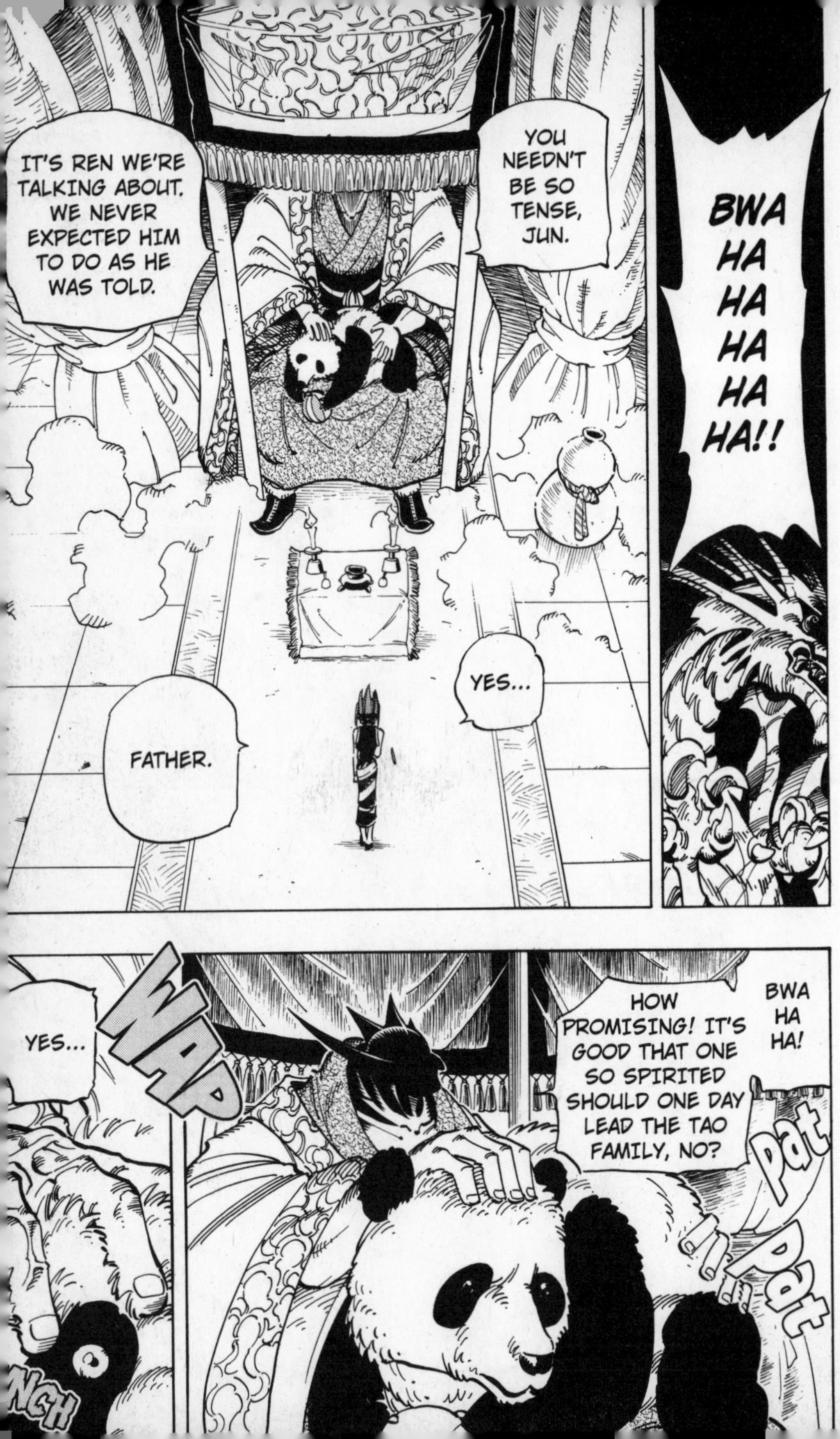
BWA HA HA HA HA HA!!
YOU NEEDN'T BE SO TENSE, JUN.
IT'S REN WE'RE TALKING ABOUT. WE NEVER EXPECTED HIM TO DO AS HE WAS TOLD.
YES...
FATHER.
BWA HA HA!
HOW PROMISING! IT'S GOOD THAT ONE SO SPIRITED SHOULD ONE DAY LEAD THE TAO FAMILY, NO?
pat
pat
WAP
YES...
NCH

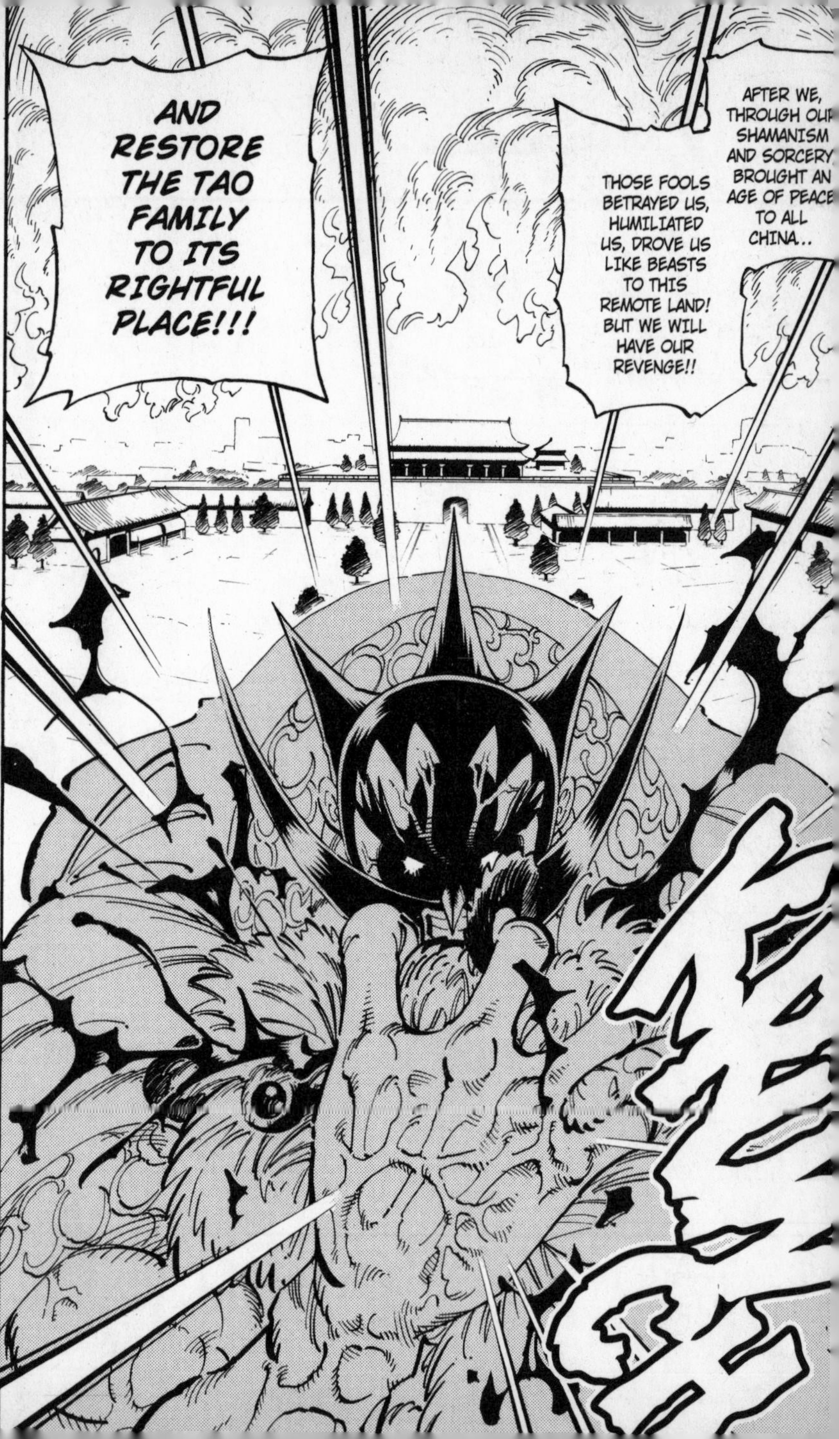
AFTER WE, THROUGH OUR SHAMANISM AND SORCERY, BROUGHT AN AGE OF PEACE TO ALL CHINA...
THOSE FOOLS BETRAYED US, HUMILIATED US, DROVE US LIKE BEASTS TO THIS REMOTE LAND! BUT WE WILL HAVE OUR REVENGE!!
AND RESTORE THE TAO FAMILY TO ITS RIGHTFUL PLACE!!!

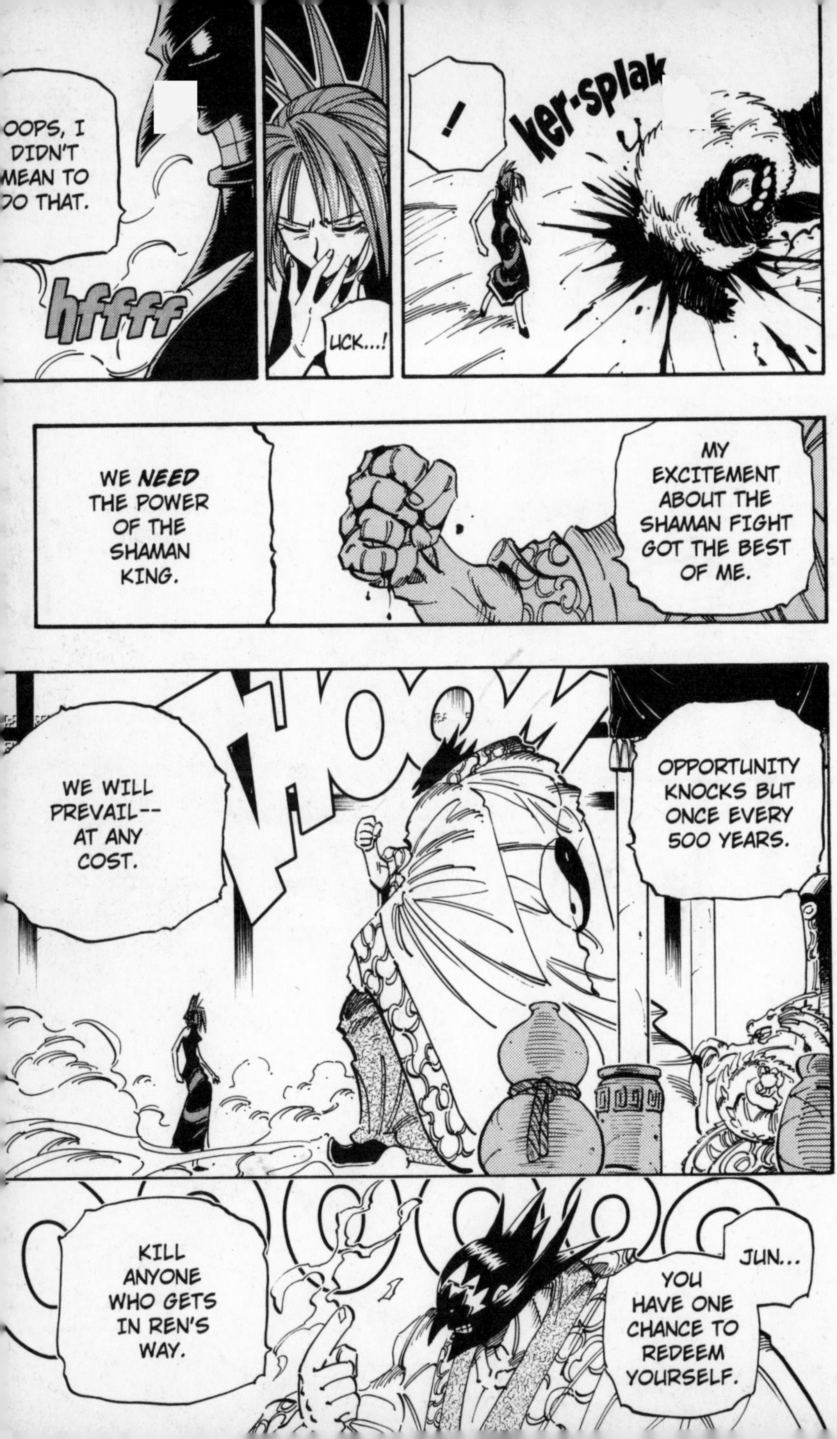
!
ker-splak
UCK...!
OOPS, I DIDN'T MEAN TO DO THAT.
hffff
MY EXCITEMENT ABOUT THE SHAMAN FIGHT GOT THE BEST OF ME.
WE *NEED* THE POWER OF THE SHAMAN KING.
OPPORTUNITY KNOCKS BUT ONCE EVERY 500 YEARS.
WE WILL PREVAIL-- AT ANY COST.
JUN...
YOU HAVE ONE CHANCE TO REDEEM YOURSELF.
KILL ANYONE WHO GETS IN REN'S WAY.

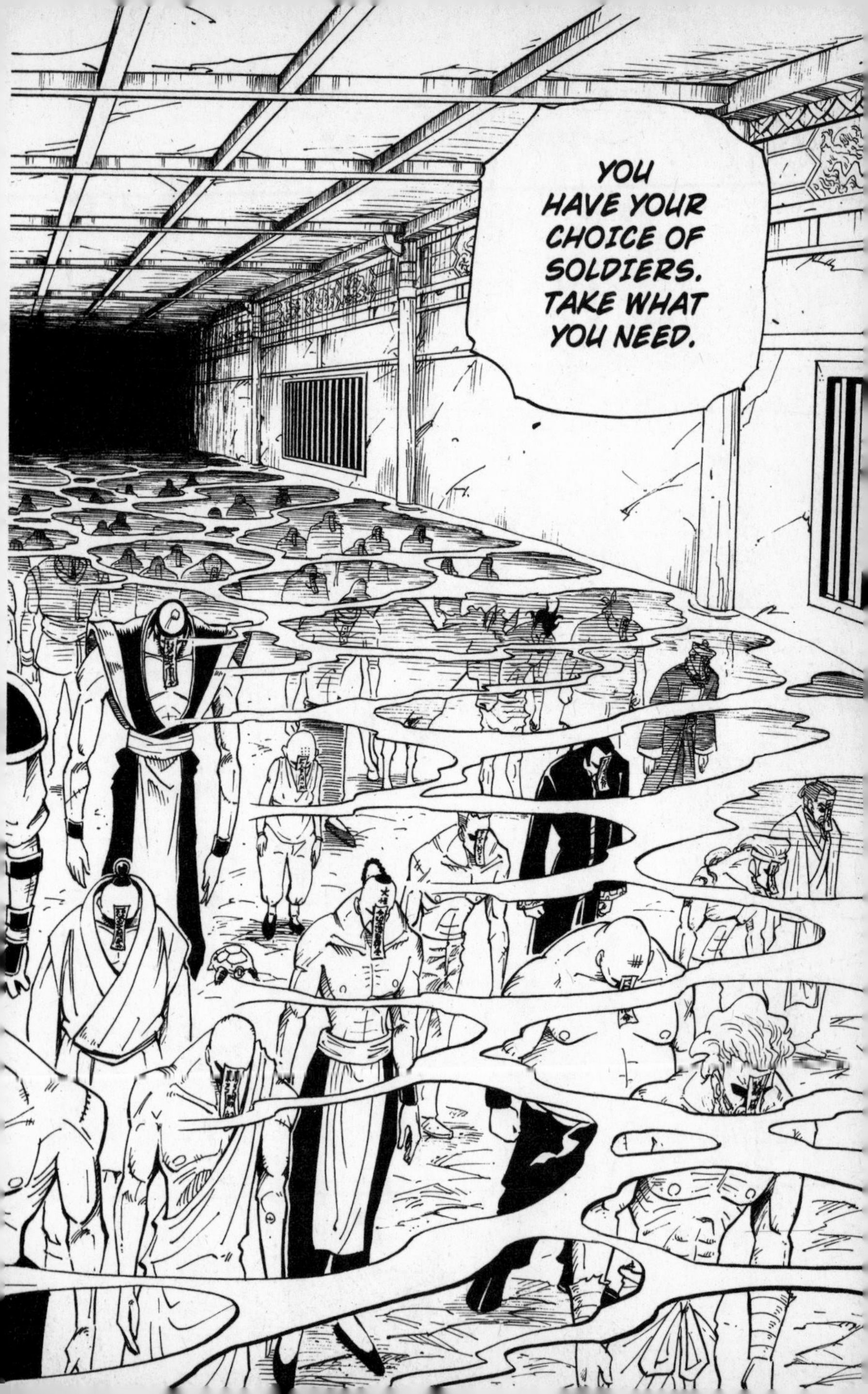
YOU HAVE YOUR CHOICE OF SOLDIERS. TAKE WHAT YOU NEED.

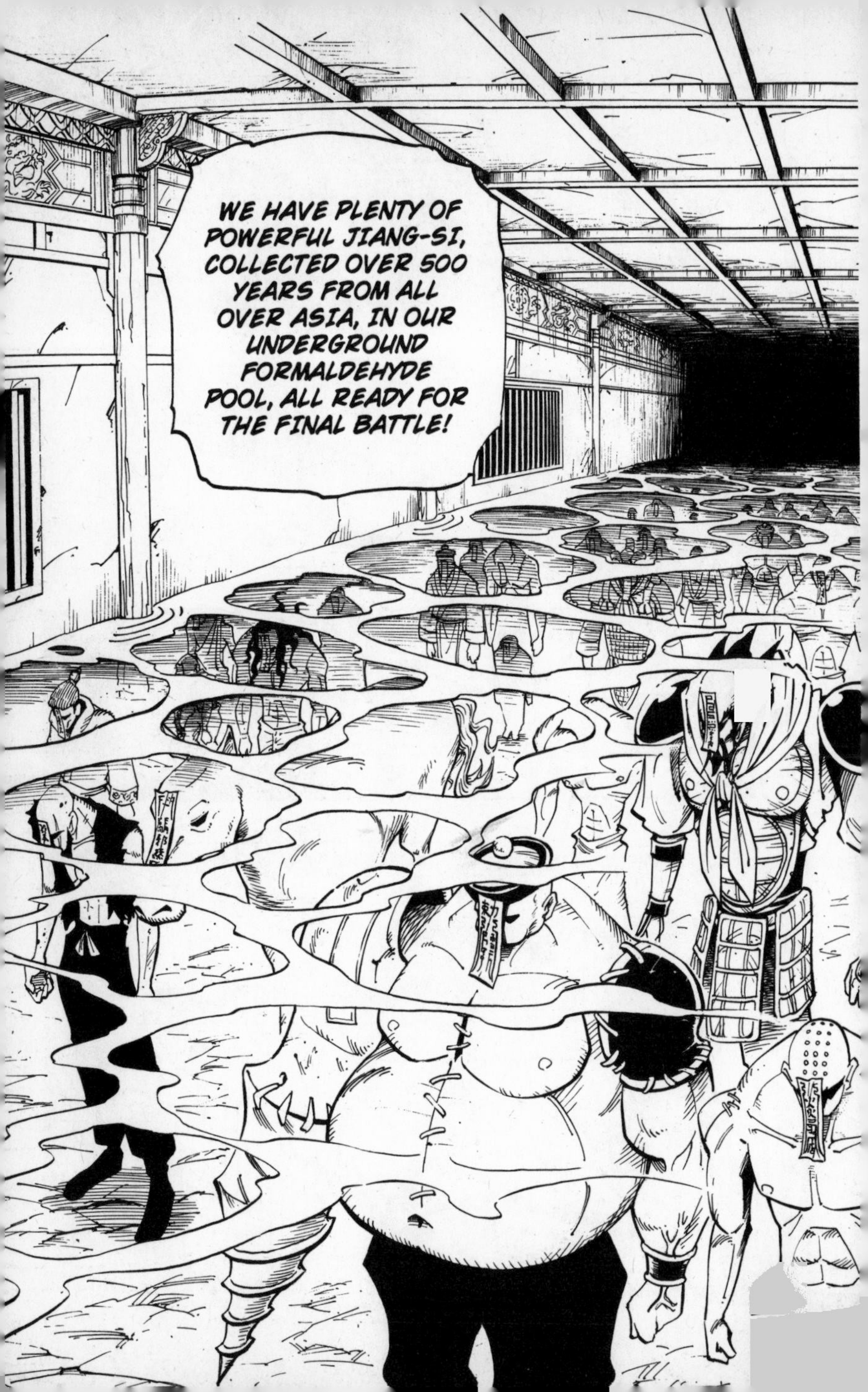
WE HAVE PLENTY OF POWERFUL JIANG-SI, COLLECTED OVER 500 YEARS FROM ALL OVER ASIA, IN OUR UNDERGROUND FORMALDEHYDE POOL, ALL READY FOR THE FINAL BATTLE!

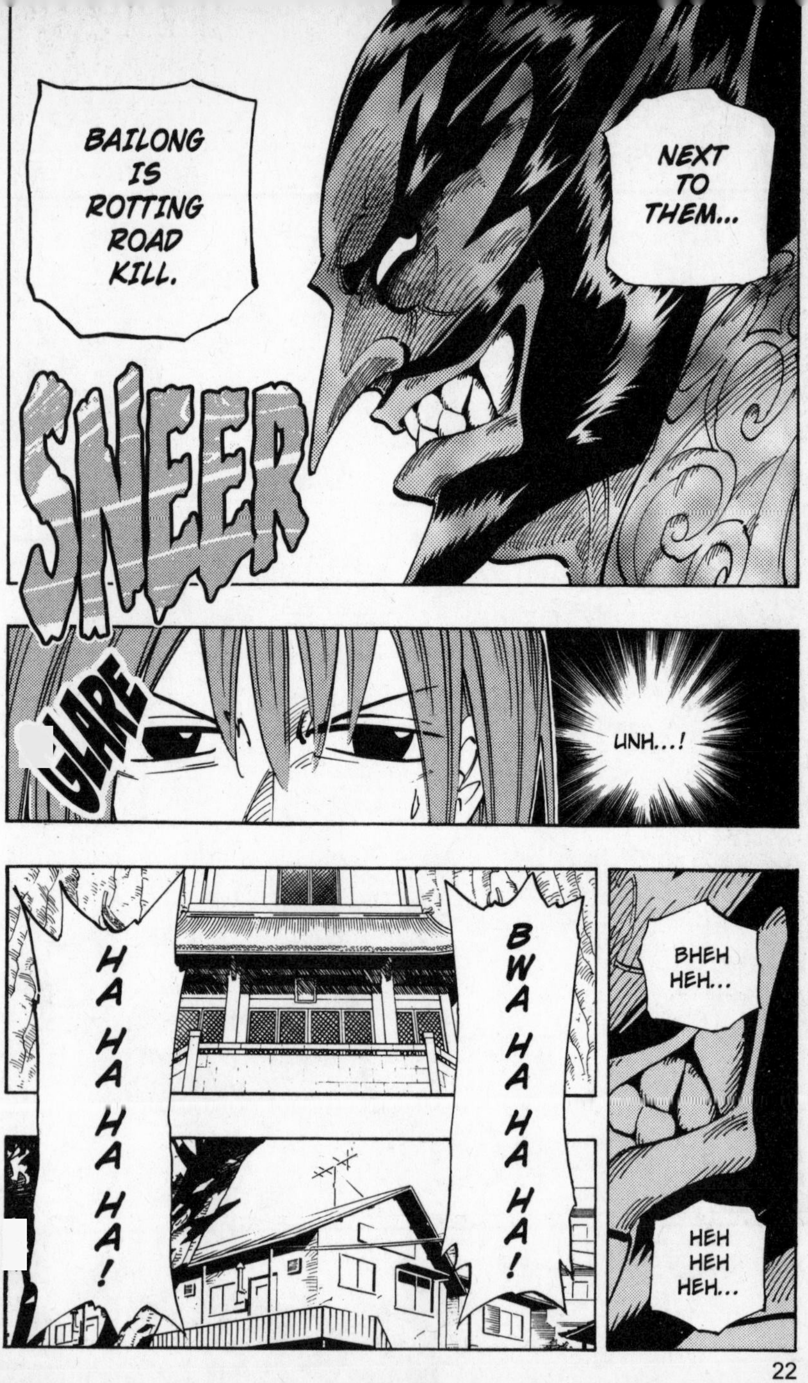
NEXT TO THEM...
BAILONG IS ROTTING ROAD KILL.
SNEER
UNH...!
GLARE
BHEH HEH...
HEH HEH HEH...
BWA HA HA HA HA HA!
HA HA HA HA HA HA!

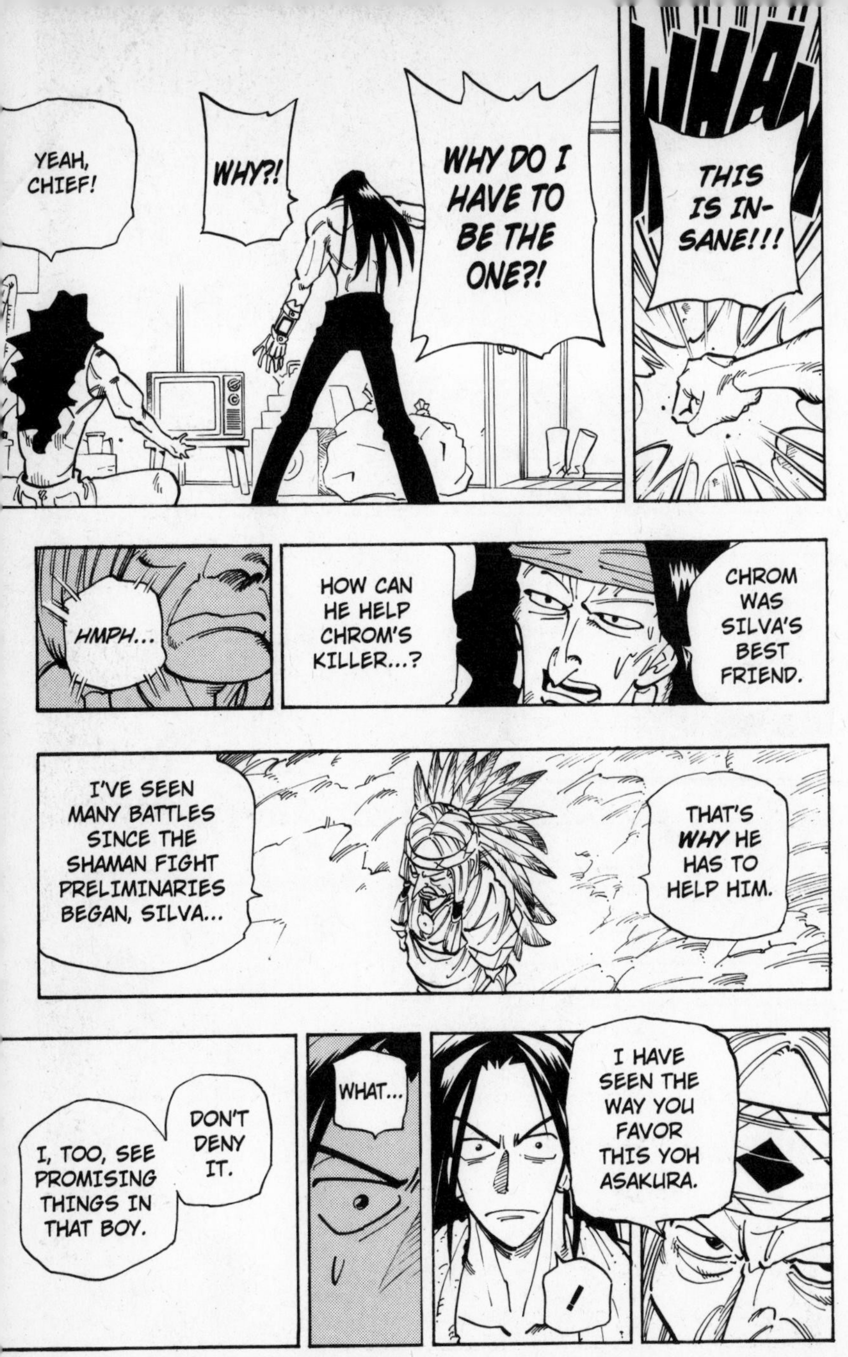
WHA
THIS IS IN-SANE!!!
WHY DO I HAVE TO BE THE ONE?!
WHY?!
YEAH, CHIEF!
CHROM WAS SILVA'S BEST FRIEND.
HOW CAN HE HELP CHROM'S KILLER...?
HMPH...
THAT'S *WHY* HE HAS TO HELP HIM.
I'VE SEEN MANY BATTLES SINCE THE SHAMAN FIGHT PRELIMINARIES BEGAN, SILVA...
I HAVE SEEN THE WAY YOU FAVOR THIS YOH ASAKURA.
!
WHAT...
DON'T DENY IT.
I, TOO, SEE PROMISING THINGS IN THAT BOY.

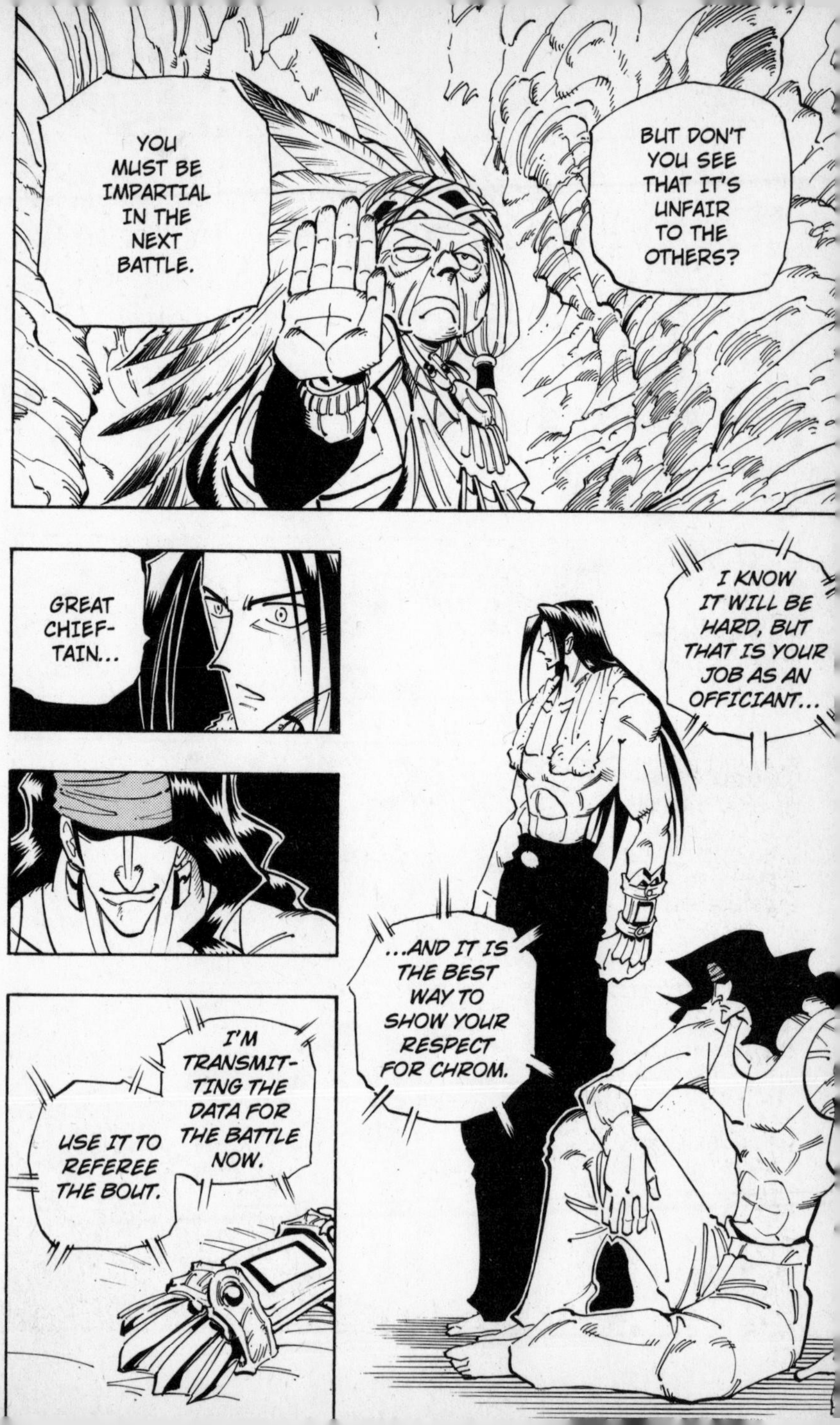
BUT DON'T YOU SEE THAT IT'S UNFAIR TO THE OTHERS?
YOU MUST BE IMPARTIAL IN THE NEXT BATTLE.
I KNOW IT WILL BE HARD, BUT THAT IS YOUR JOB AS AN OFFICIANT...
...AND IT IS THE BEST WAY TO SHOW YOUR RESPECT FOR CHROM.
GREAT CHIEF-TAIN...
I'M TRANSMIT-TING THE DATA FOR THE BATTLE NOW.
USE IT TO REFEREE THE BOUT.

READ THIS WAY

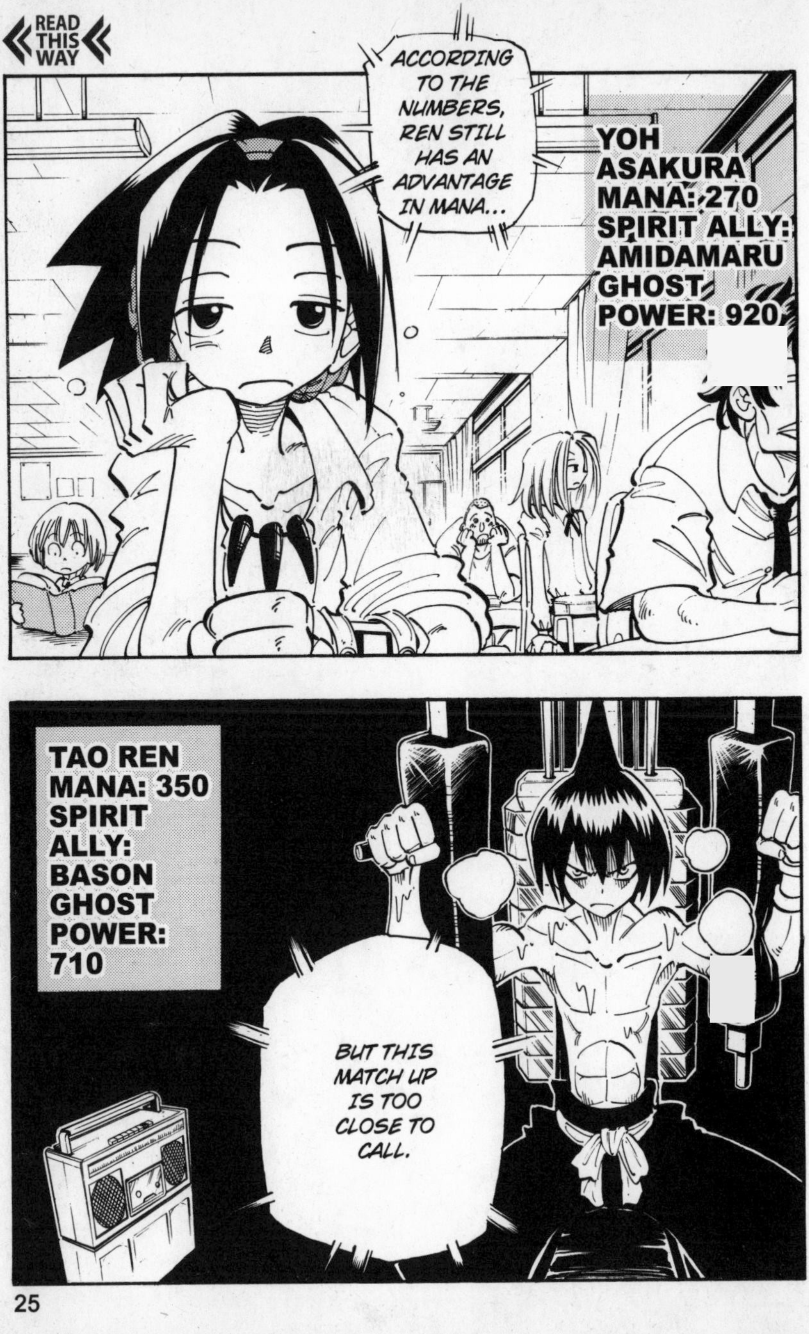
YOH ASAKURA MANA: 270 SPIRIT ALLY: AMIDAMARU GHOST POWER: 920
ACCORDING TO THE NUMBERS, REN STILL HAS AN ADVANTAGE IN MANA...
TAO REN MANA: 350 SPIRIT ALLY: BASON GHOST POWER: 710
BUT THIS MATCH UP IS TOO CLOSE TO CALL.

SHAMAN KING

7

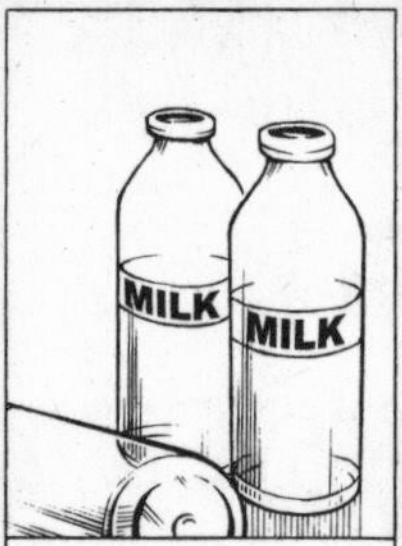
MILK
MILK

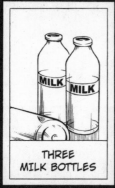

THREE MILK BOTTLES

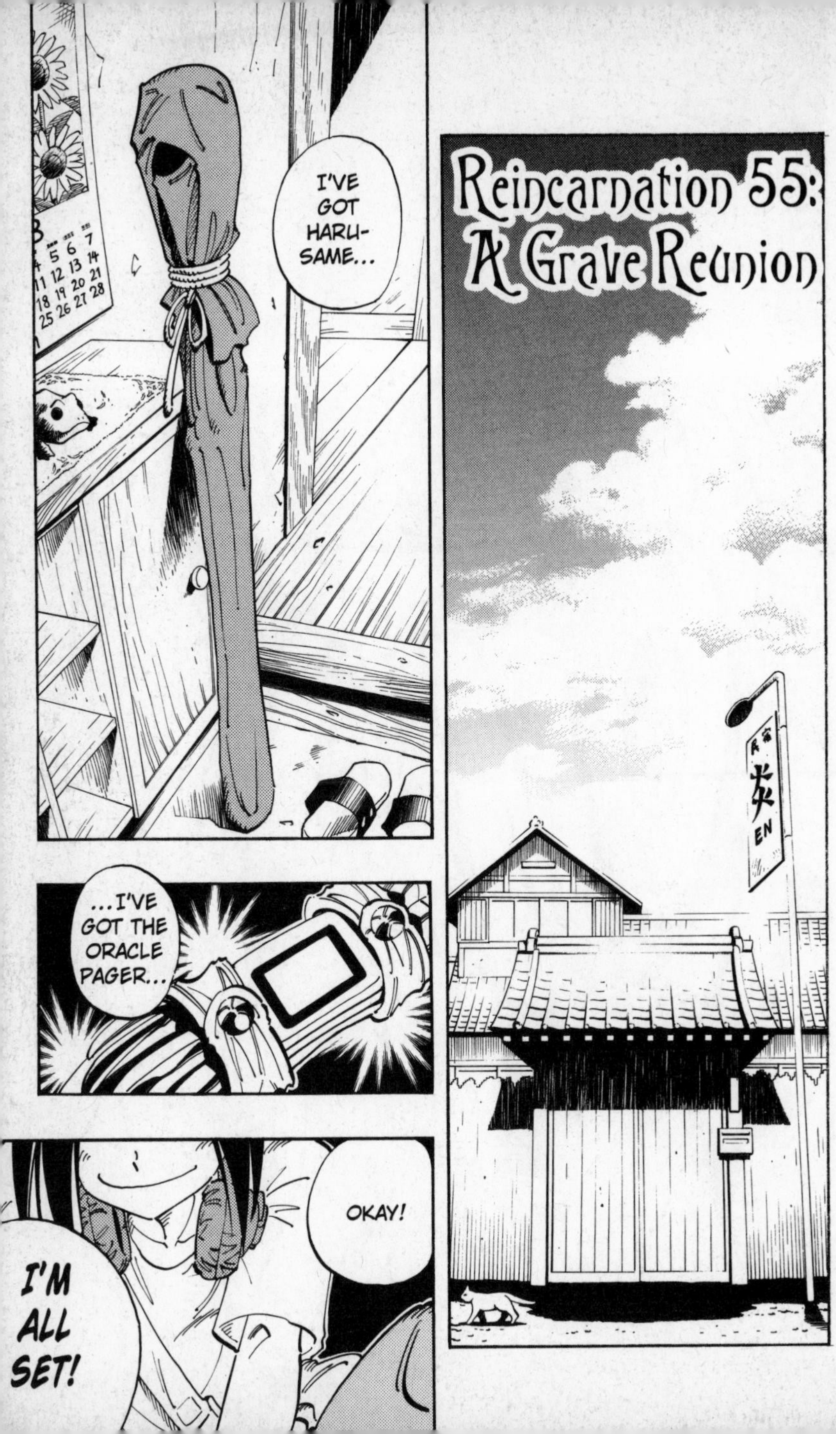
Reincarnation 55:
A Grave Reunion
民宿
炎
EN
I'VE GOT HARU-SAME...
...I'VE GOT THE ORACLE PAGER...
OKAY!
I'M ALL SET!

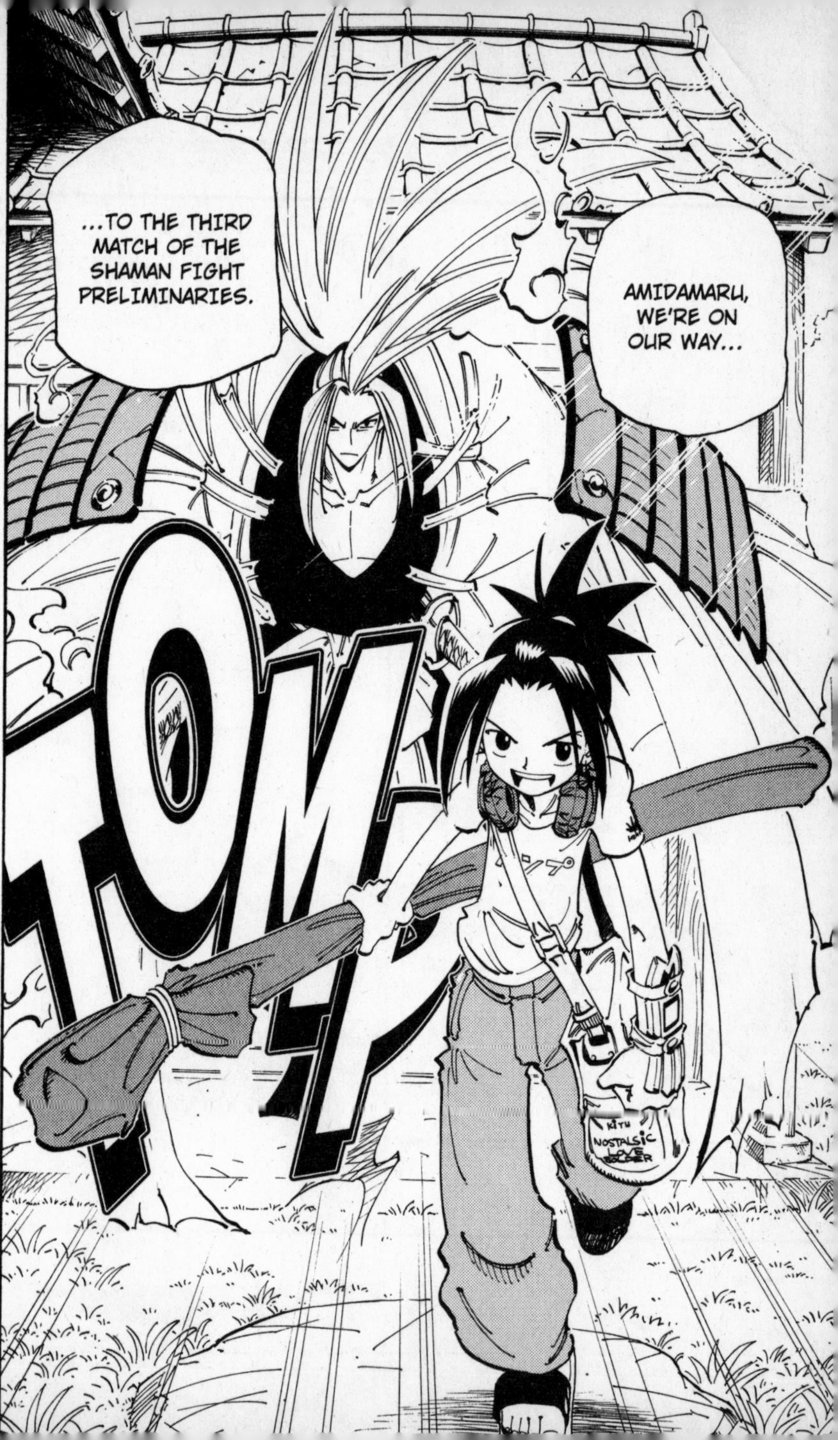
AMIDAMARU, WE'RE ON OUR WAY...
...TO THE THIRD MATCH OF THE SHAMAN FIGHT PRELIMINARIES.
TOM

Reincarnation 55:

A Grave Reunion

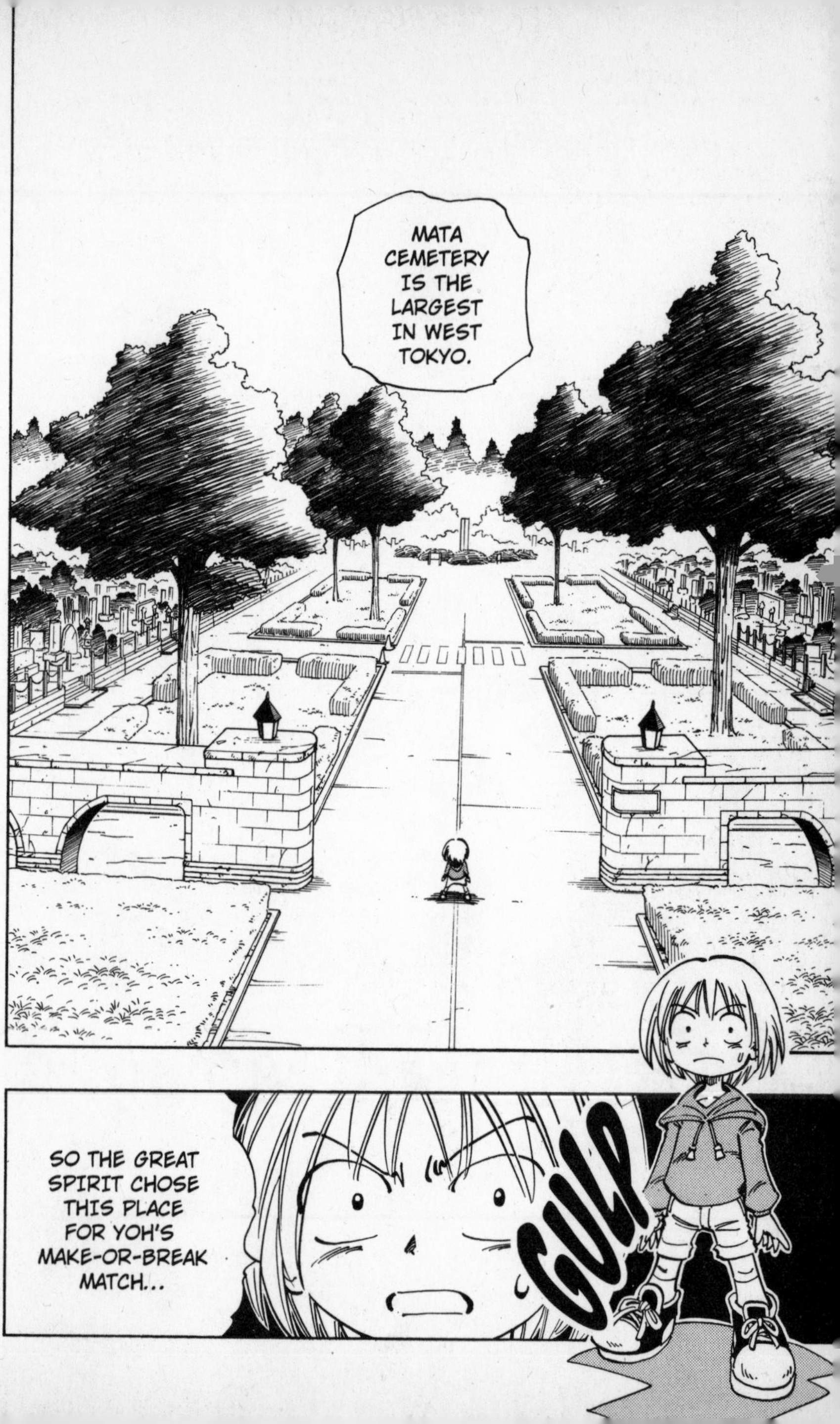
MATA CEMETERY IS THE LARGEST IN WEST TOKYO.
GULP
SO THE GREAT SPIRIT CHOSE THIS PLACE FOR YOH'S MAKE-OR-BREAK MATCH...

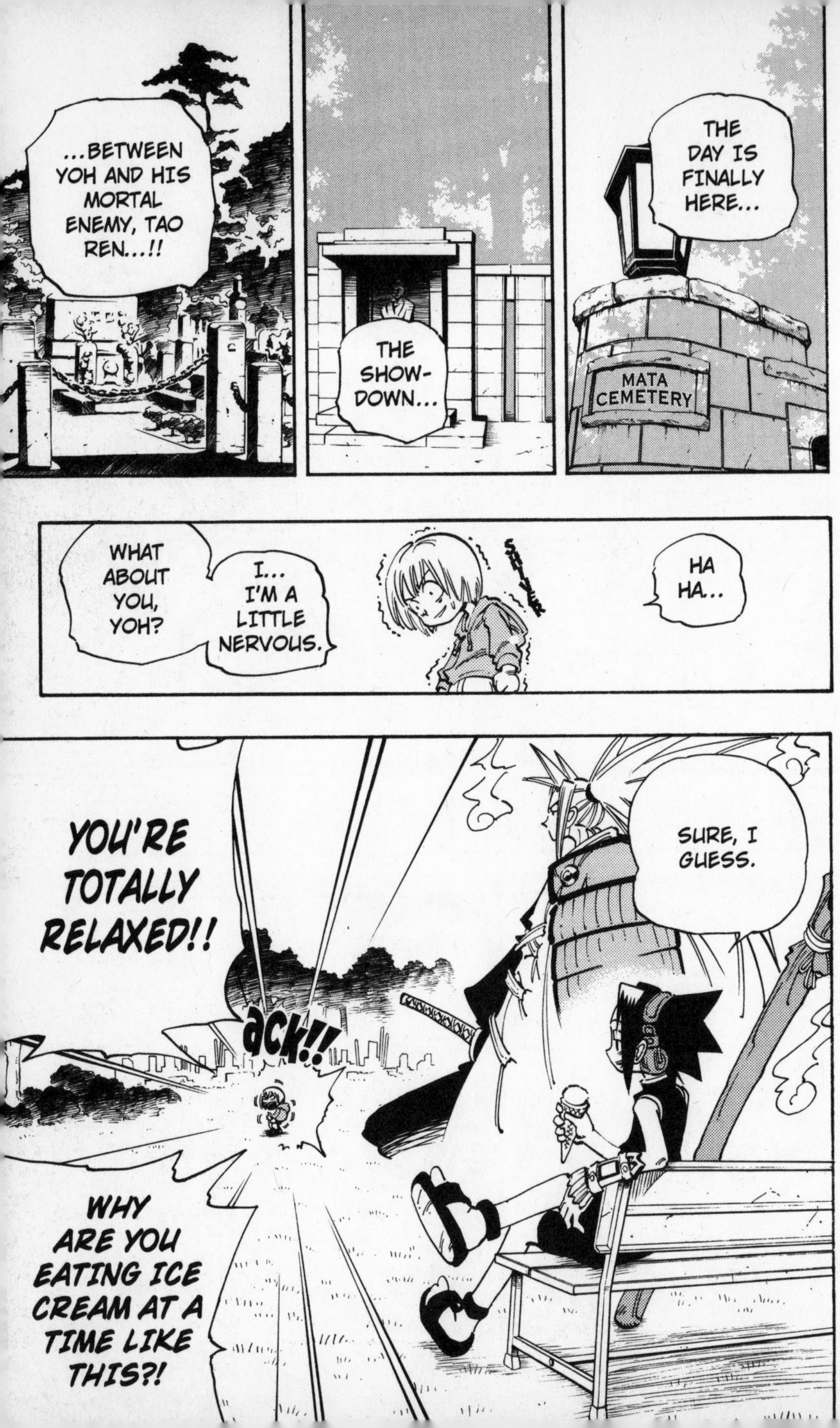
THE DAY IS FINALLY HERE...
MATA CEMETERY
THE SHOW-DOWN...
...BETWEEN YOH AND HIS MORTAL ENEMY, TAO REN...!!
HA HA...
SHIVER
I... I'M A LITTLE NERVOUS.
WHAT ABOUT YOU, YOH?
SURE, I GUESS.
YOU'RE TOTALLY RELAXED!!
ack!!
WHY ARE YOU EATING ICE CREAM AT A TIME LIKE THIS?!

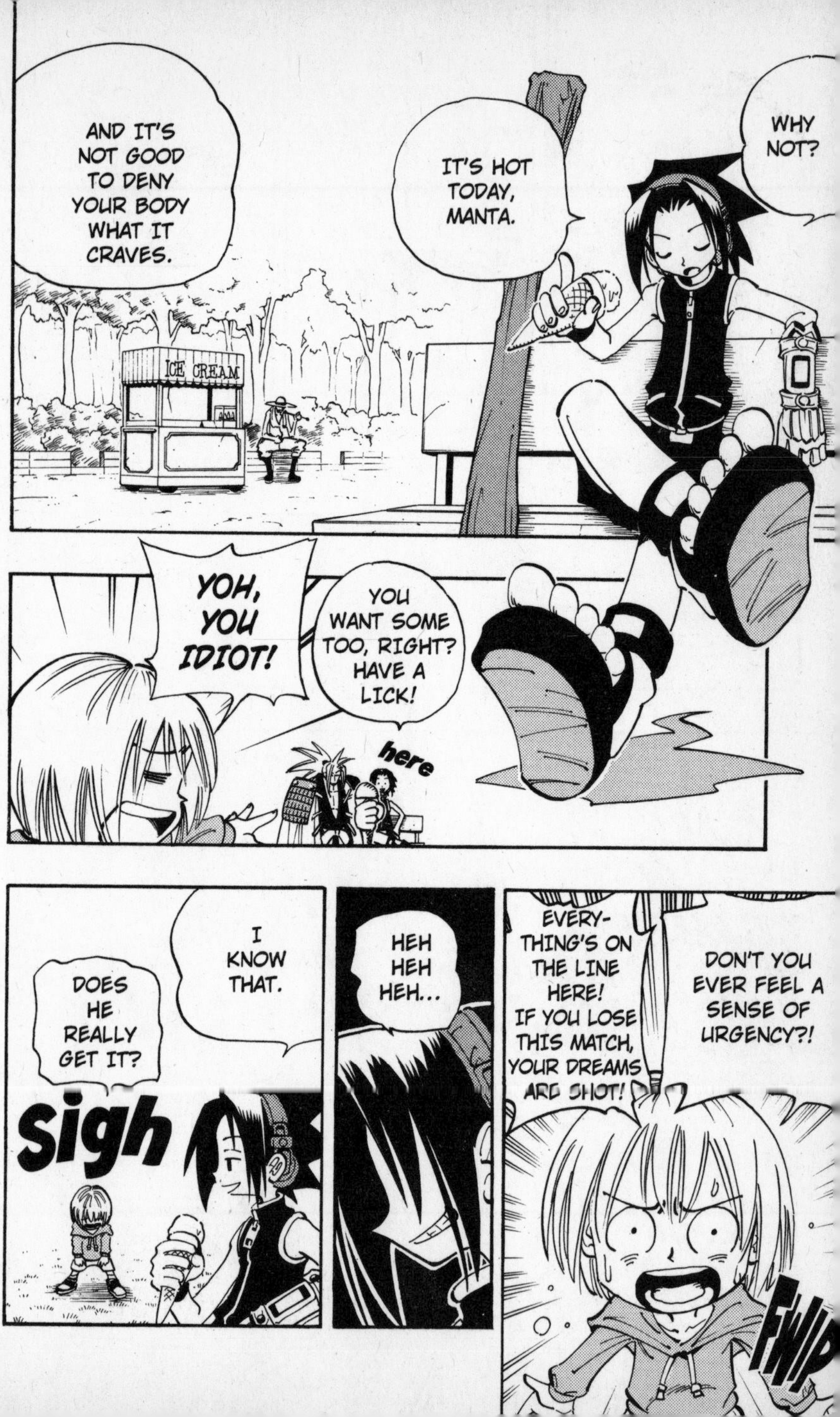
WHY NOT?
IT'S HOT TODAY, MANTA.
AND IT'S NOT GOOD TO DENY YOUR BODY WHAT IT CRAVES.
ICE CREAM
YOU WANT SOME TOO, RIGHT? HAVE A LICK!
here
YOH, YOU IDIOT!
EVERY-THING'S ON THE LINE HERE! IF YOU LOSE THIS MATCH, YOUR DREAMS ARE SHOT!
DON'T YOU EVER FEEL A SENSE OF URGENCY?!
FWIP
HEH HEH HEH...
I KNOW THAT.
DOES HE REALLY GET IT?
Sigh

READ THIS WAY

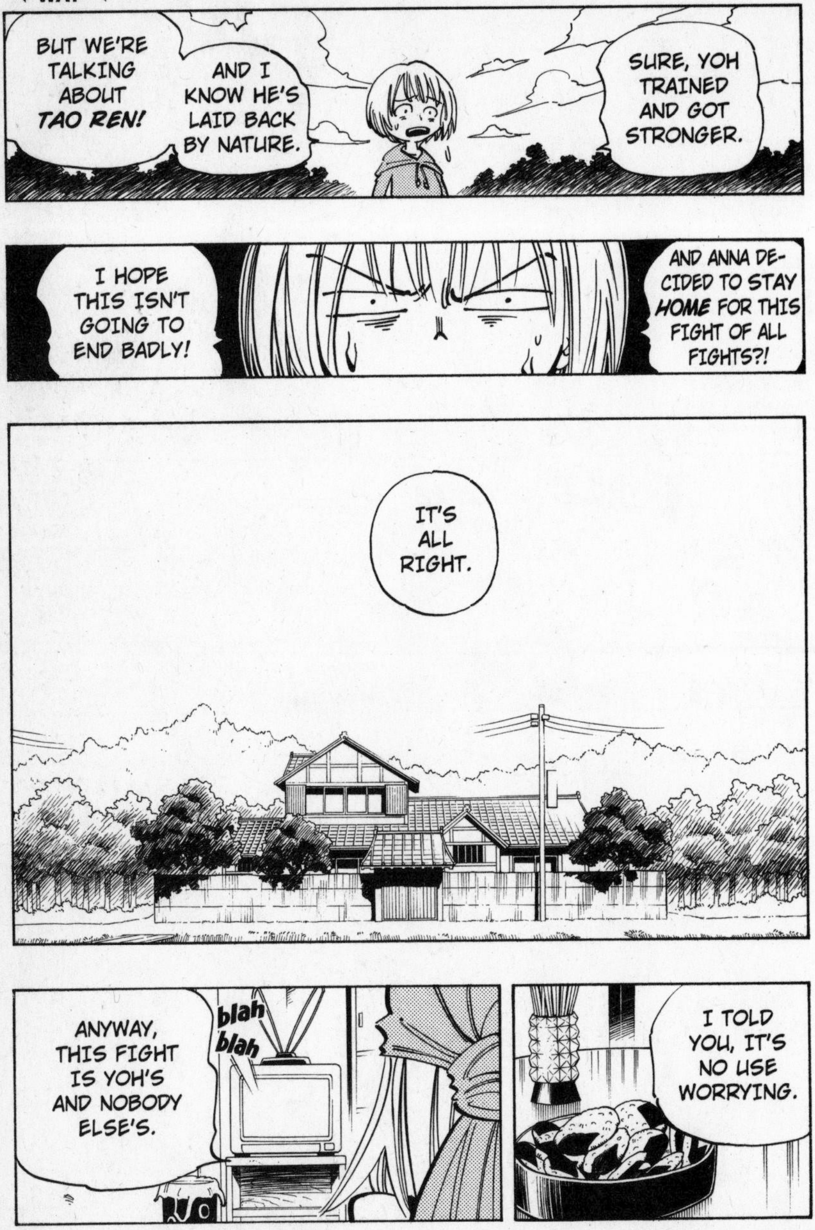

SURE, YOH TRAINED AND GOT STRONGER.
AND I KNOW HE'S LAID BACK BY NATURE.
BUT WE'RE TALKING ABOUT *TAO REN!*
AND ANNA DE-CIDED TO STAY *HOME* FOR THIS FIGHT OF ALL FIGHTS?!
I HOPE THIS ISN'T GOING TO END BADLY!
IT'S ALL RIGHT.
I TOLD YOU, IT'S NO USE WORRYING.
blah blah
ANYWAY, THIS FIGHT IS YOH'S AND NOBODY ELSE'S.

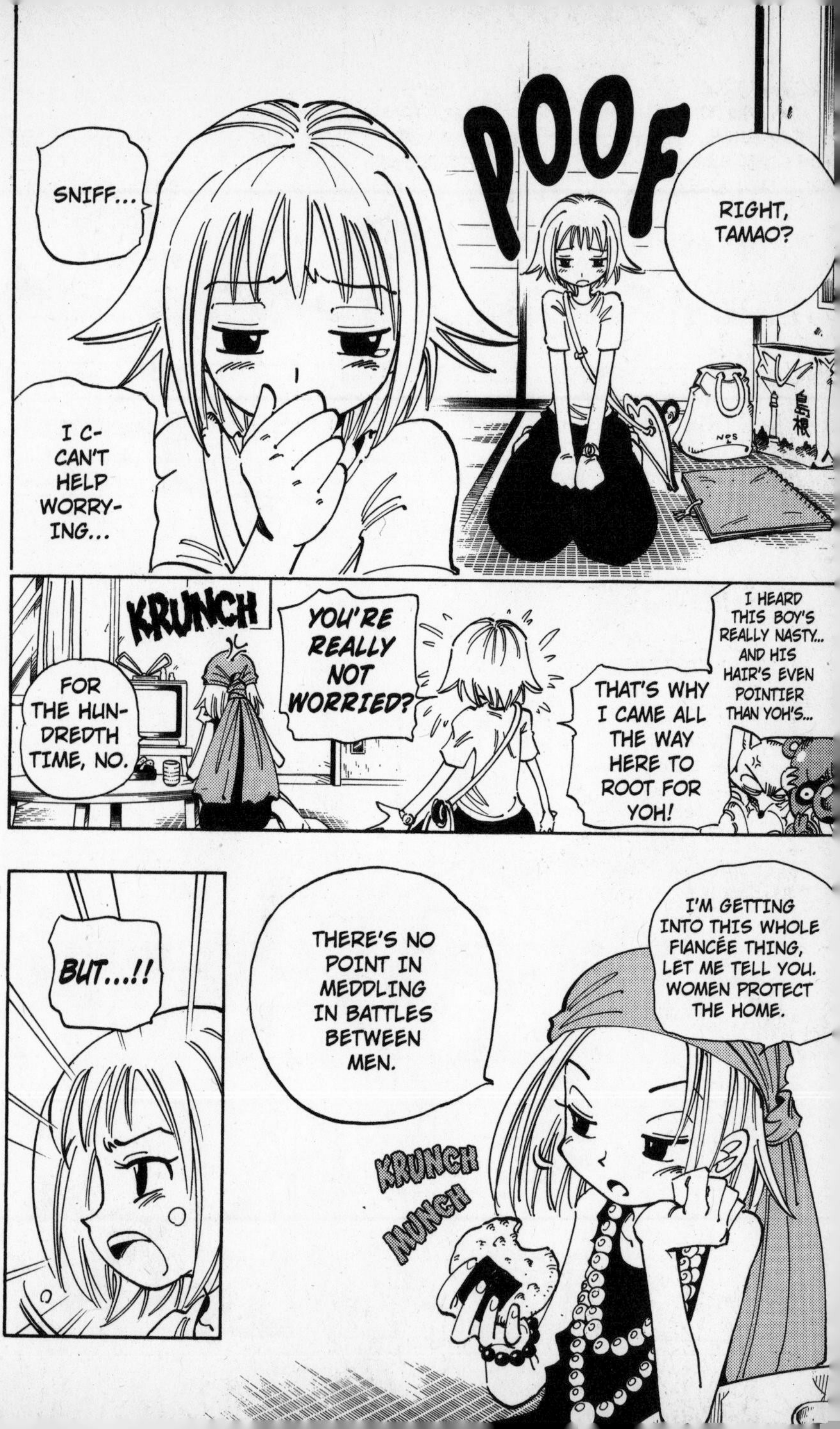
POOF
RIGHT, TAMAO?
島根
SNIFF...
I C-CAN'T HELP WORRYING...
I HEARD THIS BOY'S REALLY NASTY... AND HIS HAIR'S EVEN POINTIER THAN YOH'S...
THAT'S WHY I CAME ALL THE WAY HERE TO ROOT FOR YOH!
YOU'RE REALLY NOT WORRIED?
KRUNCH
FOR THE HUNDREDTH TIME, NO.
I'M GETTING INTO THIS WHOLE FIANCÉE THING, LET ME TELL YOU. WOMEN PROTECT THE HOME.
THERE'S NO POINT IN MEDDLING IN BATTLES BETWEEN MEN.
KRUNCH
MUNCH
BUT...!!

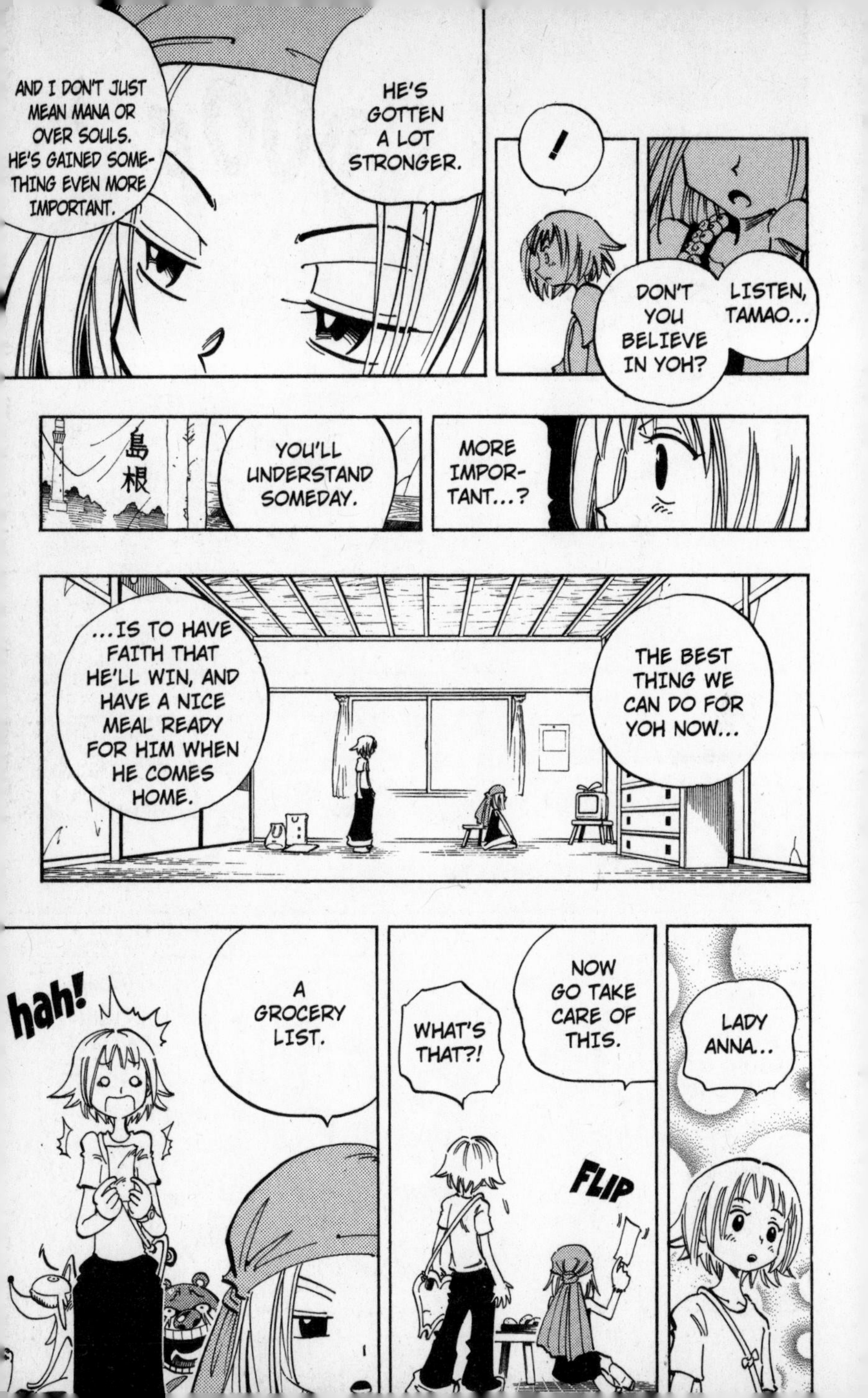
LISTEN, TAMAO...
DON'T YOU BELIEVE IN YOH?
!
HE'S GOTTEN A LOT STRONGER.
AND I DON'T JUST MEAN MANA OR OVER SOULS. HE'S GAINED SOMETHING EVEN MORE IMPORTANT.
MORE IMPORTANT...?
YOU'LL UNDERSTAND SOMEDAY.
島根
THE BEST THING WE CAN DO FOR YOH NOW...
...IS TO HAVE FAITH THAT HE'LL WIN, AND HAVE A NICE MEAL READY FOR HIM WHEN HE COMES HOME.
LADY ANNA...
NOW GO TAKE CARE OF THIS.
FLIP
WHAT'S THAT?!
A GROCERY LIST.
hah!

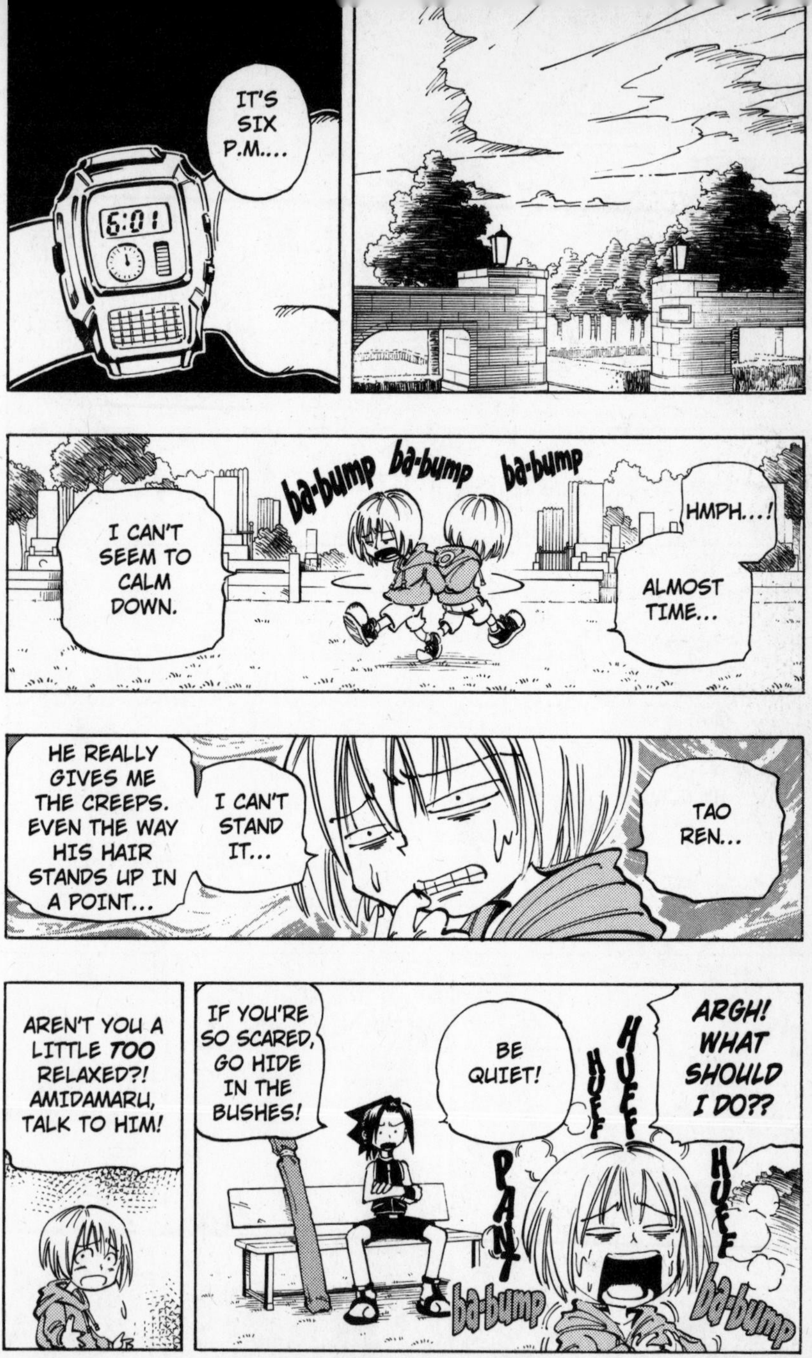
IT'S SIX P.M....
6:01
HMPH...!
ALMOST TIME...
ba-bump
ba-bump
ba-bump
I CAN'T SEEM TO CALM DOWN.
TAO REN...
I CAN'T STAND IT...
HE REALLY GIVES ME THE CREEPS. EVEN THE WAY HIS HAIR STANDS UP IN A POINT...
ARGH! WHAT SHOULD I DO??
HUFF
HUFF
HUFF
BE QUIET!
PANT
ba-bump
ba-bump
IF YOU'RE SO SCARED, GO HIDE IN THE BUSHES!
AREN'T YOU A LITTLE *TOO* RELAXED?! AMIDAMARU, TALK TO HIM!

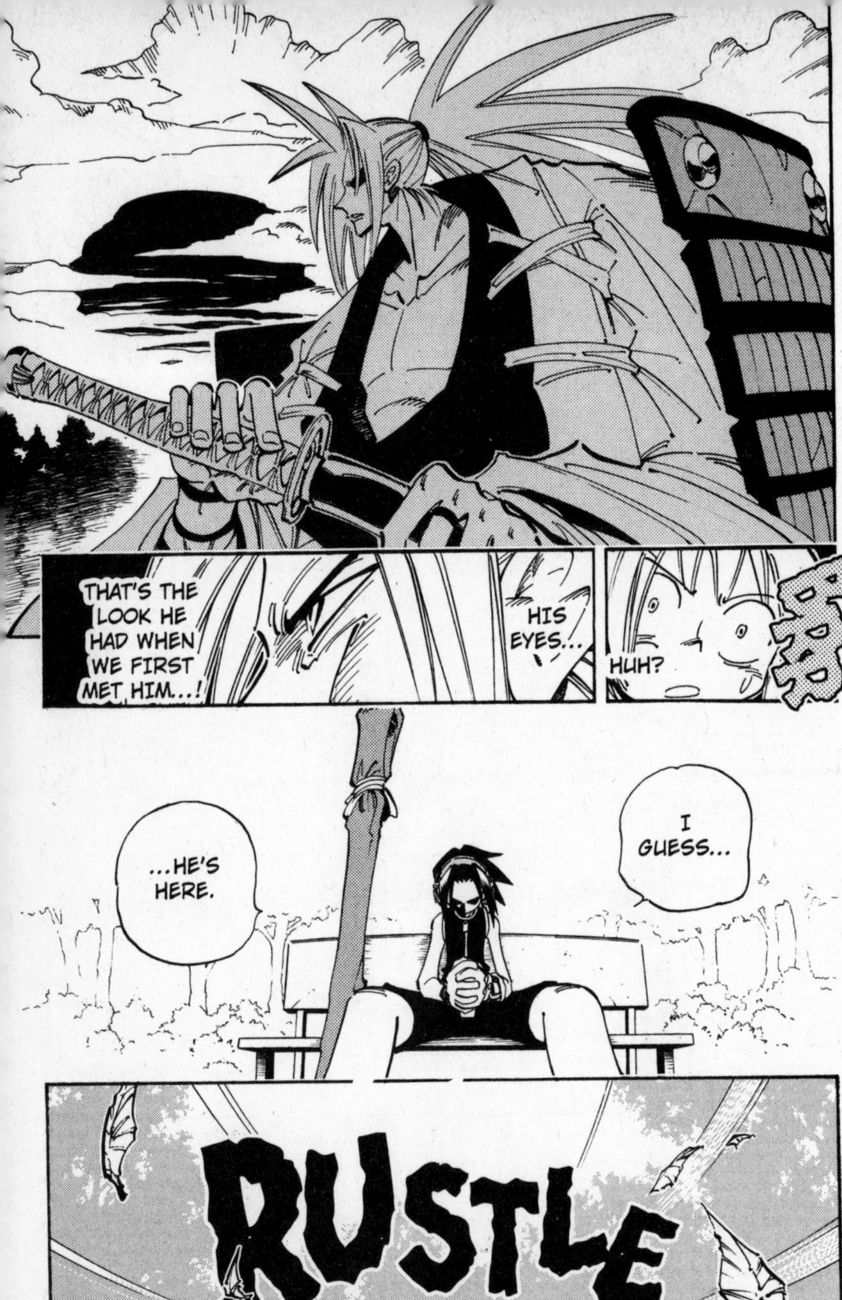
BRRR
HUH?
HIS EYES...
THAT'S THE LOOK HE HAD WHEN WE FIRST MET HIM...!
I GUESS...
...HE'S HERE.
RUSTLE

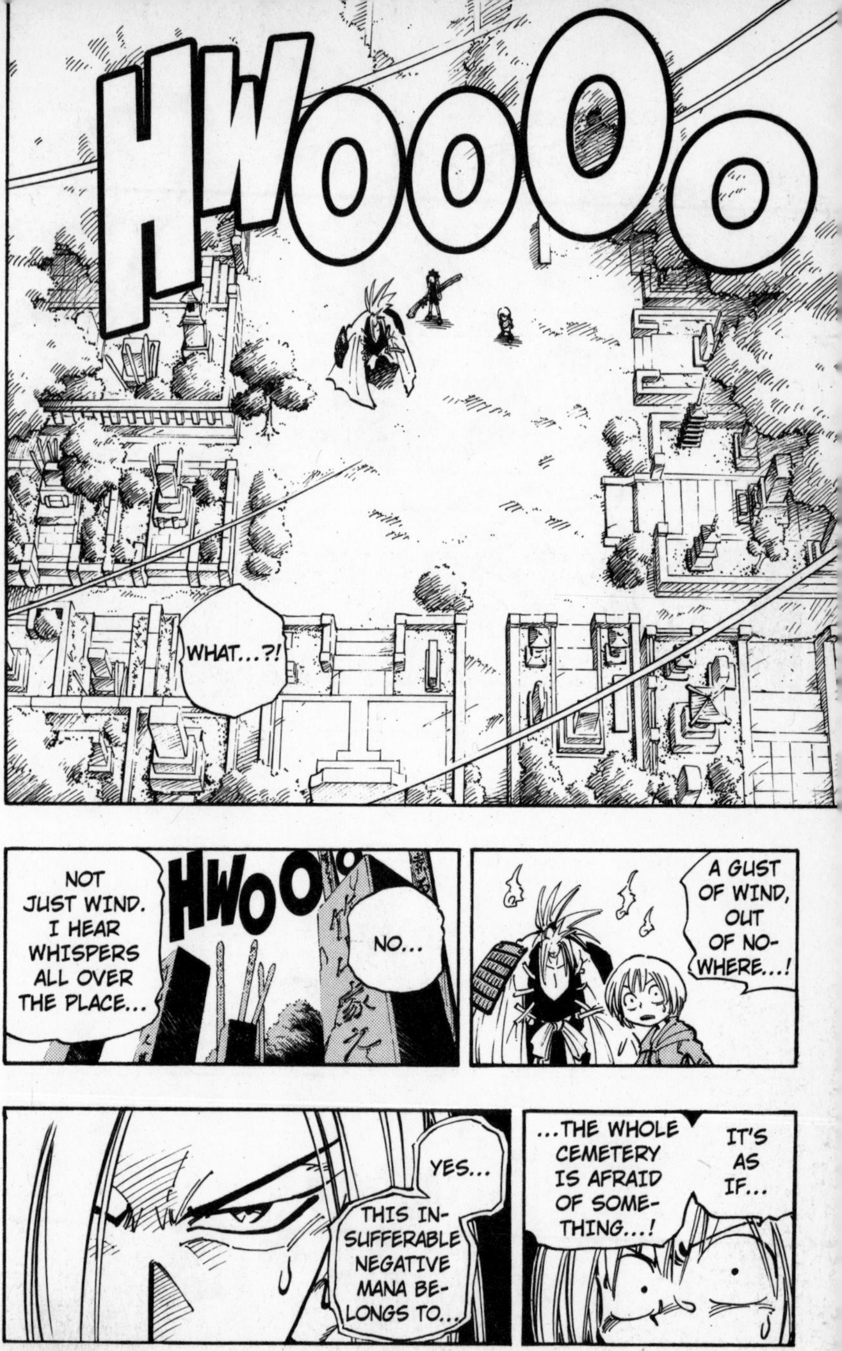
HWOOOOO
WHAT...?!
A GUST OF WIND, OUT OF NO-WHERE...!
NO...
HWOO
NOT JUST WIND. I HEAR WHISPERS ALL OVER THE PLACE...
IT'S AS IF...
...THE WHOLE CEMETERY IS AFRAID OF SOME-THING...!
YES...
THIS IN-SUFFERABLE NEGATIVE MANA BE-LONGS TO...

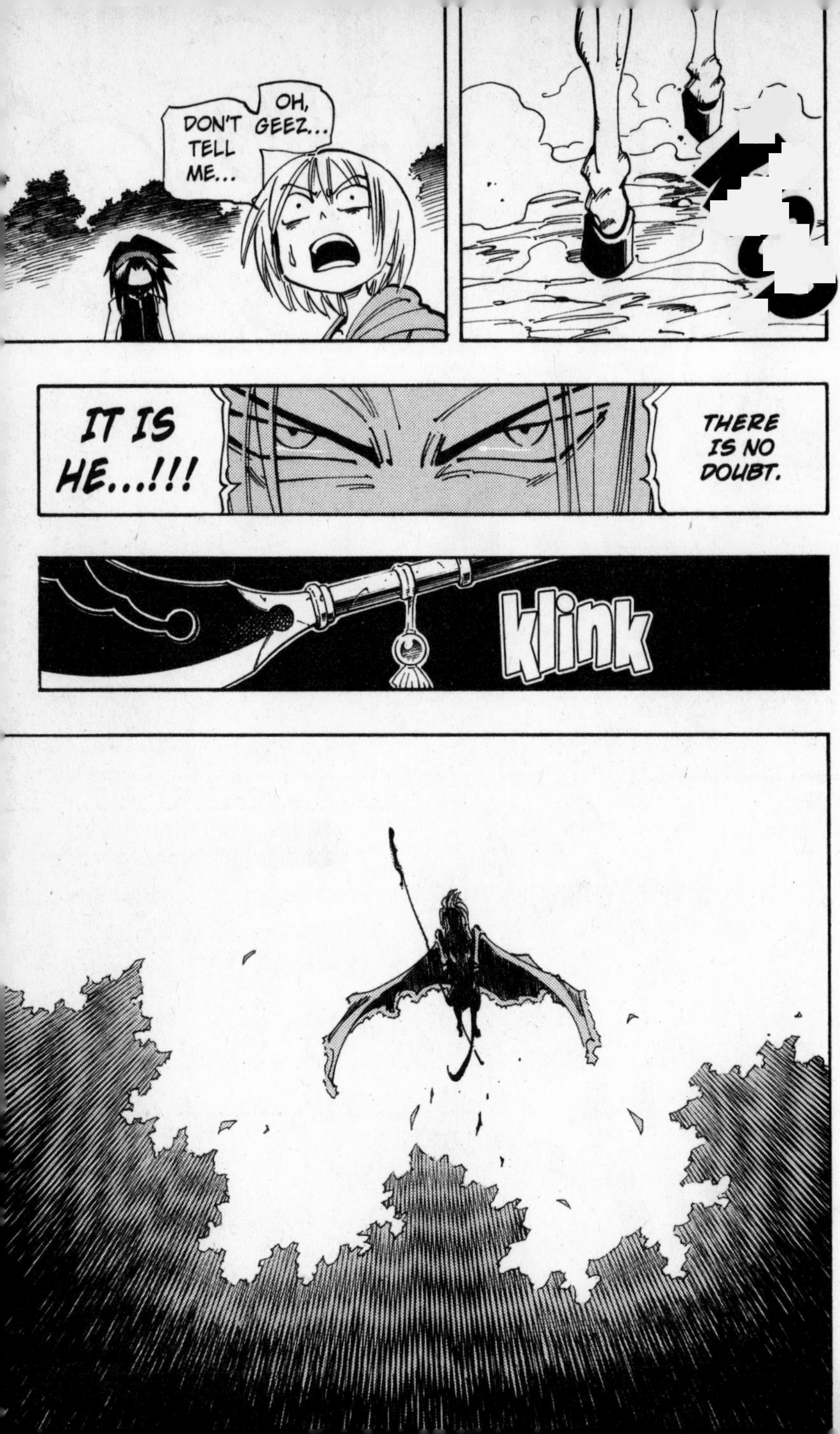
OH, GEEZ...
DON'T TELL ME...
THERE IS NO DOUBT.
IT IS HE...!!!
klink

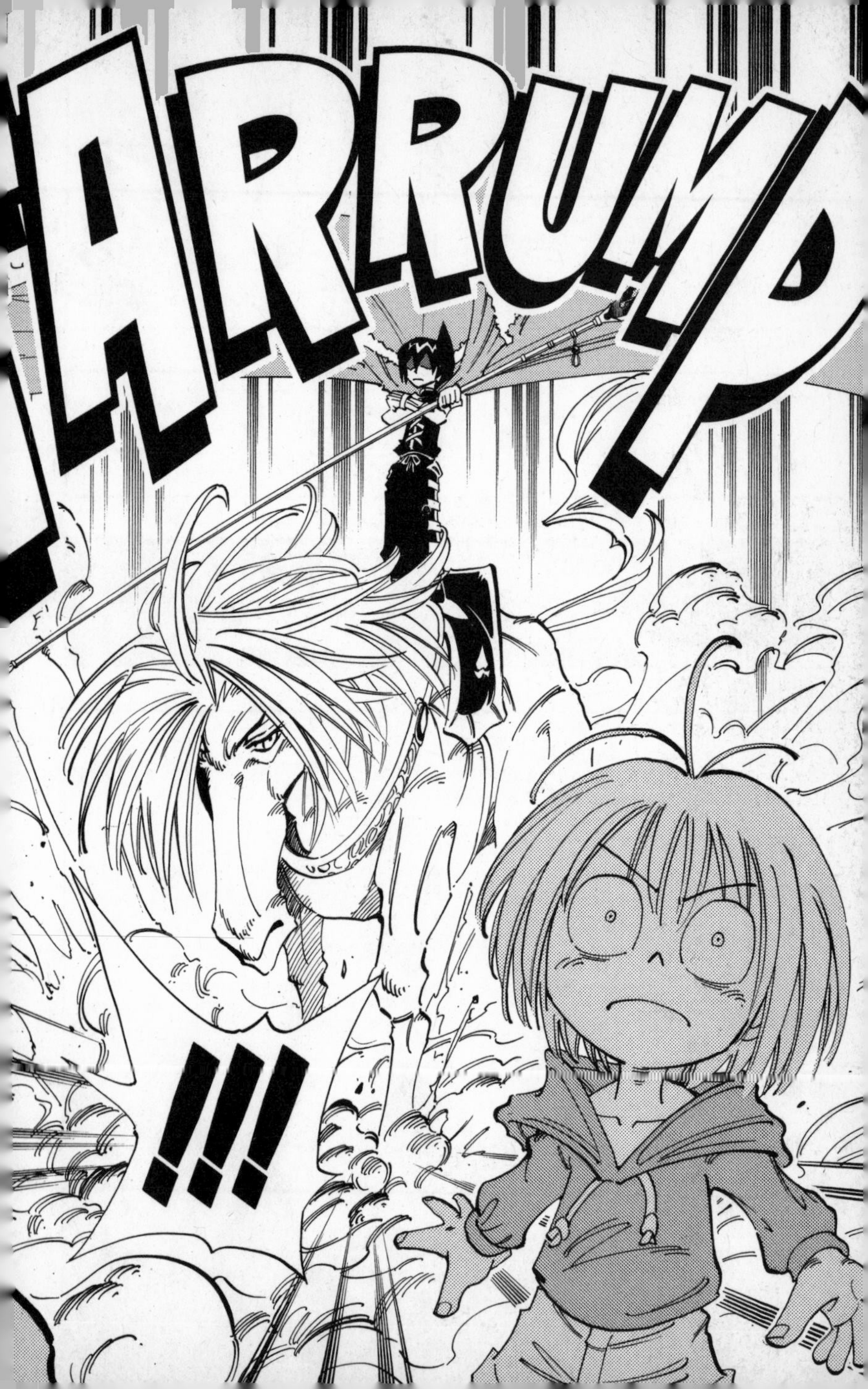
ARRUMP
!!!

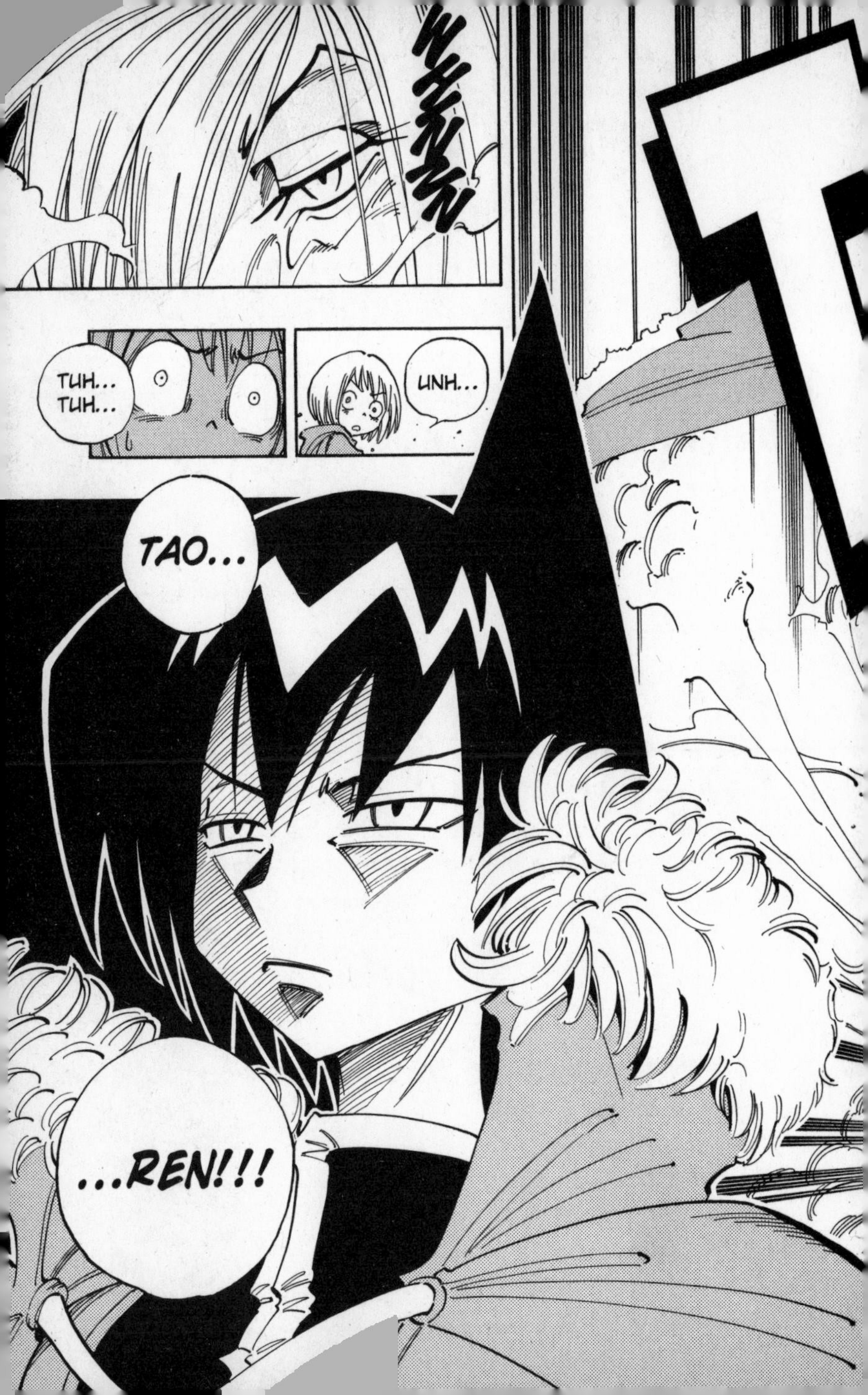
UNH...
TUH... TUH...
TAO...
...REN!!!

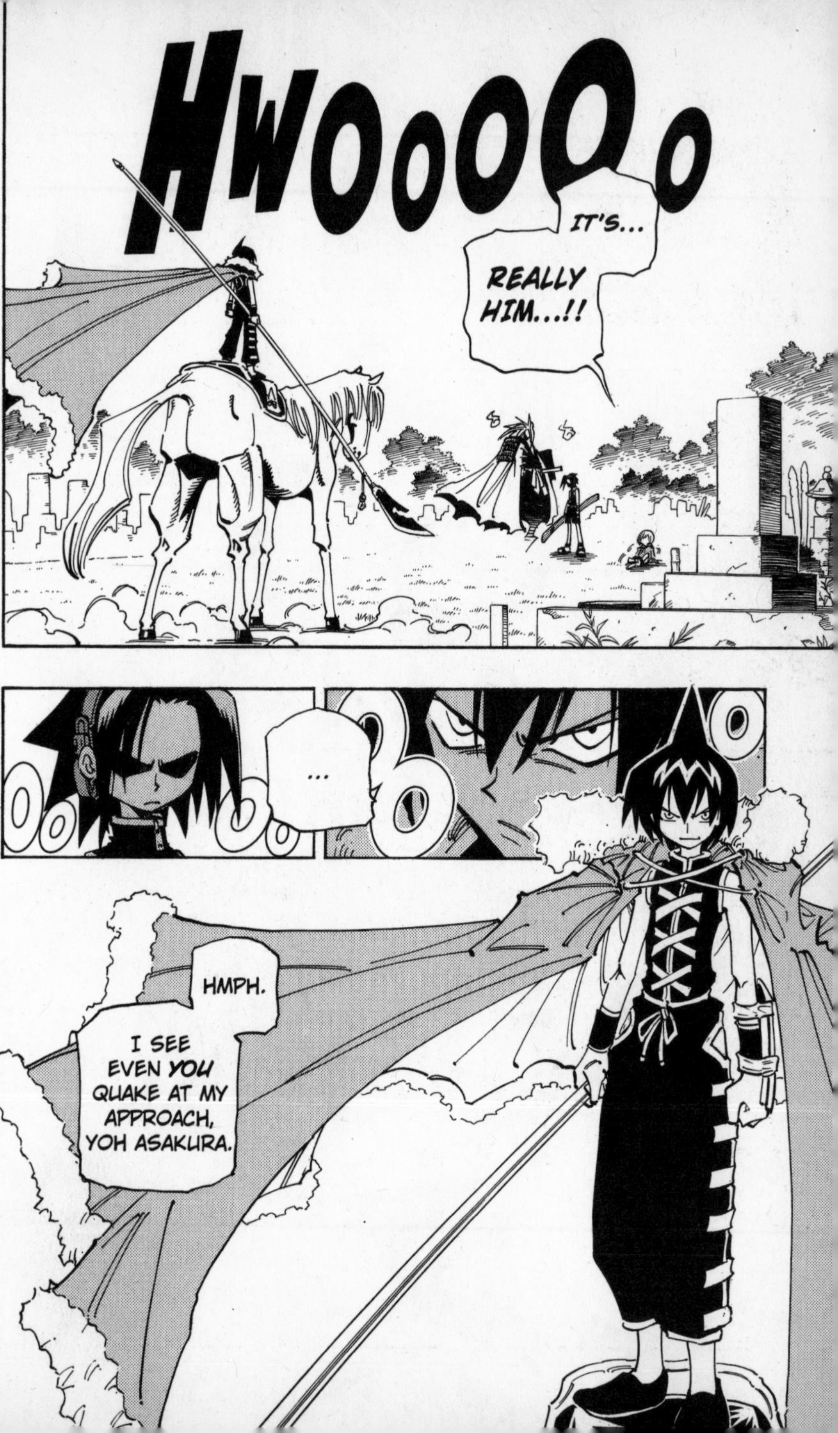
HWOOOOO
IT'S... REALLY HIM...!!
...
HMPH.
I SEE EVEN YOU QUAKE AT MY APPROACH, YOH ASAKURA.

READ THIS WAY

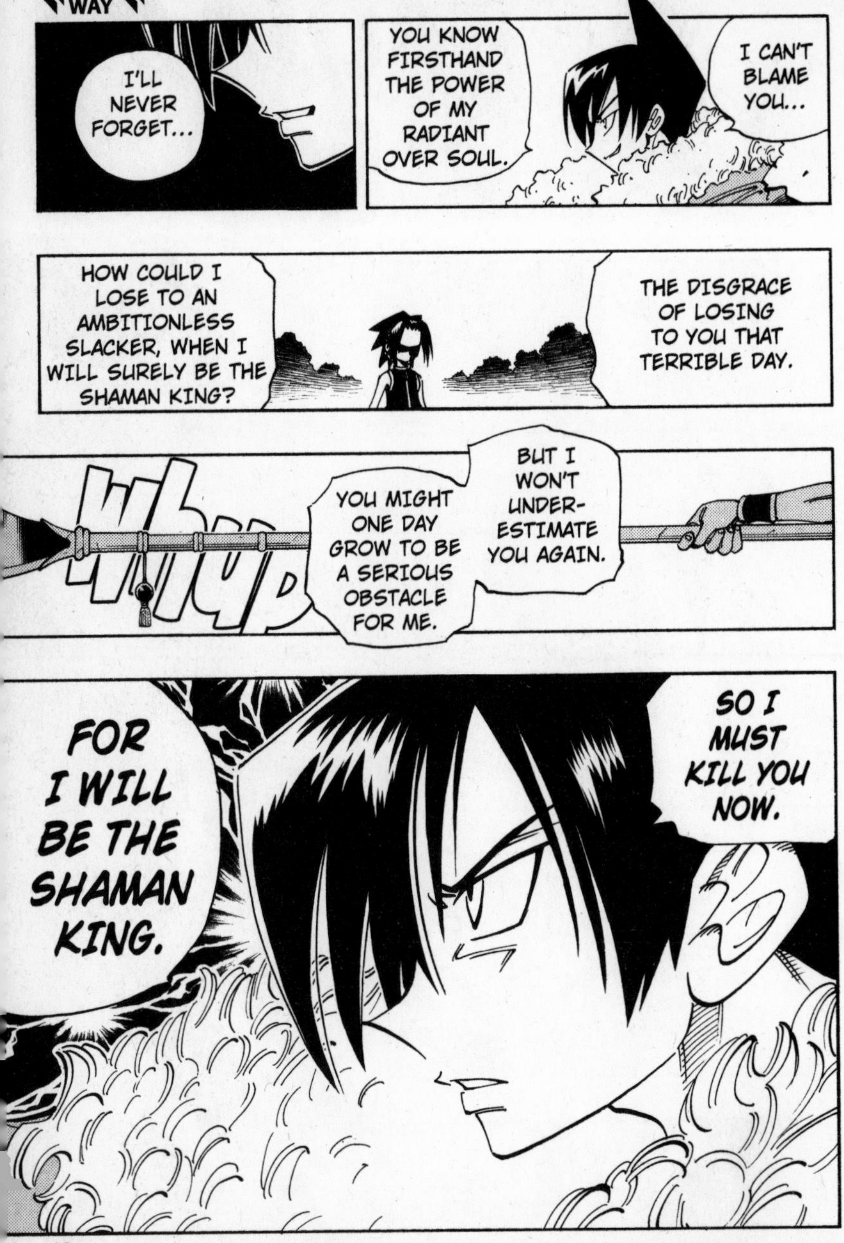
I CAN'T BLAME YOU...
YOU KNOW FIRSTHAND THE POWER OF MY RADIANT OVER SOUL.
I'LL NEVER FORGET...
THE DISGRACE OF LOSING TO YOU THAT TERRIBLE DAY.
HOW COULD I LOSE TO AN AMBITIONLESS SLACKER, WHEN I WILL SURELY BE THE SHAMAN KING?
BUT I WON'T UNDER-ESTIMATE YOU AGAIN.
YOU MIGHT ONE DAY GROW TO BE A SERIOUS OBSTACLE FOR ME.
WHUP
SO I MUST KILL YOU NOW.
FOR I WILL BE THE SHAMAN KING.

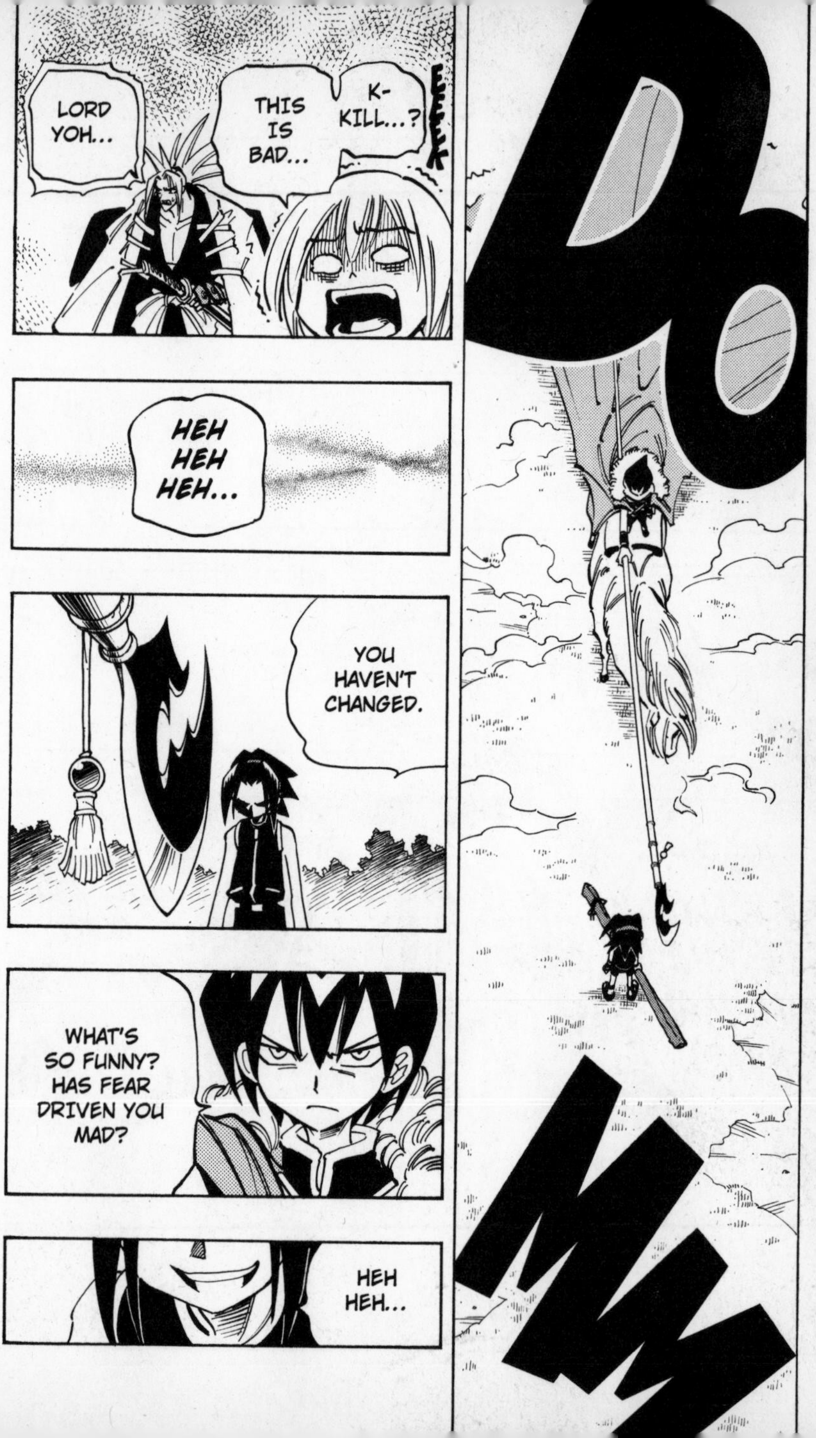

DOMM
EEEEK
K- KILL...?
THIS IS BAD...
LORD YOH...
HEH HEH HEH...
YOU HAVEN'T CHANGED.
WHAT'S SO FUNNY? HAS FEAR DRIVEN YOU MAD?
HEH HEH...

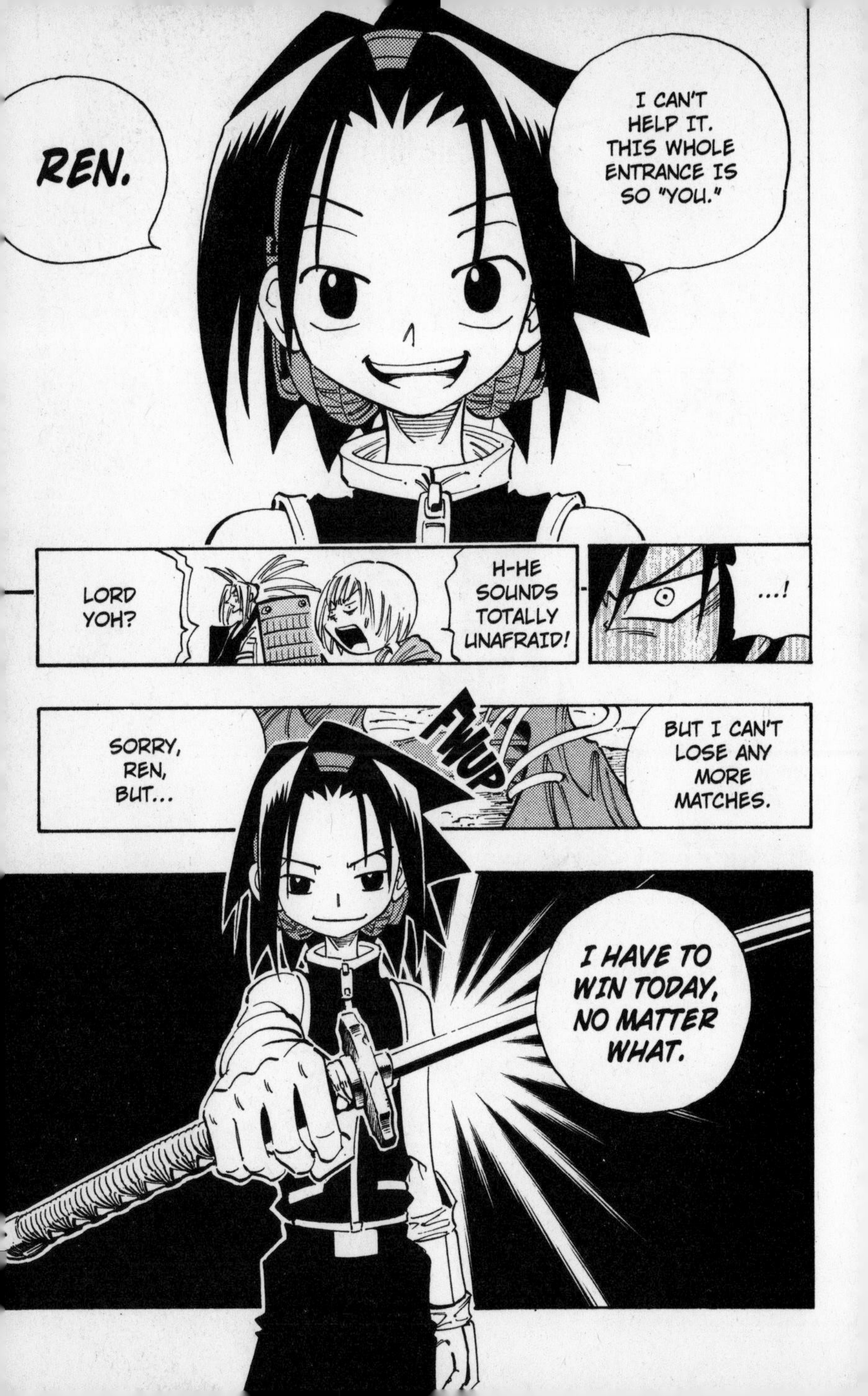
I CAN'T HELP IT. THIS WHOLE ENTRANCE IS SO "YOU."
REN.
...!
H-HE SOUNDS TOTALLY UNAFRAID!
LORD YOH?
BUT I CAN'T LOSE ANY MORE MATCHES.
FWUP
SORRY, REN, BUT...
I HAVE TO WIN TODAY, NO MATTER WHAT.

SHAMAN KING CHARACTER FILE No.29

道円

タオ エン

1999
(FEB)

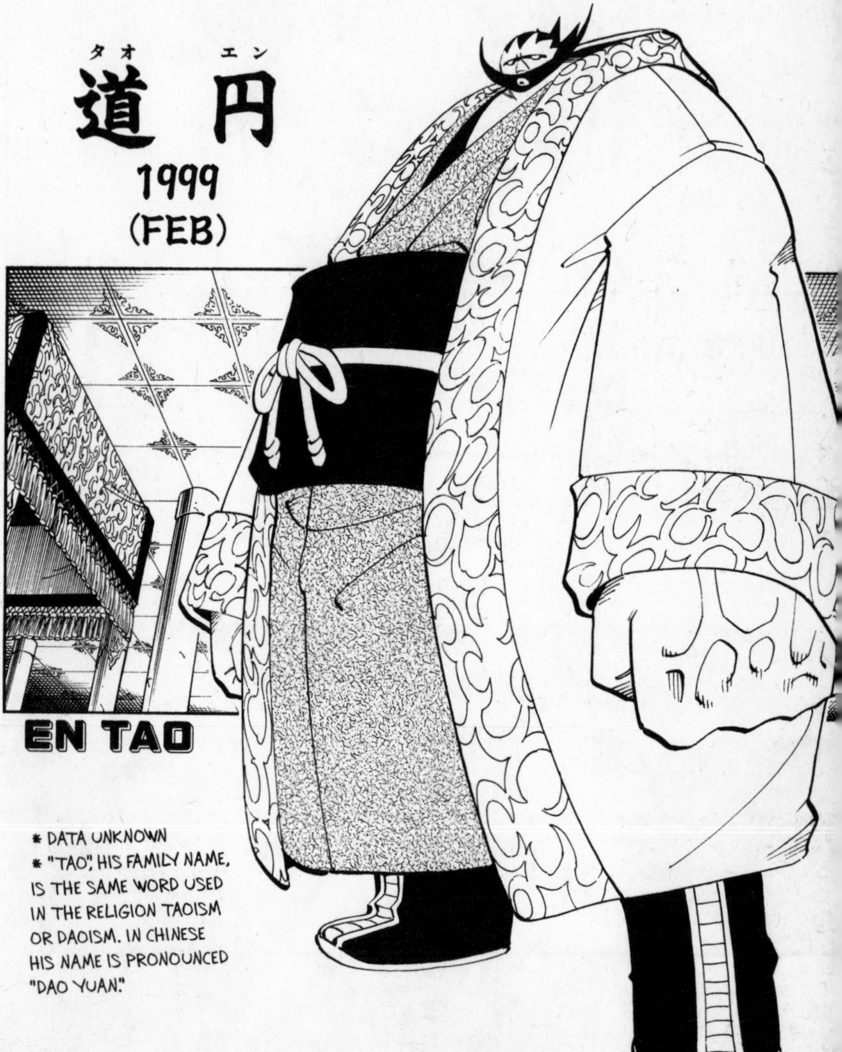

EN TAO

* DATA UNKNOWN
* "TAO," HIS FAMILY NAME, IS THE SAME WORD USED IN THE RELIGION TAOISM OR DAOISM. IN CHINESE HIS NAME IS PRONOUNCED "DAO YUAN."

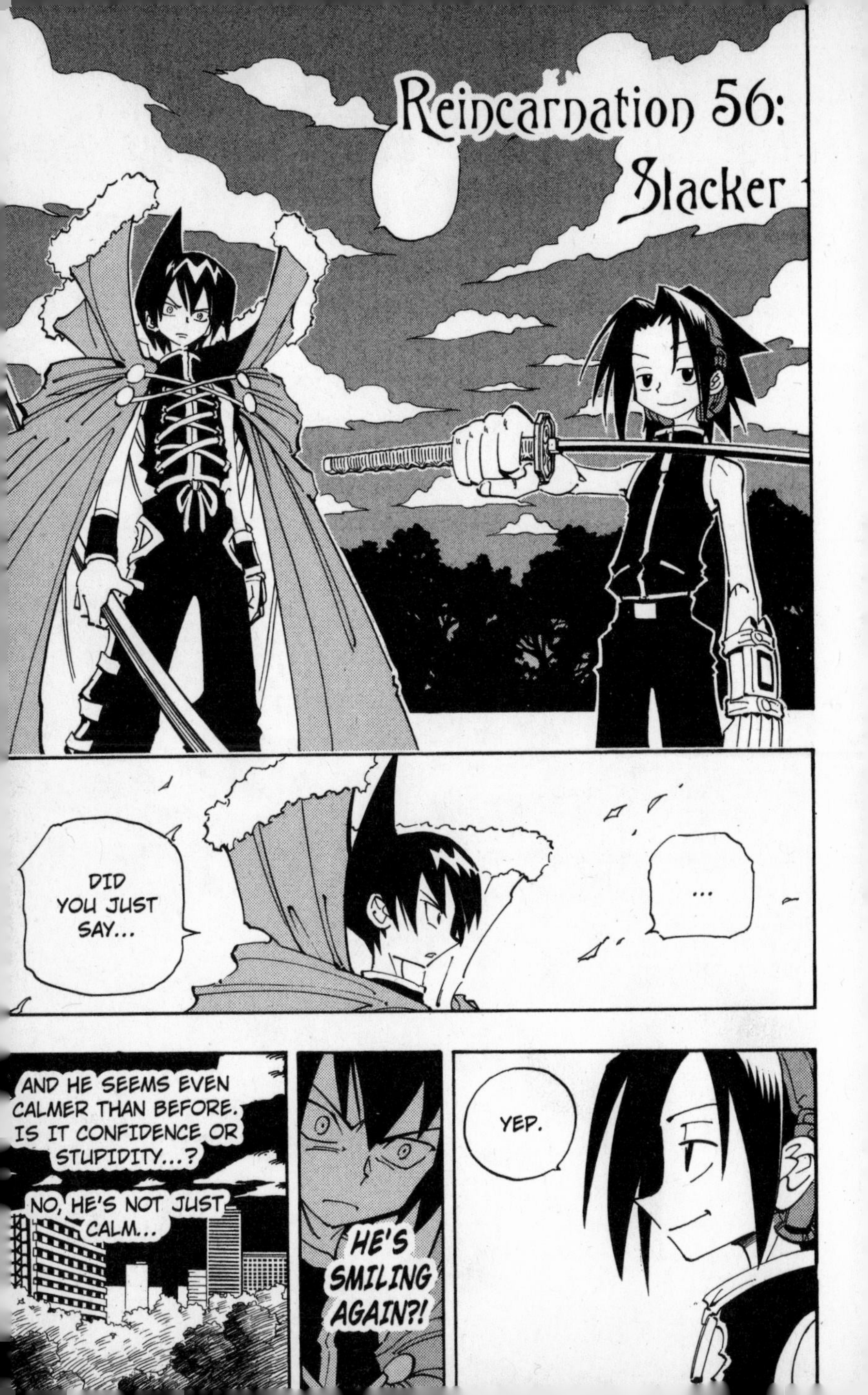
Reincarnation 56:
Slacker
...
DID YOU JUST SAY...
YEP.
HE'S SMILING AGAIN?!
AND HE SEEMS EVEN CALMER THAN BEFORE. IS IT CONFIDENCE OR STUPIDITY...?
NO, HE'S NOT JUST CALM...

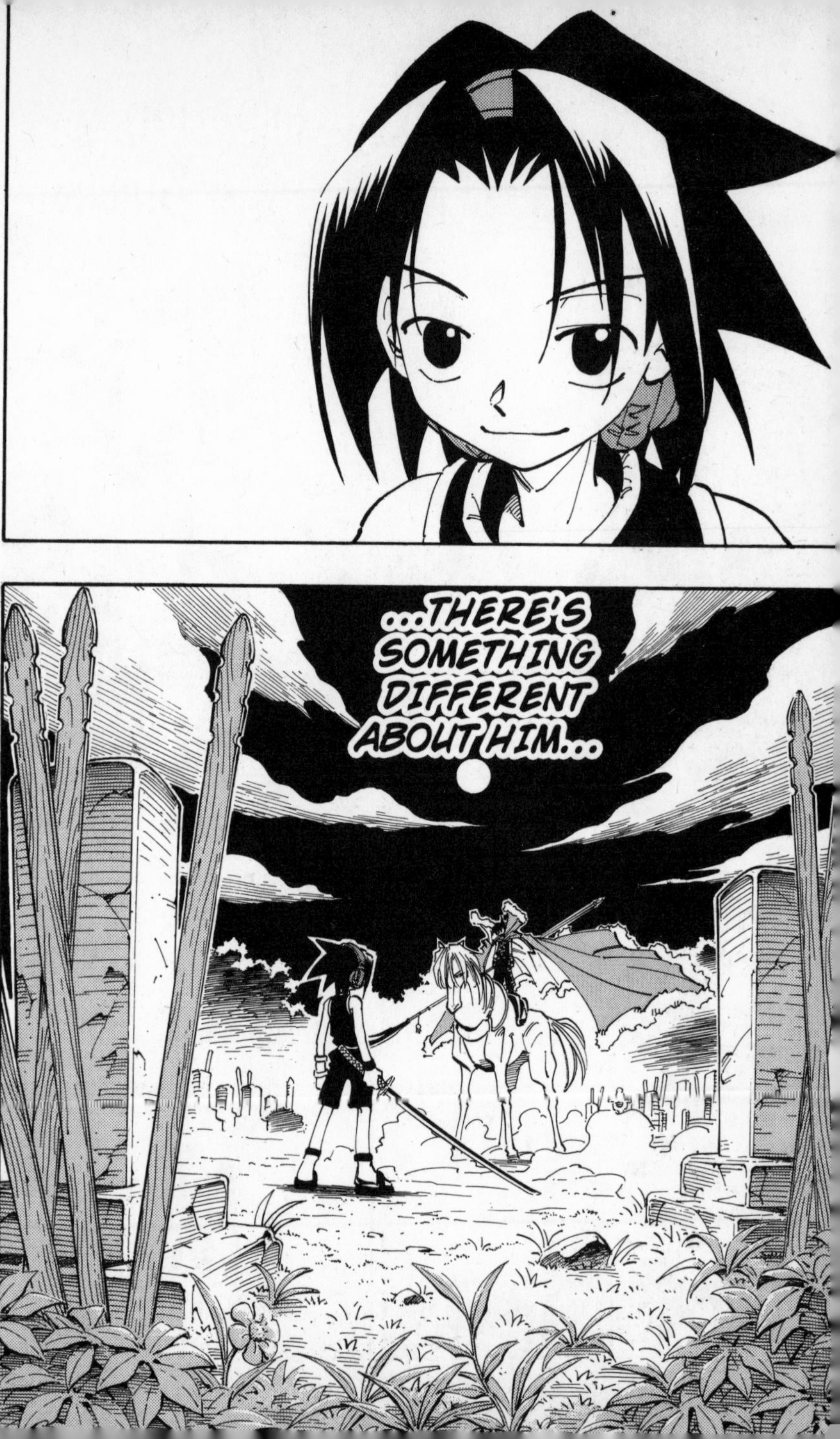
...THERE'S SOMETHING DIFFERENT ABOUT HIM...

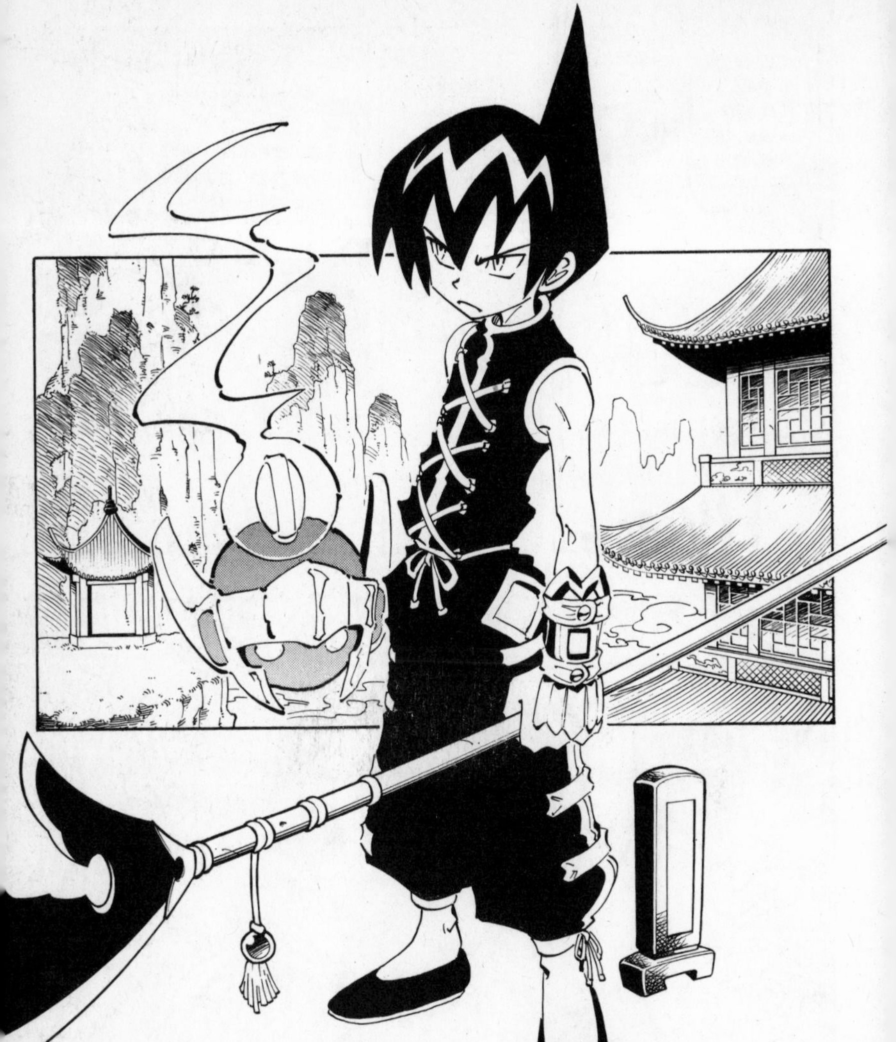

Reincarnation 56: Slacker

READ THIS WAY

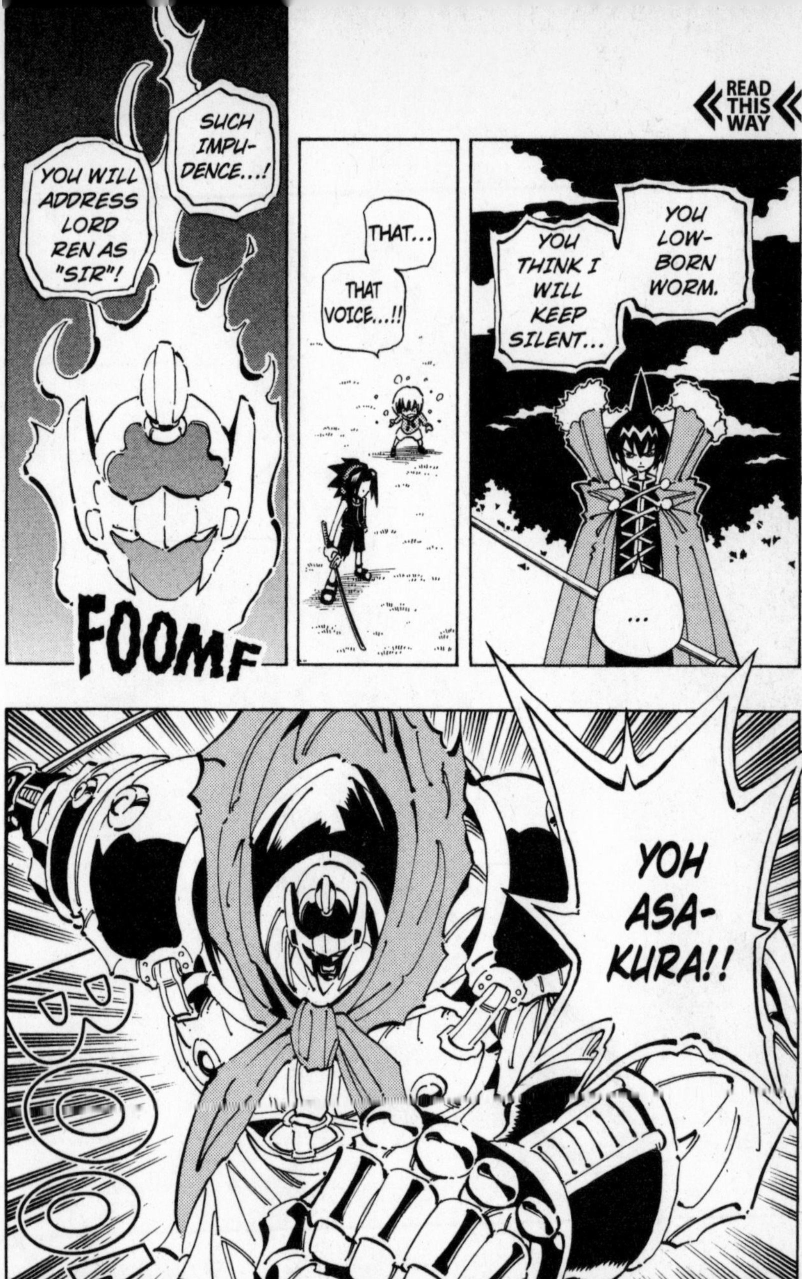
YOU LOW-BORN WORM.
YOU THINK I WILL KEEP SILENT...
...
THAT...
THAT VOICE...!!
SUCH IMPU-DENCE...!
YOU WILL ADDRESS LORD REN AS "SIR"!
FOOMF
YOH ASA-KURA!!
BOOM

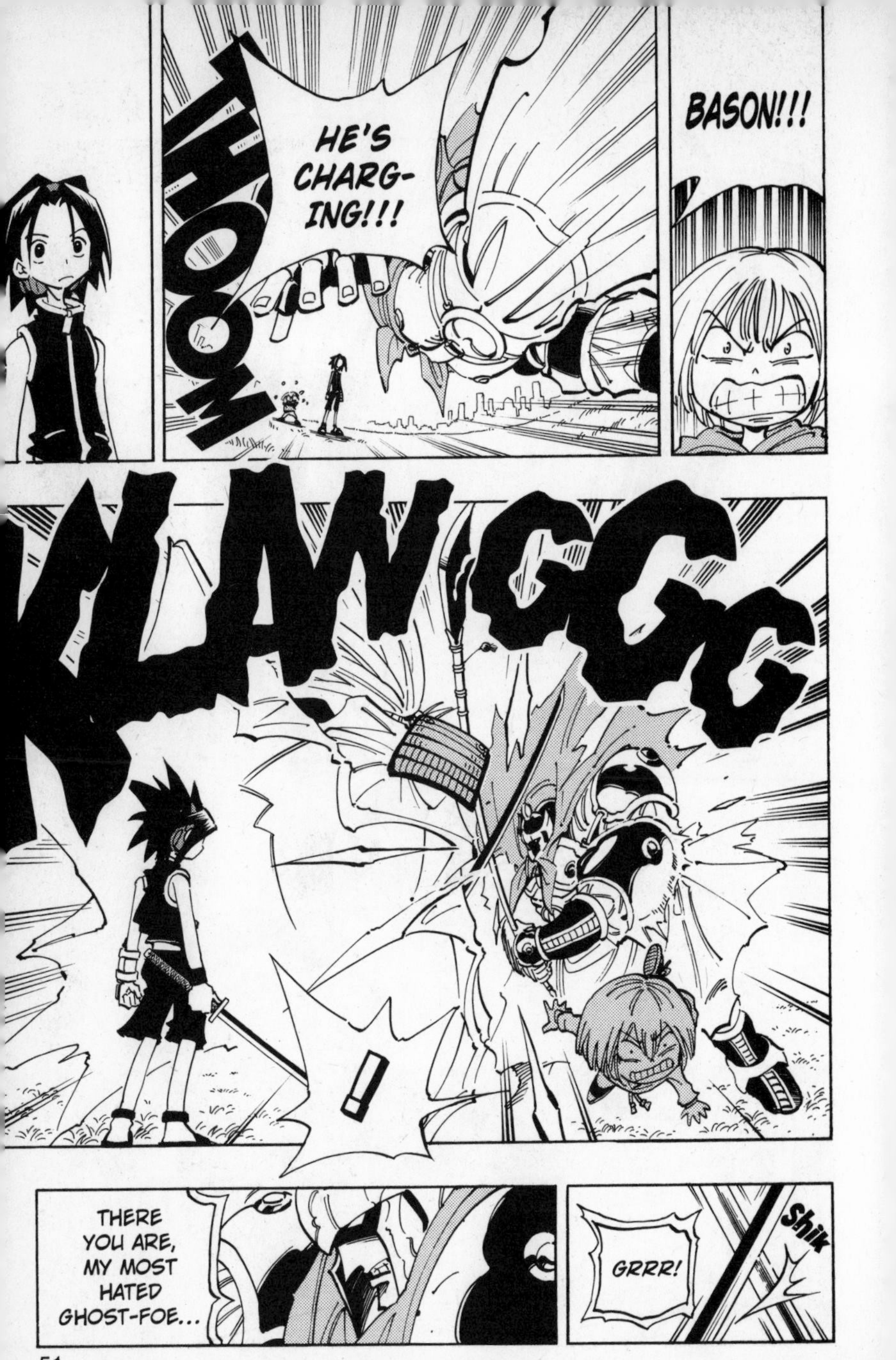
BASON!!!
THOOM
HE'S CHARG-ING!!!
KLANGG
!
Shik
GRRR!
THERE YOU ARE, MY MOST HATED GHOST-FOE...

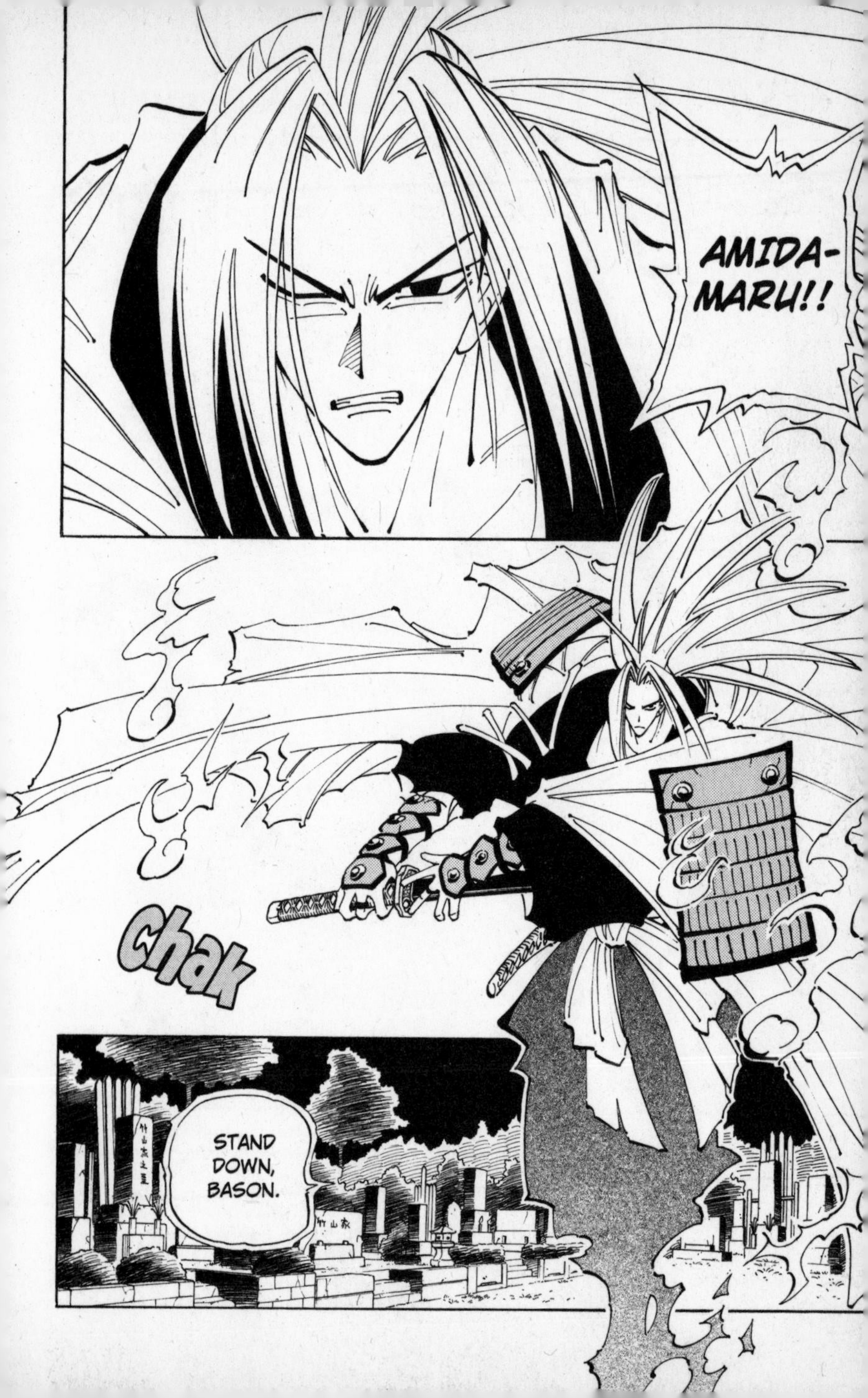
AMIDA-MARU!!
Chak
STAND DOWN, BASON.

READ THIS WAY

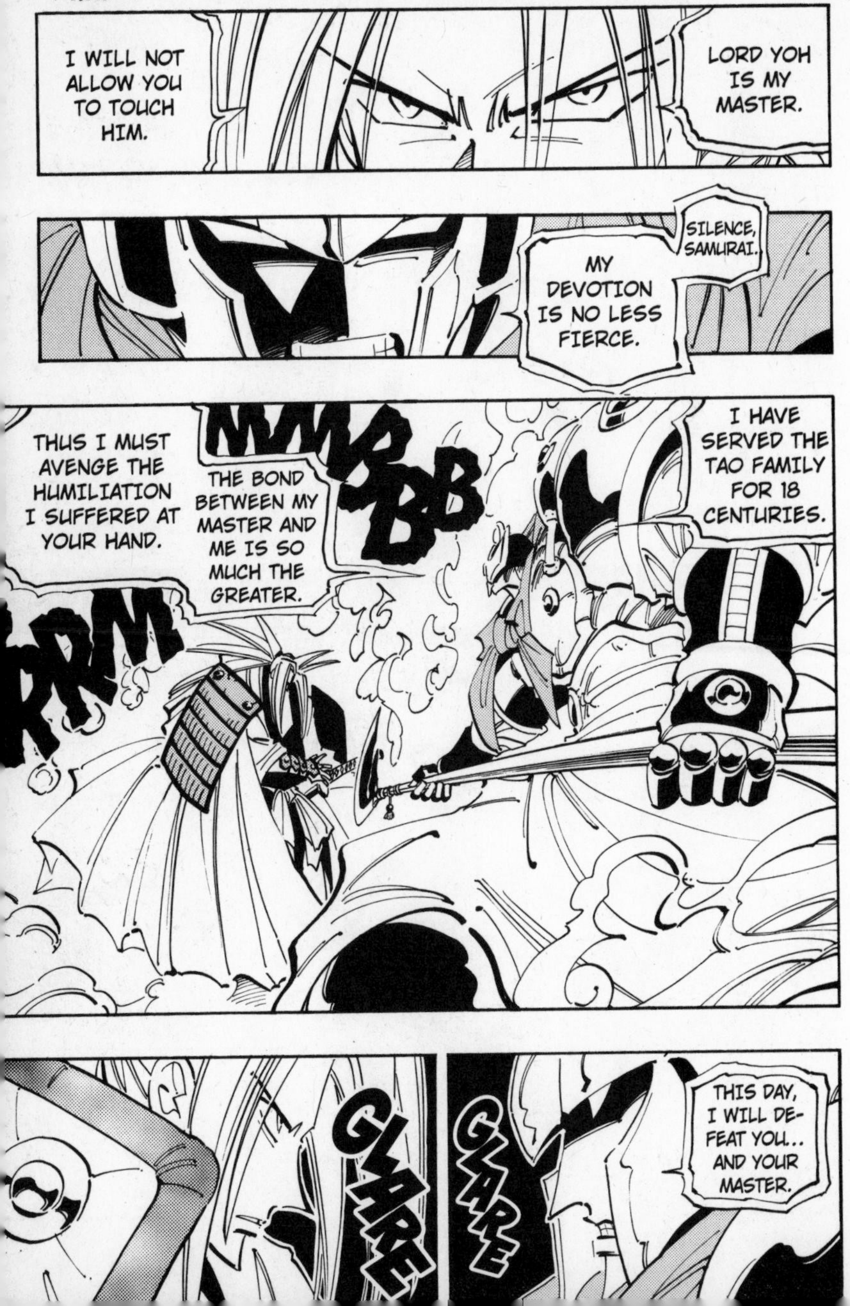

LORD YOH IS MY MASTER.
I WILL NOT ALLOW YOU TO TOUCH HIM.
SILENCE, SAMURAI.
MY DEVOTION IS NO LESS FIERCE.
I HAVE SERVED THE TAO FAMILY FOR 18 CENTURIES.
THE BOND BETWEEN MY MASTER AND ME IS SO MUCH THE GREATER.
THUS I MUST AVENGE THE HUMILIATION I SUFFERED AT YOUR HAND.
THIS DAY, I WILL DE-FEAT YOU... AND YOUR MASTER.
GLARE
GLARE

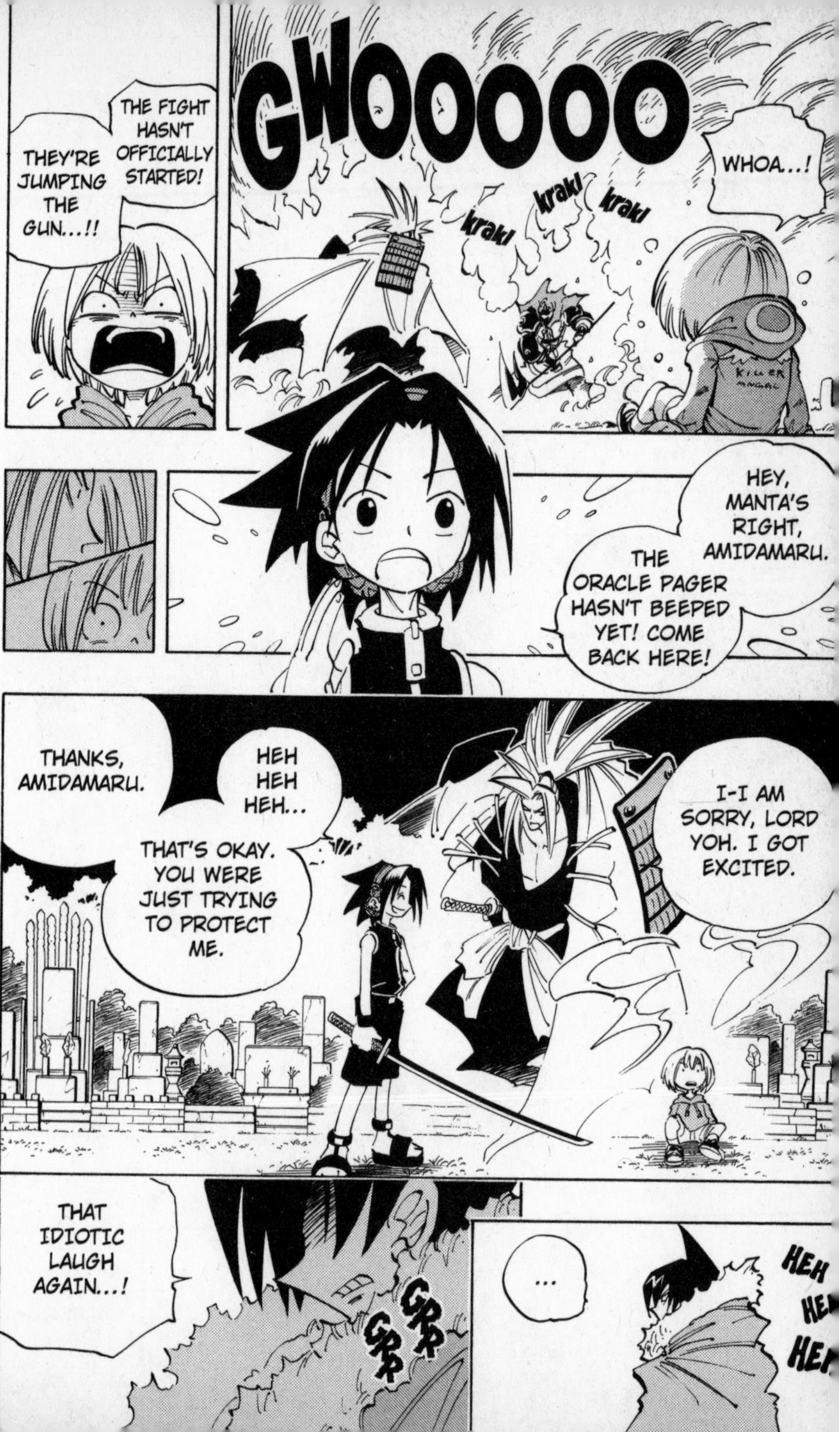
GWOOOOO
WHOA...!
krak!
krak!
krak!
THE FIGHT HASN'T OFFICIALLY STARTED!
THEY'RE JUMPING THE GUN...!!
HEY, MANTA'S RIGHT, AMIDAMARU.
THE ORACLE PAGER HASN'T BEEPED YET! COME BACK HERE!
I-I AM SORRY, LORD YOH. I GOT EXCITED.
HEH HEH HEH...
THANKS, AMIDAMARU.
THAT'S OKAY. YOU WERE JUST TRYING TO PROTECT ME.
HEH
...
THAT IDIOTIC LAUGH AGAIN...!
GRR
GRR

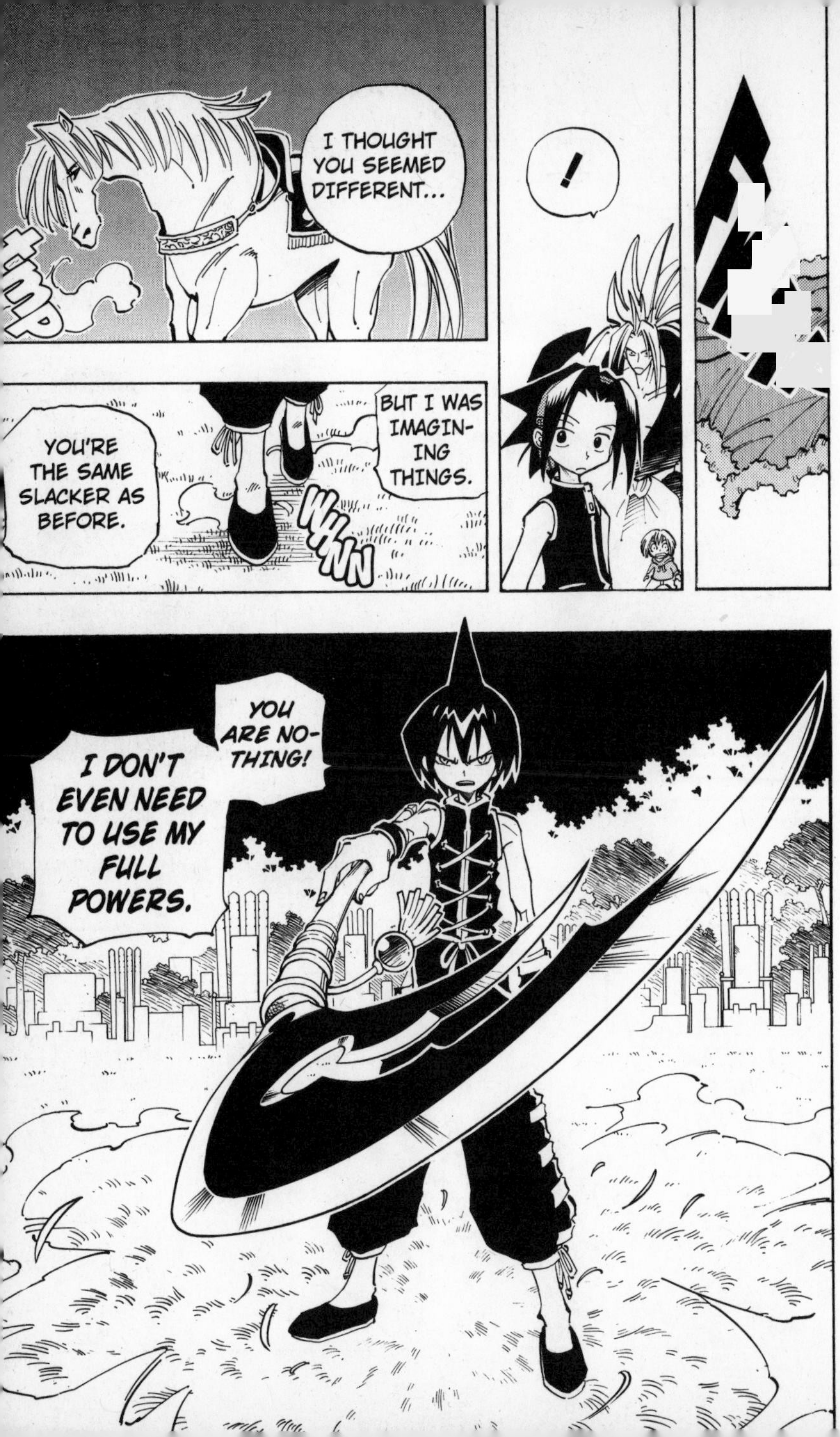
!
I THOUGHT YOU SEEMED DIFFERENT...
tmp
BUT I WAS IMAGINING THINGS.
YOU'RE THE SAME SLACKER AS BEFORE.
WHNN
YOU ARE NO-THING!
I DON'T EVEN NEED TO USE MY FULL POWERS.

READ THIS WAY

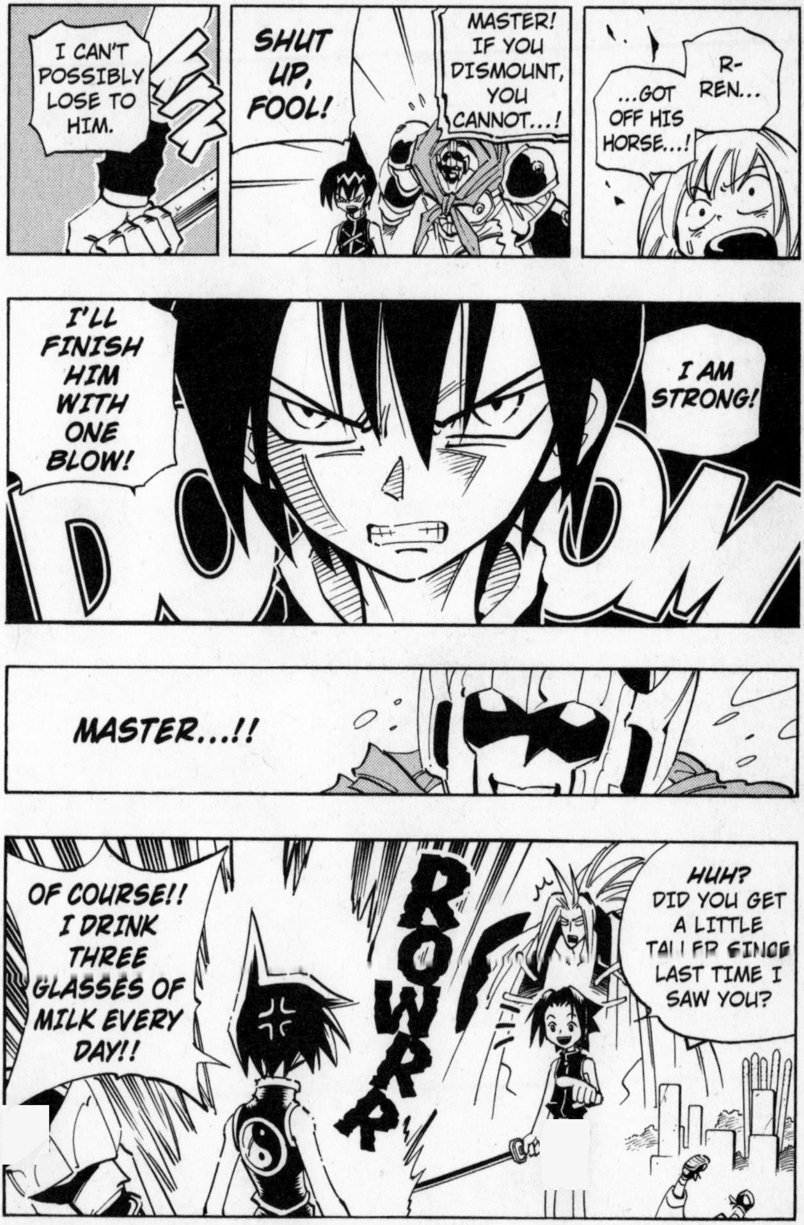
R- REN...
...GOT OFF HIS HORSE...!
MASTER! IF YOU DISMOUNT, YOU CANNOT...!
SHUT UP, FOOL!
I CAN'T POSSIBLY LOSE TO HIM.
I AM STRONG!
I'LL FINISH HIM WITH ONE BLOW!
MASTER...!!
HUH? DID YOU GET A LITTLE TALLER SINCE LAST TIME I SAW YOU?
ROWRR
OF COURSE!! I DRINK THREE GLASSES OF MILK EVERY DAY!!

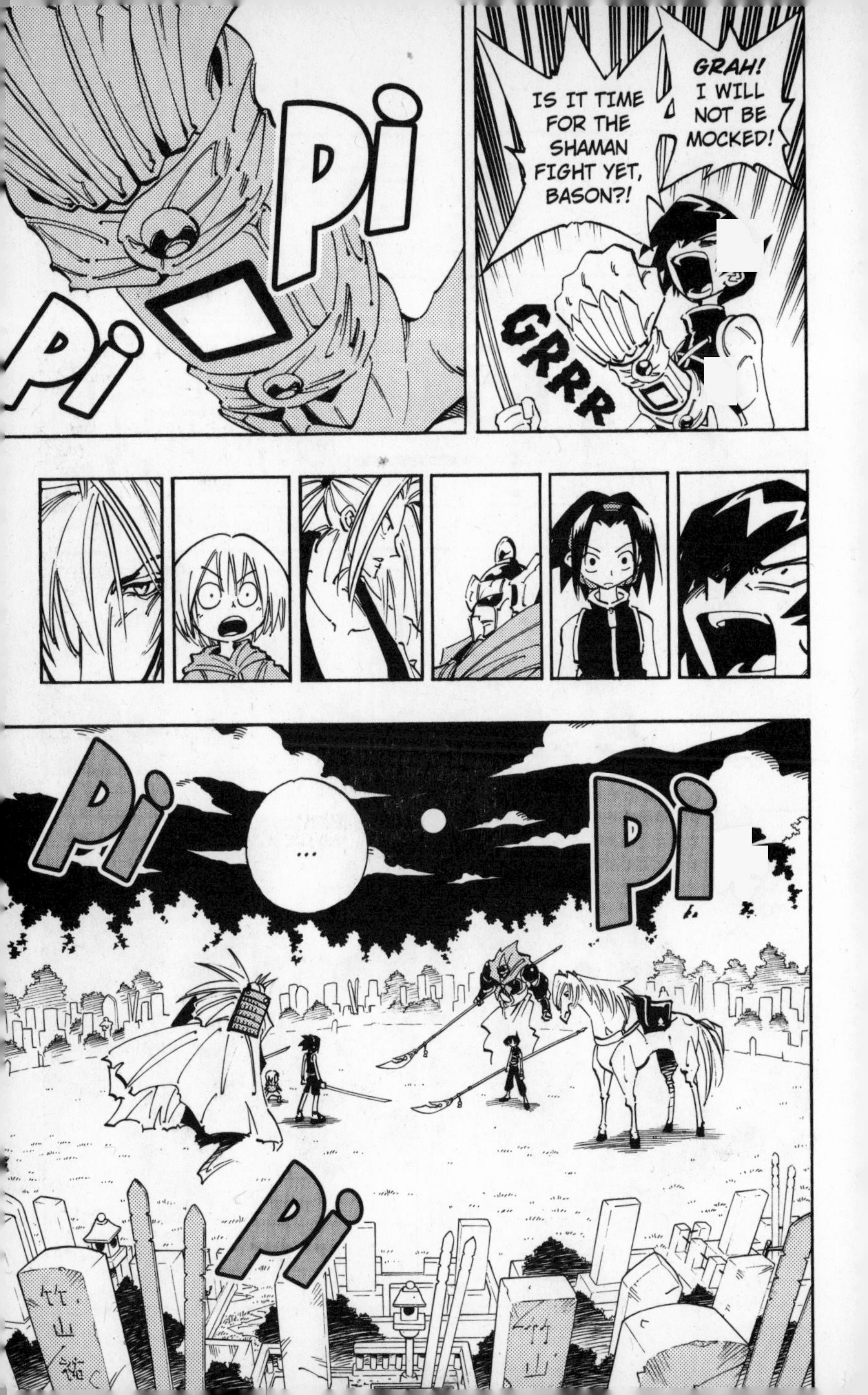

GRAH! I WILL NOT BE MOCKED!
IS IT TIME FOR THE SHAMAN FIGHT YET, BASON?!
GRRR
PI
PI
PI
...
PI
PI

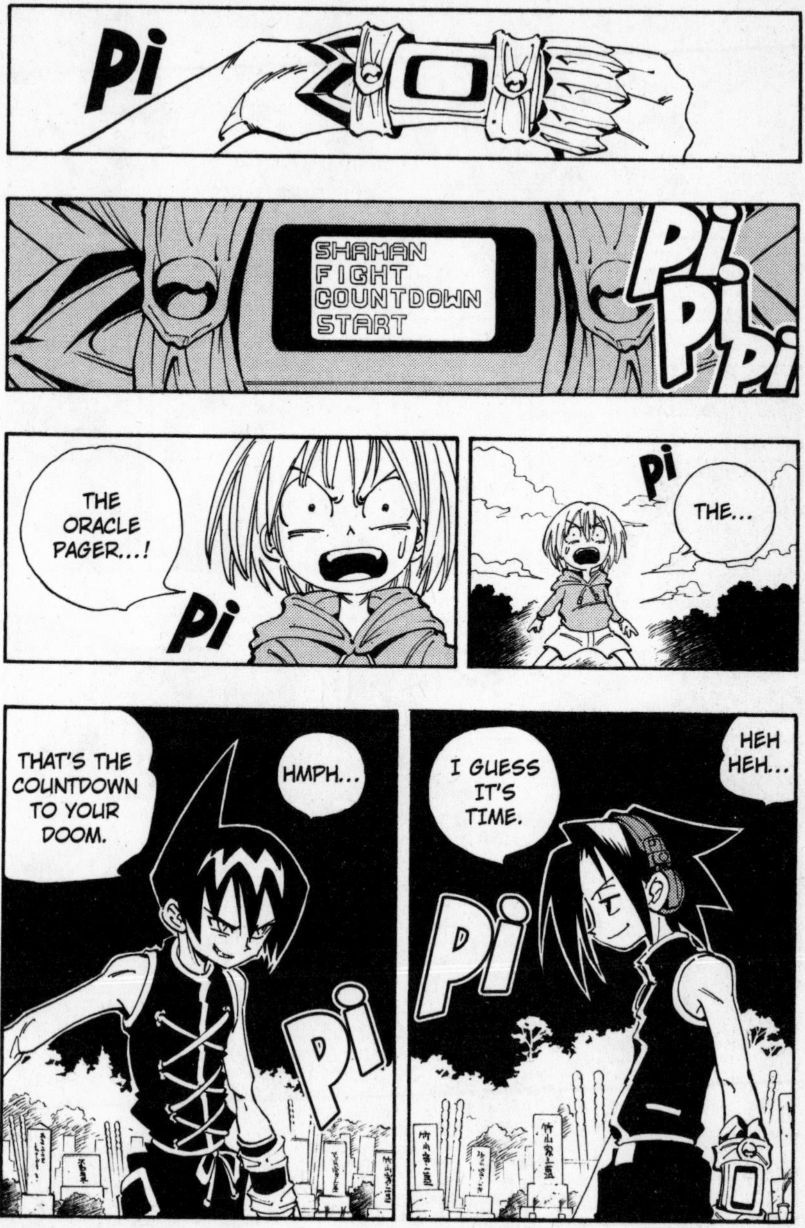
Pi
SHAMAN FIGHT COUNTDOWN START
Pi Pi Pi Pi
Pi
THE...
THE ORACLE PAGER...!
Pi
HEH HEH...
I GUESS IT'S TIME.
Pi
HMPH...
THAT'S THE COUNTDOWN TO YOUR DOOM.
Pi

READ THIS WAY

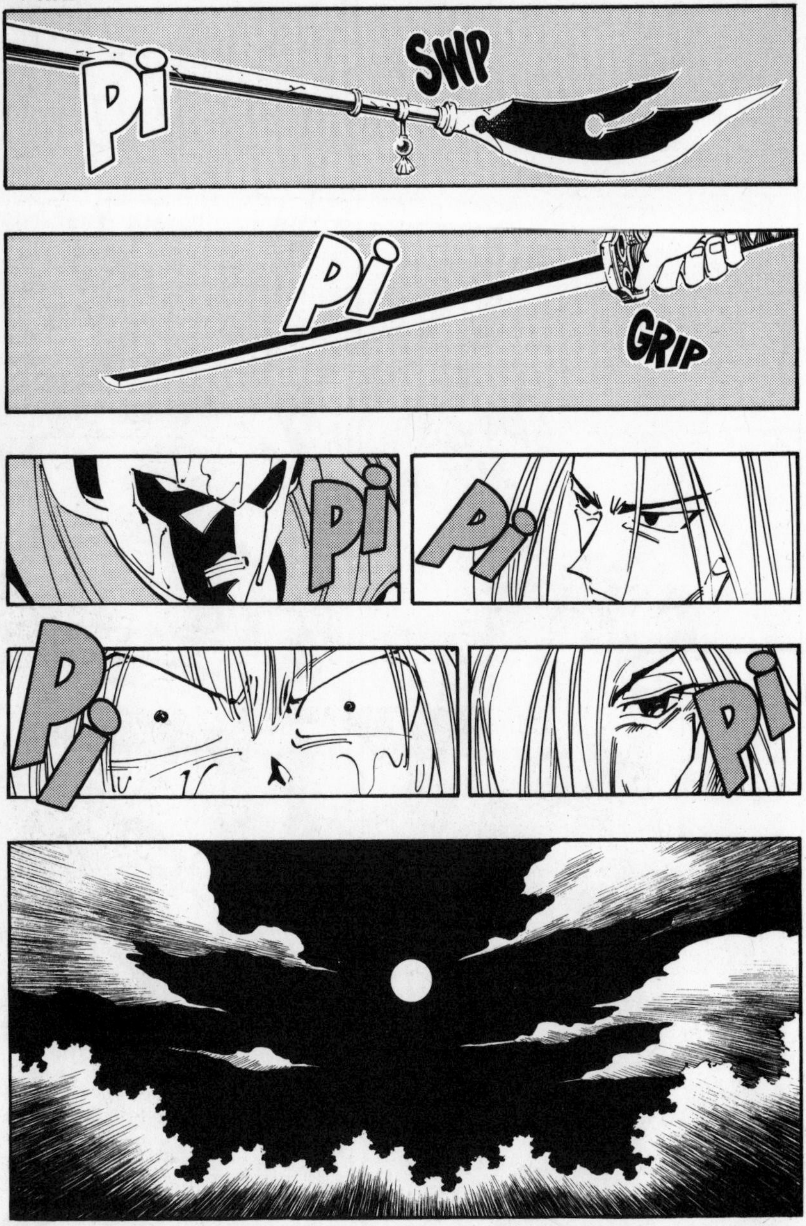
SWP
Pi
GRIP
Pi
Pi
Pi
Pi
Pi

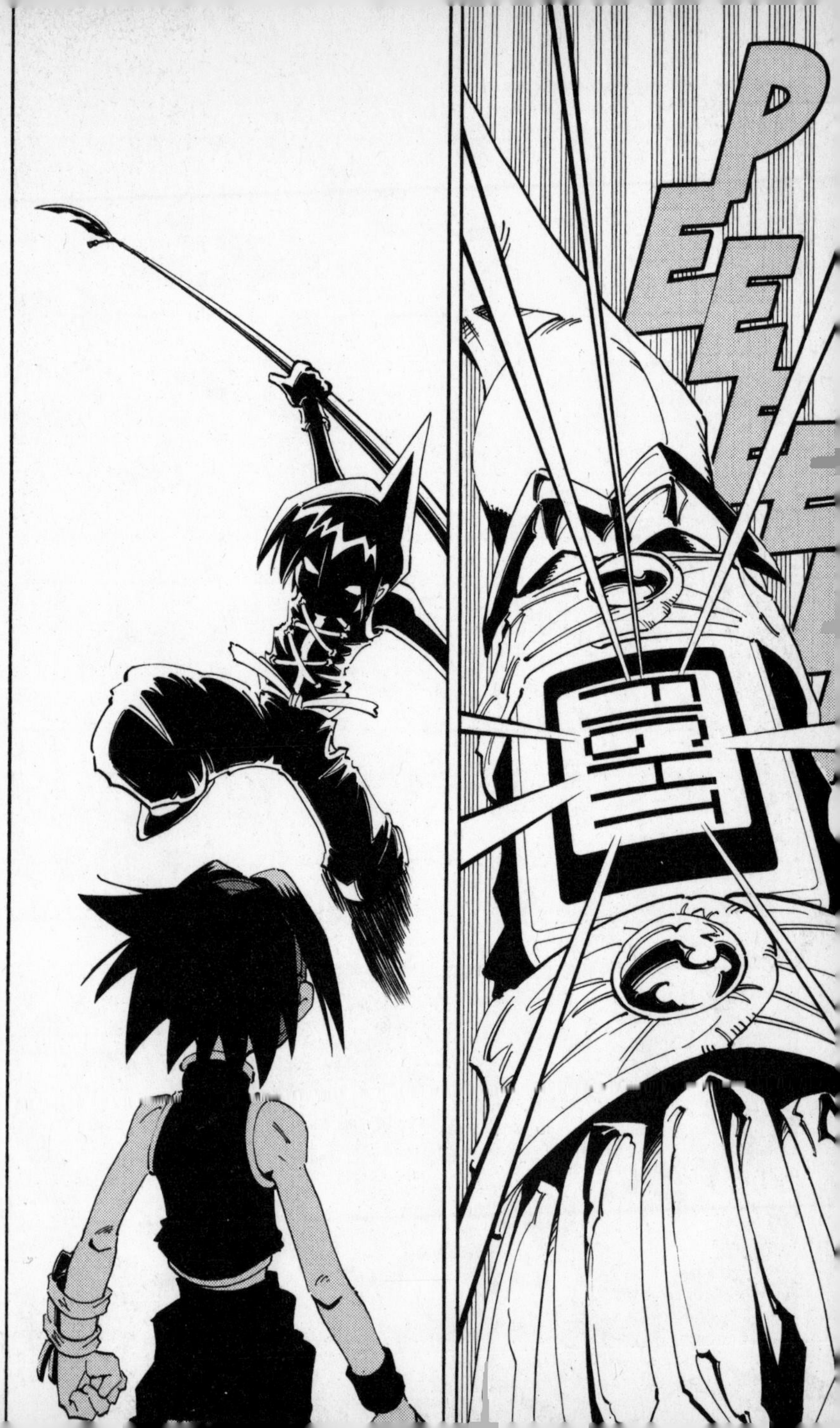
PEEEE
FIGHT

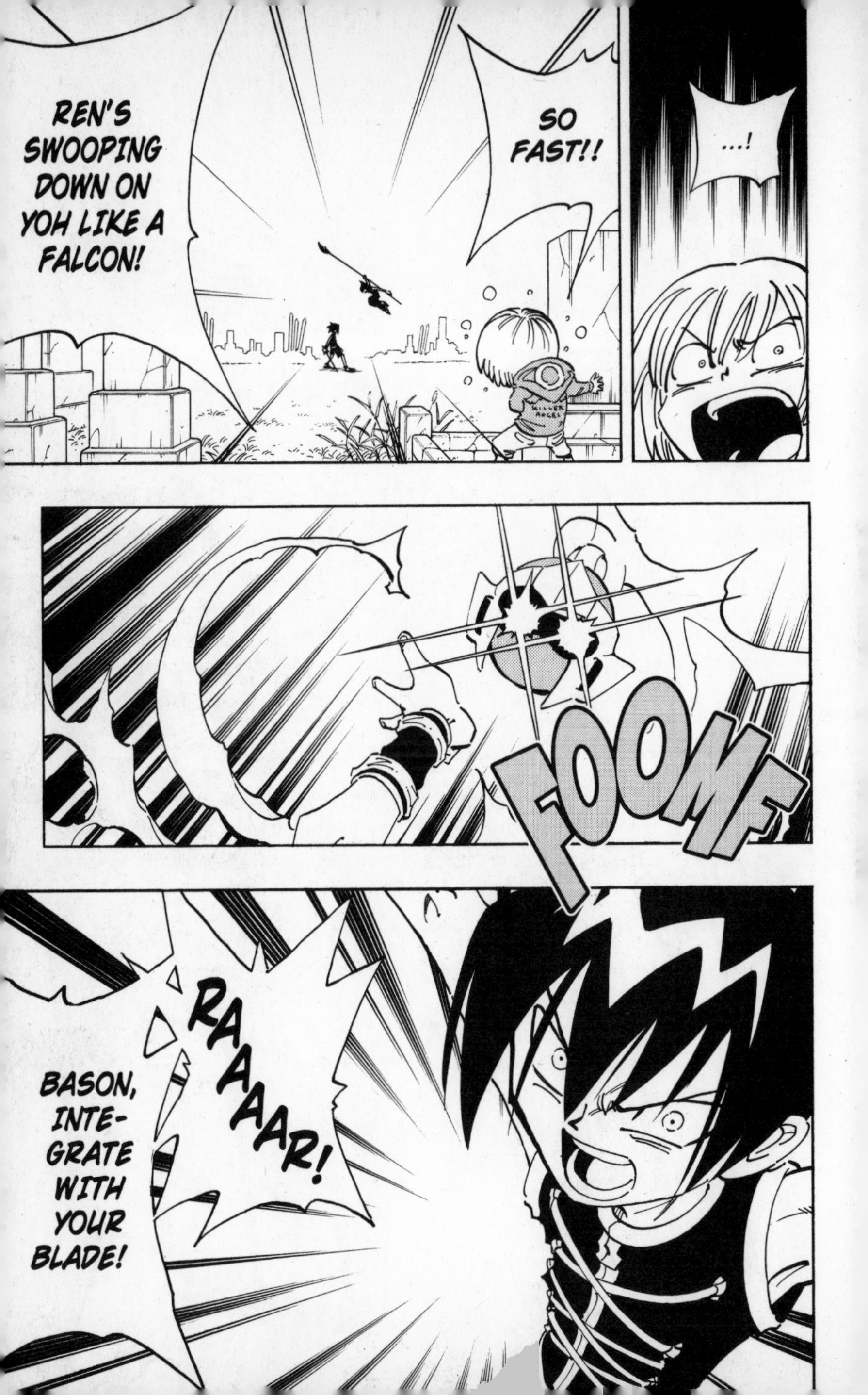
...!
SO FAST!!
REN'S SWOOPING DOWN ON YOH LIKE A FALCON!
FOOMF
RAAAAR!
BASON, INTE-GRATE WITH YOUR BLADE!

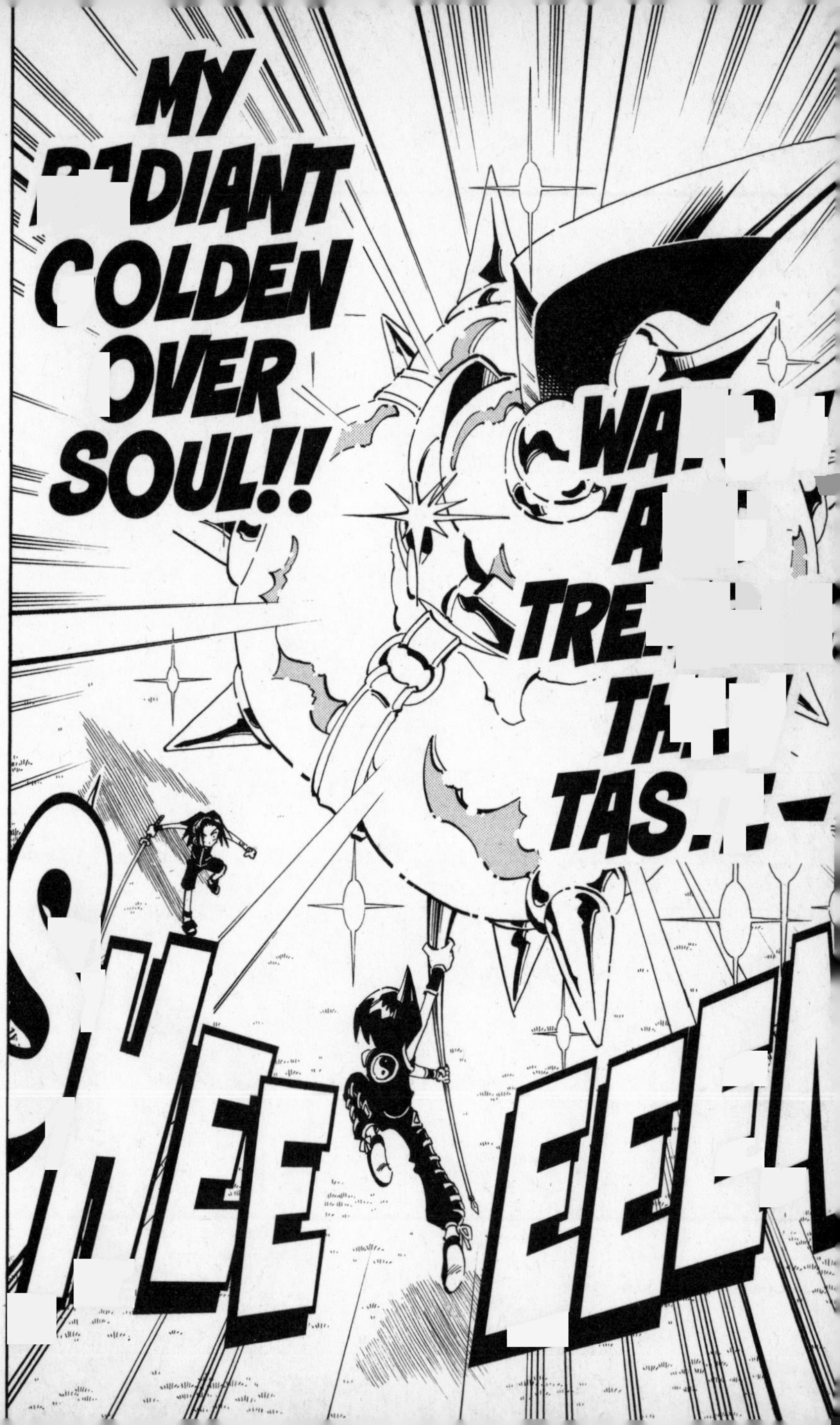
MY RADIANT GOLDEN OVER SOUL!!

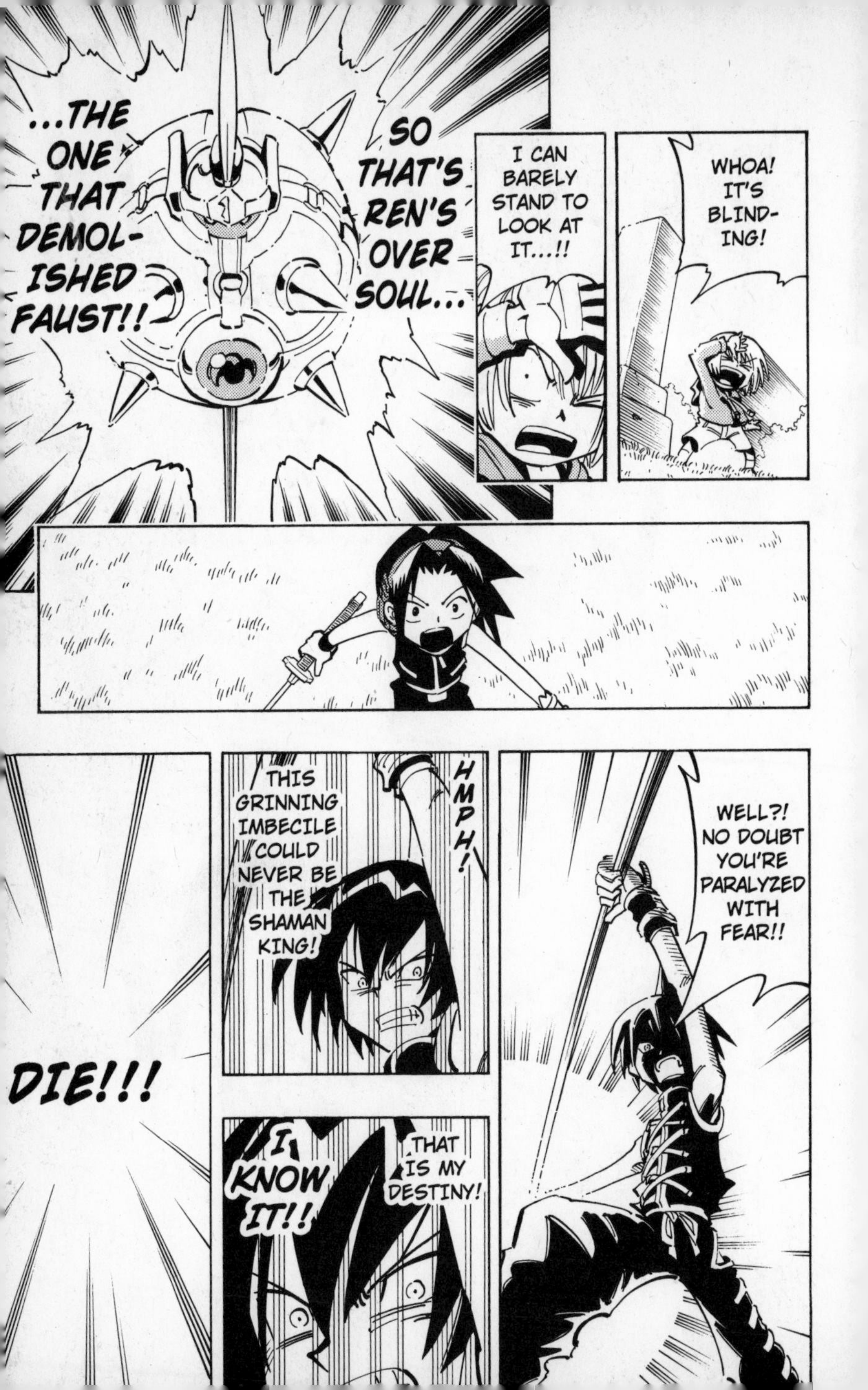
WHOA! IT'S BLINDING!
I CAN BARELY STAND TO LOOK AT IT...!!
SO THAT'S REN'S OVER SOUL...
...THE ONE THAT DEMOLISHED FAUST!!
WELL?! NO DOUBT YOU'RE PARALYZED WITH FEAR!!
HMPH!
THIS GRINNING IMBECILE COULD NEVER BE THE SHAMAN KING!
THAT IS MY DESTINY!
I KNOW IT!!
DIE!!!

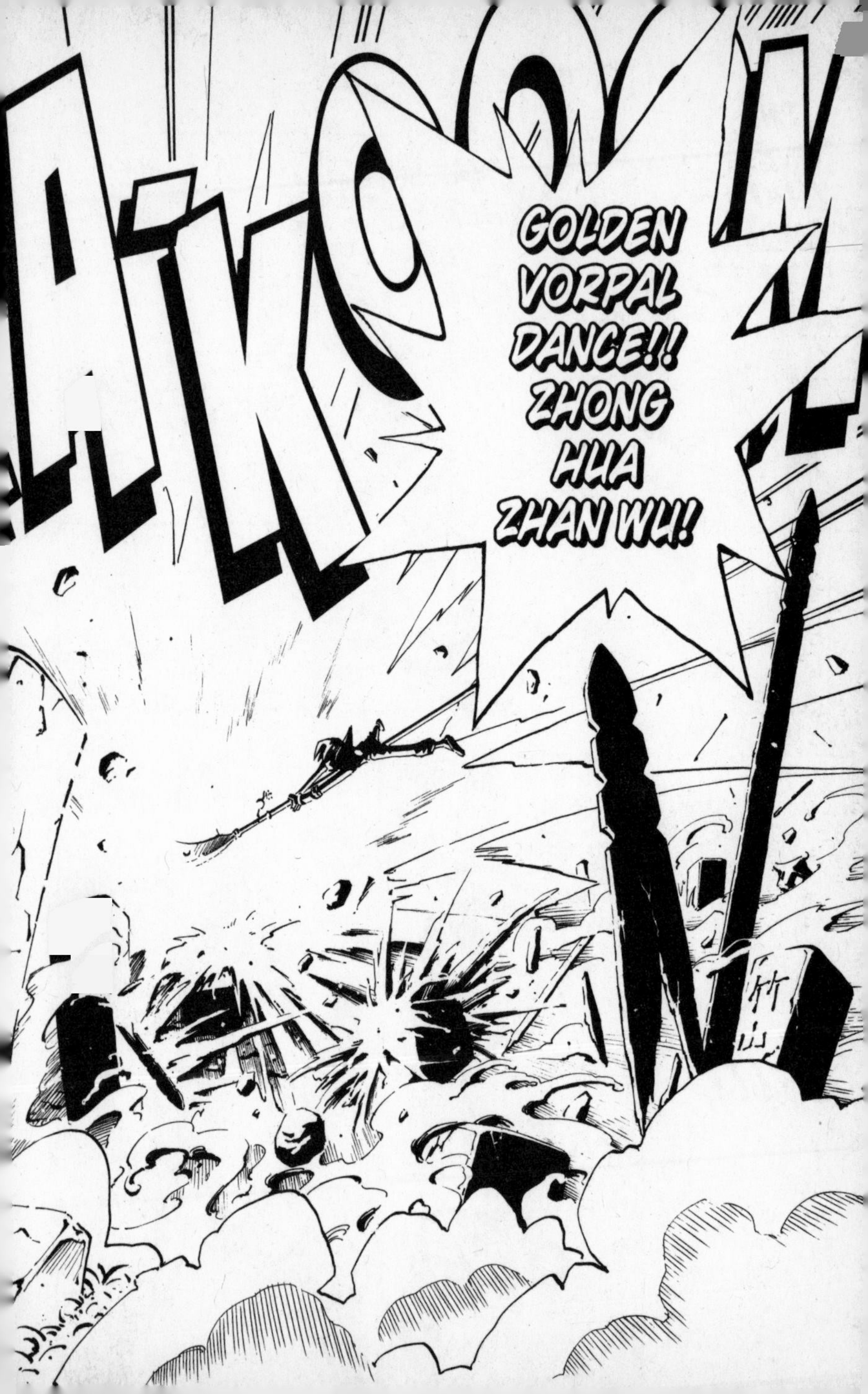
GOLDEN VORPAL DANCE!! ZHONG HUA ZHAN WU!

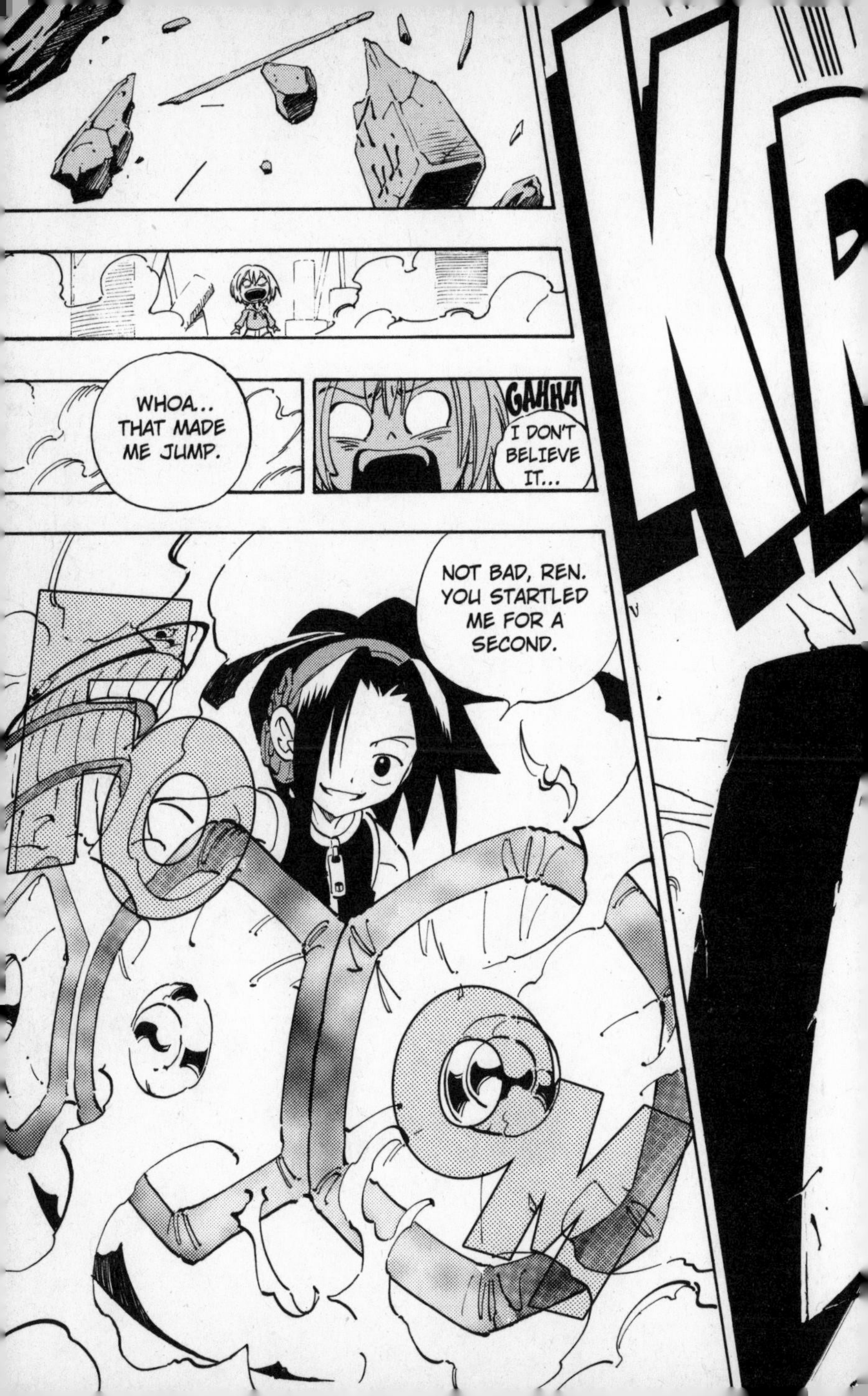
GAHHH
I DON'T BELIEVE IT...
WHOA... THAT MADE ME JUMP.
NOT BAD, REN. YOU STARTLED ME FOR A SECOND.

SHAMAN
KING
7

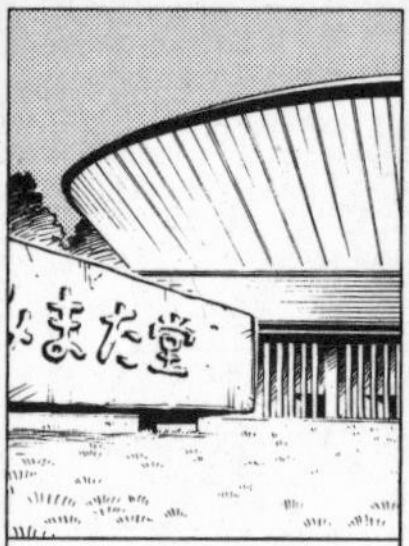

みまた堂

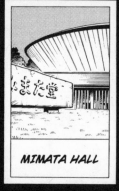

MIMATA HALL

Reincarnation 57: Clash at Mata Cemetery

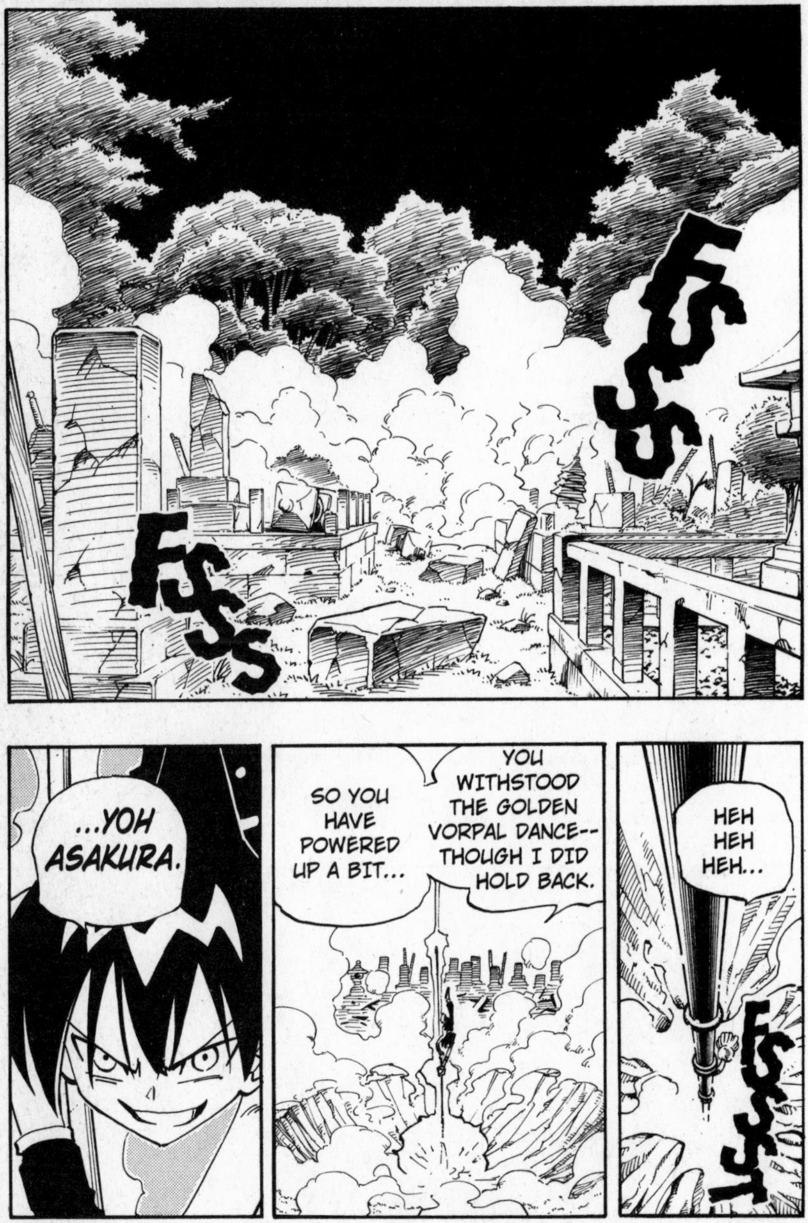
FSSS
FSSS
HEH HEH HEH...
FSSST
YOU WITHSTOOD THE GOLDEN VORPAL DANCE--THOUGH I DID HOLD BACK.
SO YOU HAVE POWERED UP A BIT...
...YOH ASAKURA.

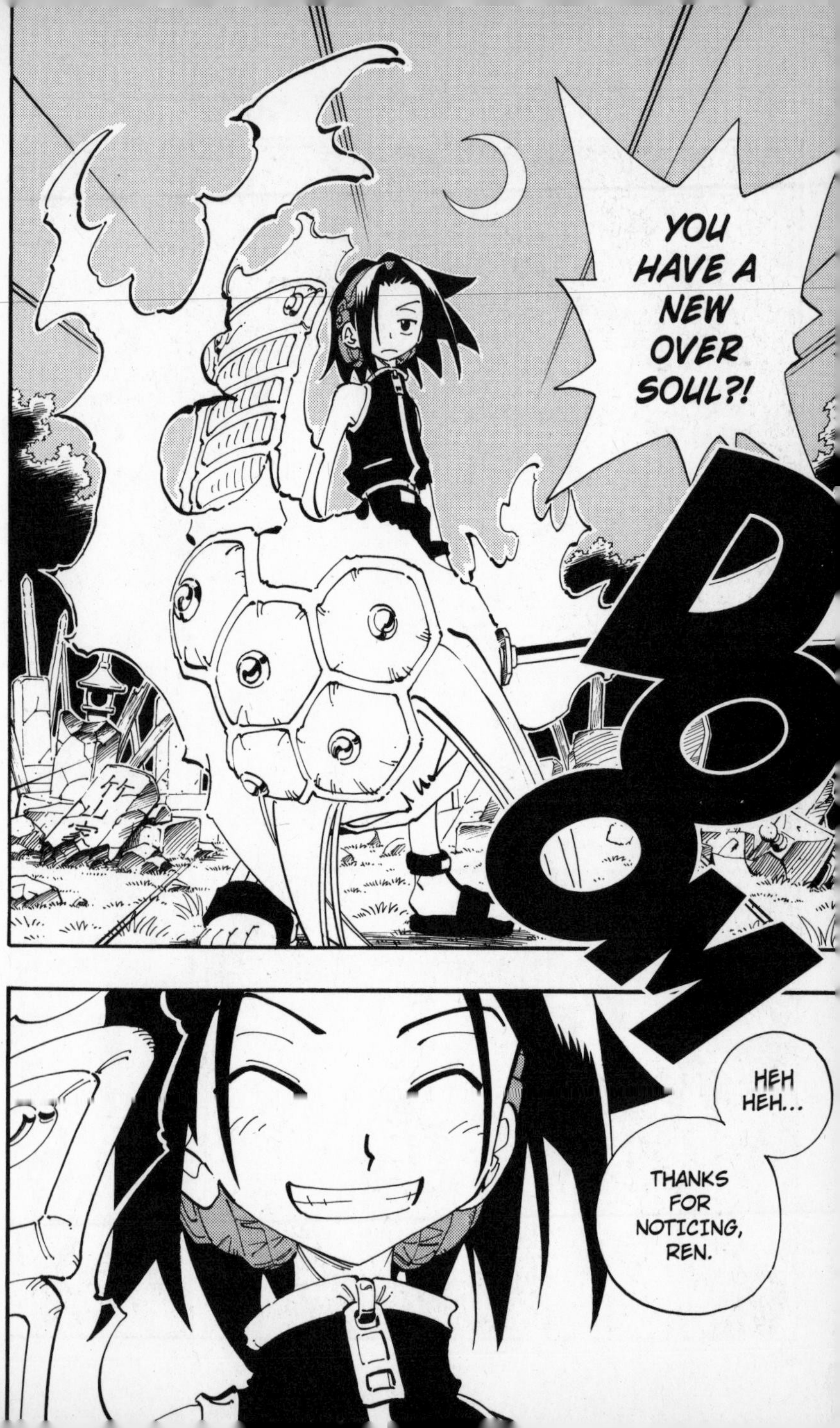
YOU HAVE A NEW OVER SOUL?!
BOOM
HEH HEH...
THANKS FOR NOTICING, REN.

Reincarnation 57: Clash at Mata Cemetery

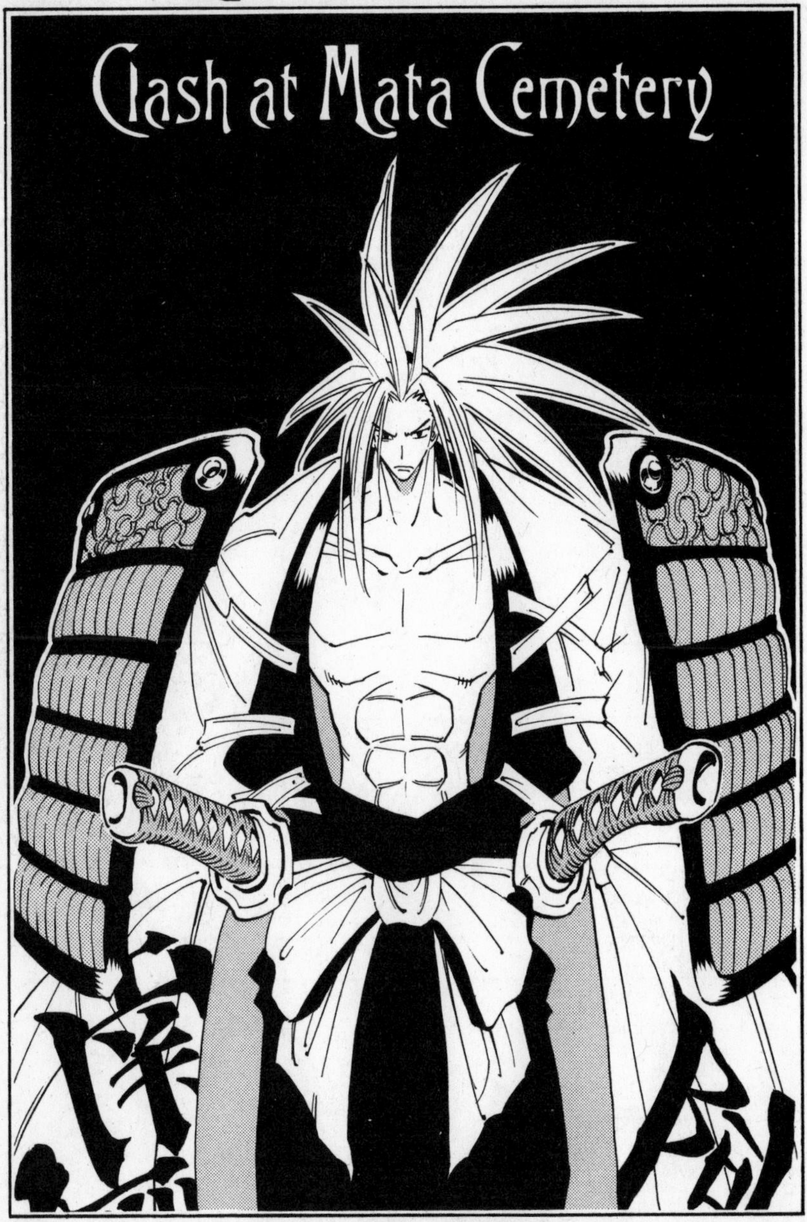

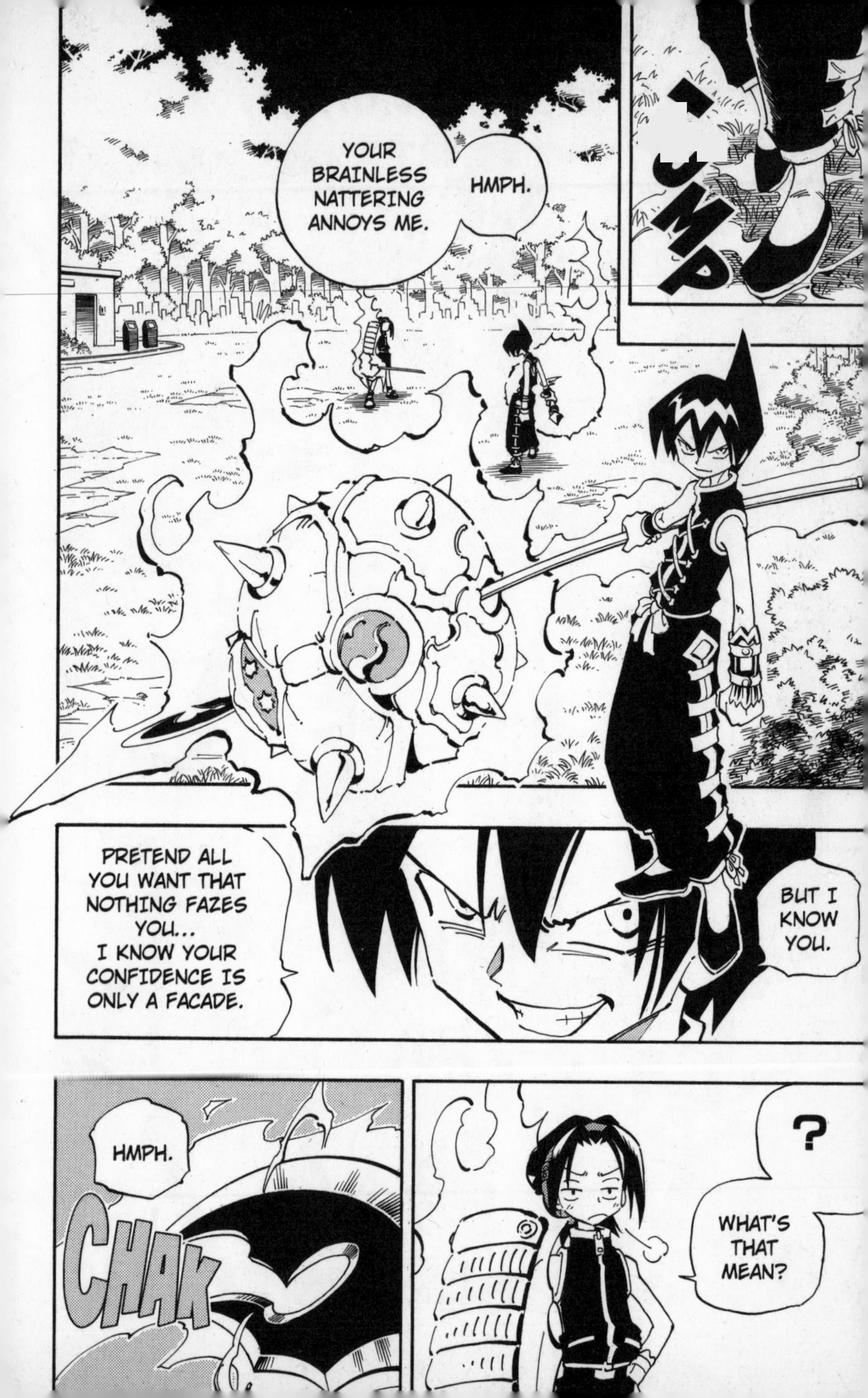
HMPH.
YOUR BRAINLESS NATTERING ANNOYS ME.
BUT I KNOW YOU.
PRETEND ALL YOU WANT THAT NOTHING FAZES YOU... I KNOW YOUR CONFIDENCE IS ONLY A FACADE.
?
WHAT'S THAT MEAN?
HMPH.
CHAK

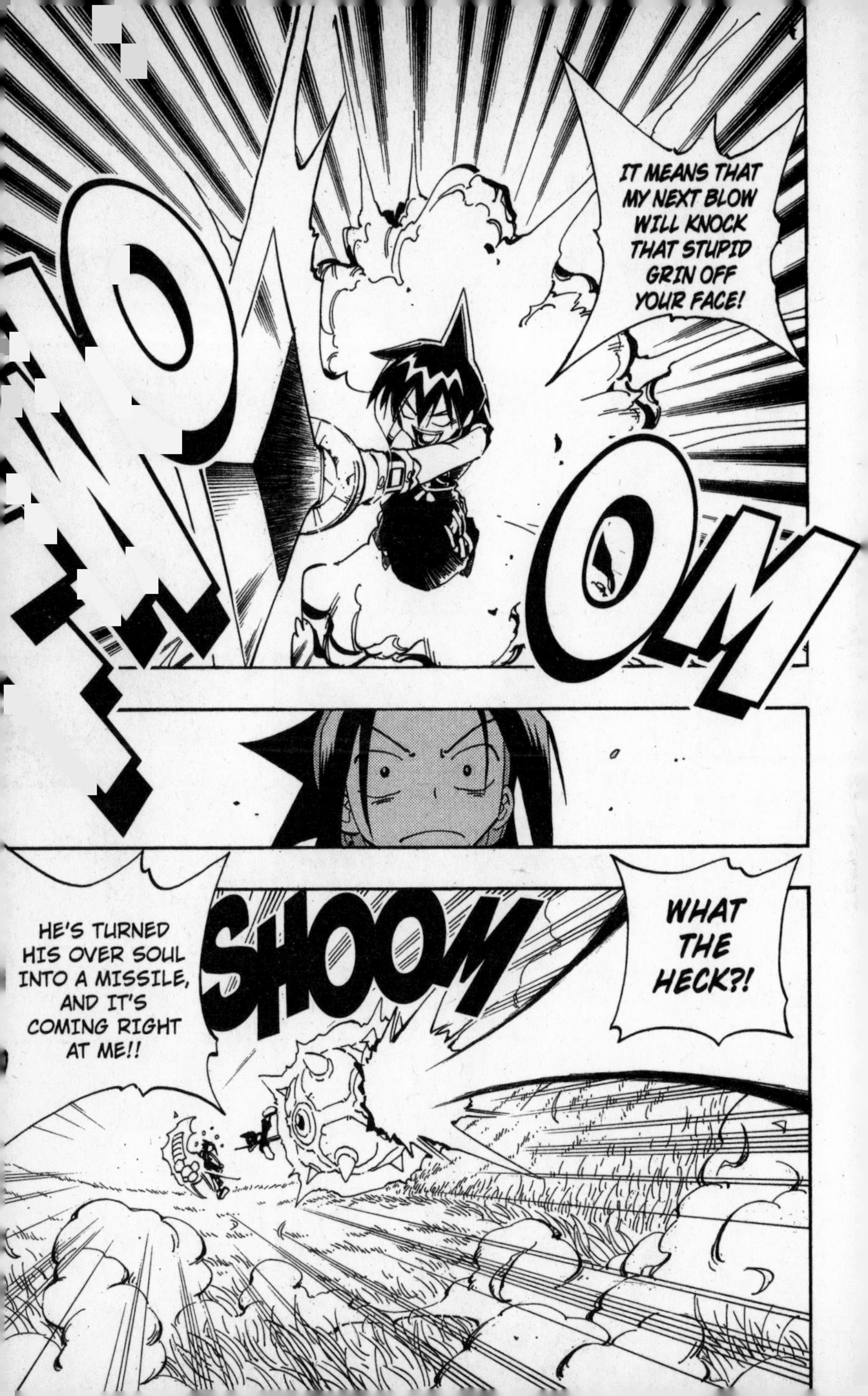
IT MEANS THAT MY NEXT BLOW WILL KNOCK THAT STUPID GRIN OFF YOUR FACE!
WHAT THE HECK?!
SHOOM
HE'S TURNED HIS OVER SOUL INTO A MISSILE, AND IT'S COMING RIGHT AT ME!!

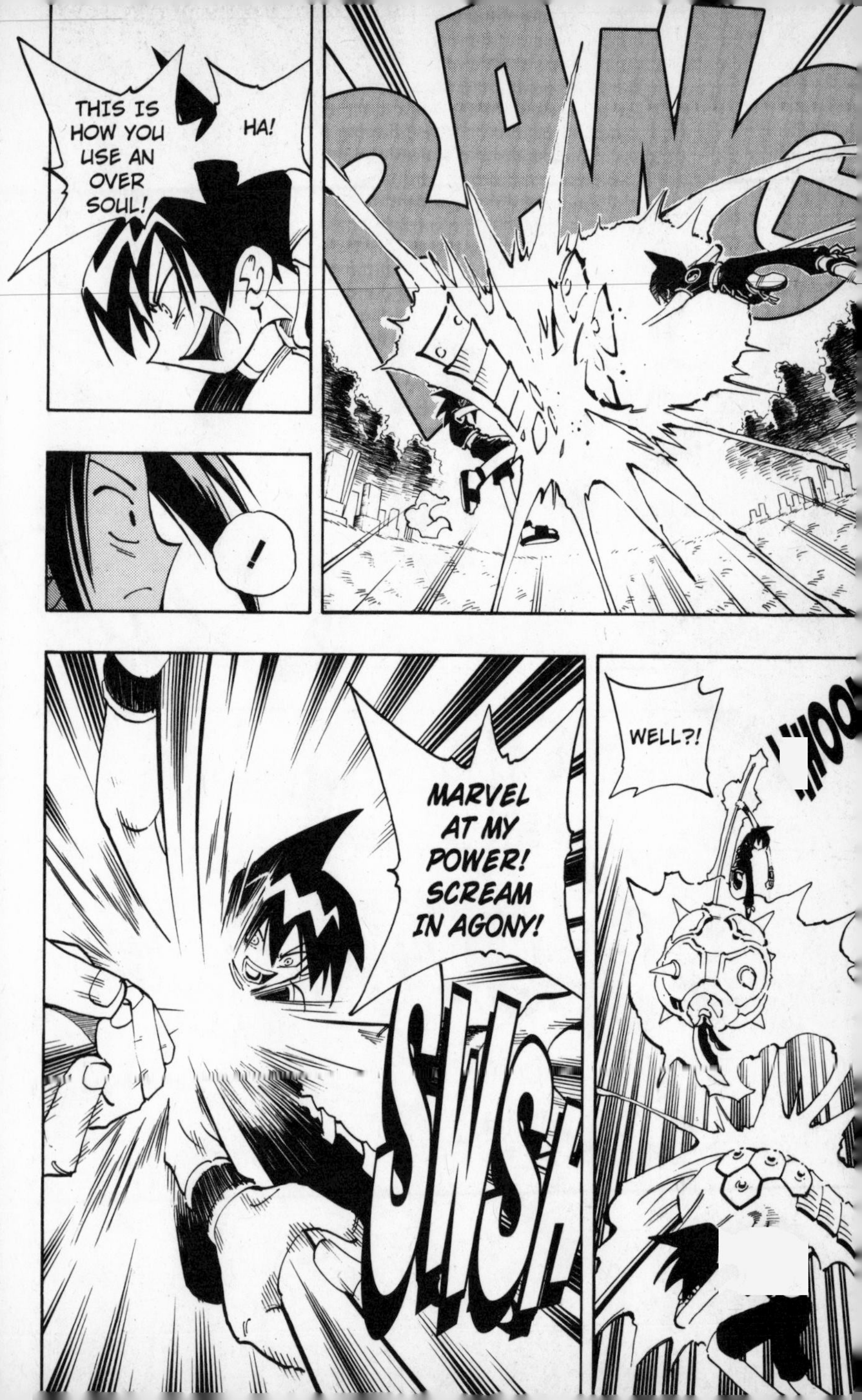
THIS IS HOW YOU USE AN OVER SOUL!
HA!
!
WELL?!
MARVEL AT MY POWER! SCREAM IN AGONY!
SWISH

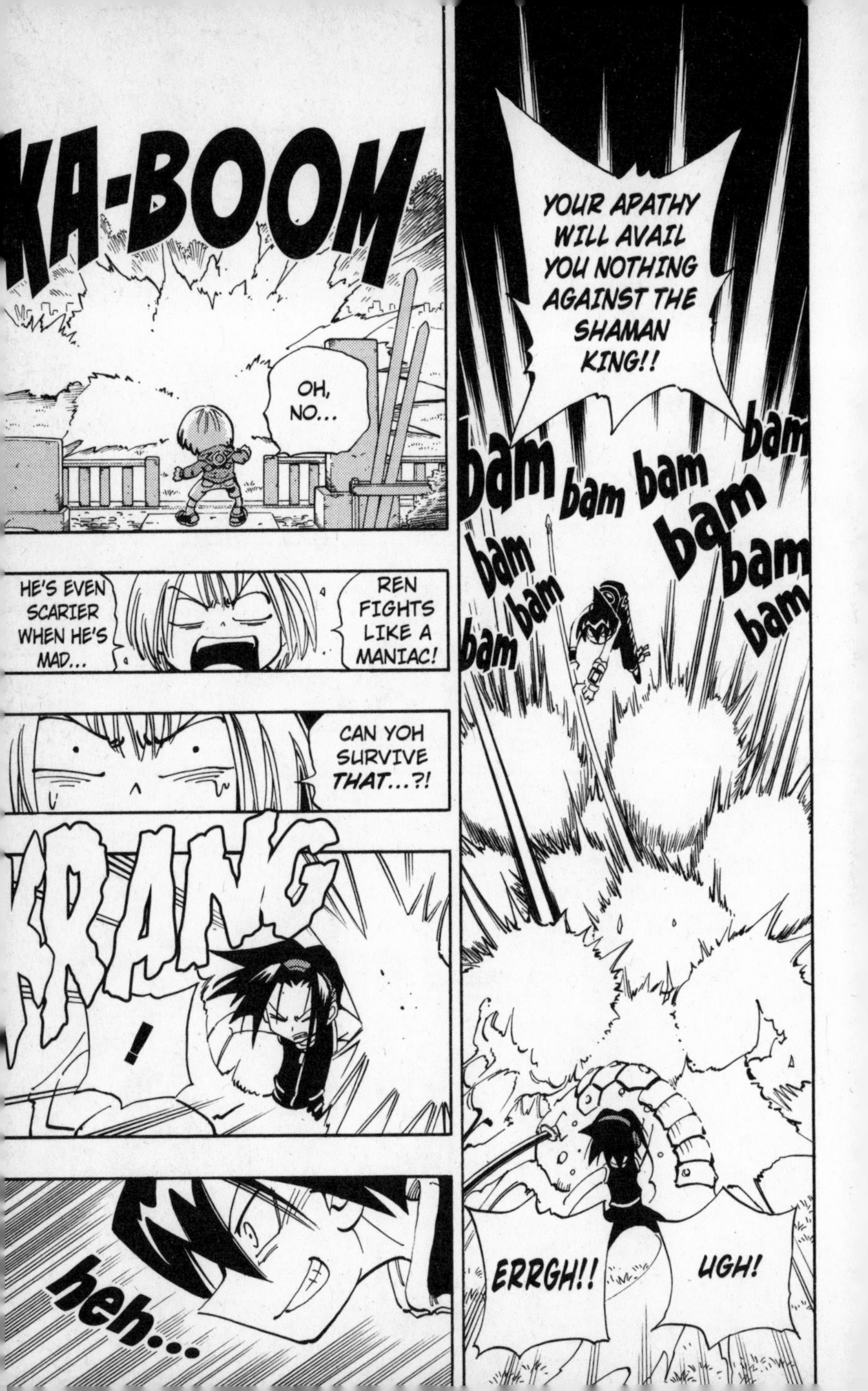
YOUR APATHY WILL AVAIL YOU NOTHING AGAINST THE SHAMAN KING!!
bam bam bam bam bam bam bam bam bam bam
UGH!
ERRGH!!
KA-BOOM
OH, NO...
REN FIGHTS LIKE A MANIAC!
HE'S EVEN SCARIER WHEN HE'S MAD...
CAN YOH SURVIVE *THAT*...?!
RANG
!
heh...

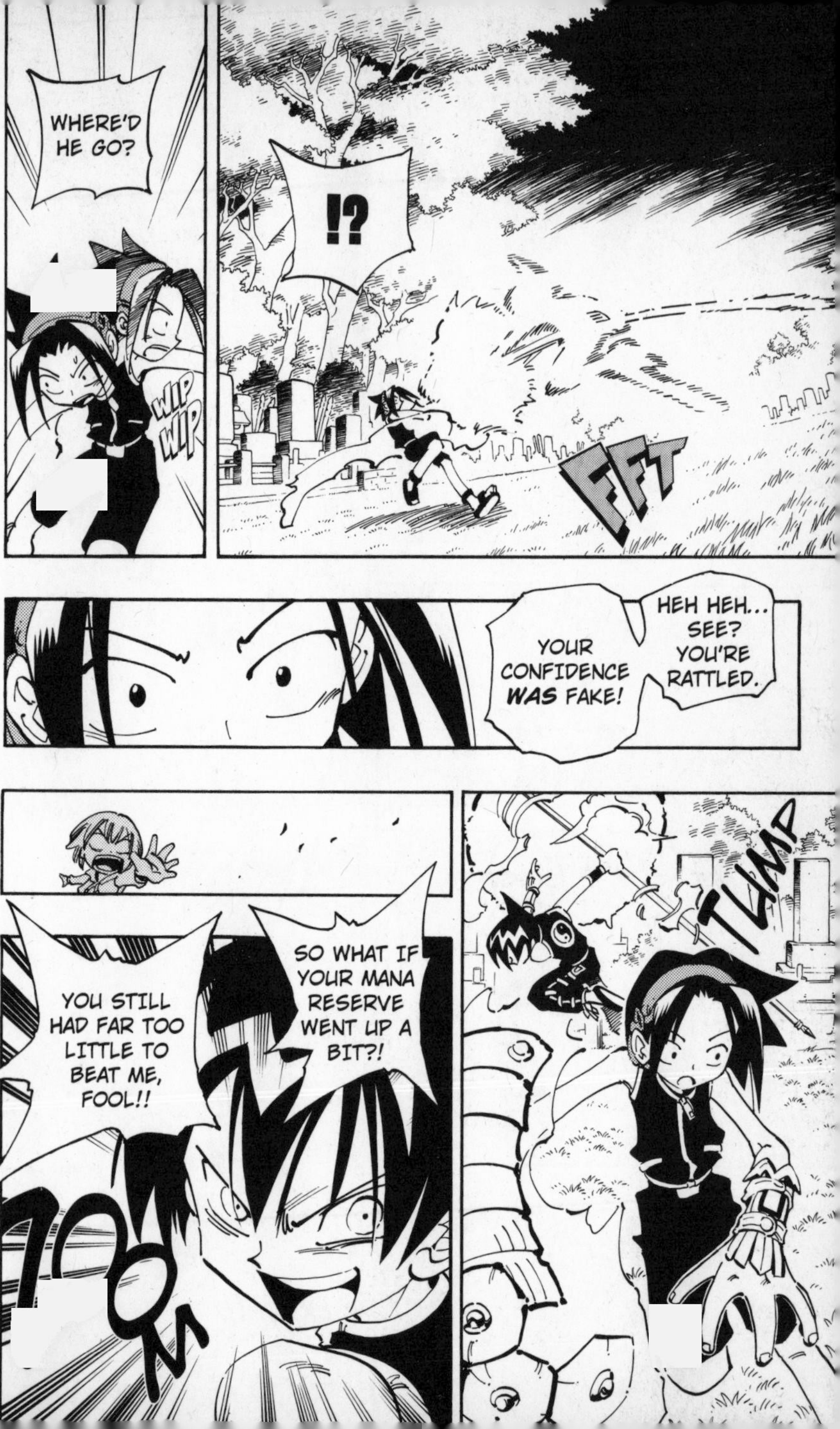
!?
FFT
WHERE'D HE GO?
WIP WIP
HEH HEH... SEE? YOU'RE RATTLED.
YOUR CONFIDENCE WAS FAKE!
TUMP
SO WHAT IF YOUR MANA RESERVE WENT UP A BIT?!
YOU STILL HAD FAR TOO LITTLE TO BEAT ME, FOOL!!

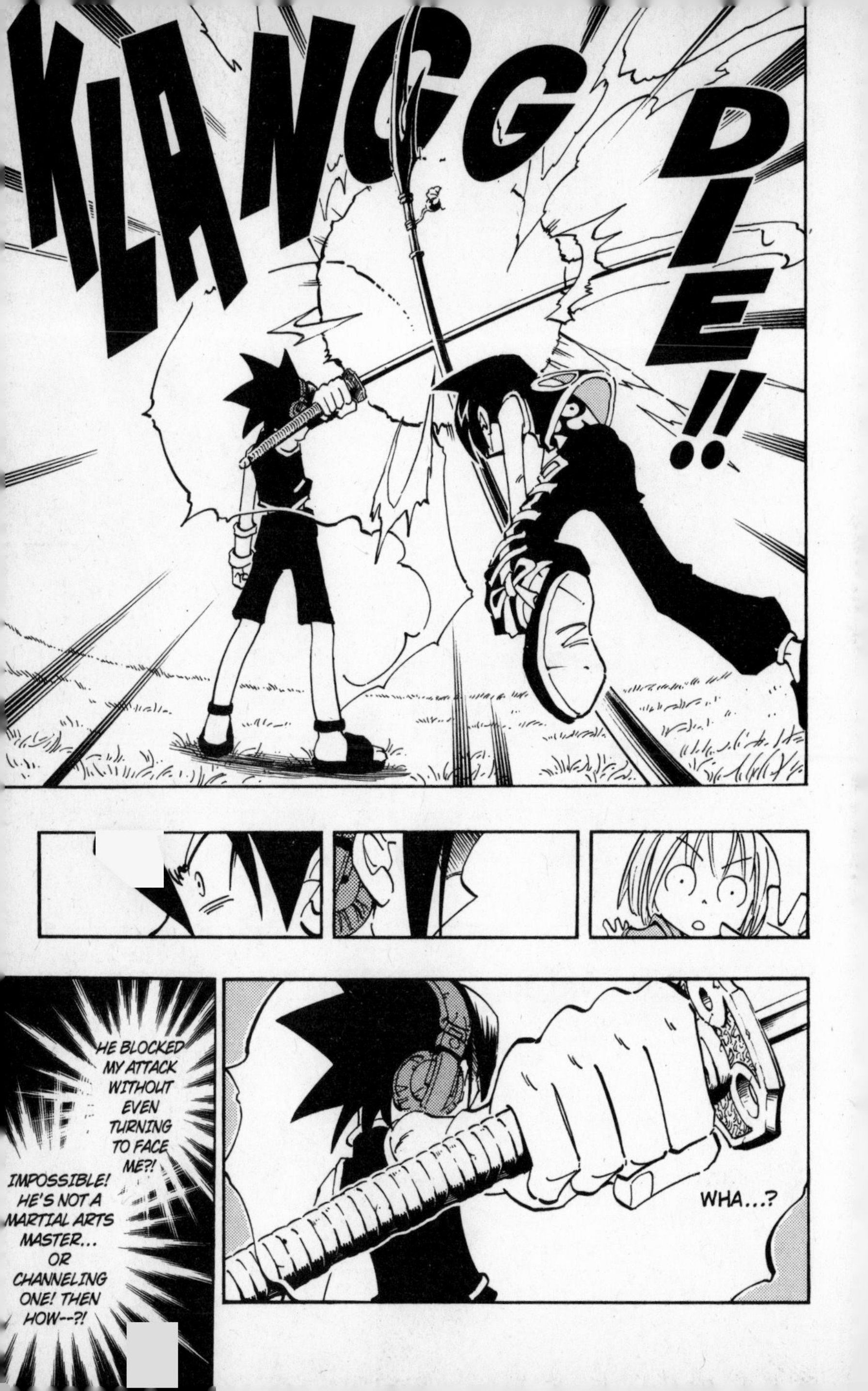
DIE!!
KLANGG
WHA...?
HE BLOCKED MY ATTACK WITHOUT EVEN TURNING TO FACE ME?!
IMPOSSIBLE! HE'S NOT A MARTIAL ARTS MASTER... OR CHANNELING ONE! THEN HOW--?!

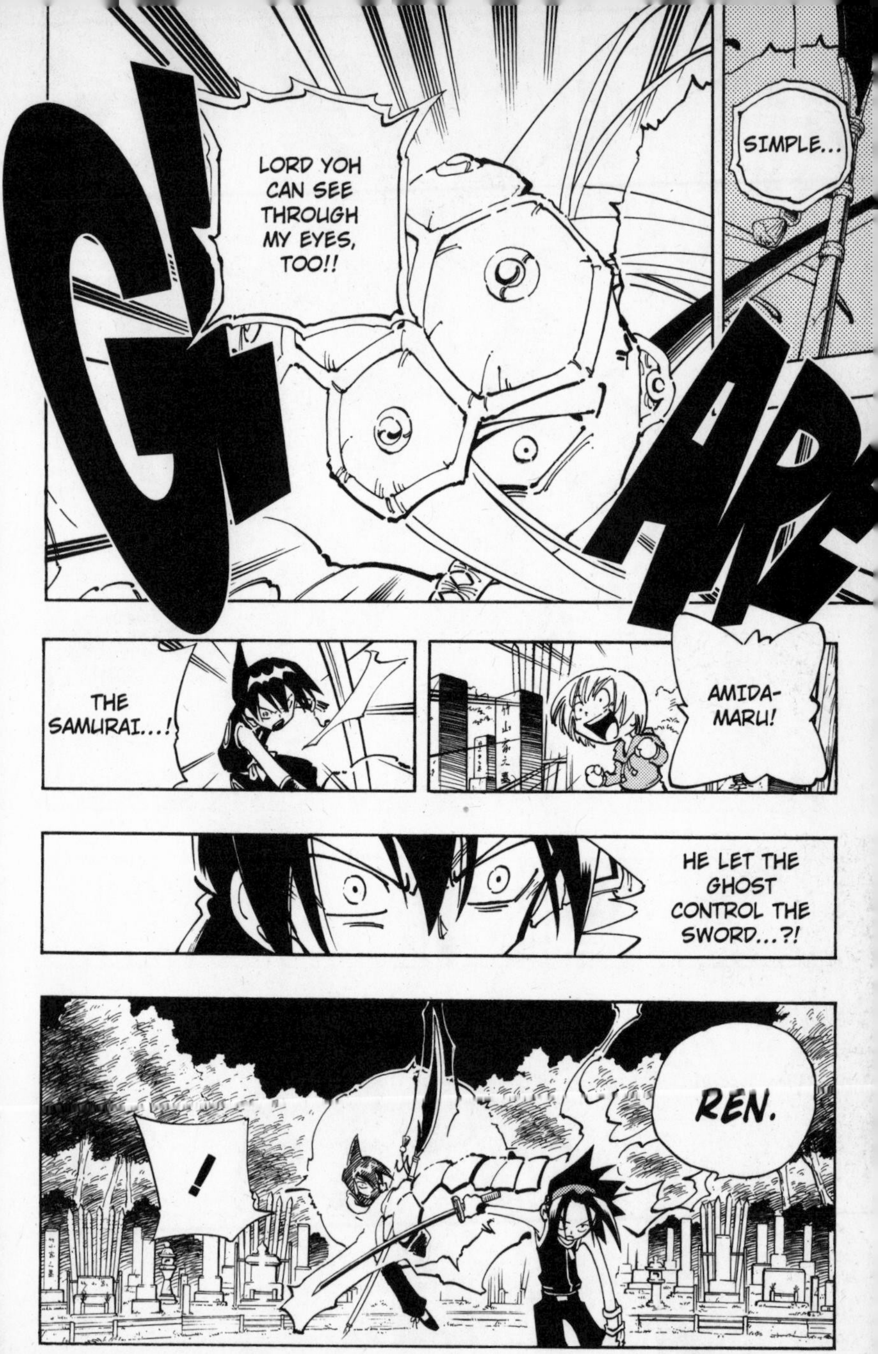
SIMPLE...
LORD YOH CAN SEE THROUGH MY EYES, TOO!!
AMIDA-MARU!
THE SAMURAI...!
HE LET THE GHOST CONTROL THE SWORD...?!
REN.
!

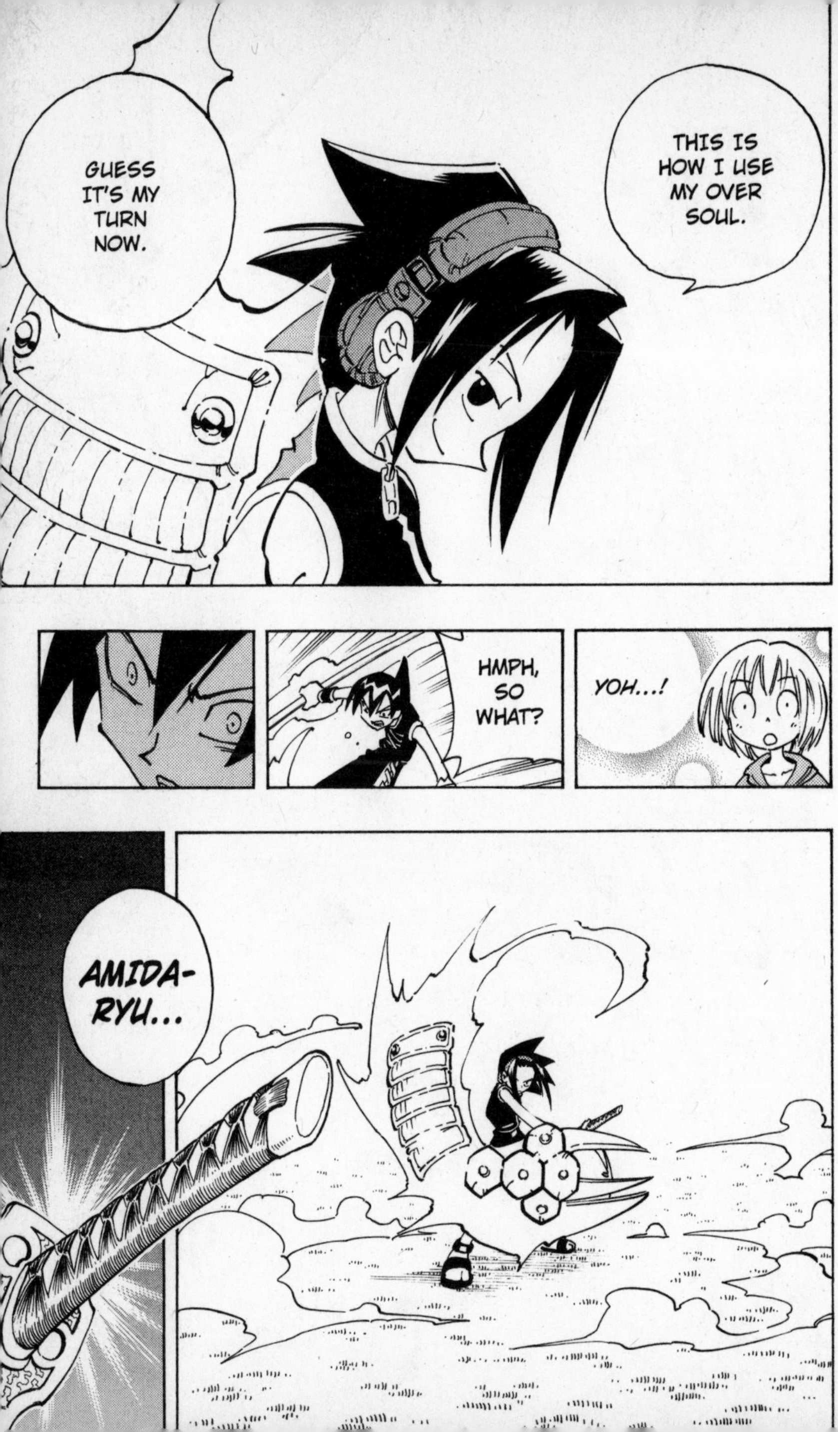
THIS IS HOW I USE MY OVER SOUL.
GUESS IT'S MY TURN NOW.
YOH...!
HMPH, SO WHAT?
AMIDA-RYU...

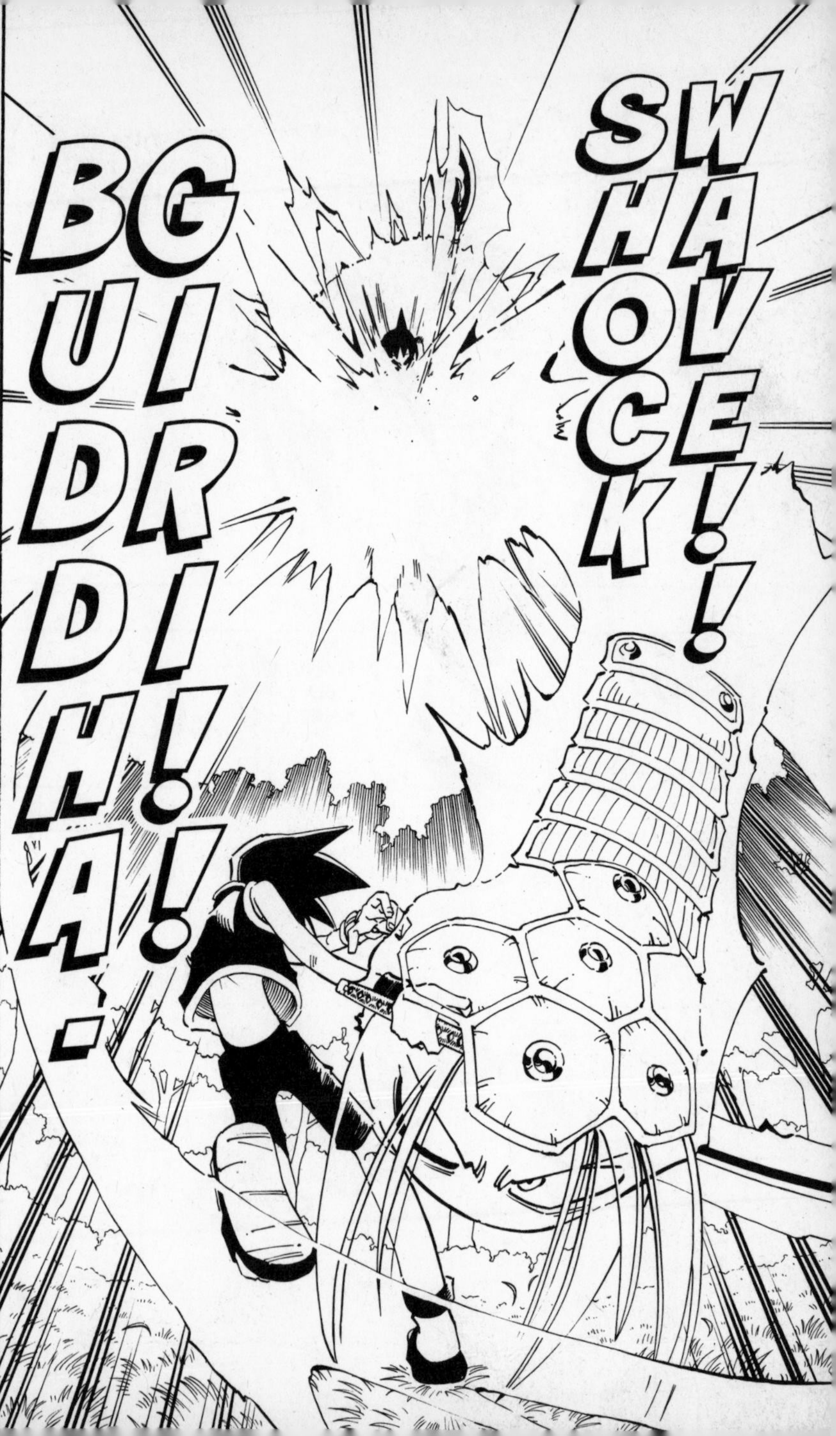
SHOCK WAVE!!
BUDDHA GIRI!!

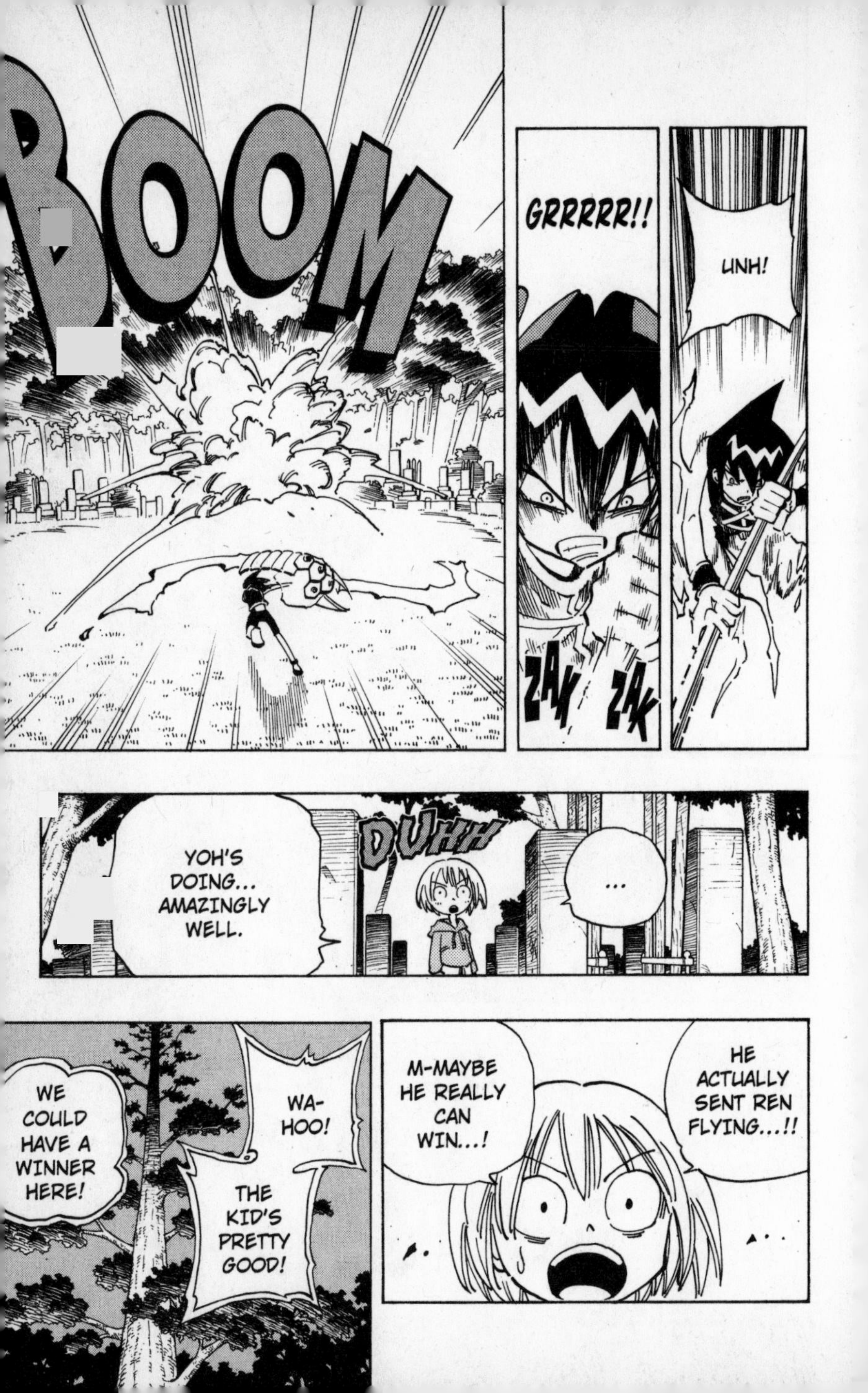
UNH!
GRRRRR!!
ZAK ZAK
BOOM
...
DUHH
YOH'S DOING... AMAZINGLY WELL.
HE ACTUALLY SENT REN FLYING...!!
M-MAYBE HE REALLY CAN WIN...!
WA-HOO!
THE KID'S PRETTY GOOD!
WE COULD HAVE A WINNER HERE!

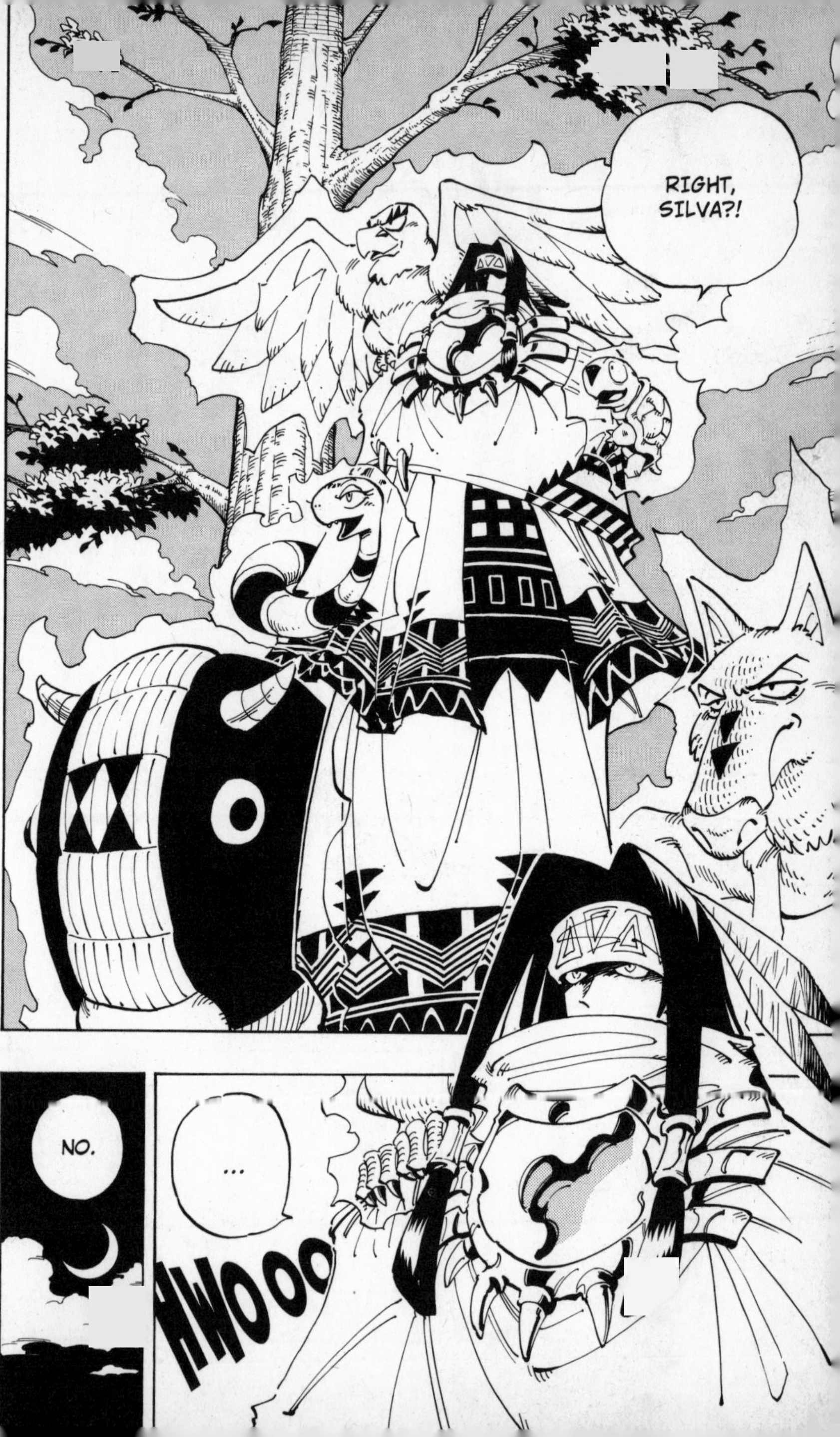
RIGHT, SILVA?!
...
NO.
HWOOO

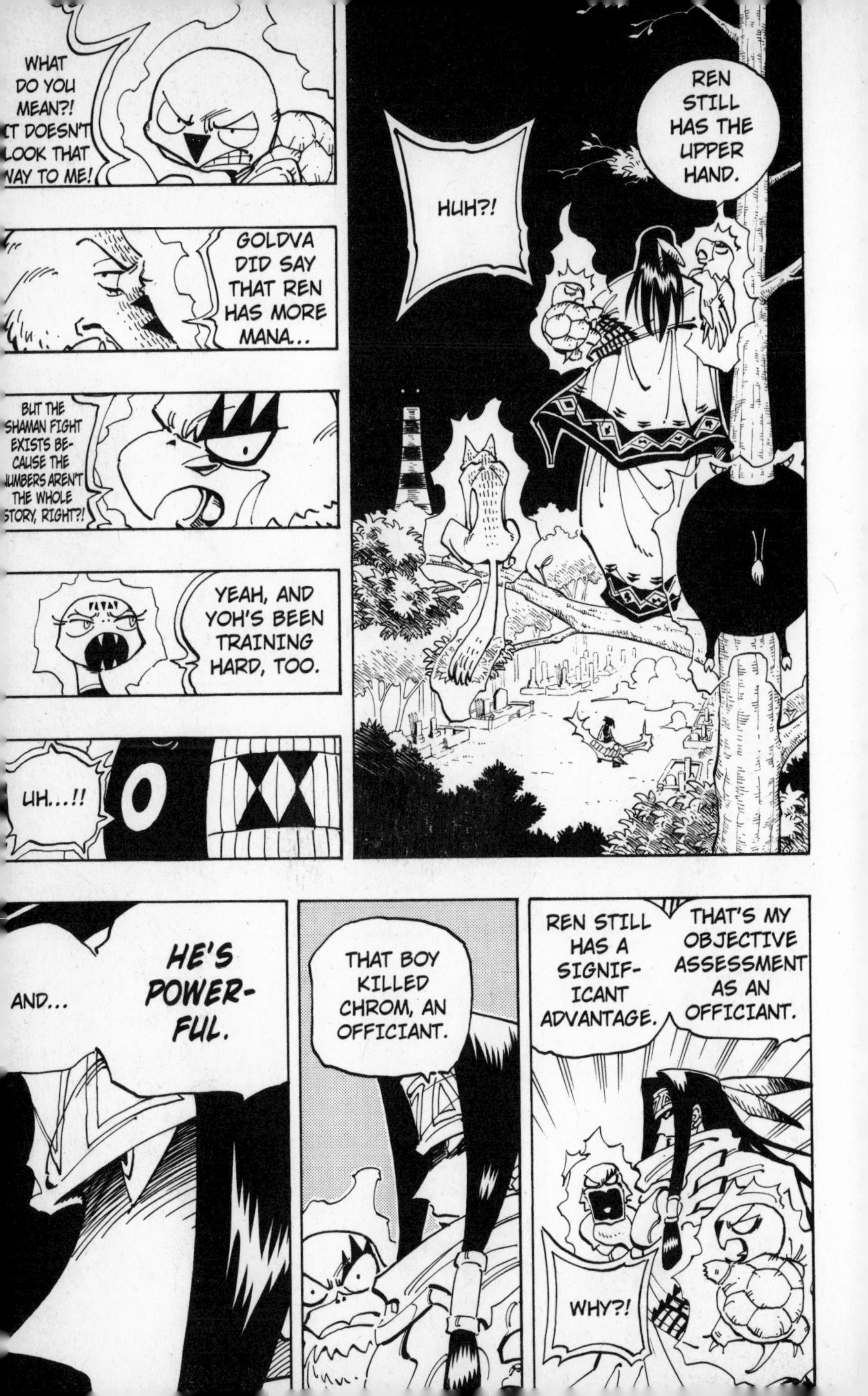
REN STILL HAS THE UPPER HAND.
HUH?!
WHAT DO YOU MEAN?! IT DOESN'T LOOK THAT WAY TO ME!
GOLDVA DID SAY THAT REN HAS MORE MANA...
BUT THE SHAMAN FIGHT EXISTS BECAUSE THE NUMBERS AREN'T THE WHOLE STORY, RIGHT?!
YEAH, AND YOH'S BEEN TRAINING HARD, TOO.
UH...!!
THAT'S MY OBJECTIVE ASSESSMENT AS AN OFFICIANT.
REN STILL HAS A SIGNIFICANT ADVANTAGE.
WHY?!
THAT BOY KILLED CHROM, AN OFFICIANT.
HE'S POWERFUL.
AND...

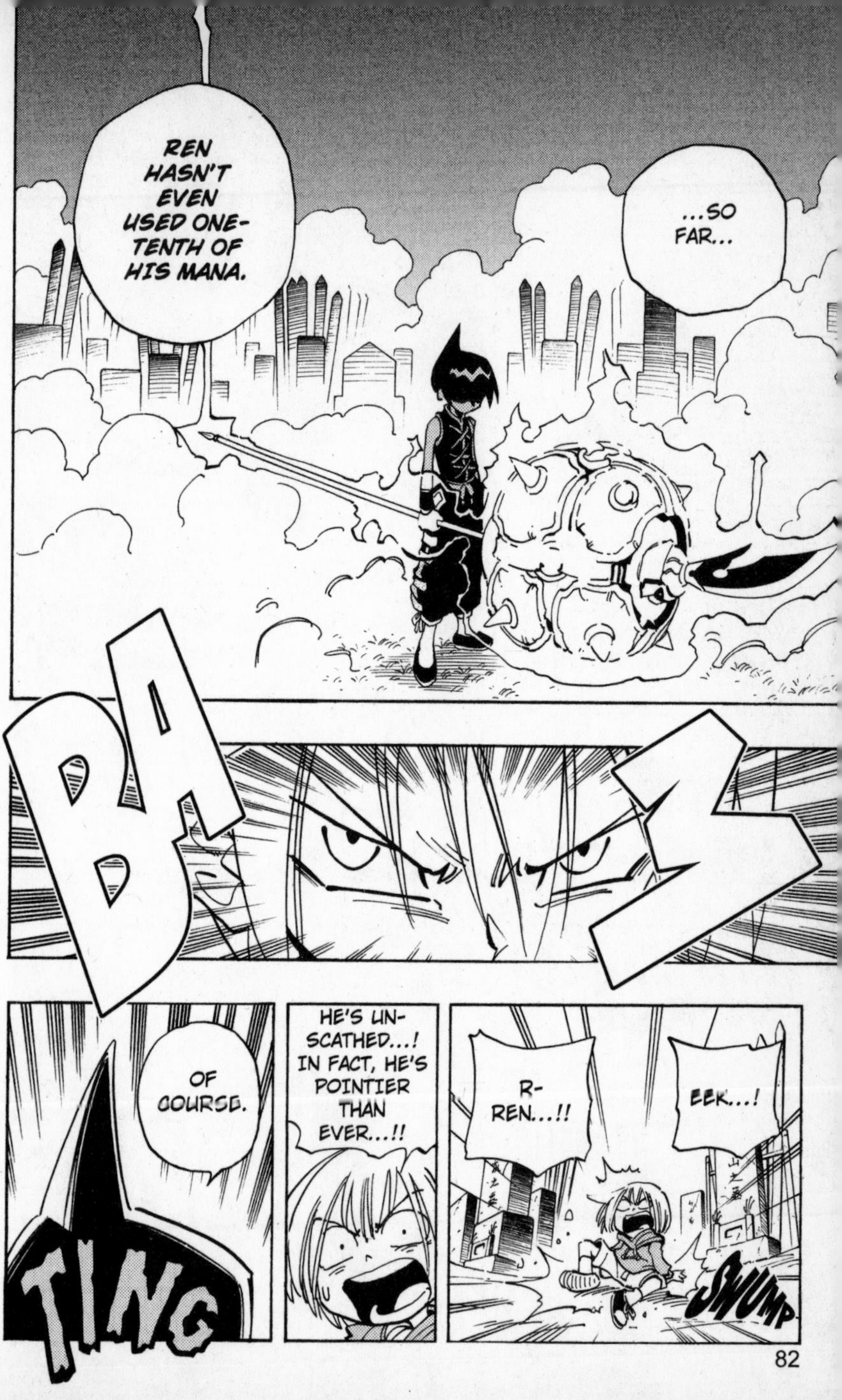
REN HASN'T EVEN USED ONE-TENTH OF HIS MANA.
...SO FAR...
BAZ
EEK...!
R-REN...!!
SWUMP
HE'S UN-SCATHED...! IN FACT, HE'S POINTIER THAN EVER...!!
OF COURSE.
TING

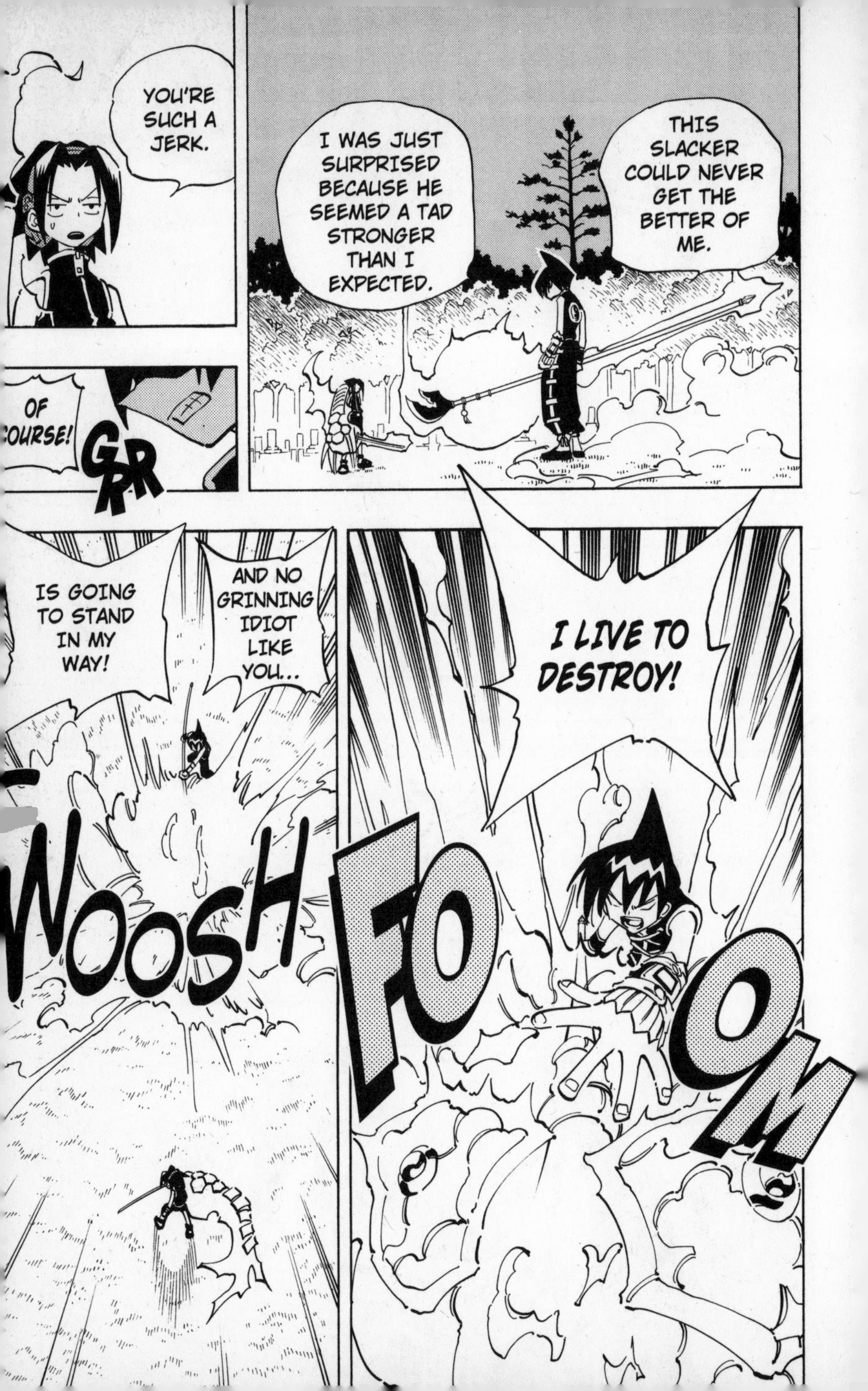
THIS SLACKER COULD NEVER GET THE BETTER OF ME.
I WAS JUST SURPRISED BECAUSE HE SEEMED A TAD STRONGER THAN I EXPECTED.
YOU'RE SUCH A JERK.
OF COURSE!
GRR
I LIVE TO DESTROY!
FOOOM
AND NO GRINNING IDIOT LIKE YOU...
IS GOING TO STAND IN MY WAY!
WOOSH

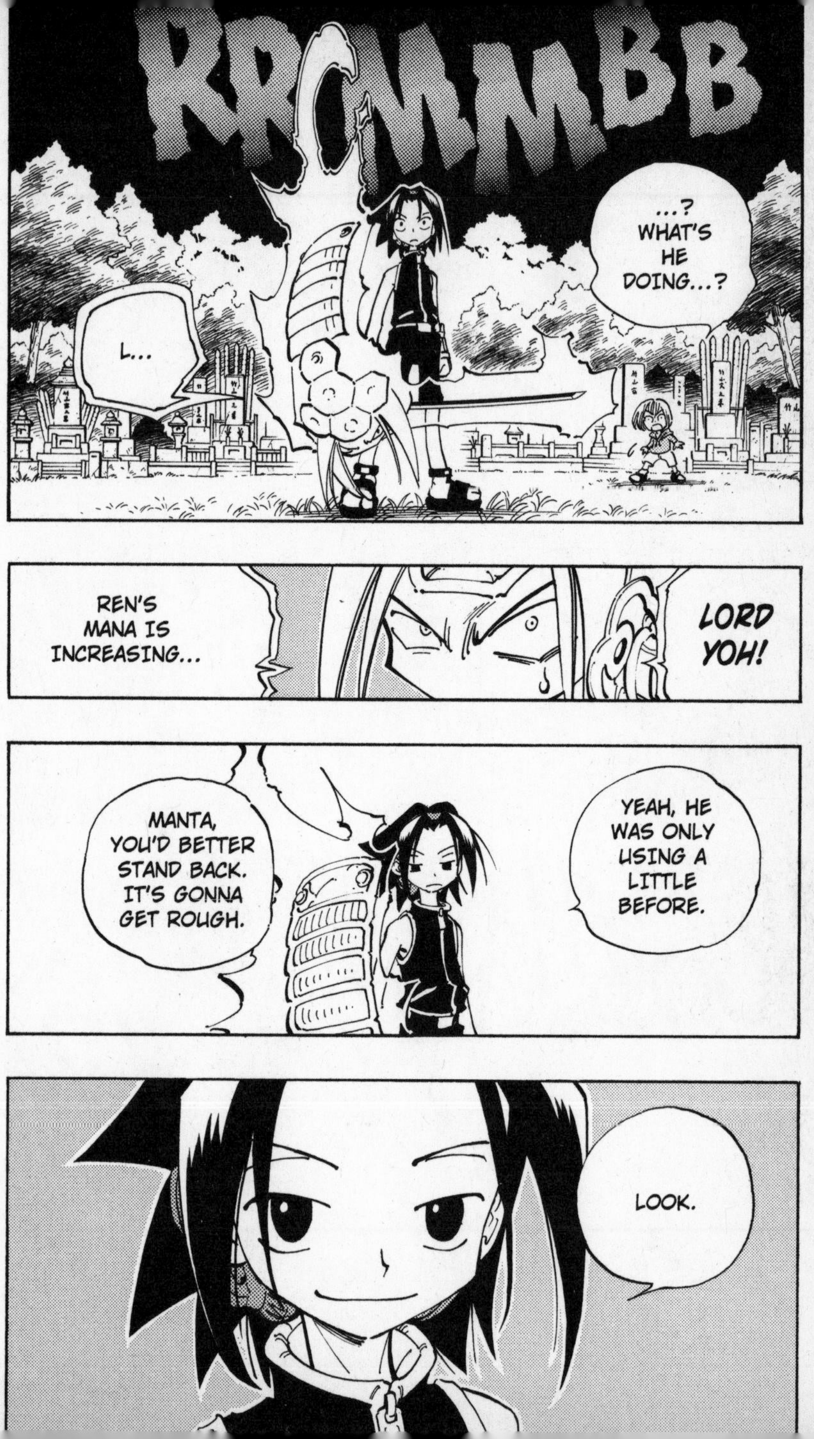
RBMMBB
...? WHAT'S HE DOING...?
I...
LORD YOH!
REN'S MANA IS INCREASING...
YEAH, HE WAS ONLY USING A LITTLE BEFORE.
MANTA, YOU'D BETTER STAND BACK. IT'S GONNA GET ROUGH.
LOOK.

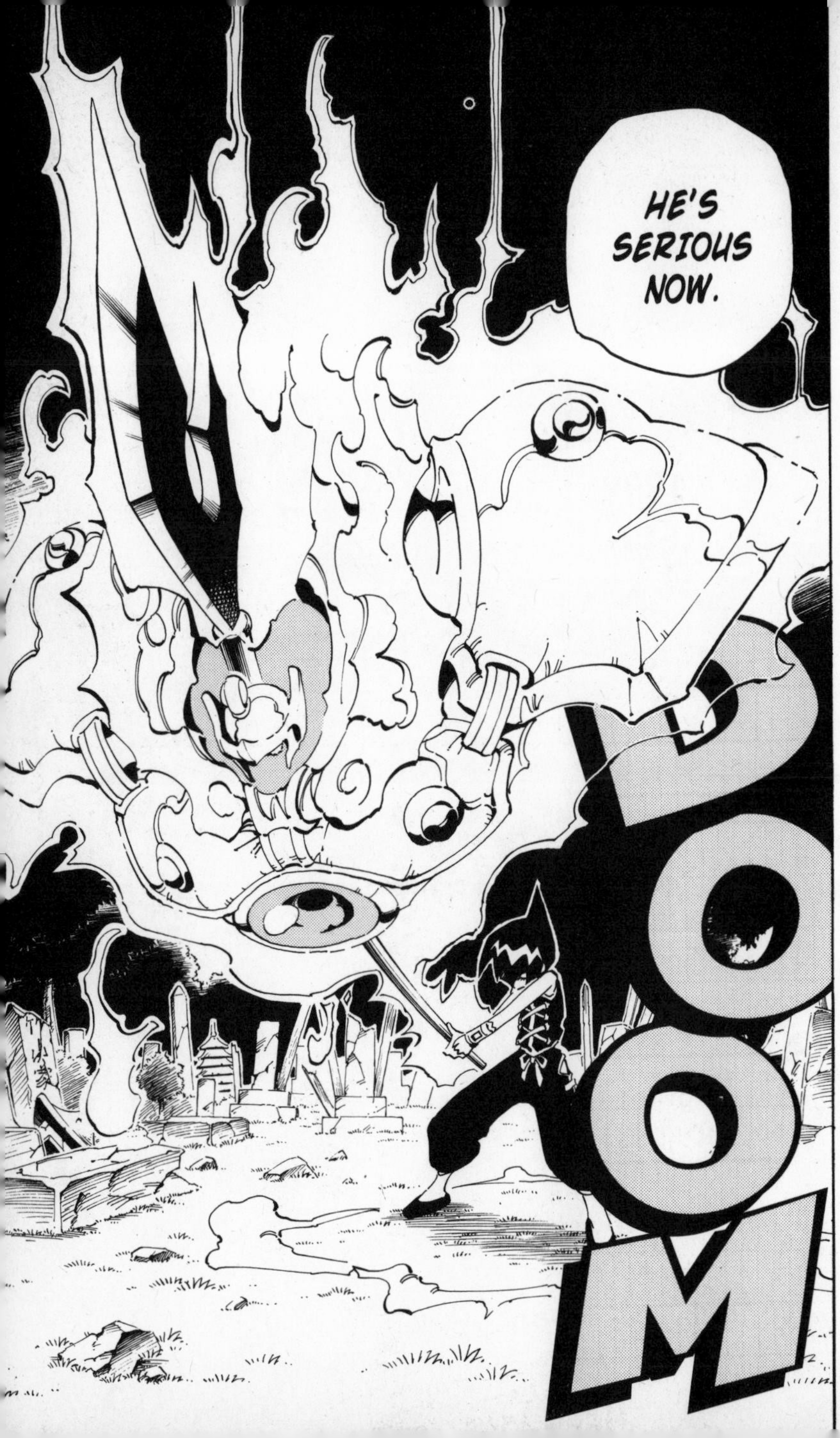
HE'S SERIOUS NOW.
DOOOM

SHAMAN KING CHARACTER FILE No.30

道(タオ)蓮(レン)

1999
(FEB)

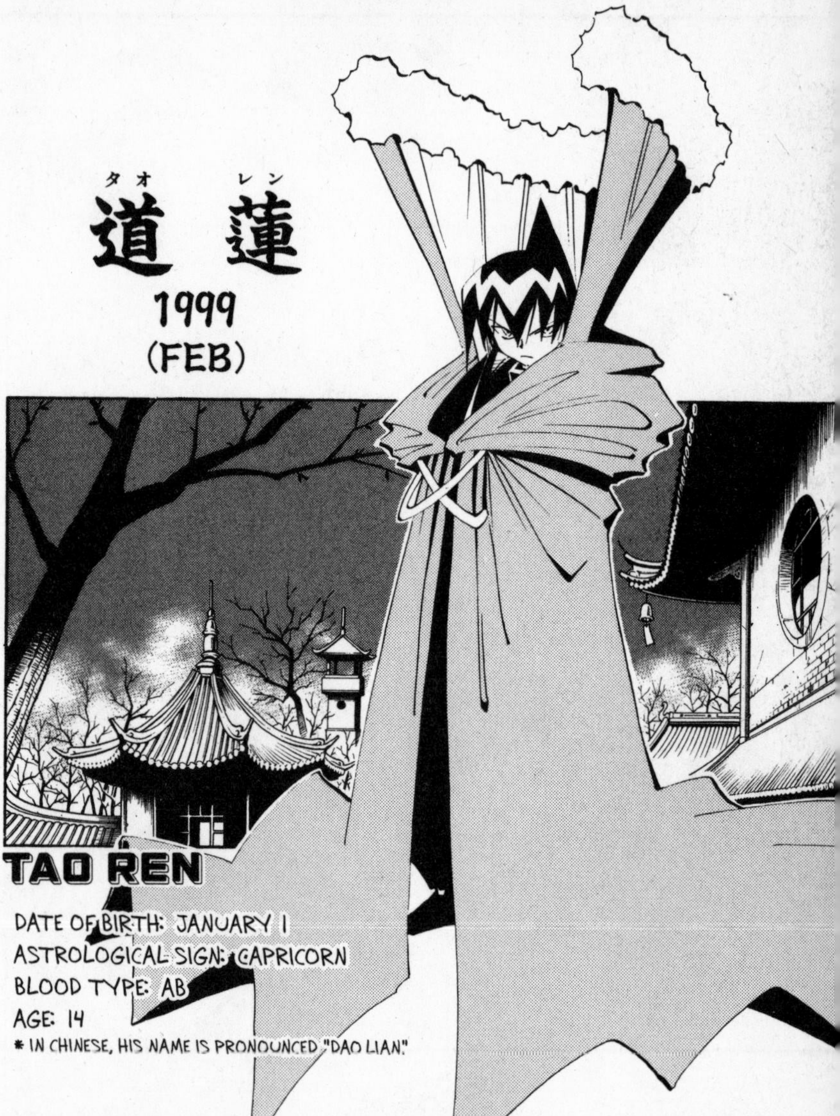

TAO REN

DATE OF BIRTH: JANUARY 1
ASTROLOGICAL SIGN: CAPRICORN
BLOOD TYPE: AB
AGE: 14

* IN CHINESE, HIS NAME IS PRONOUNCED "DAO LIAN."

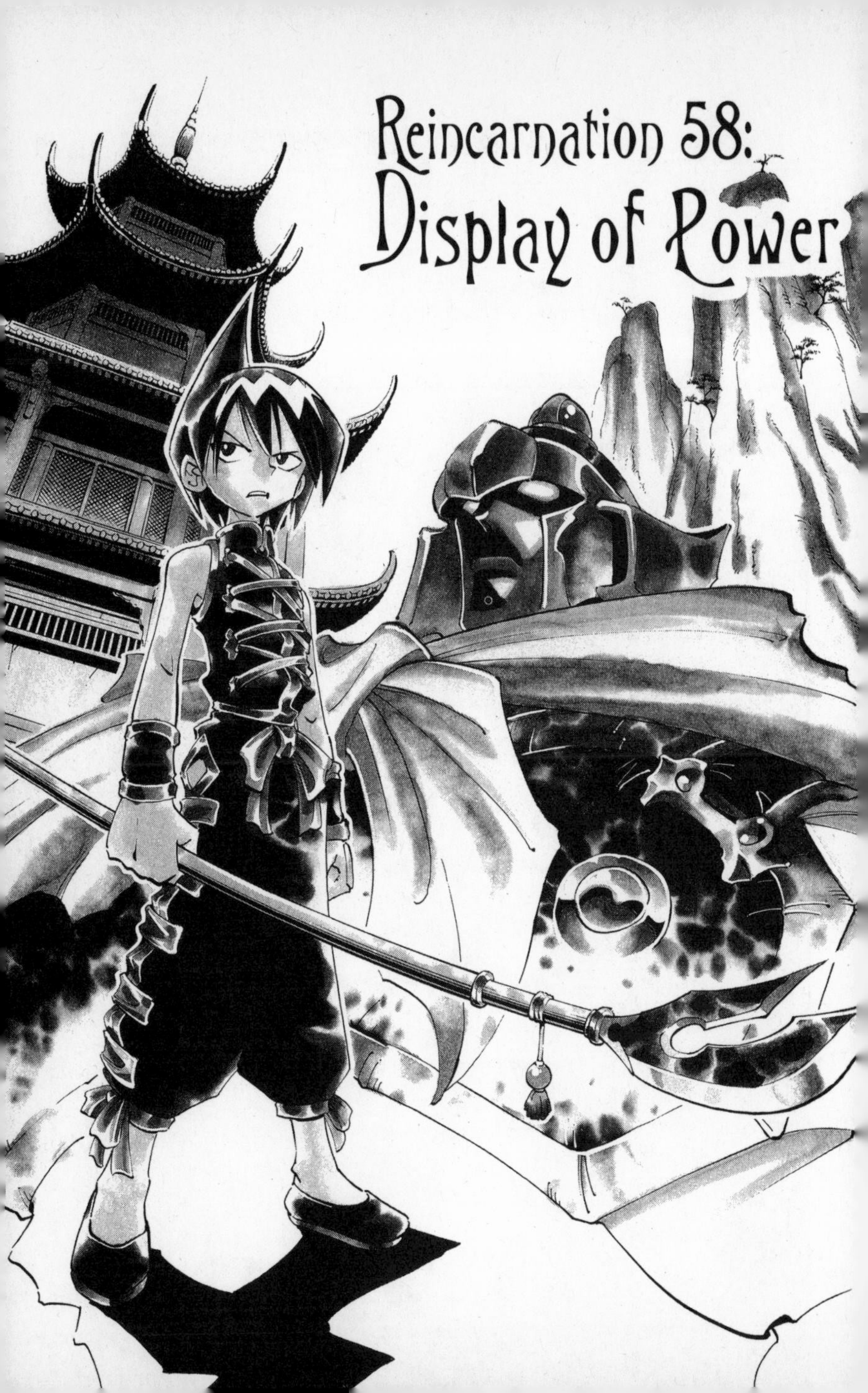
Reincarnation 58:
Display of Power

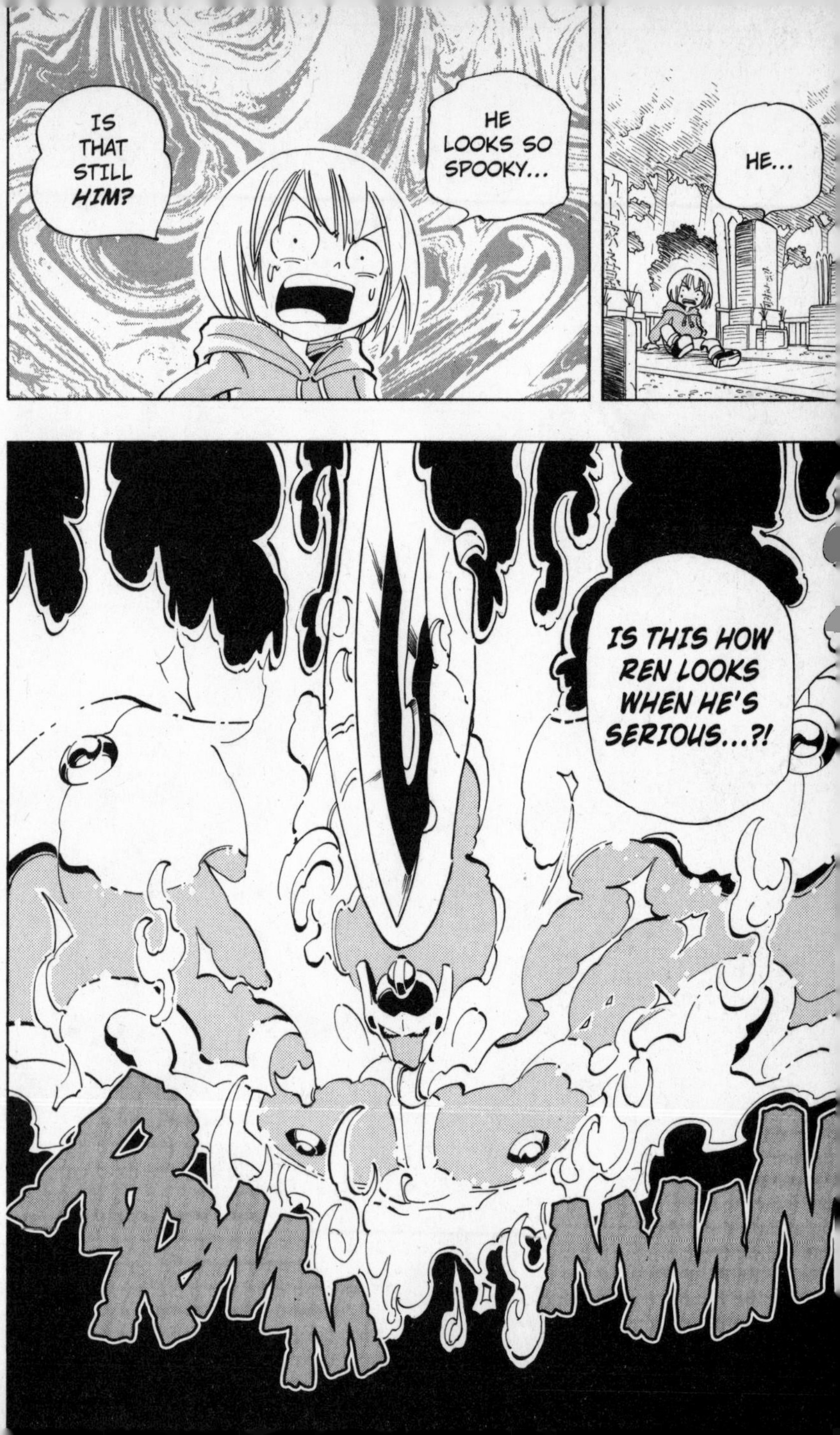
HE...
HE LOOKS SO SPOOKY...
IS THAT STILL *HIM?*
IS THIS HOW REN LOOKS WHEN HE'S SERIOUS...?!

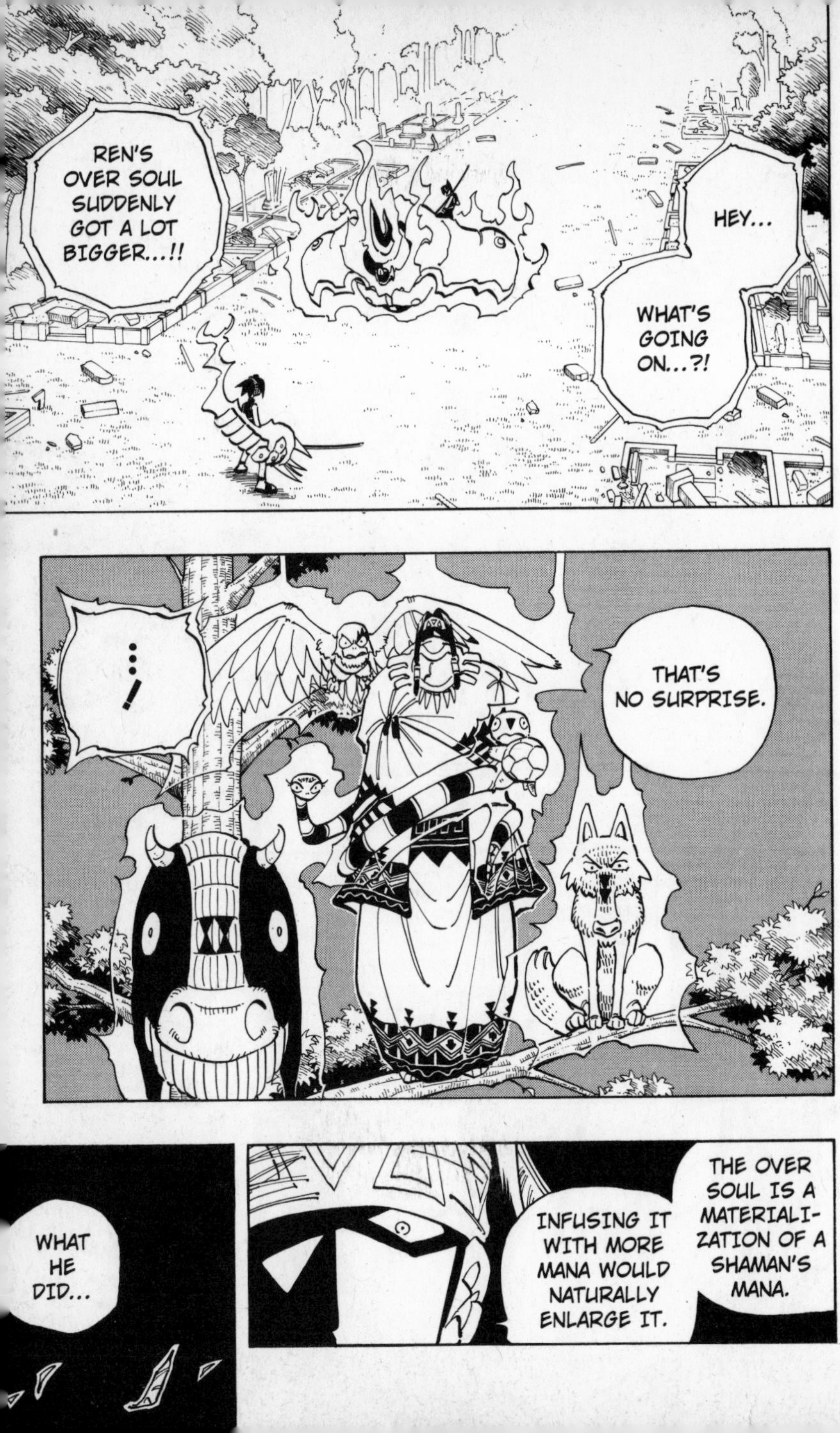
HEY...
WHAT'S GOING ON...?!
REN'S OVER SOUL SUDDENLY GOT A LOT BIGGER...!!
THAT'S NO SURPRISE.
...!
THE OVER SOUL IS A MATERIALI-ZATION OF A SHAMAN'S MANA.
INFUSING IT WITH MORE MANA WOULD NATURALLY ENLARGE IT.
WHAT HE DID...

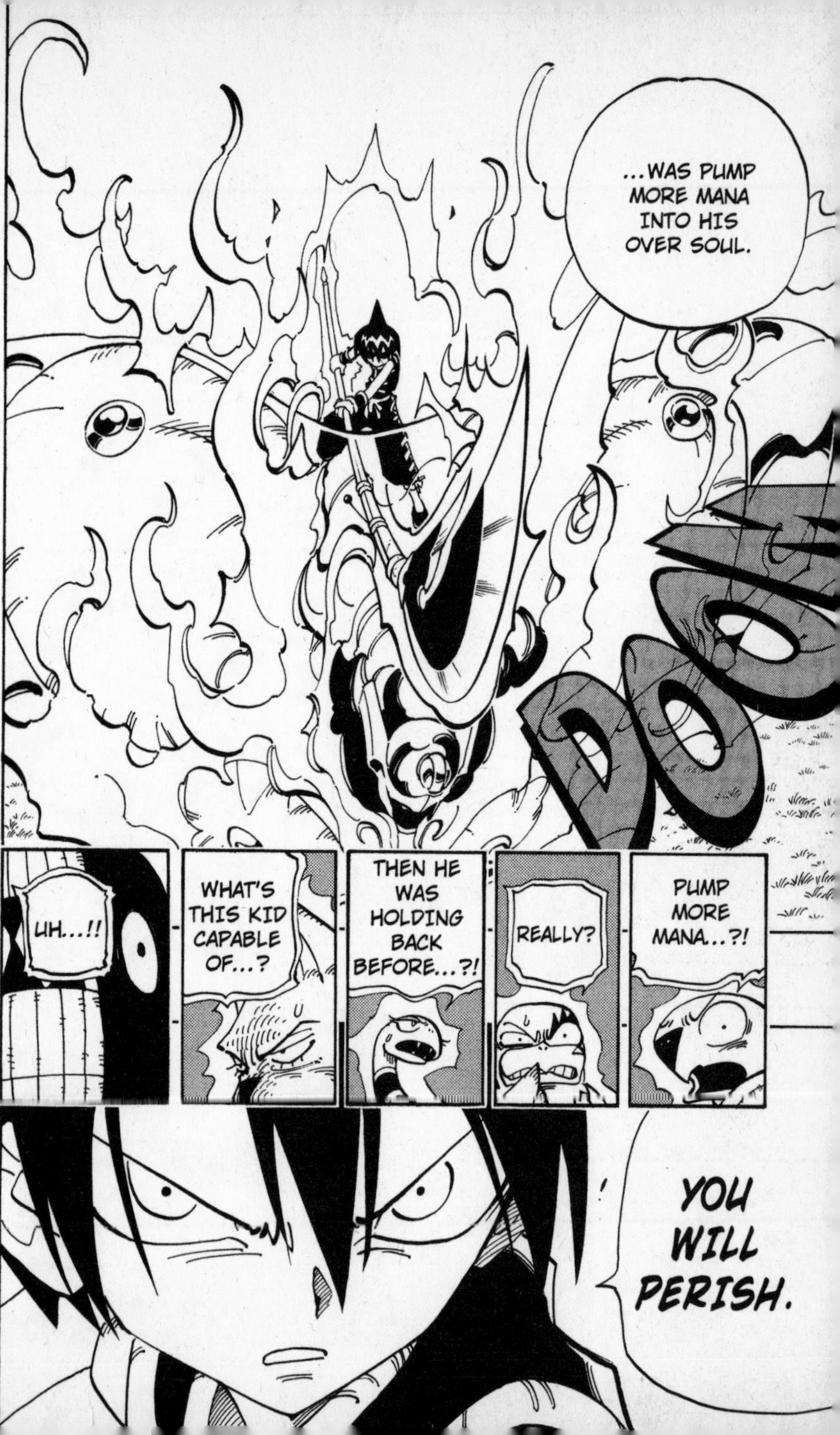
...WAS PUMP MORE MANA INTO HIS OVER SOUL.
DOOM
PUMP MORE MANA...?!
REALLY?
THEN HE WAS HOLDING BACK BEFORE...?!
WHAT'S THIS KID CAPABLE OF...?
UH...!!
YOU WILL PERISH.

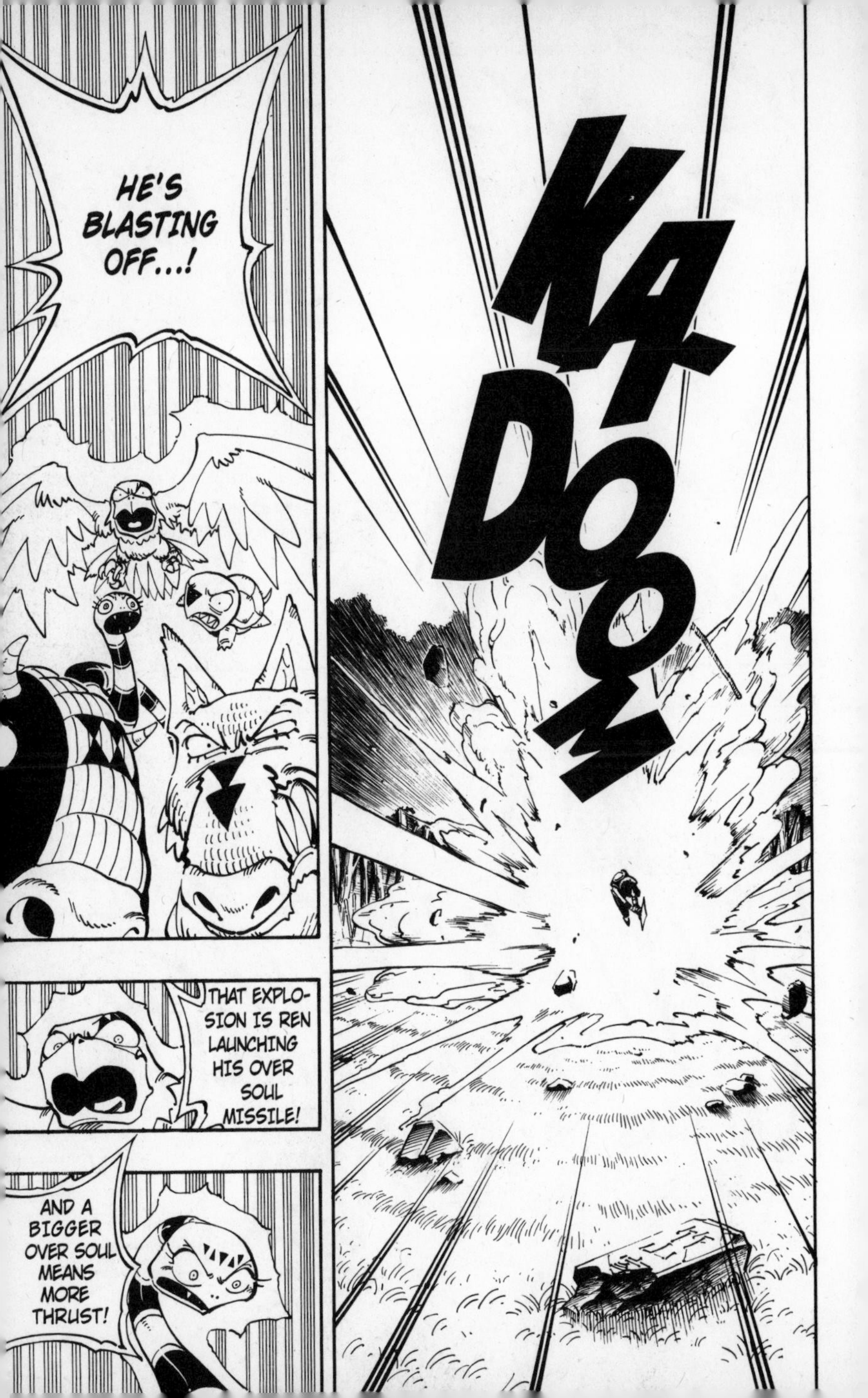
KA-DOOM
HE'S BLASTING OFF...!
THAT EXPLOSION IS REN LAUNCHING HIS OVER SOUL MISSILE!
AND A BIGGER OVER SOUL MEANS MORE THRUST!

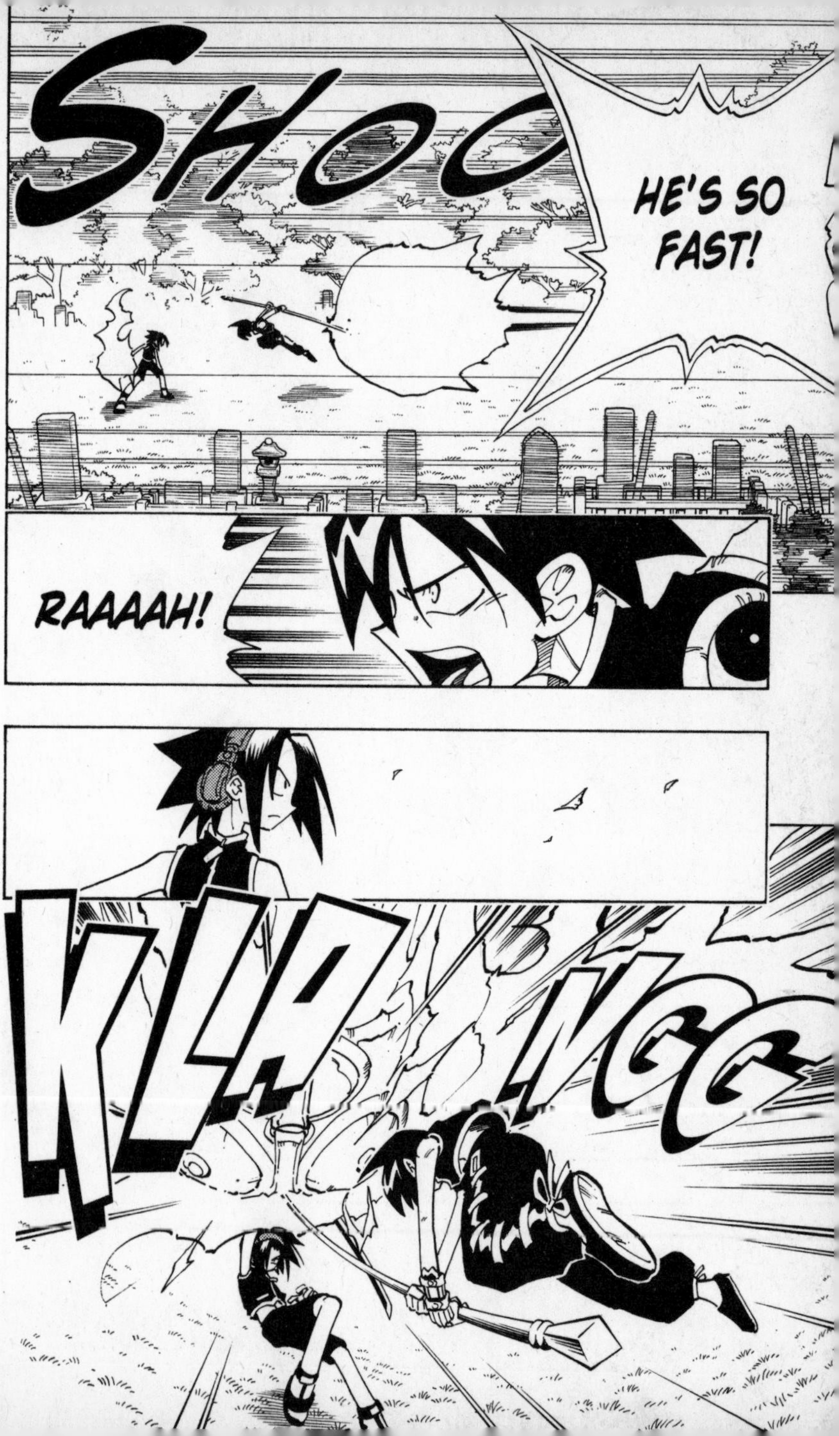
HE'S SO FAST!
SHOO
RAAAAH!
KLANGG

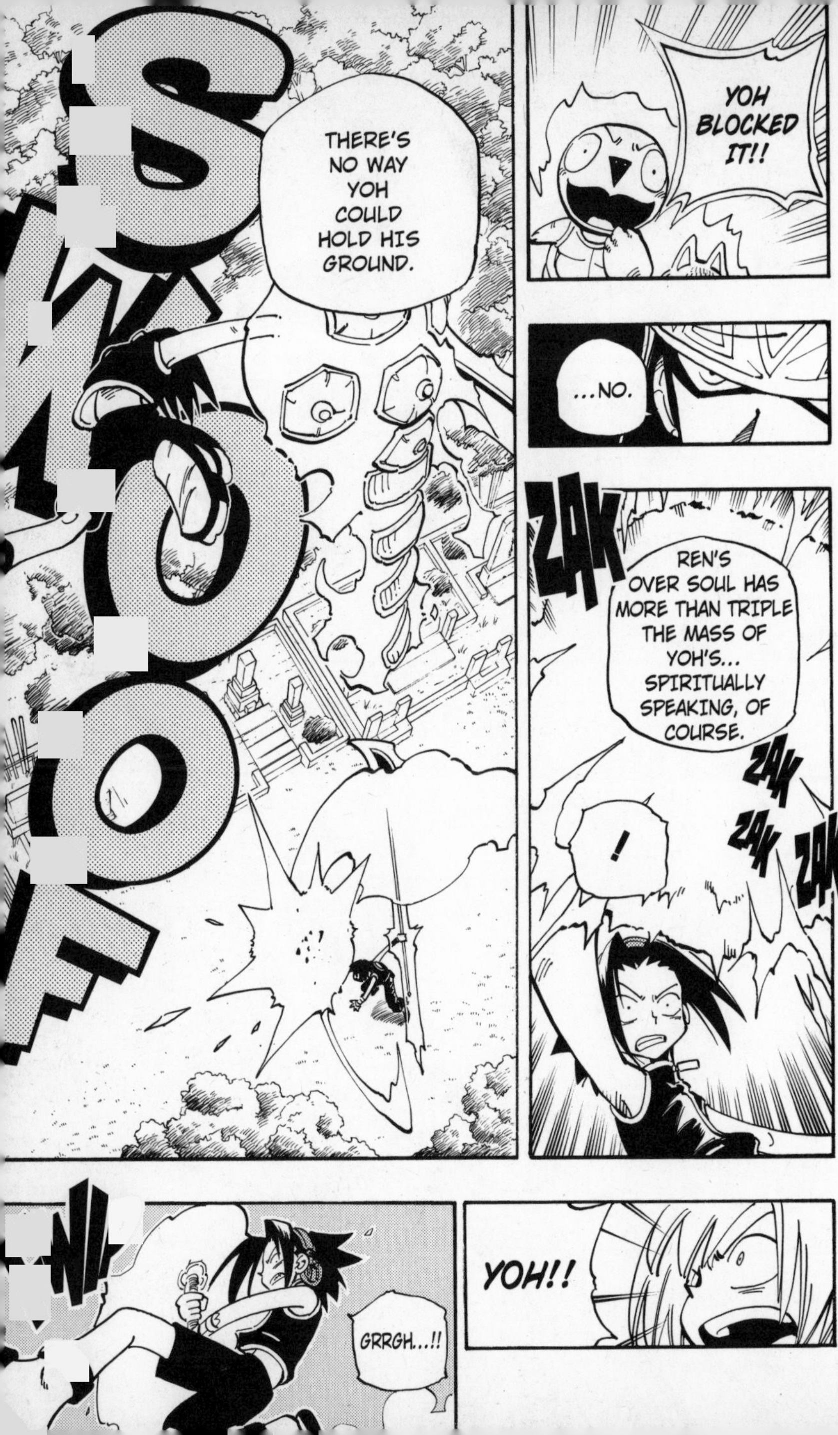
YOH BLOCKED IT!!
...NO.
ZAK
REN'S OVER SOUL HAS MORE THAN TRIPLE THE MASS OF YOH'S... SPIRITUALLY SPEAKING, OF COURSE.
ZAK
ZAK
ZAK
!
THERE'S NO WAY YOH COULD HOLD HIS GROUND.
YOH!!
GRRGH...!!

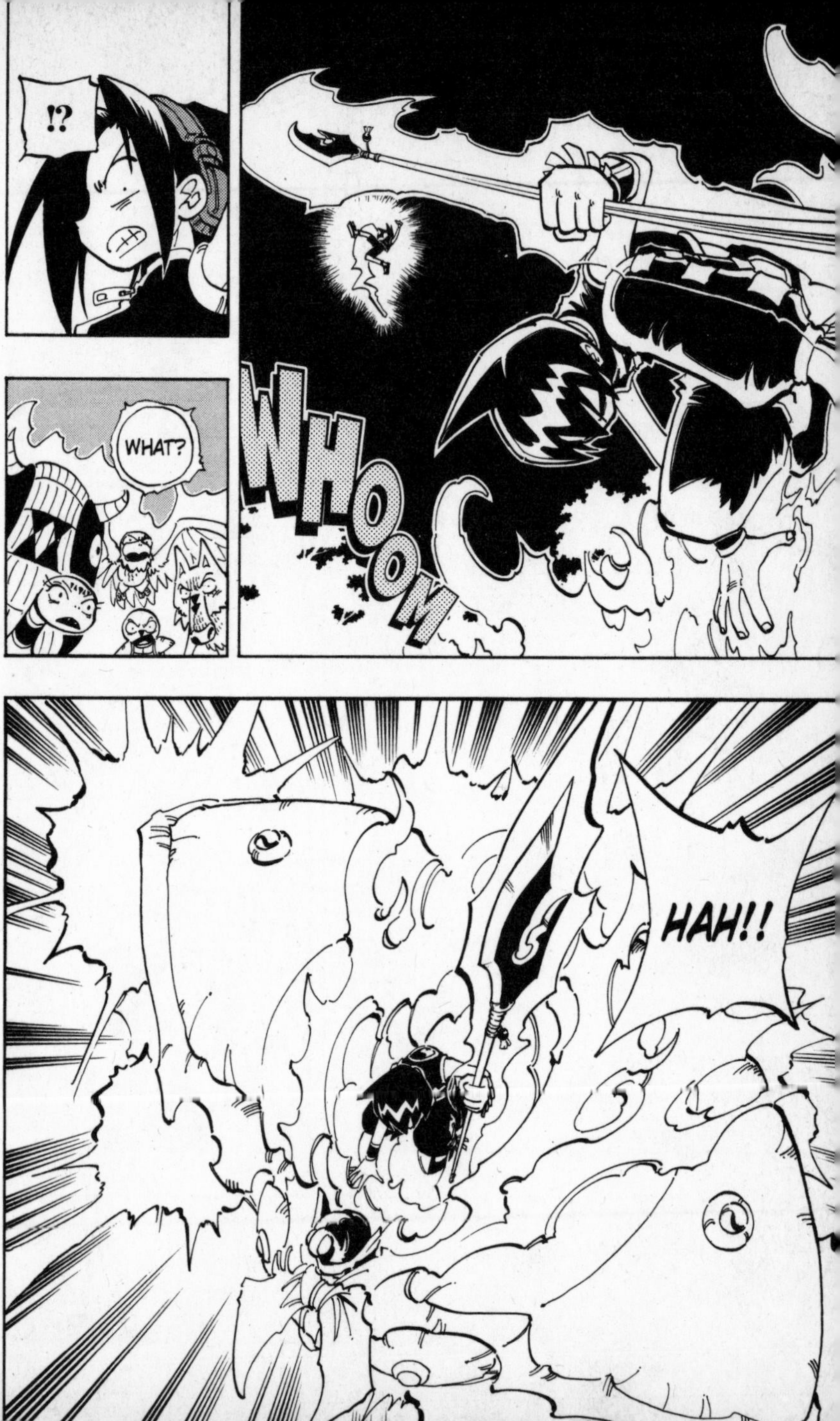
WHOOM
!?
WHAT?
HAH!!

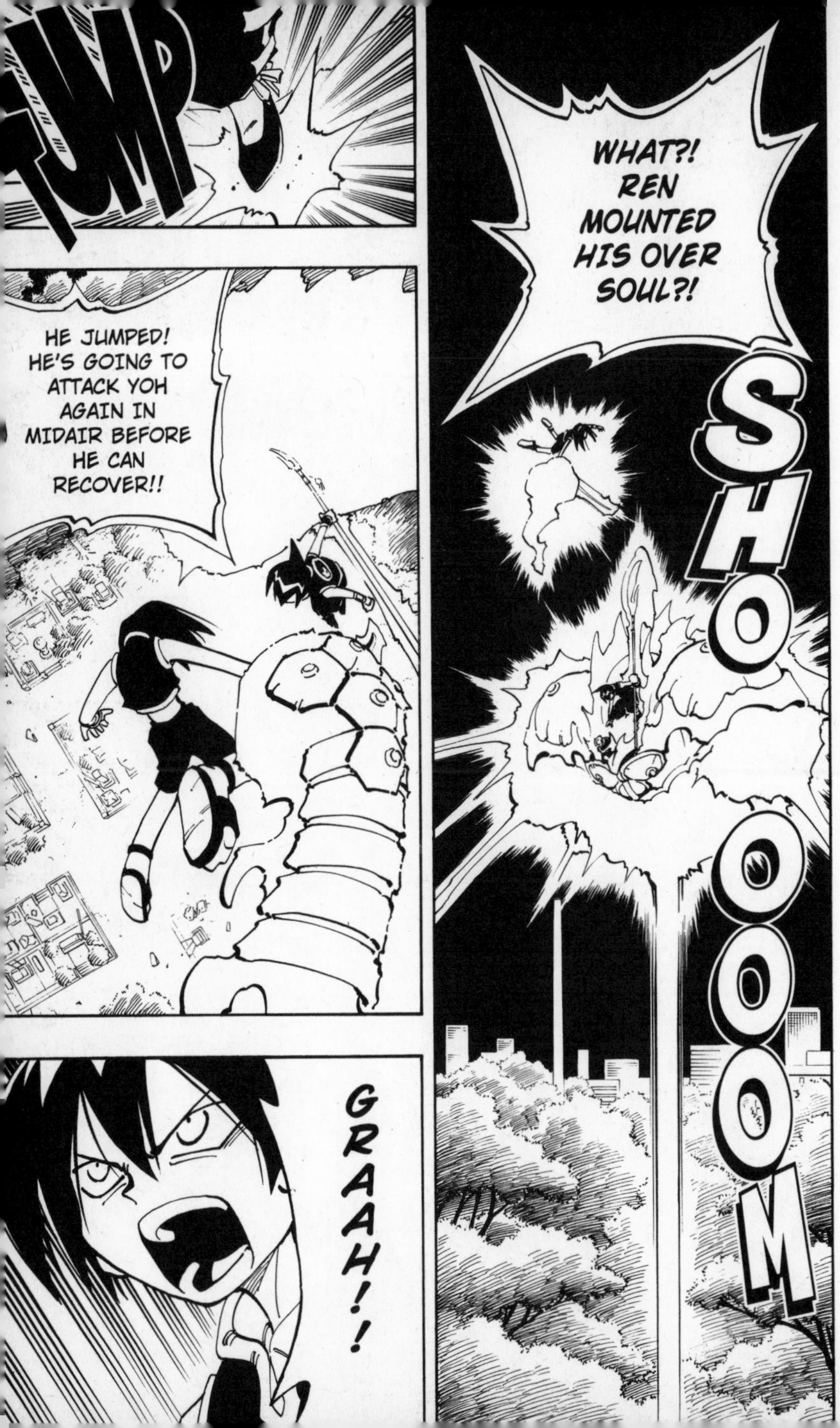
WHAT?! REN MOUNTED HIS OVER SOUL?!
SHOOOOOM
TUMP
HE JUMPED! HE'S GOING TO ATTACK YOH AGAIN IN MIDAIR BEFORE HE CAN RECOVER!!
GRAAAH!!

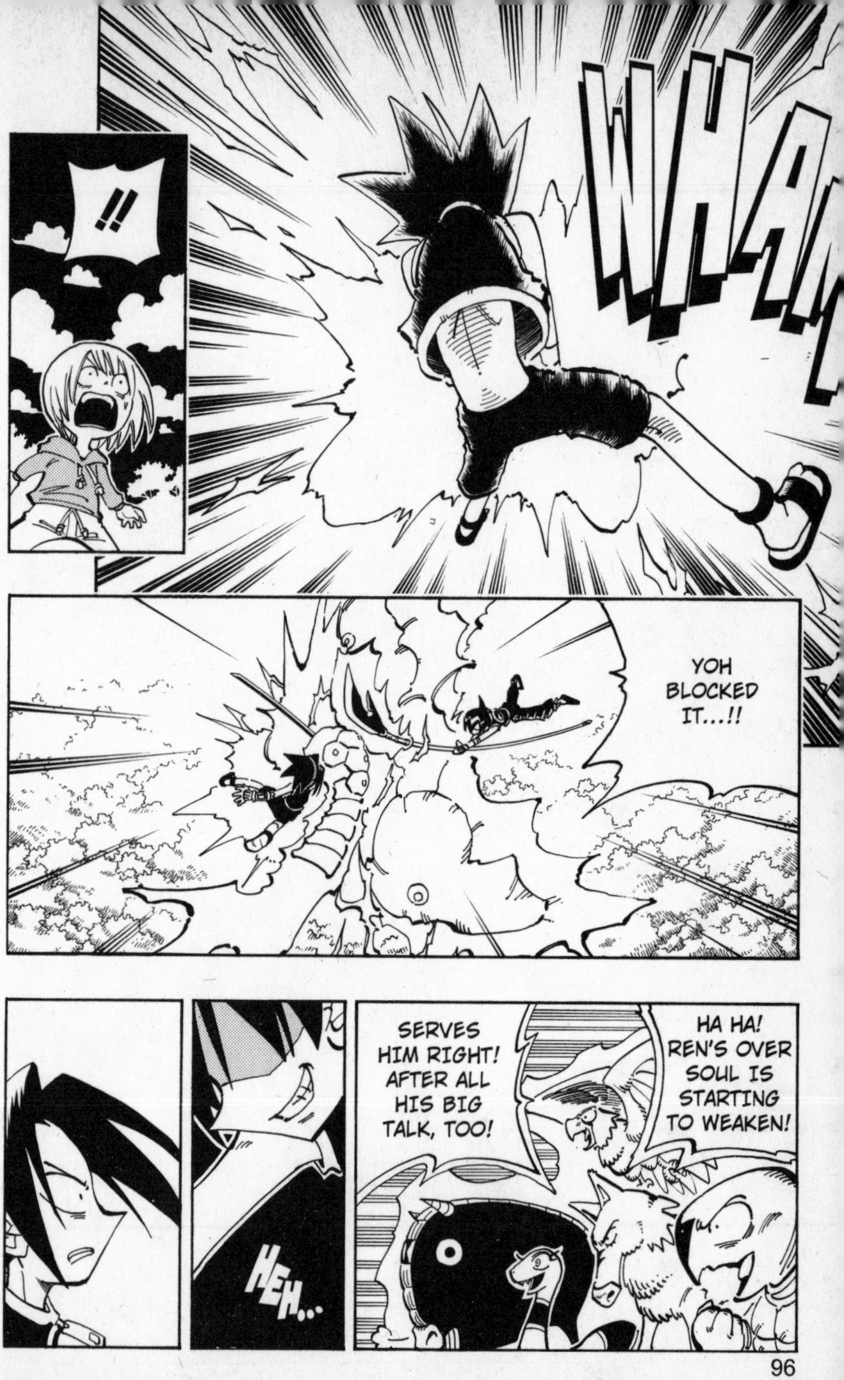
WHA
!!
YOH BLOCKED IT...!!
HA HA! REN'S OVER SOUL IS STARTING TO WEAKEN!
SERVES HIM RIGHT! AFTER ALL HIS BIG TALK, TOO!
HEH...

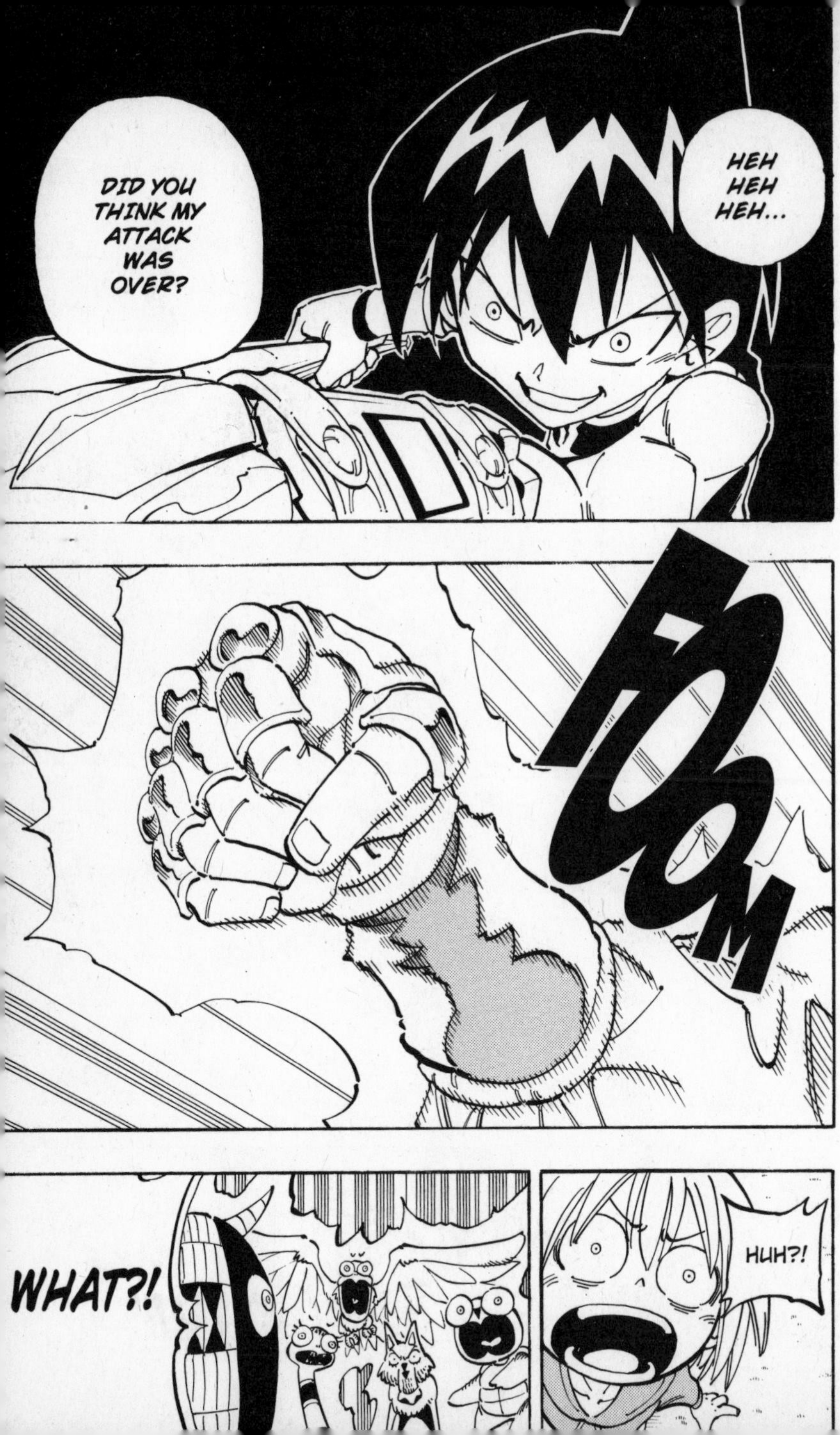
HEH HEH HEH...
DID YOU THINK MY ATTACK WAS OVER?
FOOM
HUH?!
WHAT?!

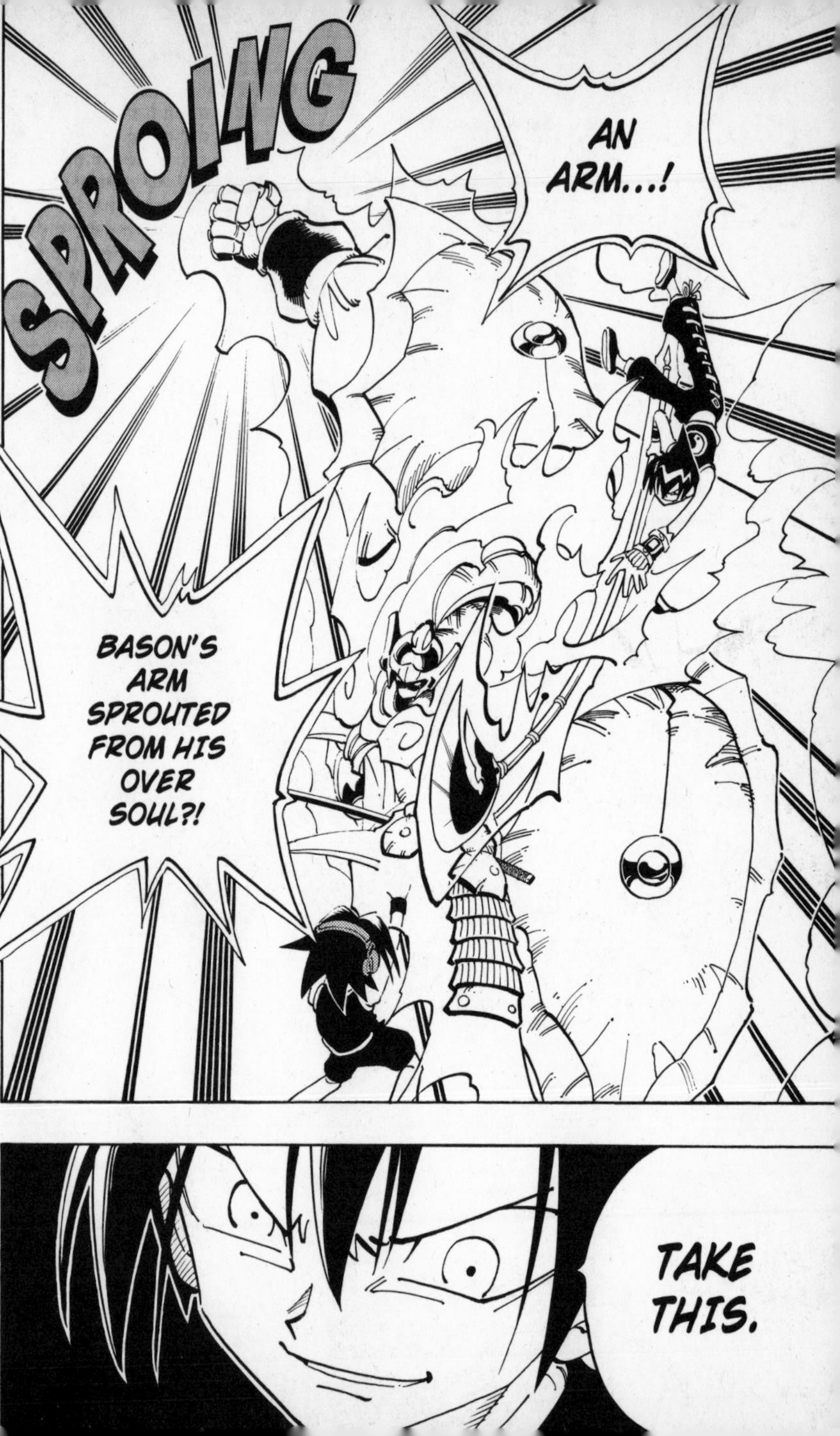
AN ARM...!
SPROING
BASON'S ARM SPROUTED FROM HIS OVER SOUL?!
TAKE THIS.

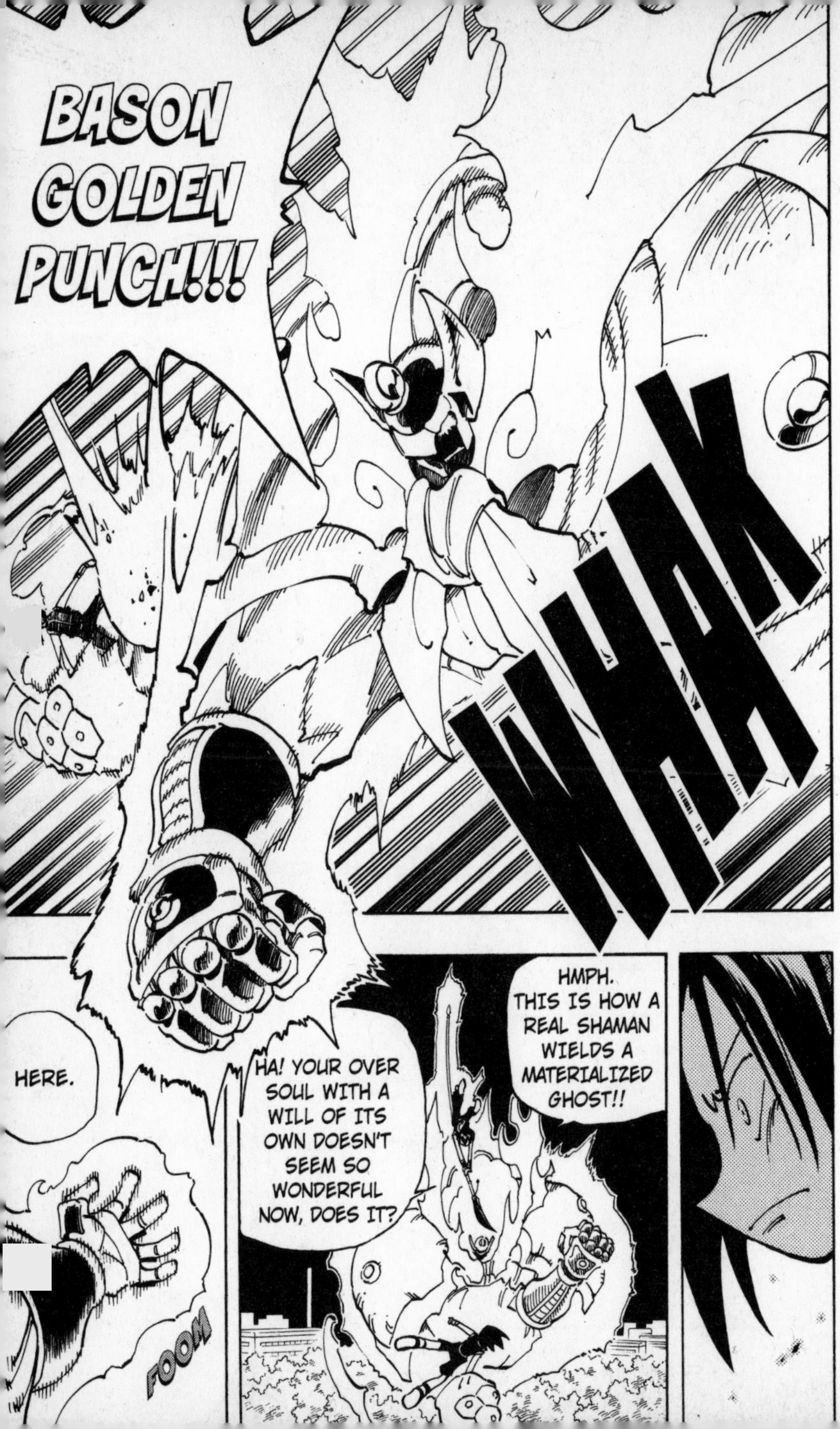
BASON GOLDEN PUNCH!!!
WHAK
HMPH. THIS IS HOW A REAL SHAMAN WIELDS A MATERIALIZED GHOST!!
HA! YOUR OVER SOUL WITH A WILL OF ITS OWN DOESN'T SEEM SO WONDERFUL NOW, DOES IT?
HERE.
FOOM

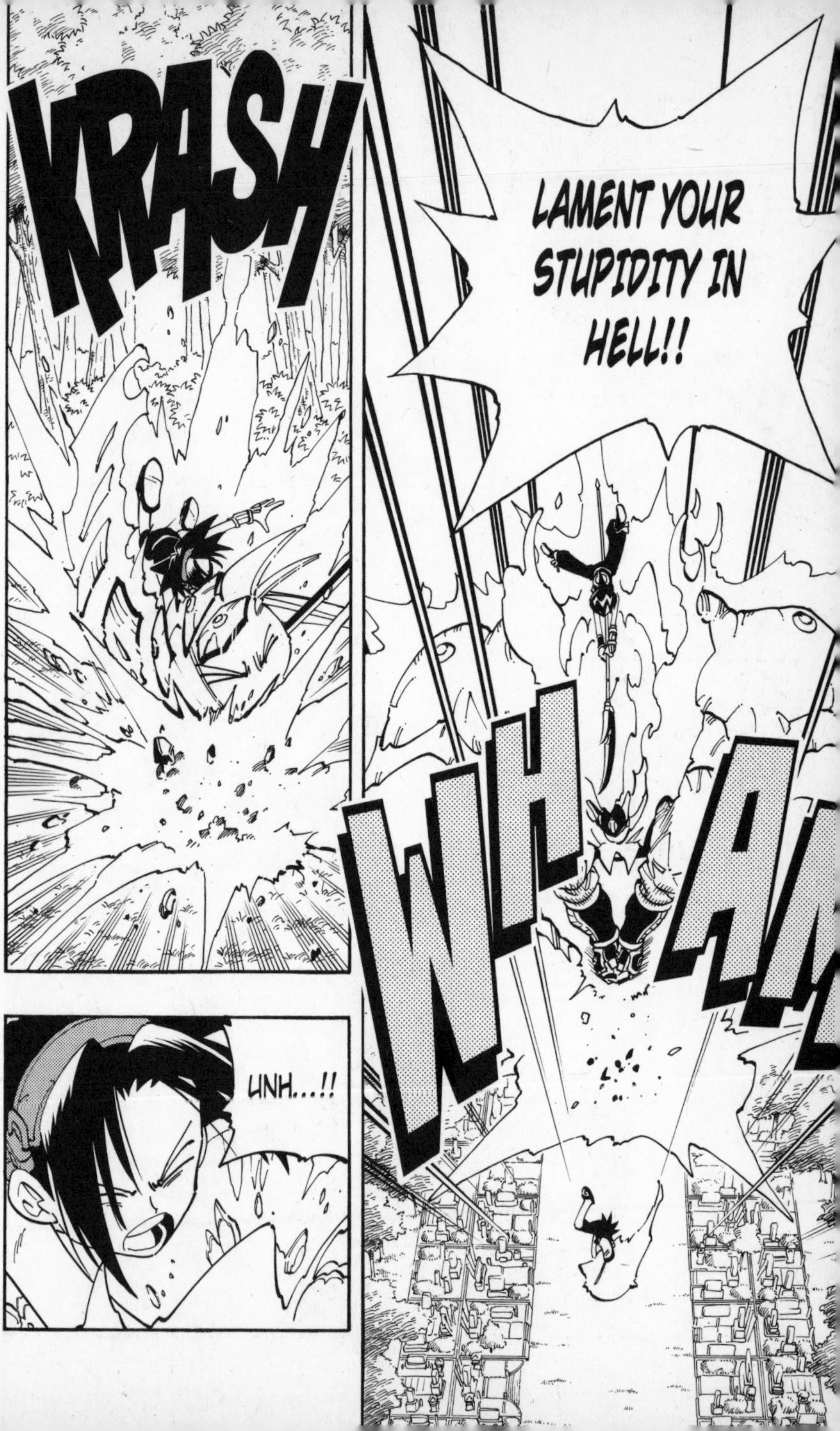
LAMENT YOUR STUPIDITY IN HELL!!
WHA
KRASH
UNH...!!

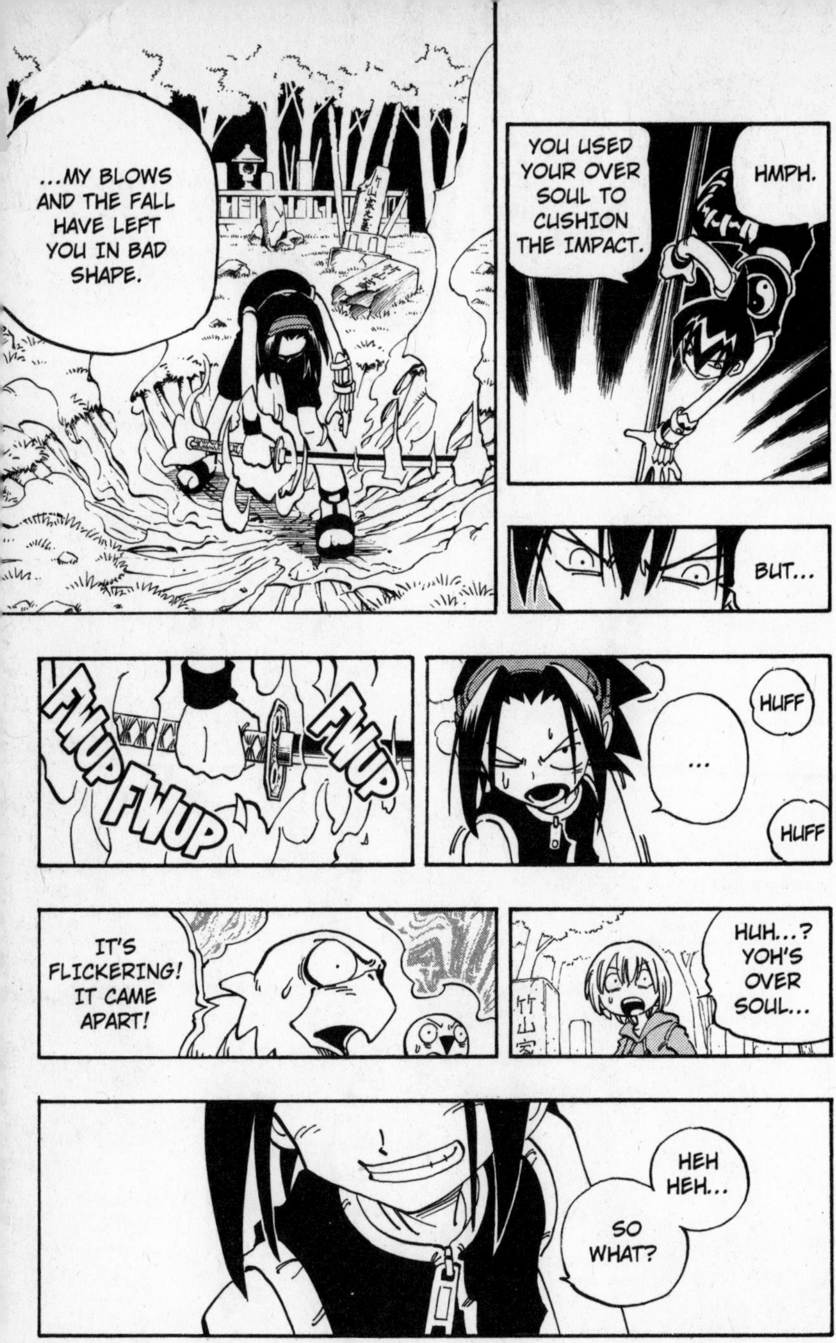
HMPH.
YOU USED YOUR OVER SOUL TO CUSHION THE IMPACT.
BUT...
...MY BLOWS AND THE FALL HAVE LEFT YOU IN BAD SHAPE.
HUFF
...
HUFF
FWUP
FWUP
FWUP
HUH...? YOH'S OVER SOUL...
IT'S FLICKERING! IT CAME APART!
HEH HEH...
SO WHAT?

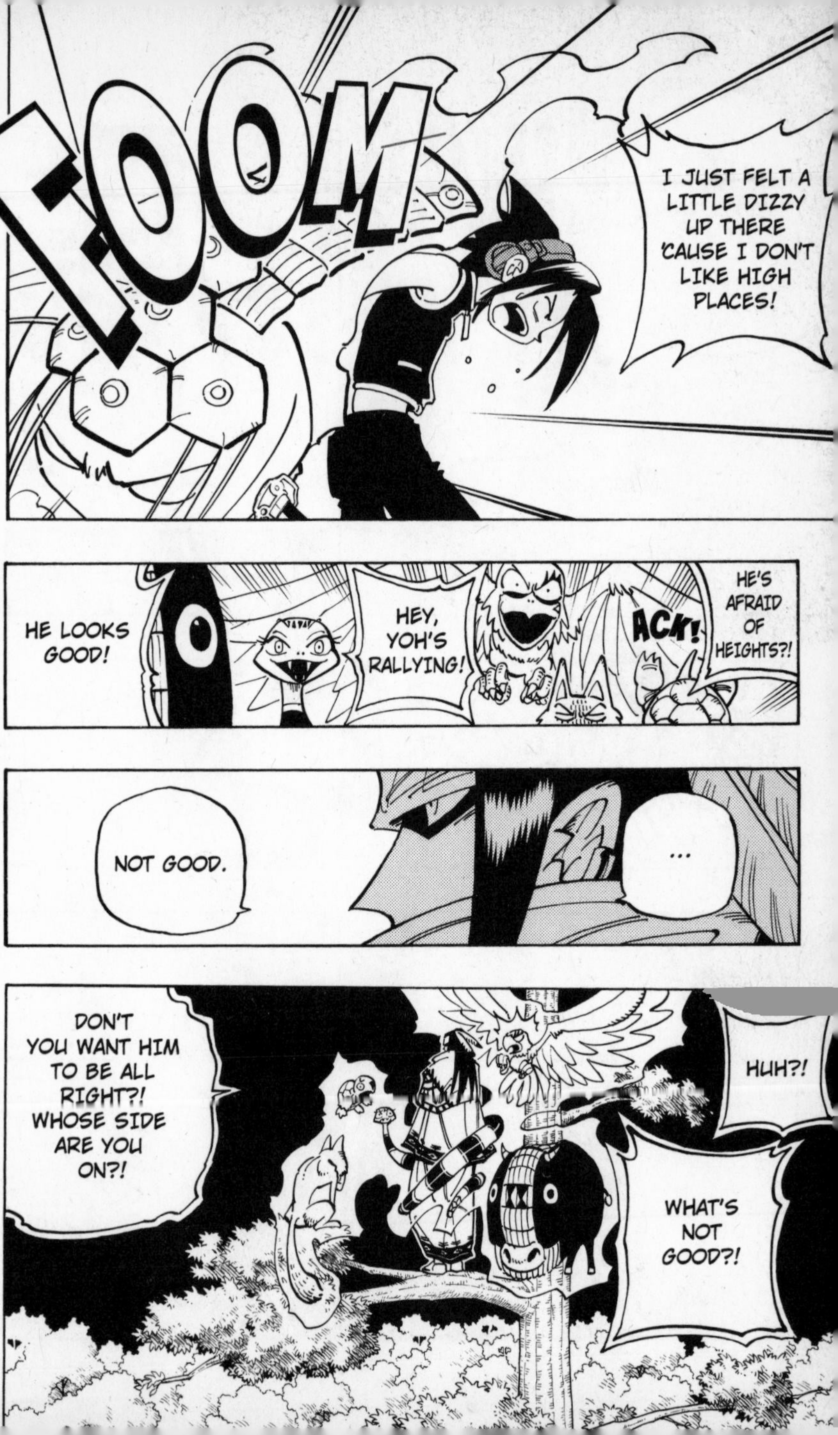
FOOM
I JUST FELT A LITTLE DIZZY UP THERE 'CAUSE I DON'T LIKE HIGH PLACES!
HE'S AFRAID OF HEIGHTS?!
ACK!
HEY, YOH'S RALLYING!
HE LOOKS GOOD!
...
NOT GOOD.
HUH?!
WHAT'S NOT GOOD?!
DON'T YOU WANT HIM TO BE ALL RIGHT?! WHOSE SIDE ARE YOU ON?!

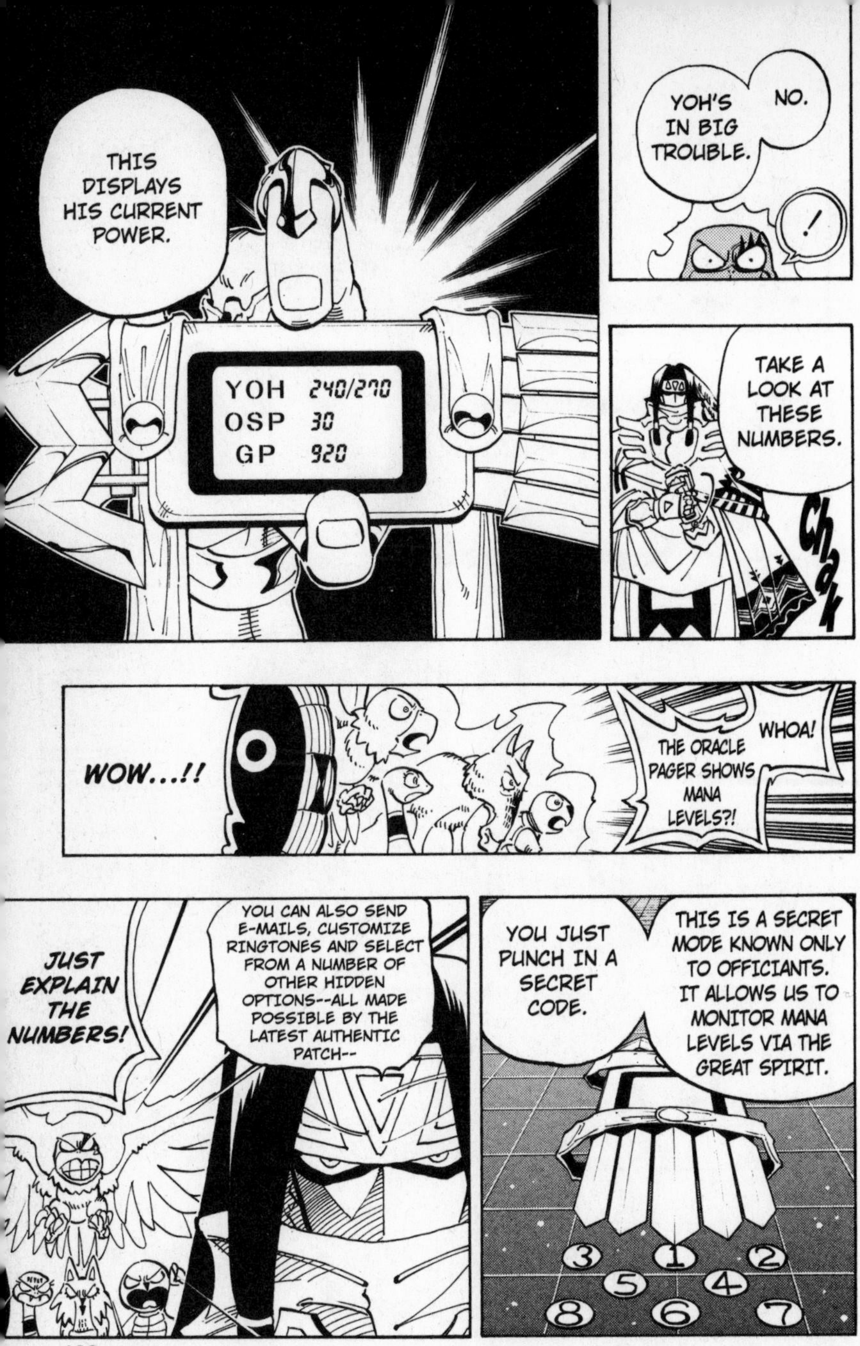
NO.
YOH'S IN BIG TROUBLE.
!
TAKE A LOOK AT THESE NUMBERS.
Chak
THIS DISPLAYS HIS CURRENT POWER.
YOH 240/270
OSP 30
GP 920
WHOA!
THE ORACLE PAGER SHOWS MANA LEVELS?!
WOW...!!
THIS IS A SECRET MODE KNOWN ONLY TO OFFICIANTS. IT ALLOWS US TO MONITOR MANA LEVELS VIA THE GREAT SPIRIT.
YOU JUST PUNCH IN A SECRET CODE.
3 1 2
5 4
8 6 7
YOU CAN ALSO SEND E-MAILS, CUSTOMIZE RINGTONES AND SELECT FROM A NUMBER OF OTHER HIDDEN OPTIONS--ALL MADE POSSIBLE BY THE LATEST AUTHENTIC PATCH--
JUST EXPLAIN THE NUMBERS!

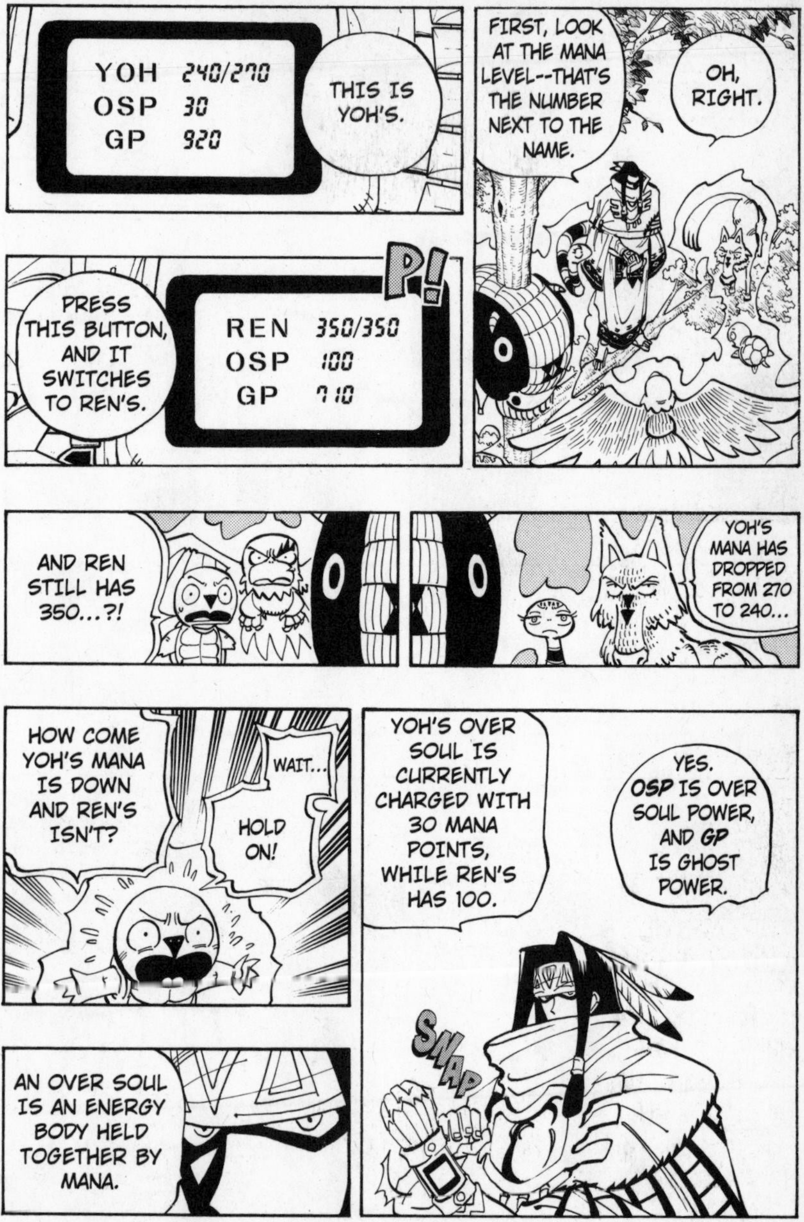
FIRST, LOOK AT THE MANA LEVEL--THAT'S THE NUMBER NEXT TO THE NAME.
OH, RIGHT.
YOH 240/270
OSP 30
GP 920
THIS IS YOH'S.
P!
REN 350/350
OSP 100
GP 710
PRESS THIS BUTTON, AND IT SWITCHES TO REN'S.
YOH'S MANA HAS DROPPED FROM 270 TO 240...
AND REN STILL HAS 350...?!
YOH'S OVER SOUL IS CURRENTLY CHARGED WITH 30 MANA POINTS, WHILE REN'S HAS 100.
YES. OSP IS OVER SOUL POWER, AND GP IS GHOST POWER.
SNAP
HOW COME YOH'S MANA IS DOWN AND REN'S ISN'T?
WAIT...
HOLD ON!
AN OVER SOUL IS AN ENERGY BODY HELD TOGETHER BY MANA.

READ THIS WAY

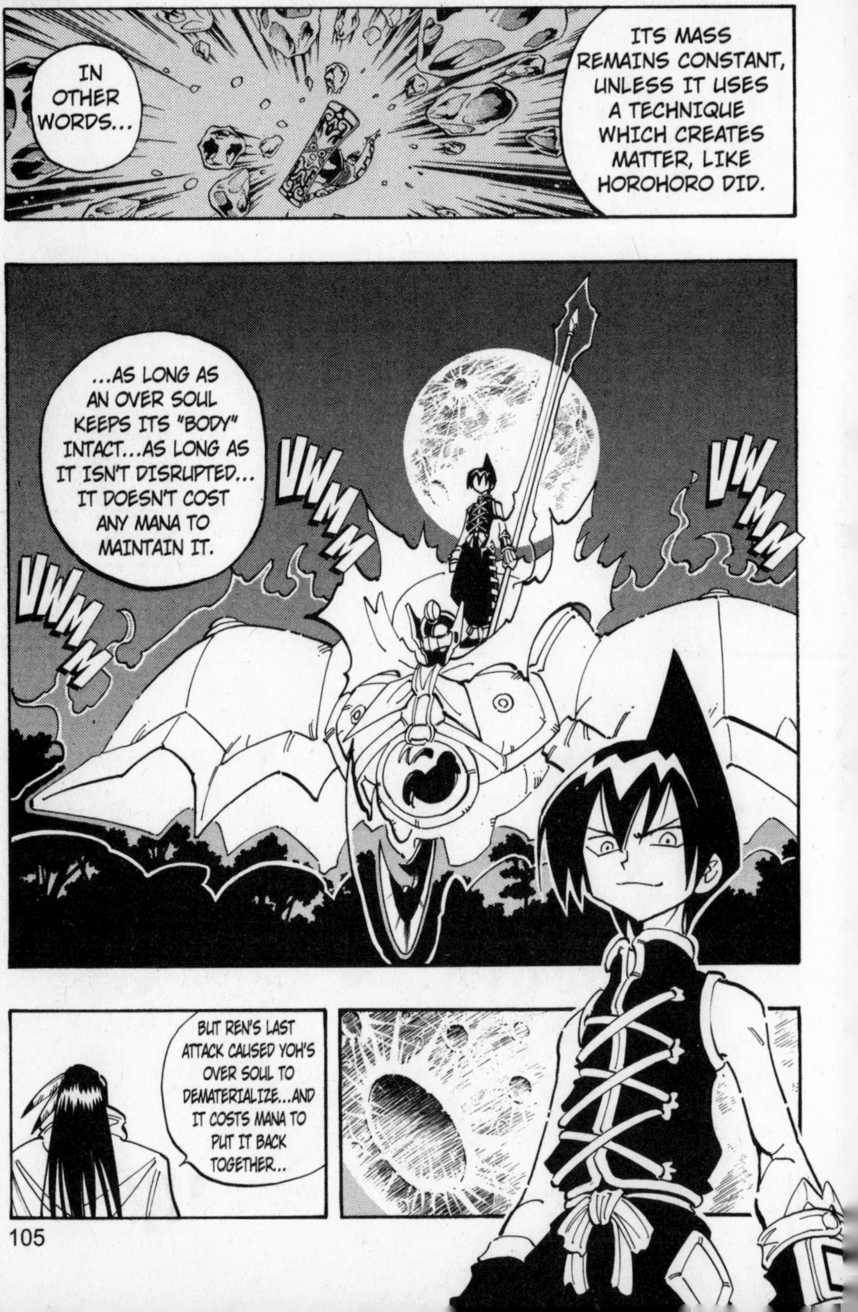
ITS MASS REMAINS CONSTANT, UNLESS IT USES A TECHNIQUE WHICH CREATES MATTER, LIKE HOROHORO DID.
IN OTHER WORDS...
UWMM
UWMM
...AS LONG AS AN OVER SOUL KEEPS ITS "BODY" INTACT...AS LONG AS IT ISN'T DISRUPTED... IT DOESN'T COST ANY MANA TO MAINTAIN IT.
UWMM
BUT REN'S LAST ATTACK CAUSED YOH'S OVER SOUL TO DEMATERIALIZE...AND IT COSTS MANA TO PUT IT BACK TOGETHER...

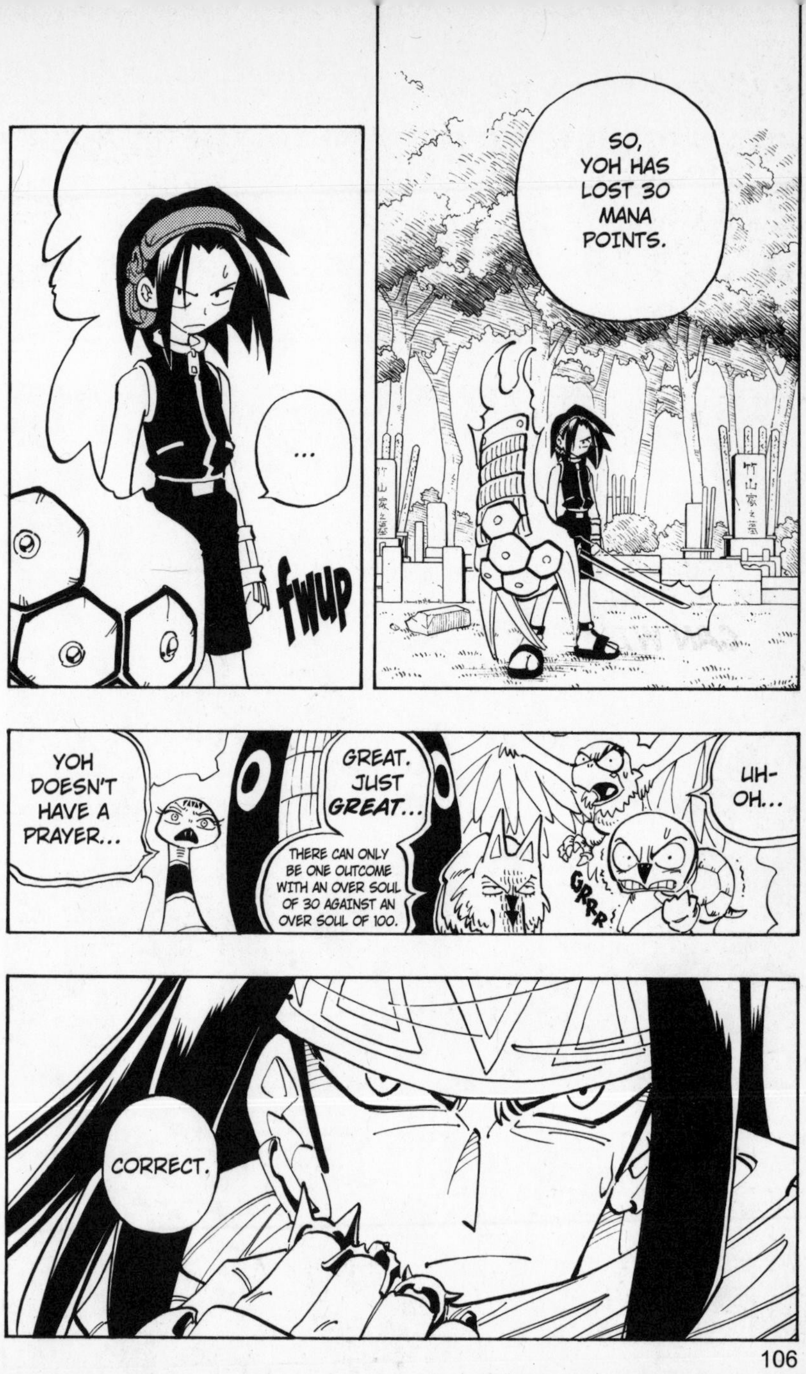
SO, YOH HAS LOST 30 MANA POINTS.
...
fwup
UH-OH...
GRRR
GREAT. JUST GREAT...
THERE CAN ONLY BE ONE OUTCOME WITH AN OVER SOUL OF 30 AGAINST AN OVER SOUL OF 100.
YOH DOESN'T HAVE A PRAYER...
CORRECT.

READ THIS WAY

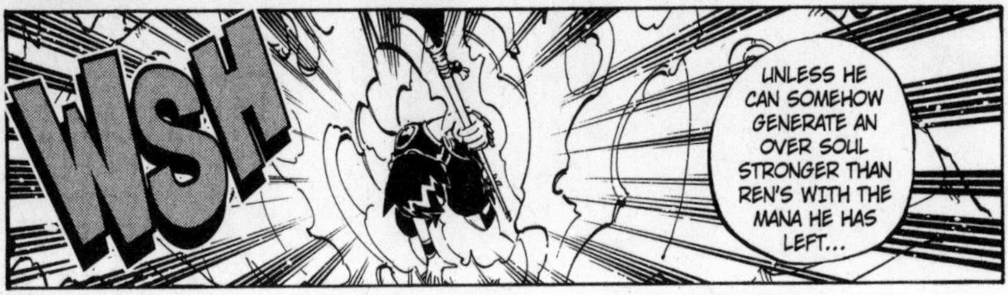
WSH
UNLESS HE CAN SOMEHOW GENERATE AN OVER SOUL STRONGER THAN REN'S WITH THE MANA HE HAS LEFT...

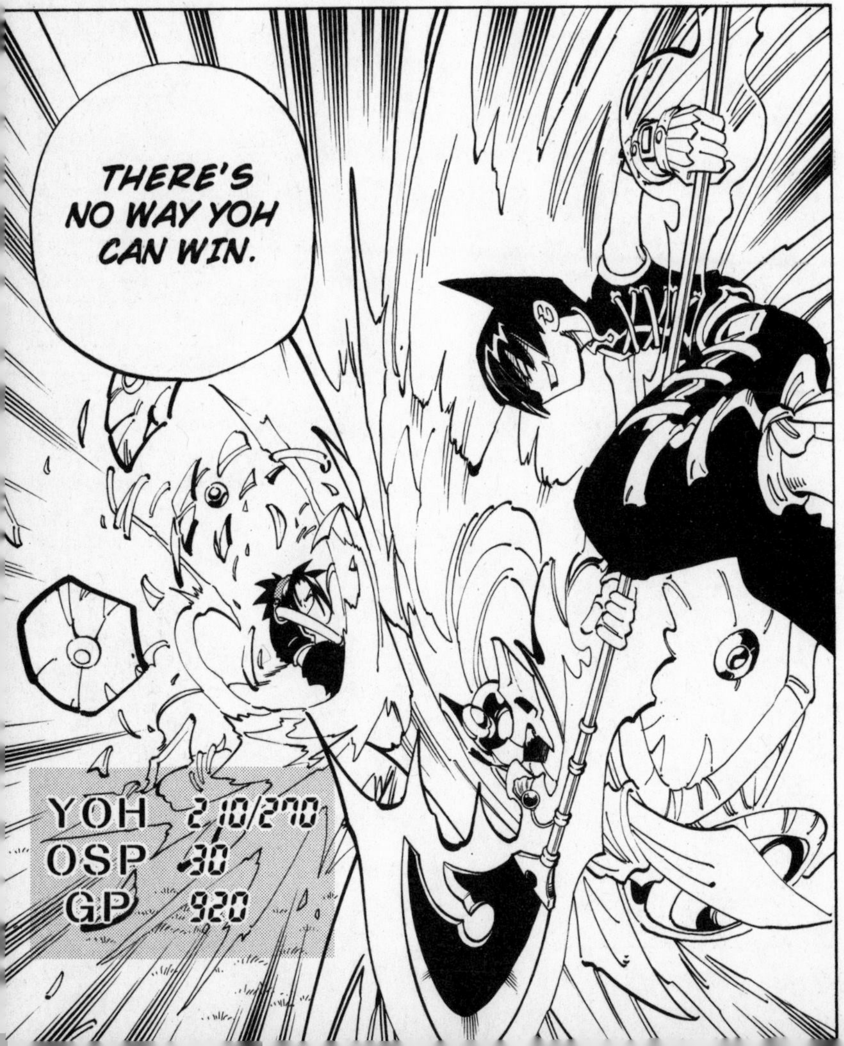
THERE'S NO WAY YOH CAN WIN.
YOH 210/270
OSP 30
GP 920

SHAMAN
KING
7

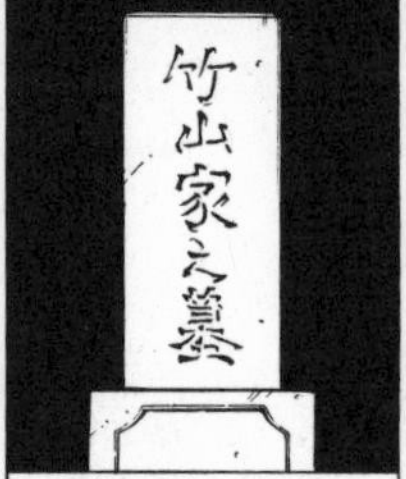
竹山家之墓

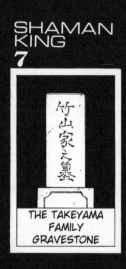

THE TAKEYAMA FAMILY GRAVESTONE

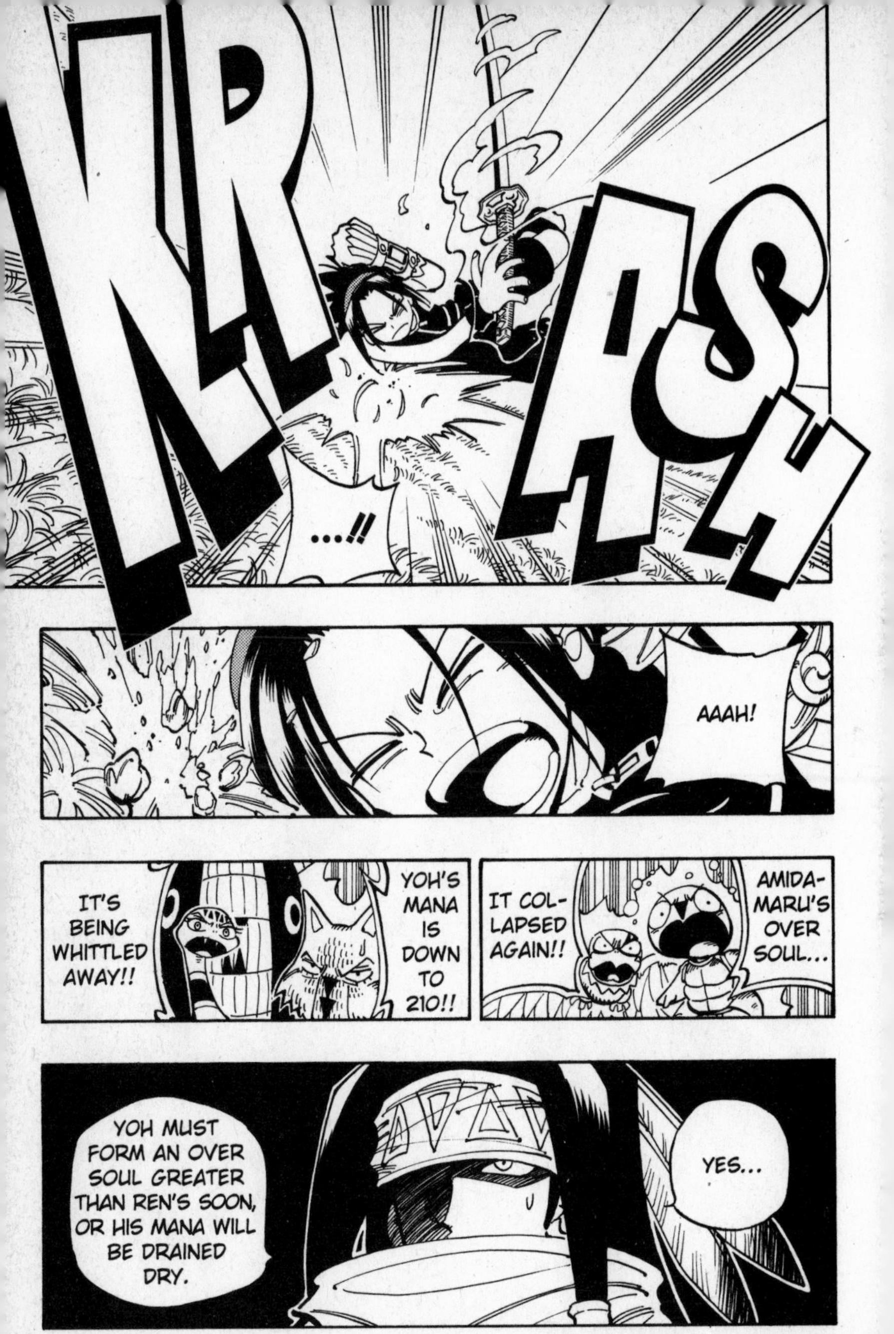
...!!
AAAH!
AMIDA-MARU'S OVER SOUL...
IT COL-LAPSED AGAIN!!
YOH'S MANA IS DOWN TO 210!!
IT'S BEING WHITTLED AWAY!!
YES...
YOH MUST FORM AN OVER SOUL GREATER THAN REN'S SOON, OR HIS MANA WILL BE DRAINED DRY.

Reincarnation 59: Too Much Work

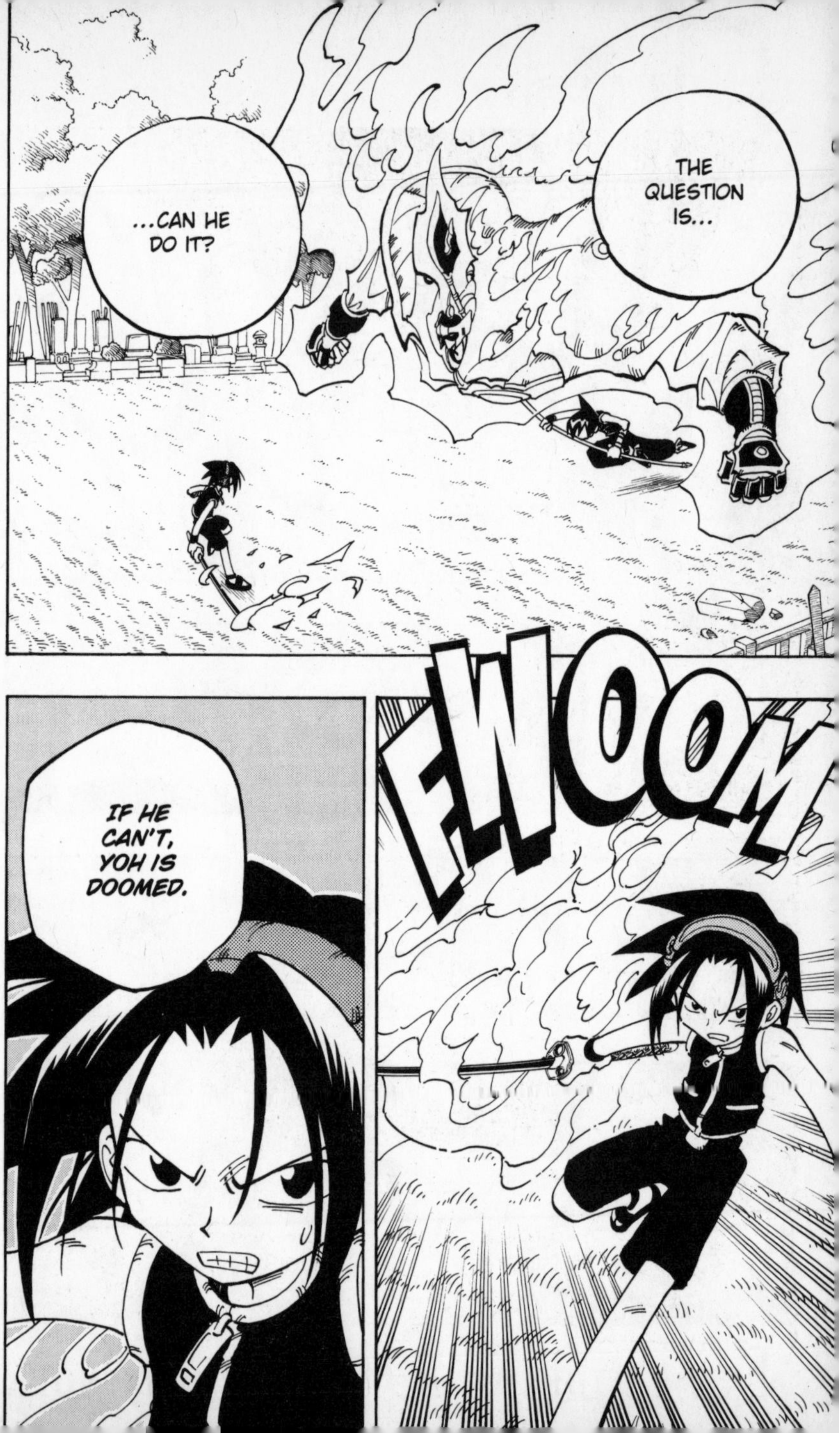
THE QUESTION IS...
...CAN HE DO IT?
FWOOM
IF HE CAN'T, YOH IS DOOMED.

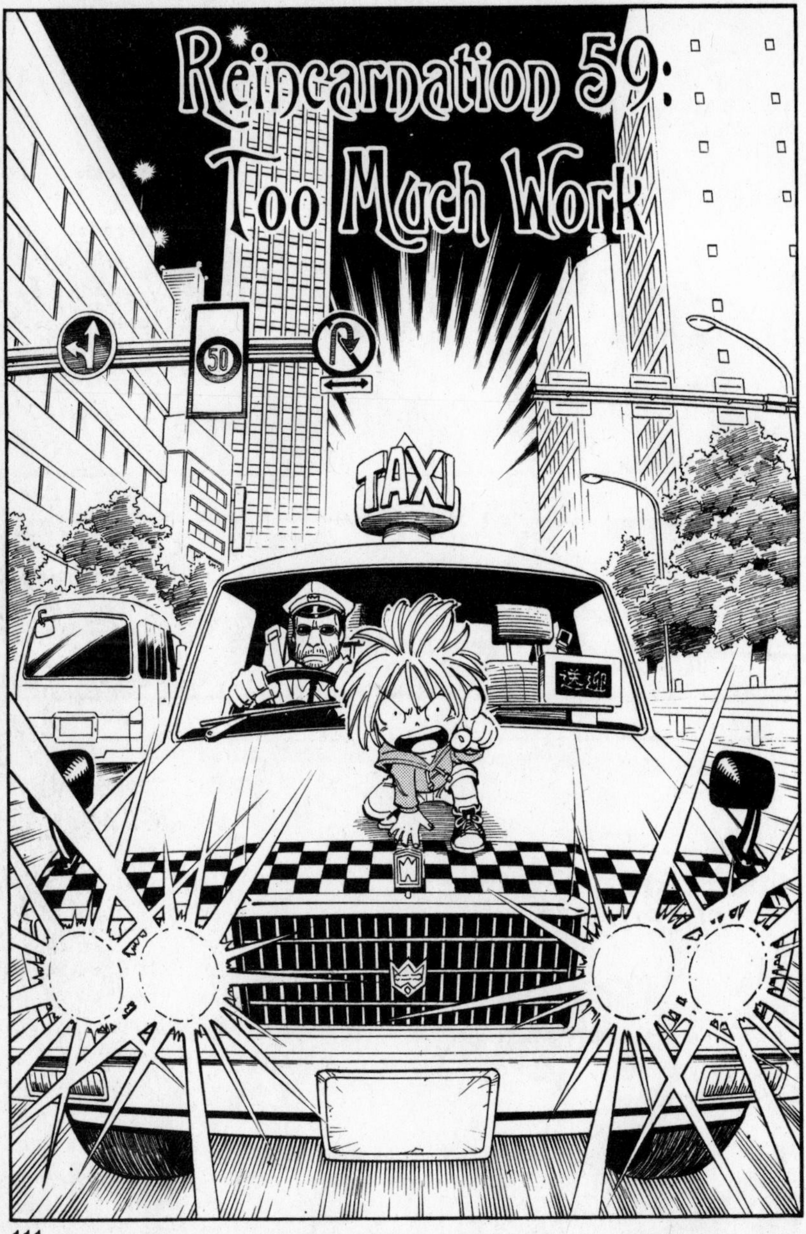
Reincarnation 59:
Too Much Work
50
TAXI
送迎

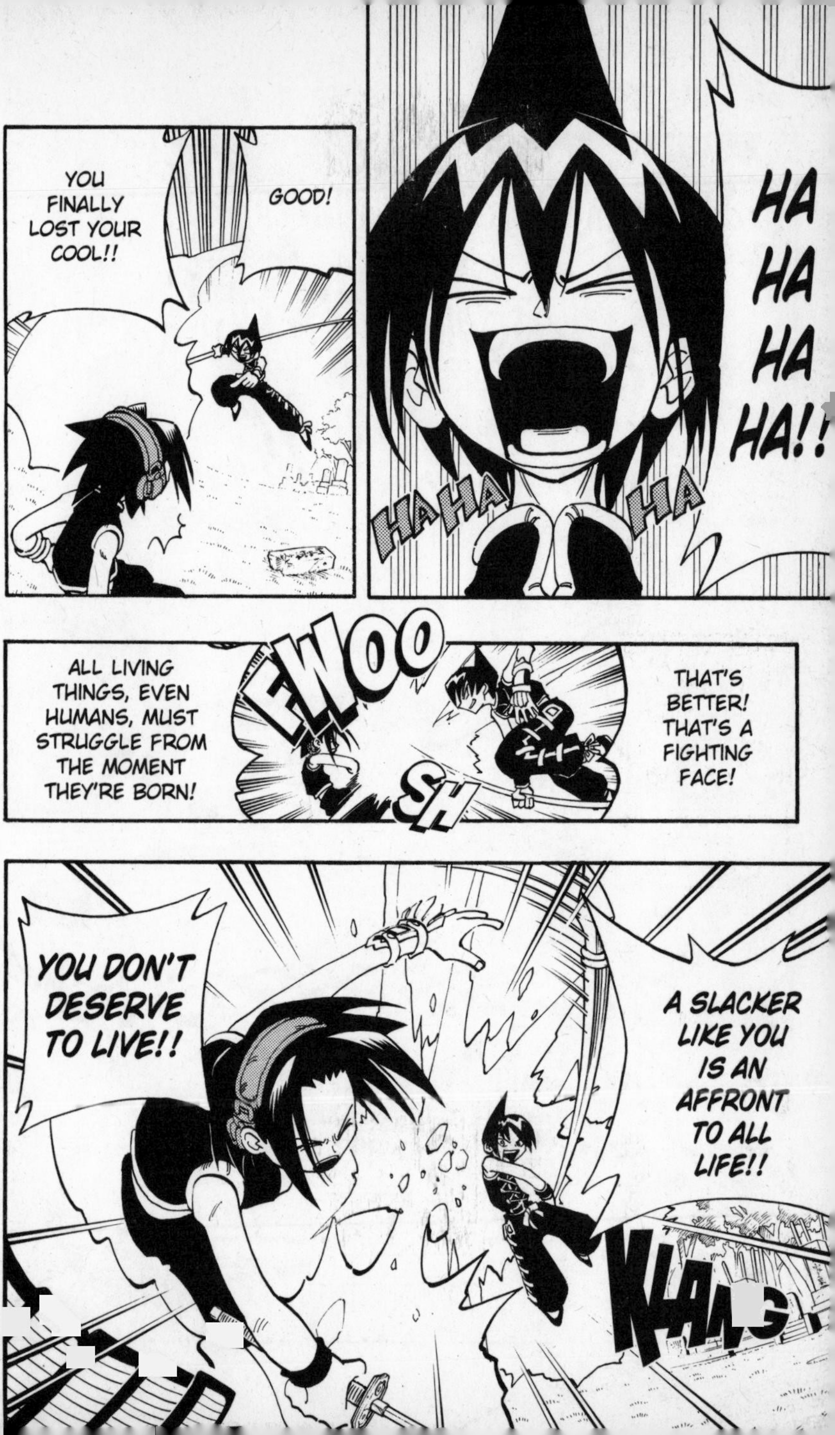
HA HA HA HA!!
HAHAHA HA
GOOD!
YOU FINALLY LOST YOUR COOL!!
THAT'S BETTER! THAT'S A FIGHTING FACE!
SWOOSH
ALL LIVING THINGS, EVEN HUMANS, MUST STRUGGLE FROM THE MOMENT THEY'RE BORN!
A SLACKER LIKE YOU IS AN AFFRONT TO ALL LIFE!!
KLANG
YOU DON'T DESERVE TO LIVE!!

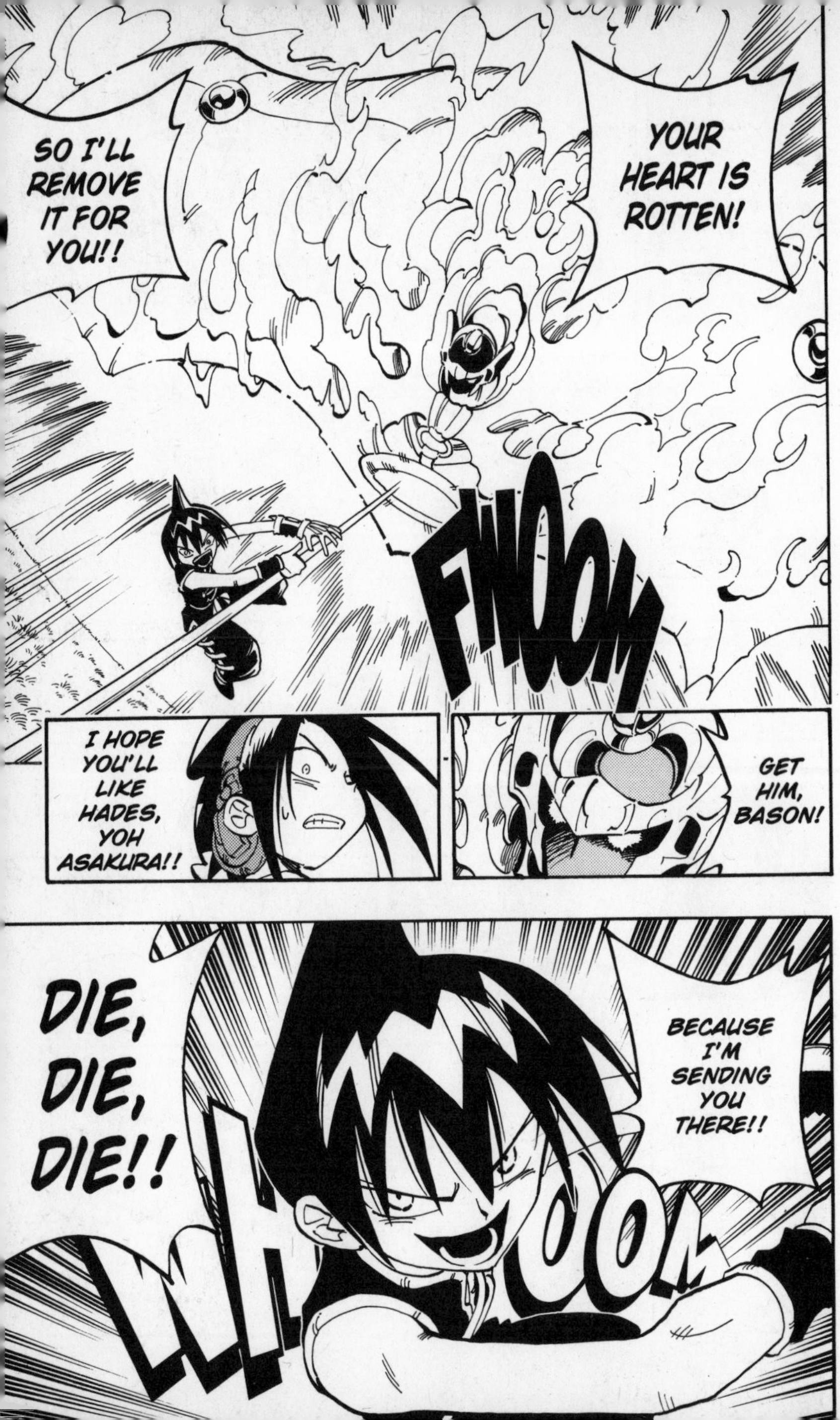
YOUR HEART IS ROTTEN!
SO I'LL REMOVE IT FOR YOU!!
FWOOM
GET HIM, BASON!
I HOPE YOU'LL LIKE HADES, YOH ASAKURA!!
BECAUSE I'M SENDING YOU THERE!!
DIE, DIE, DIE!!
WHOOOM

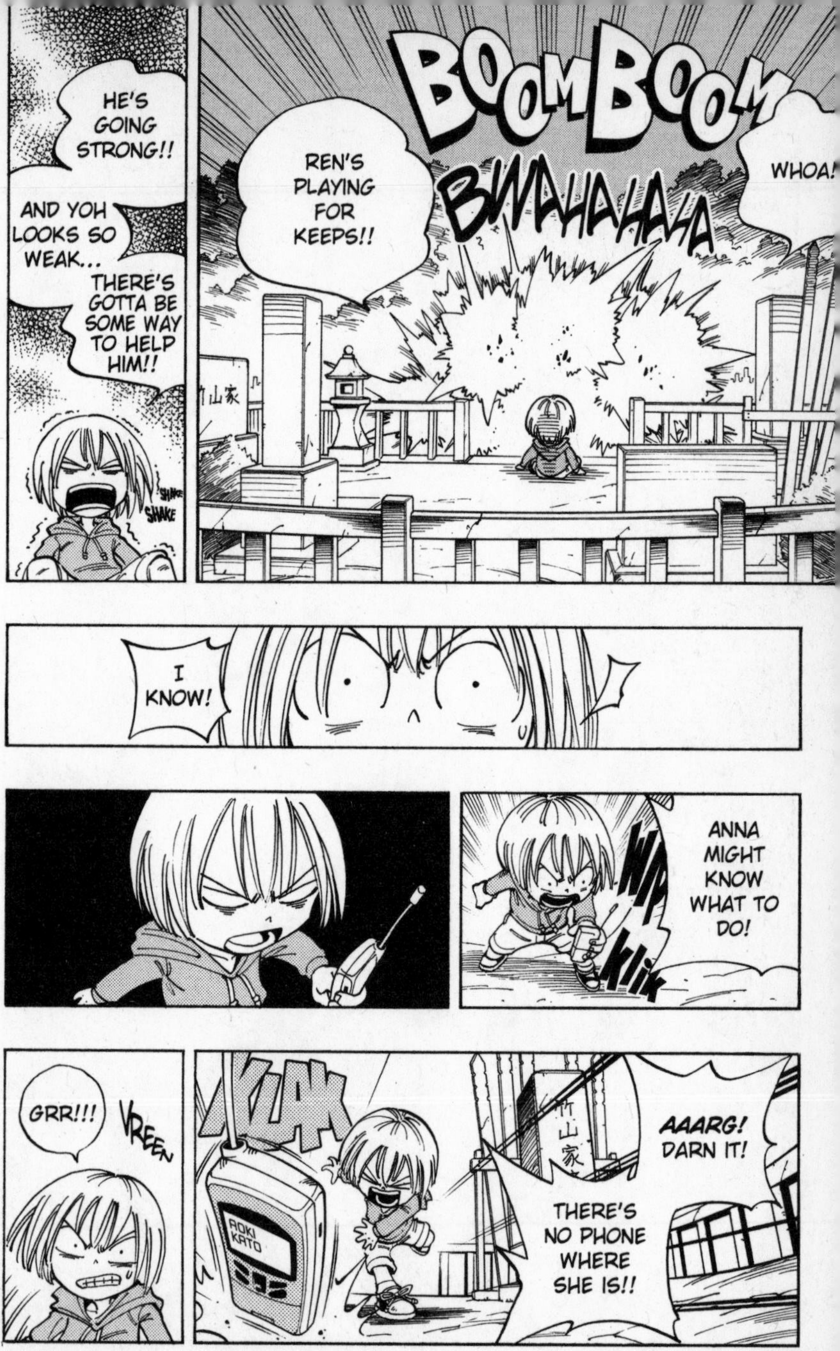
BOOM BOOM
WHOA!
BWAHAHAHAHA
REN'S PLAYING FOR KEEPS!!
HE'S GOING STRONG!!
AND YOH LOOKS SO WEAK...
THERE'S GOTTA BE SOME WAY TO HELP HIM!!
SHAKE SHAKE
I KNOW!
ANNA MIGHT KNOW WHAT TO DO!
KLIK
AAARG! DARN IT!
THERE'S NO PHONE WHERE SHE IS!!
KLAK
AOKI KATO
VREEEN
GRR!!!

READ THIS WAY

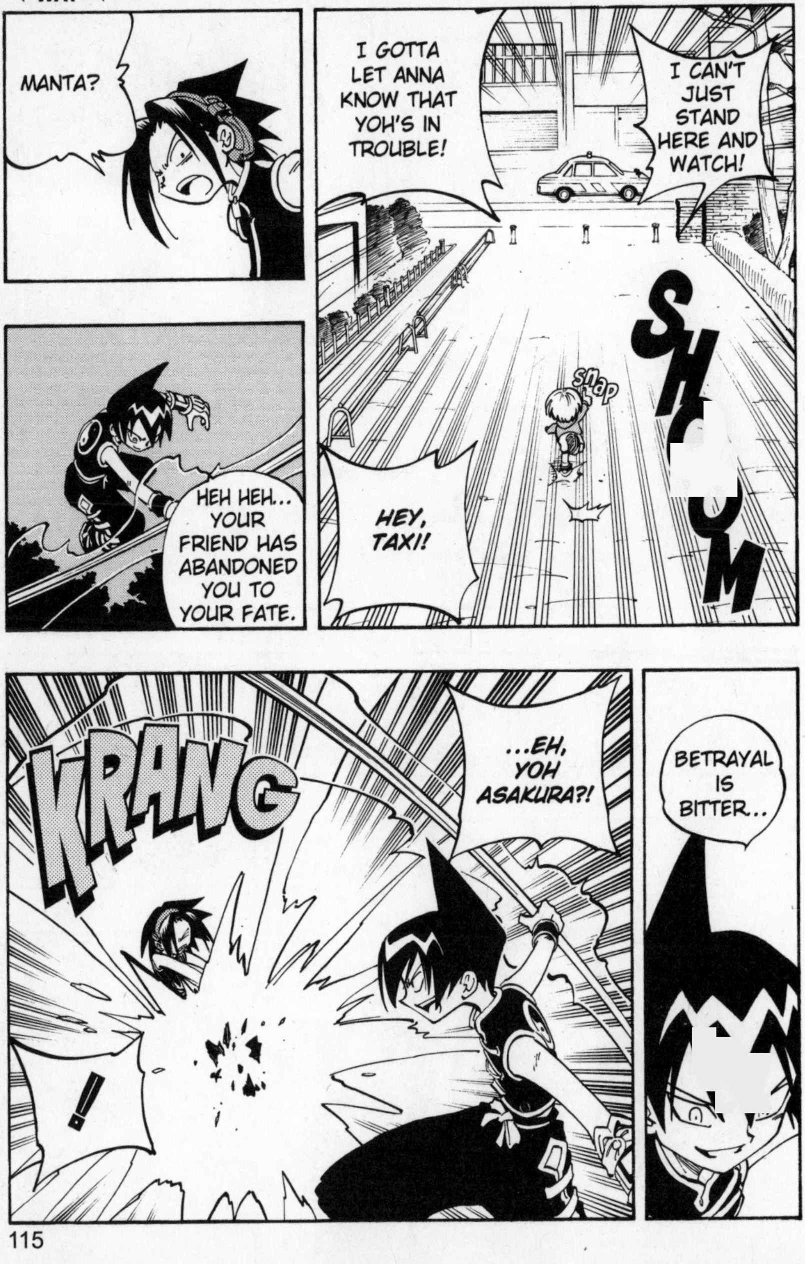
I CAN'T JUST STAND HERE AND WATCH!
I GOTTA LET ANNA KNOW THAT YOH'S IN TROUBLE!
SHOOM
snap
HEY, TAXI!!
MANTA?
HEH HEH... YOUR FRIEND HAS ABANDONED YOU TO YOUR FATE.
BETRAYAL IS BITTER...
...EH, YOH ASAKURA?!
KRANG
!

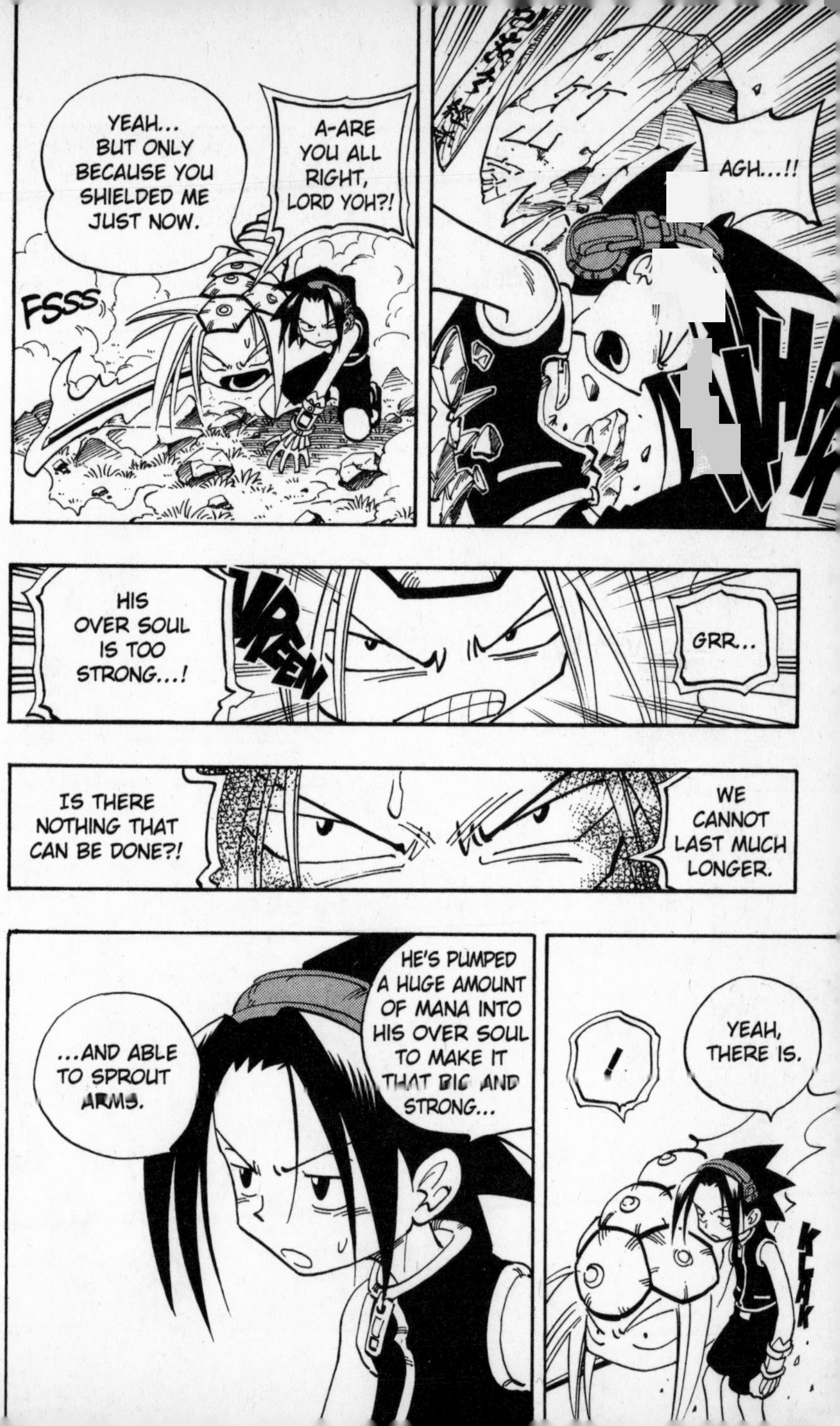
AGH...!!
A-ARE YOU ALL RIGHT, LORD YOH?!
YEAH... BUT ONLY BECAUSE YOU SHIELDED ME JUST NOW.
FSSS
GRR...
VREEN
HIS OVER SOUL IS TOO STRONG...!
WE CANNOT LAST MUCH LONGER.
IS THERE NOTHING THAT CAN BE DONE?!
YEAH, THERE IS.
!
HE'S PUMPED A HUGE AMOUNT OF MANA INTO HIS OVER SOUL TO MAKE IT THAT BIG AND STRONG...
...AND ABLE TO SPROUT ARMS.

READ THIS WAY

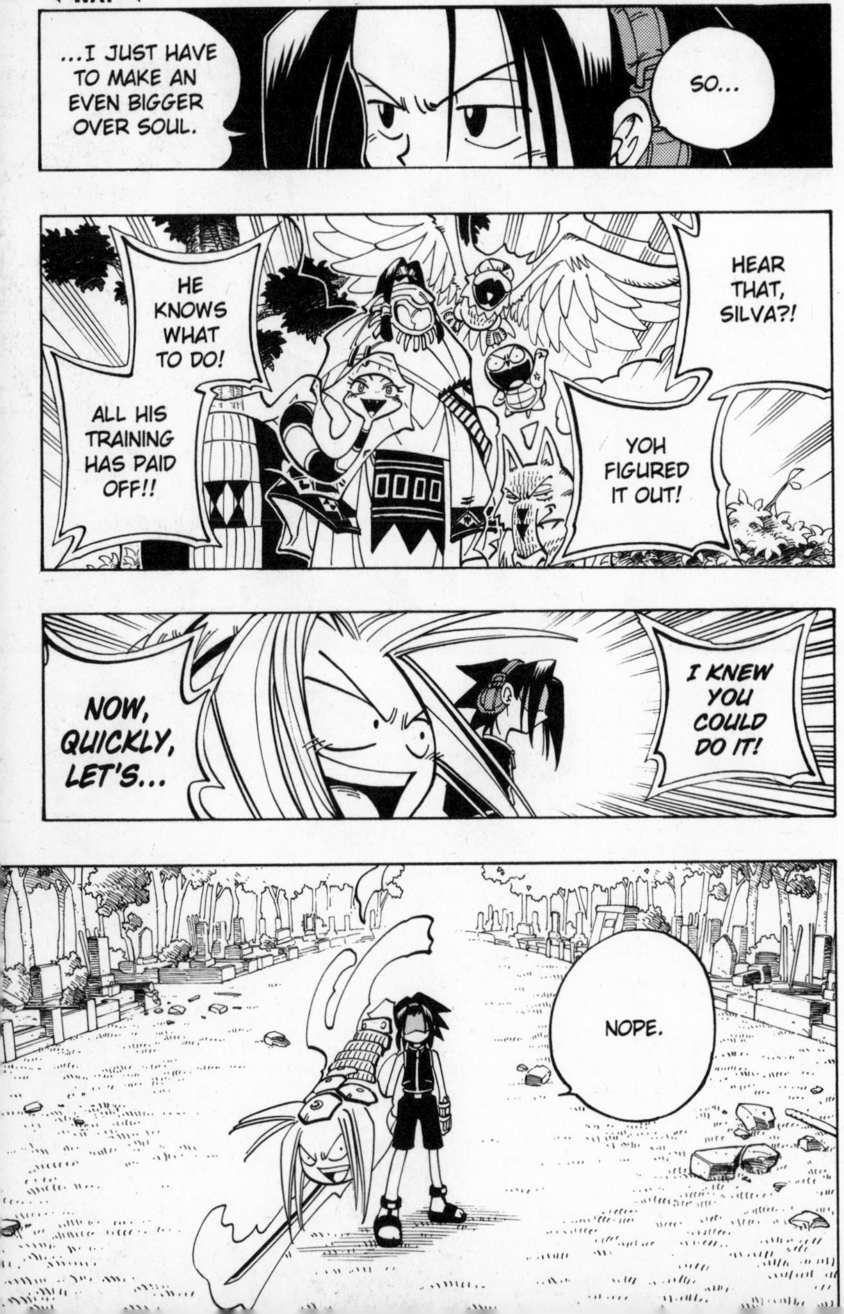
SO...
...I JUST HAVE TO MAKE AN EVEN BIGGER OVER SOUL.
HEAR THAT, SILVA?!
YOH FIGURED IT OUT!
HE KNOWS WHAT TO DO!
ALL HIS TRAINING HAS PAID OFF!!
I KNEW YOU COULD DO IT!
NOW, QUICKLY, LET'S...
NOPE.

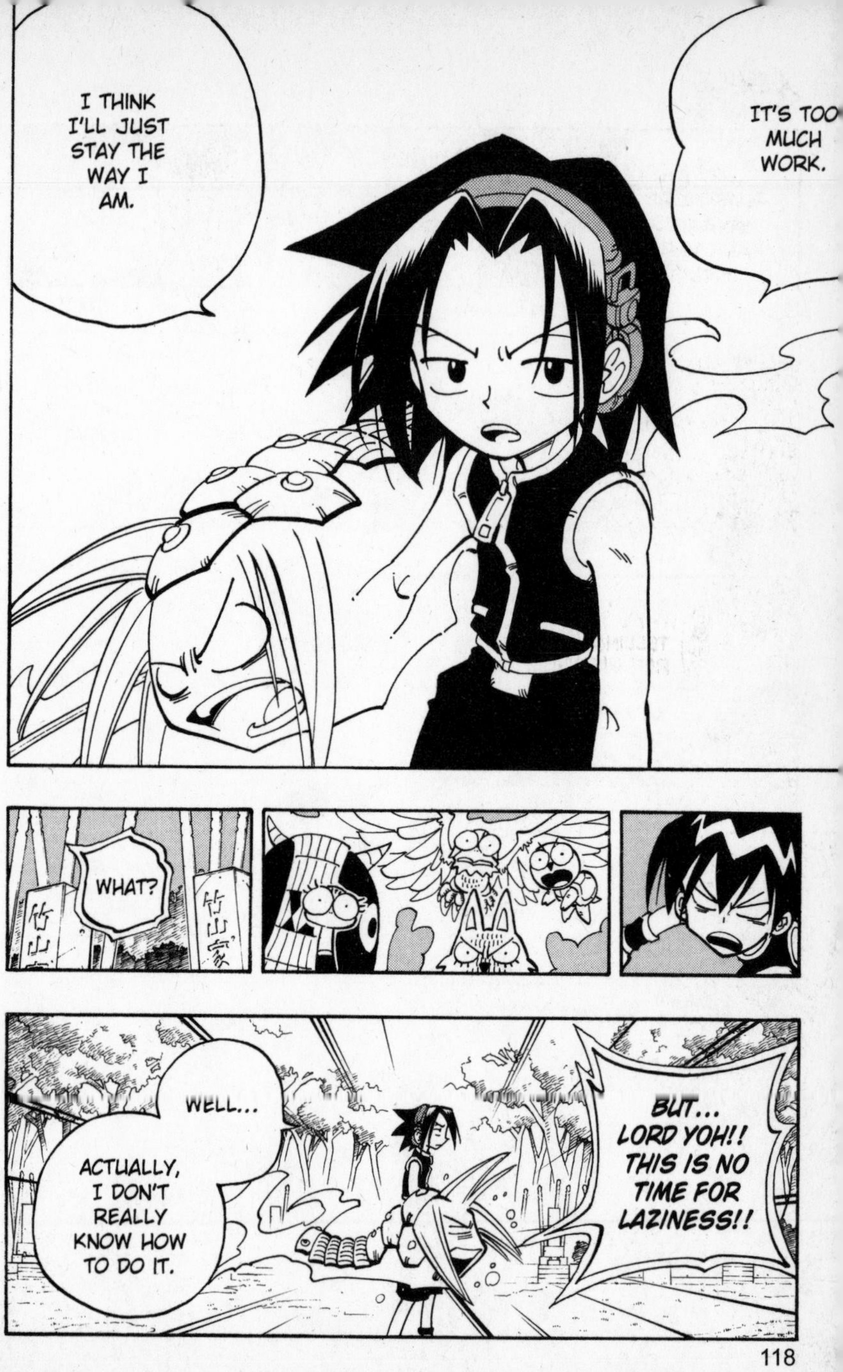
IT'S TOO MUCH WORK.
I THINK I'LL JUST STAY THE WAY I AM.
WHAT?
BUT... LORD YOH!! THIS IS NO TIME FOR LAZINESS!!
WELL...
ACTUALLY, I DON'T REALLY KNOW HOW TO DO IT.

READ THIS WAY

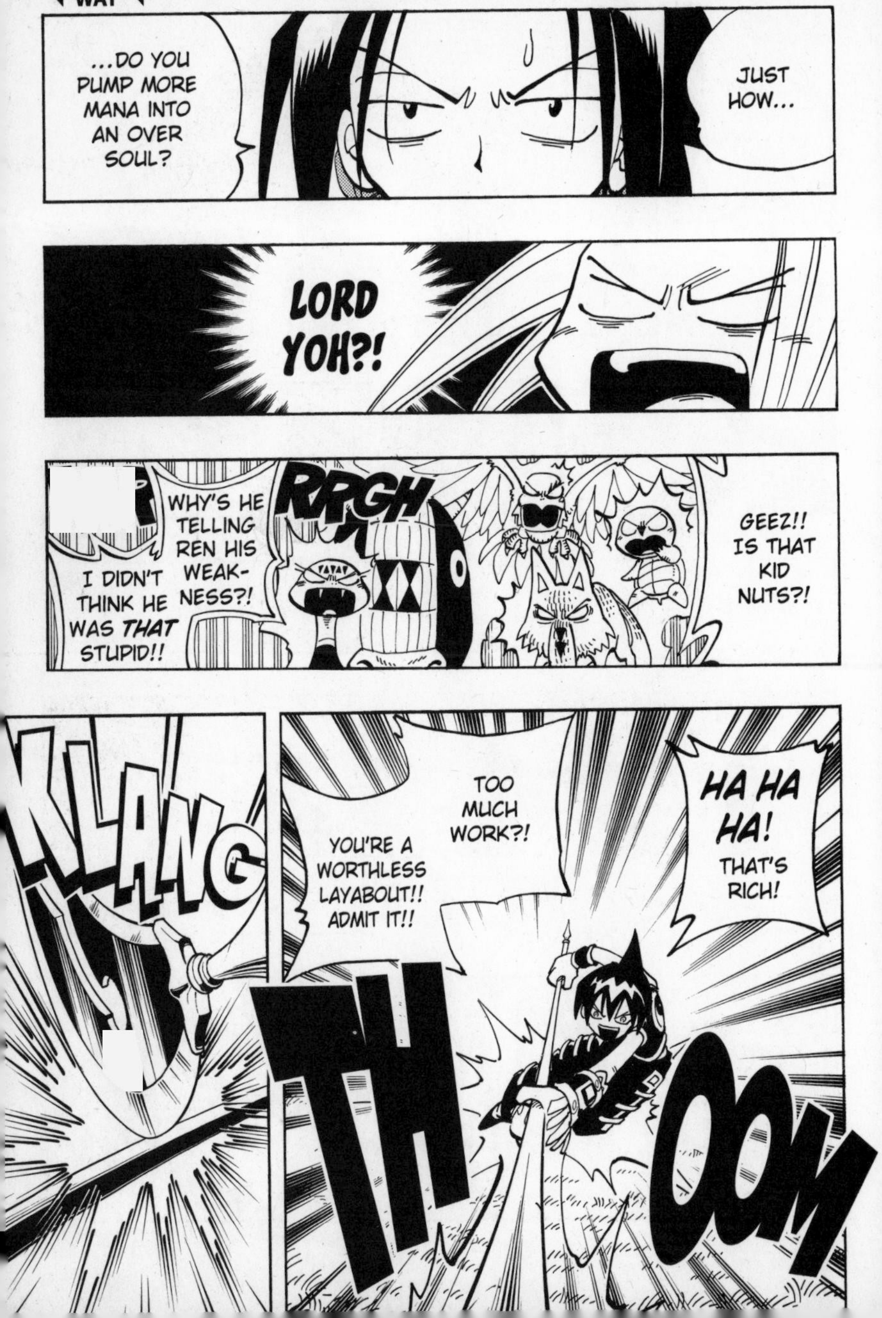
JUST HOW...
...DO YOU PUMP MORE MANA INTO AN OVER SOUL?
LORD YOH?!
GEEZ!! IS THAT KID NUTS?!
RPGH
WHY'S HE TELLING REN HIS WEAK-NESS?!
I DIDN'T THINK HE WAS *THAT* STUPID!!
HA HA HA! THAT'S RICH!
TOO MUCH WORK?!
YOU'RE A WORTHLESS LAYABOUT!! ADMIT IT!!
THOOM
KLANG

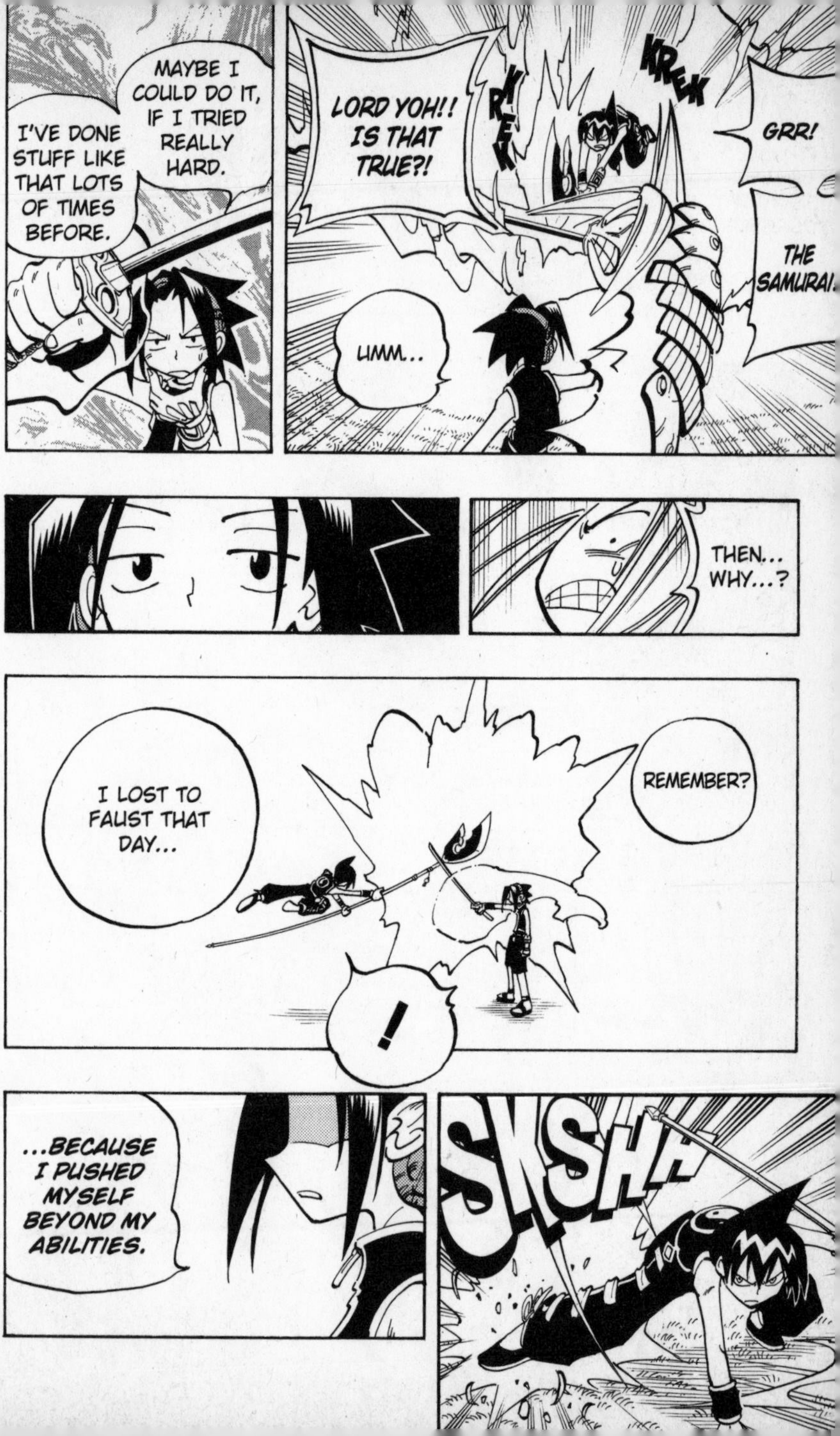
KREK
KREK
GRR!
THE SAMURAI.
LORD YOH!! IS THAT TRUE?!
UMM...
MAYBE I COULD DO IT, IF I TRIED REALLY HARD.
I'VE DONE STUFF LIKE THAT LOTS OF TIMES BEFORE.
THEN... WHY...?
REMEMBER?
I LOST TO FAUST THAT DAY...
!
SKSHA
...BECAUSE I PUSHED MYSELF BEYOND MY ABILITIES.

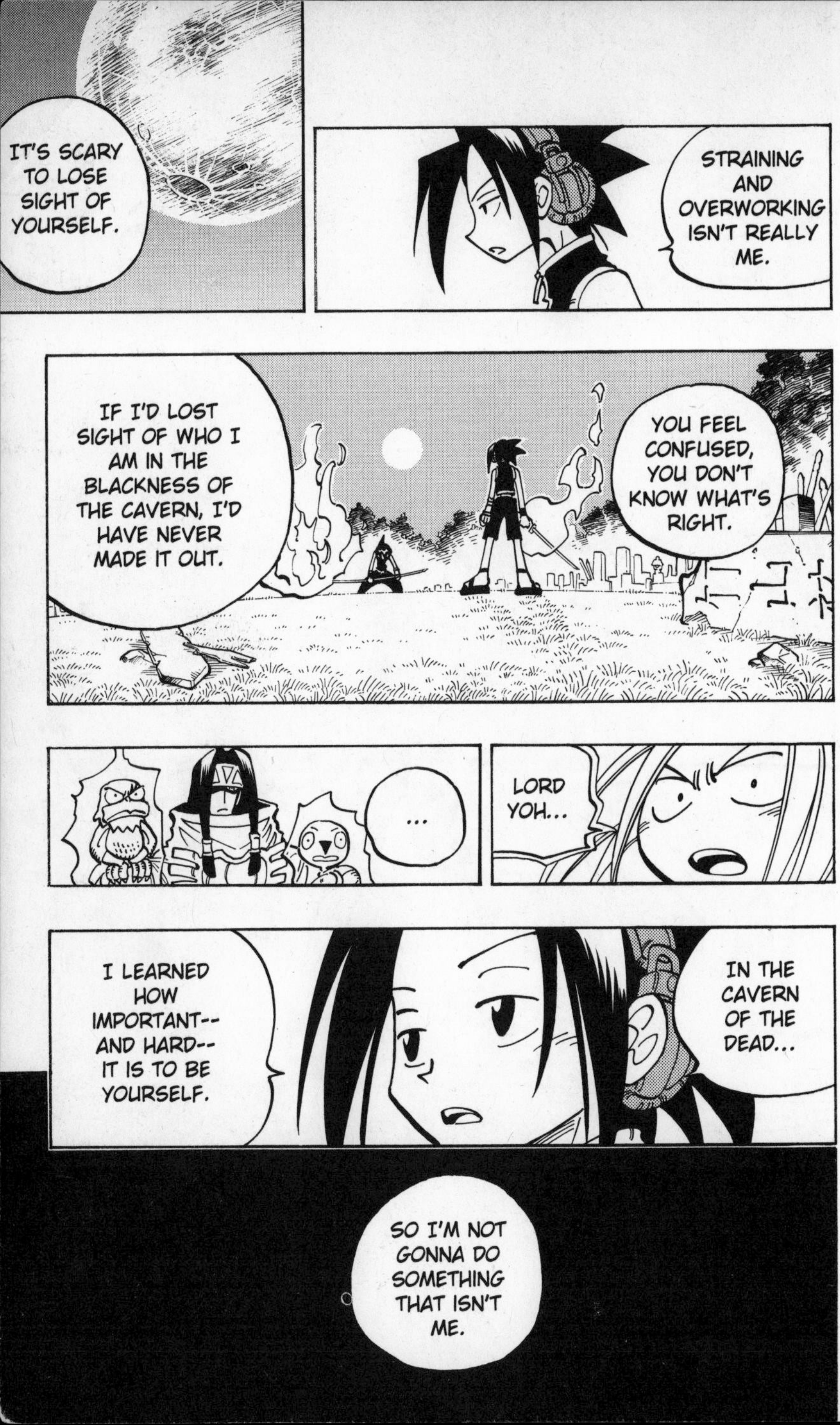
STRAINING AND OVERWORKING ISN'T REALLY ME.
IT'S SCARY TO LOSE SIGHT OF YOURSELF.
YOU FEEL CONFUSED, YOU DON'T KNOW WHAT'S RIGHT.
IF I'D LOST SIGHT OF WHO I AM IN THE BLACKNESS OF THE CAVERN, I'D HAVE NEVER MADE IT OUT.
LORD YOH...
...
IN THE CAVERN OF THE DEAD...
I LEARNED HOW IMPORTANT-- AND HARD-- IT IS TO BE YOURSELF.
SO I'M NOT GONNA DO SOMETHING THAT ISN'T ME.

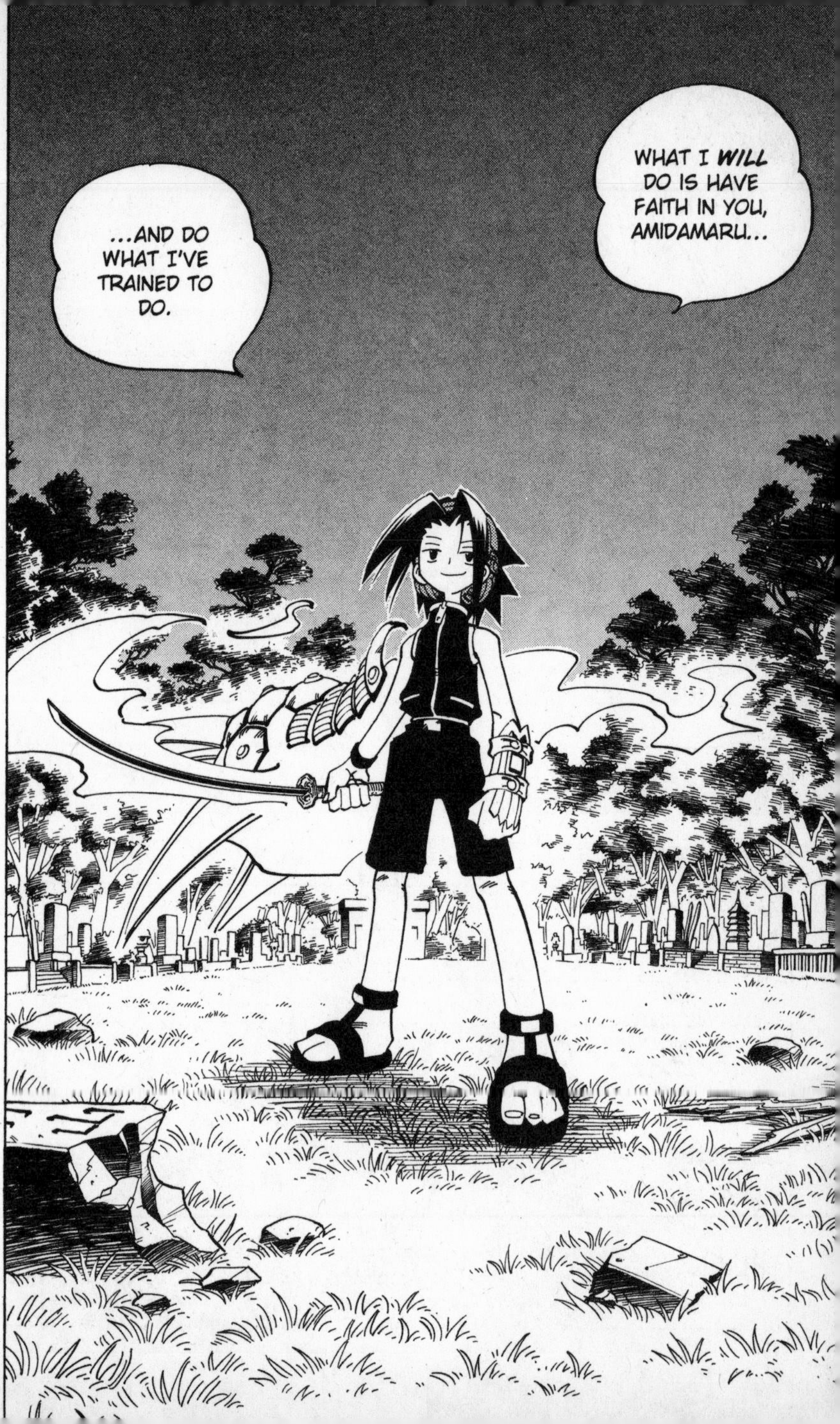
WHAT I WILL DO IS HAVE FAITH IN YOU, AMIDAMARU...
...AND DO WHAT I'VE TRAINED TO DO.

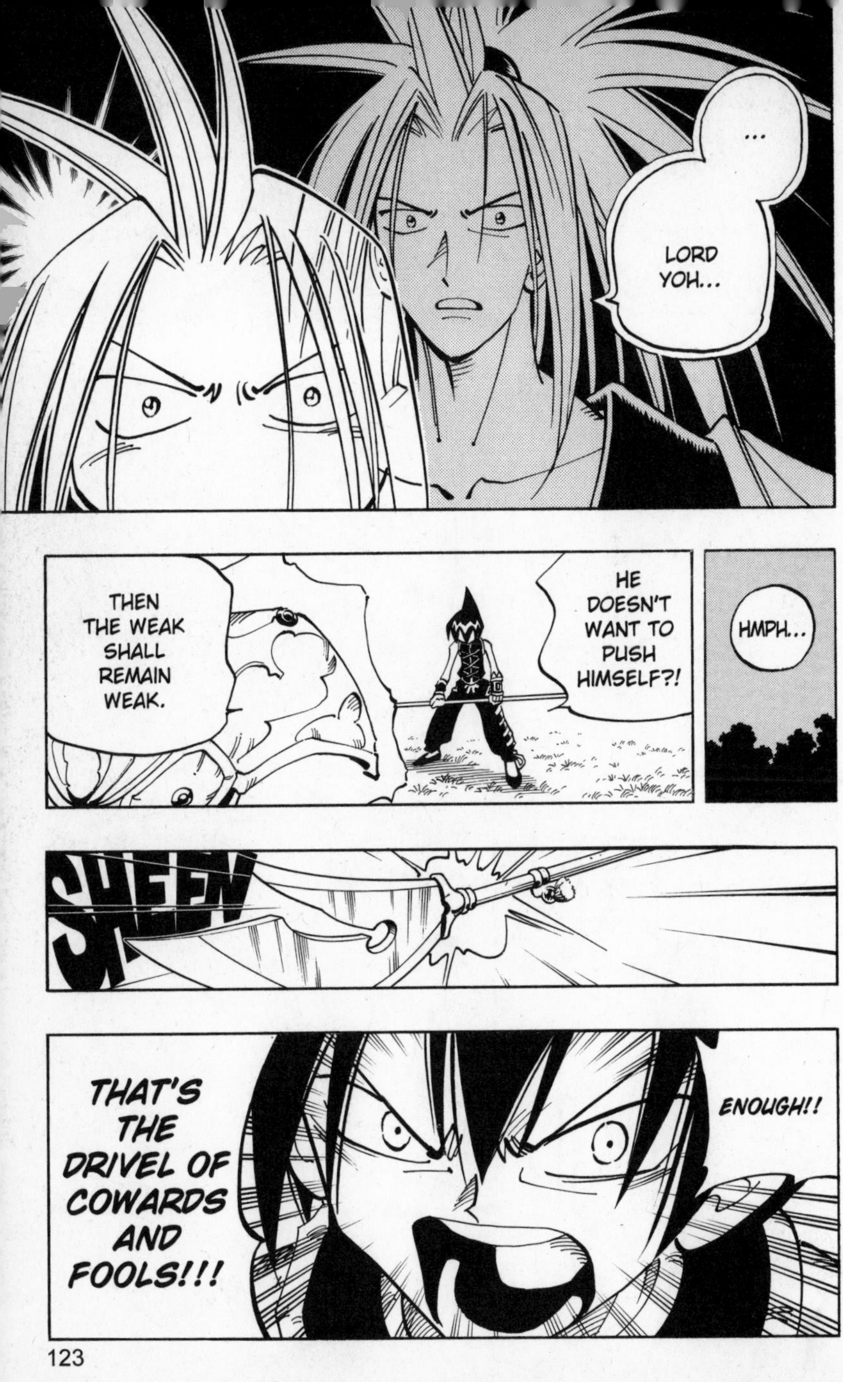
...
LORD YOH...
HMPH...
HE DOESN'T WANT TO PUSH HIMSELF?!
THEN THE WEAK SHALL REMAIN WEAK.
SHEEN
ENOUGH!!
THAT'S THE DRIVEL OF COWARDS AND FOOLS!!!

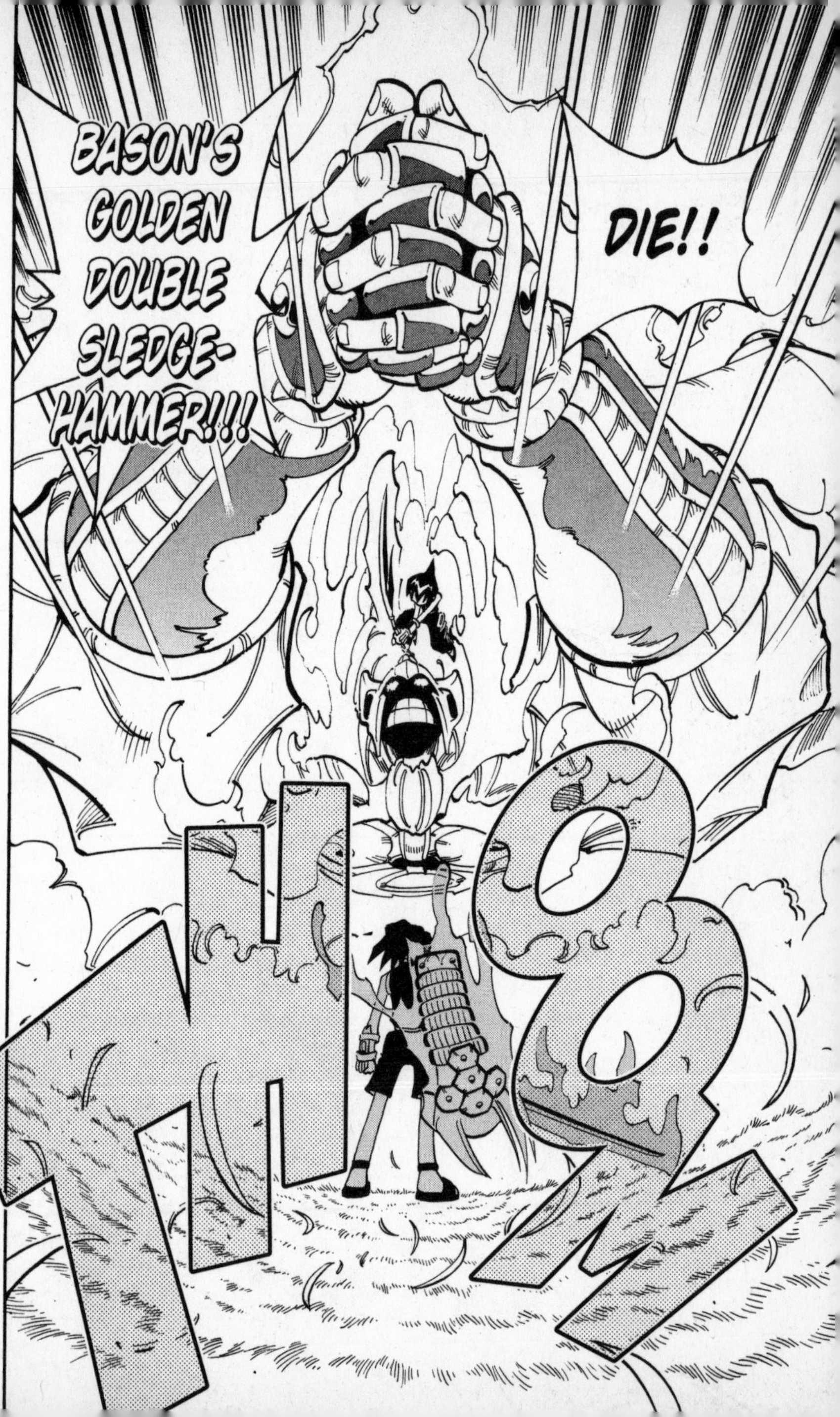
DIE!!
BASON'S GOLDEN DOUBLE SLEDGE-HAMMER!!!
THOOM

READ THIS WAY

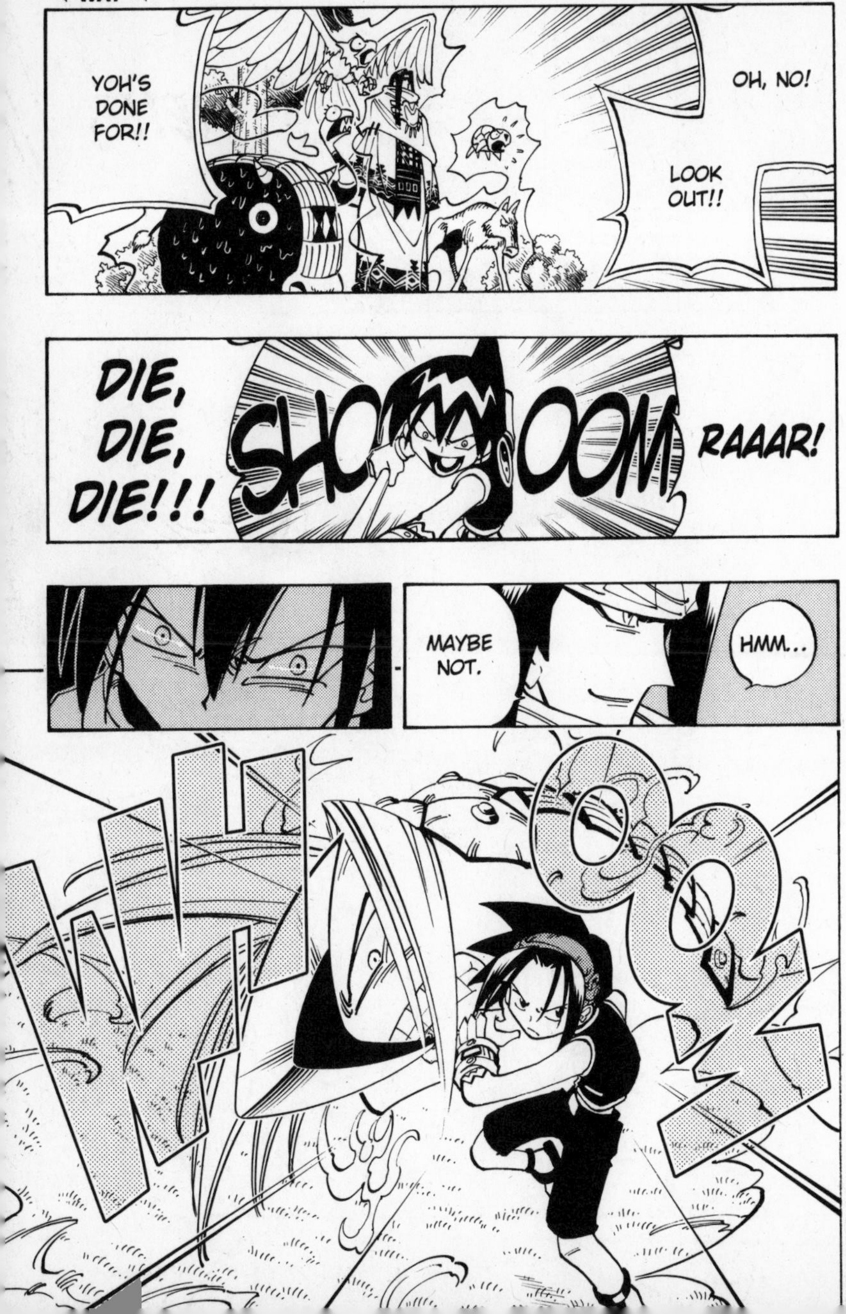
OH, NO!
LOOK OUT!!
YOH'S DONE FOR!!
RAAAR!
SHO
OOM
DIE, DIE, DIE!!!
HMM...
MAYBE NOT.

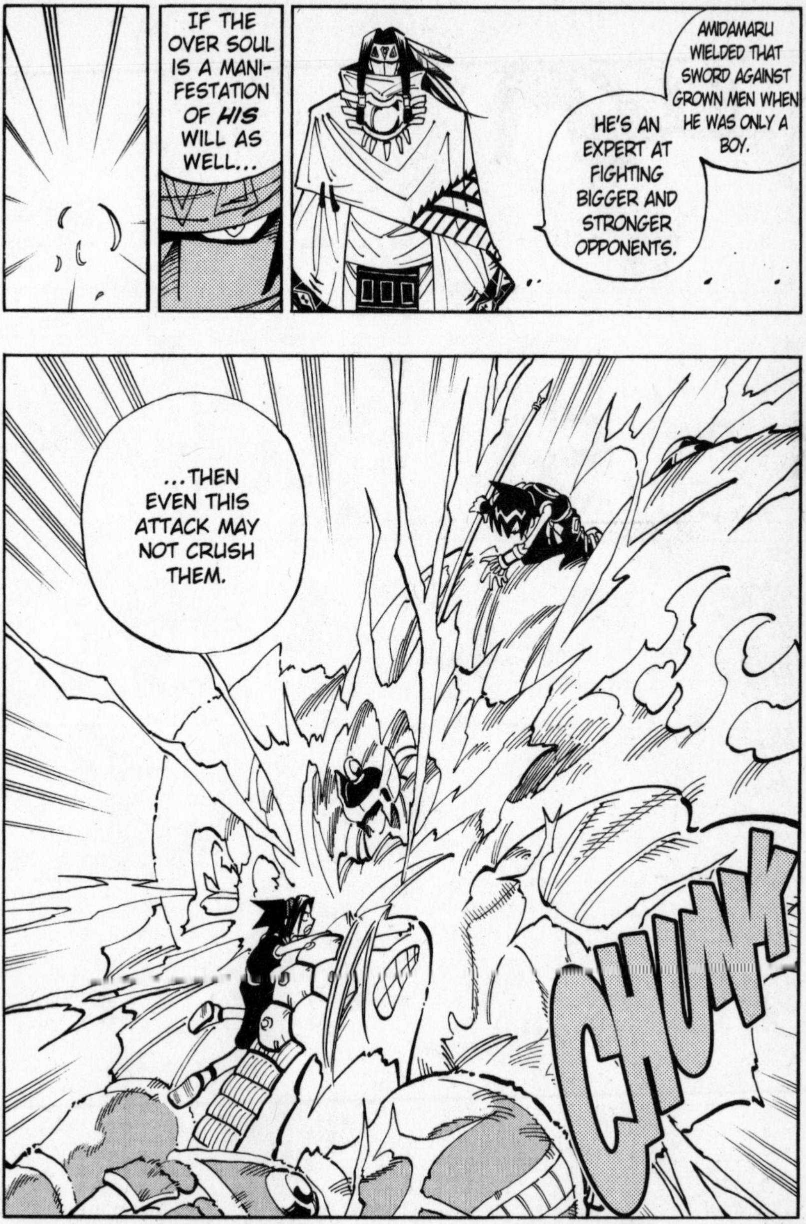
AMIDAMARU WIELDED THAT SWORD AGAINST GROWN MEN WHEN HE WAS ONLY A BOY.
HE'S AN EXPERT AT FIGHTING BIGGER AND STRONGER OPPONENTS.
IF THE OVER SOUL IS A MANI-FESTATION OF *HIS* WILL AS WELL...
...THEN EVEN THIS ATTACK MAY NOT CRUSH THEM.
CHUNK

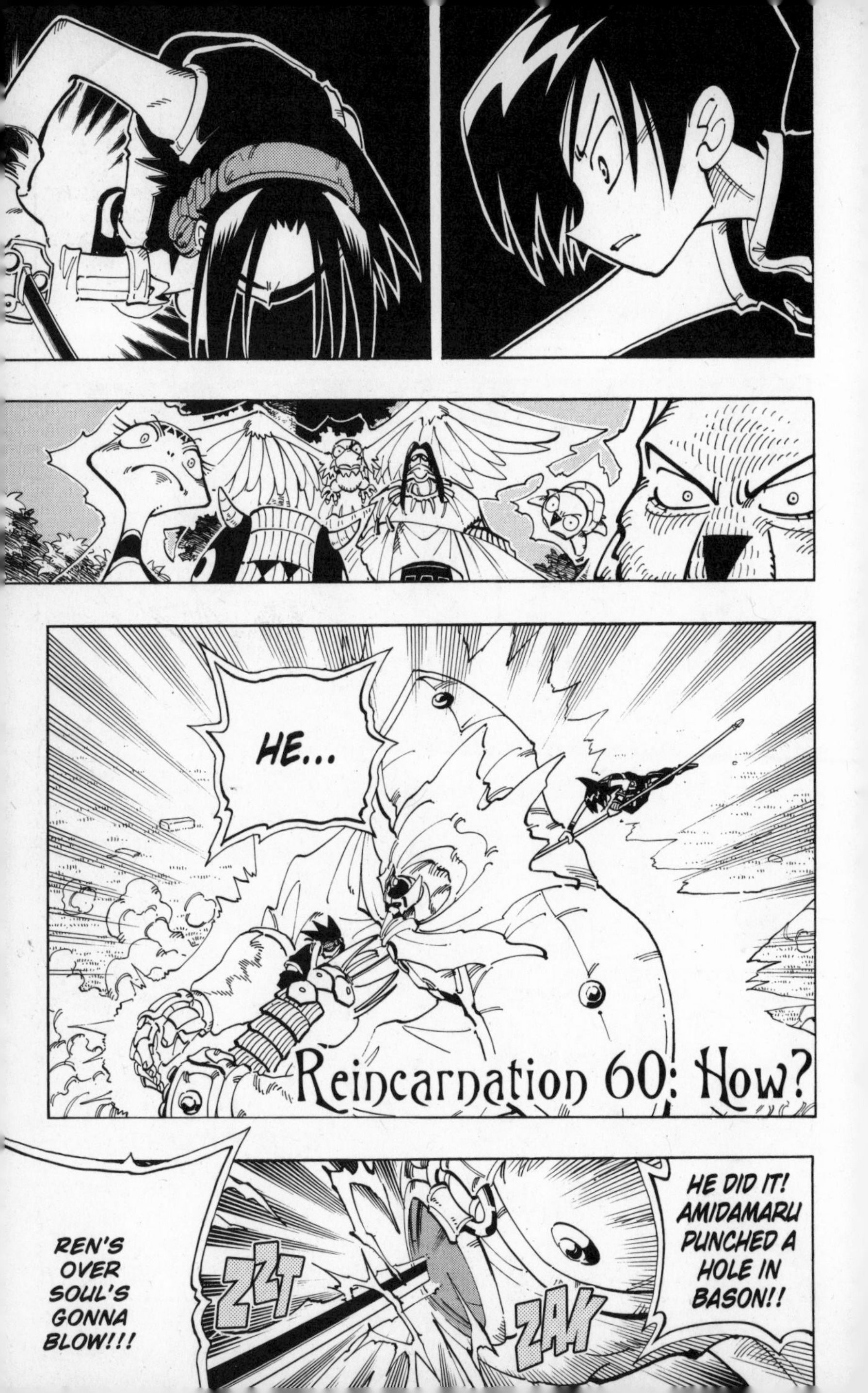
HE...
Reincarnation 60: How?
HE DID IT! AMIDAMARU PUNCHED A HOLE IN BASON!!
ZAK
ZZT
REN'S OVER SOUL'S GONNA BLOW!!!

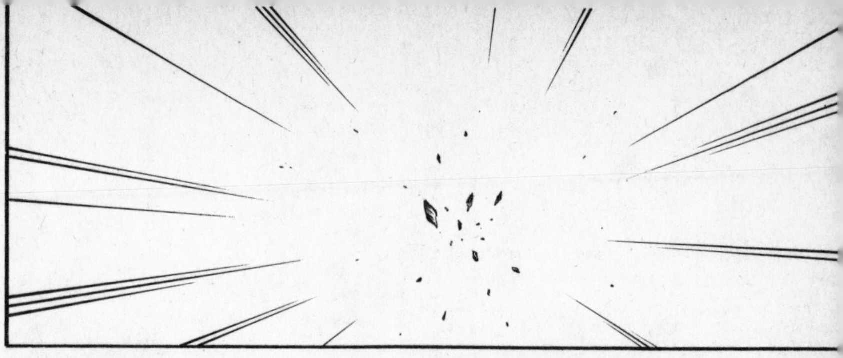
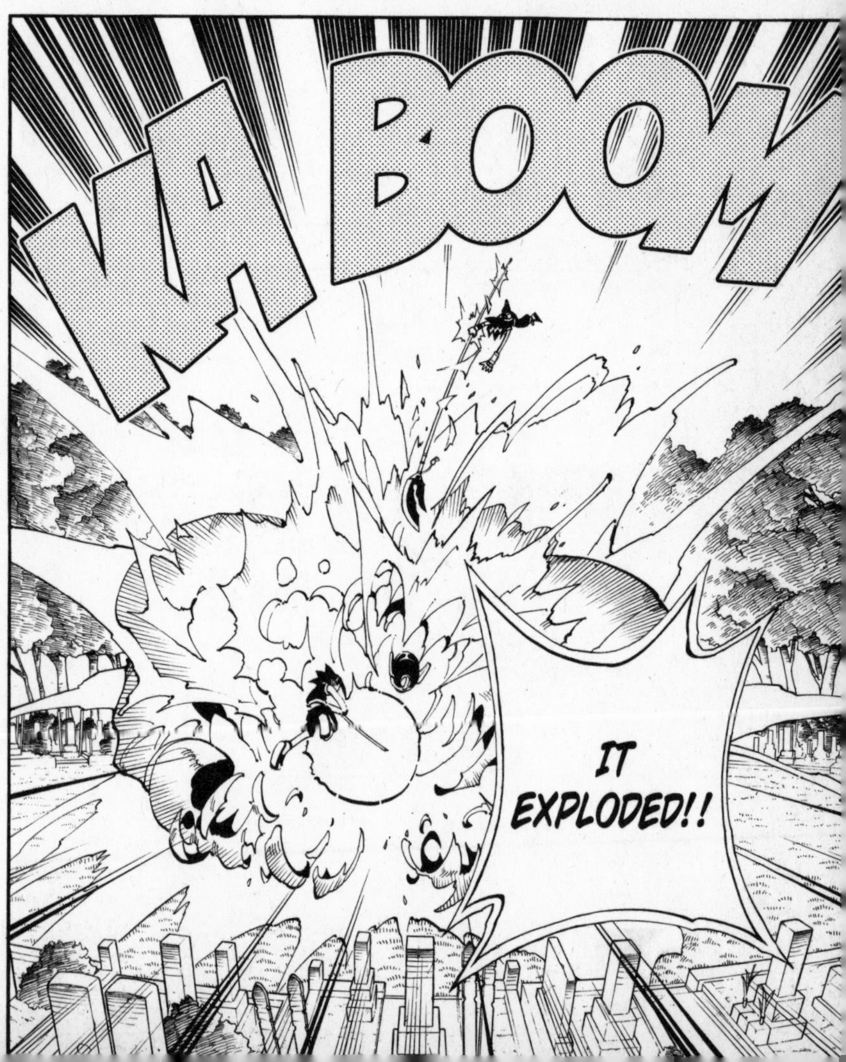
KA BOOM
IT EXPLODED!!

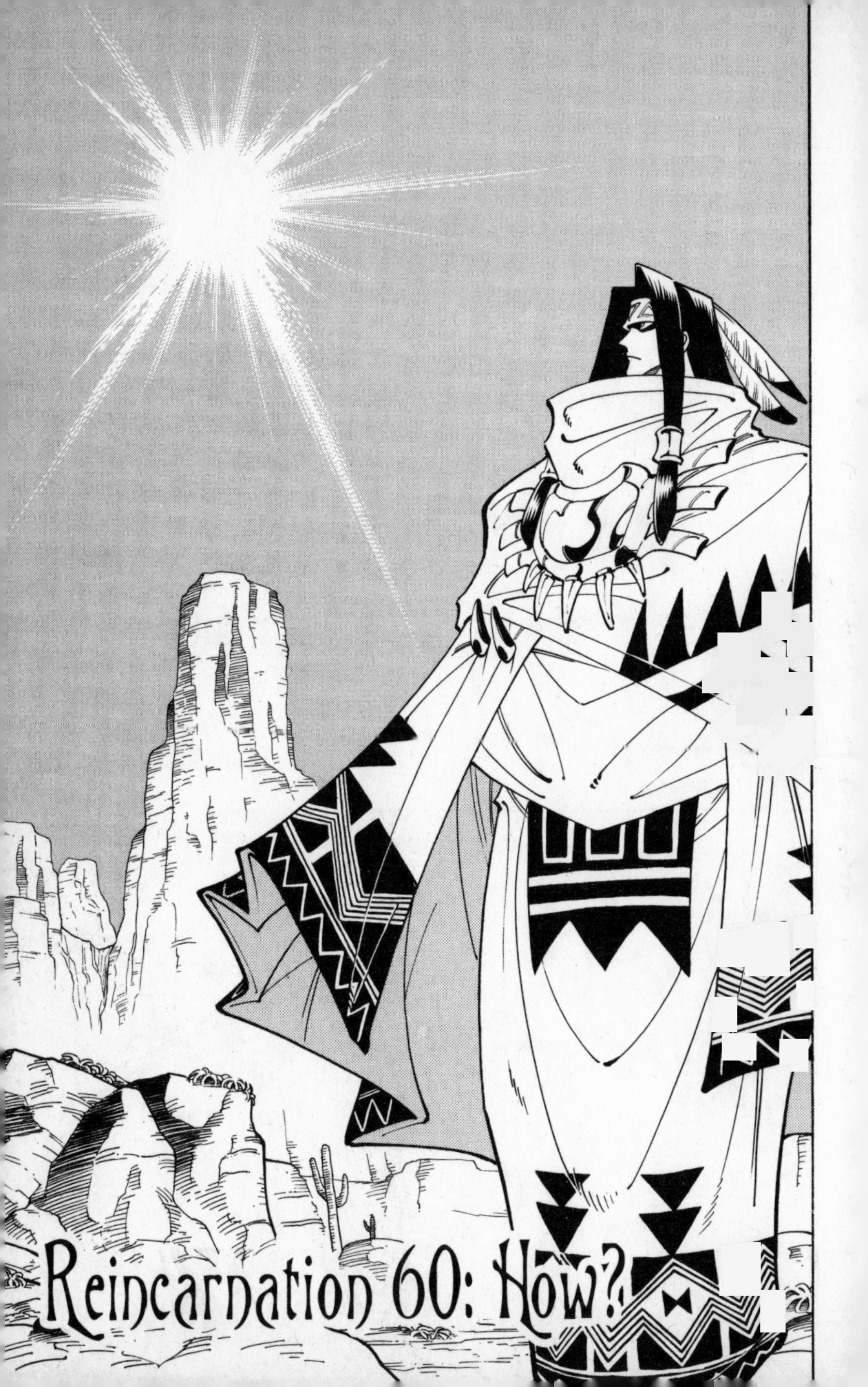
Reincarnation 60: How?

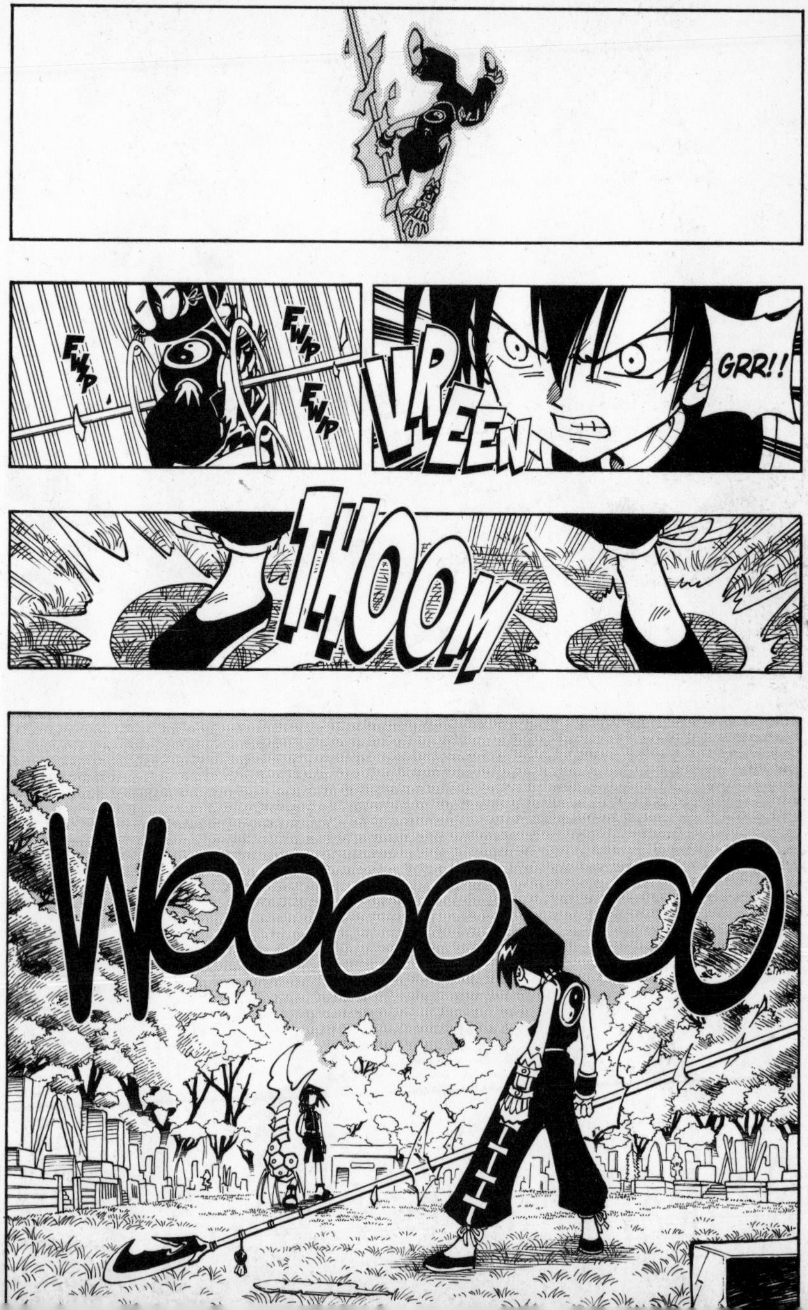
GRR!!
VREEN
FWIP
FWIP
FWIP
THOOM
WOOOOOO

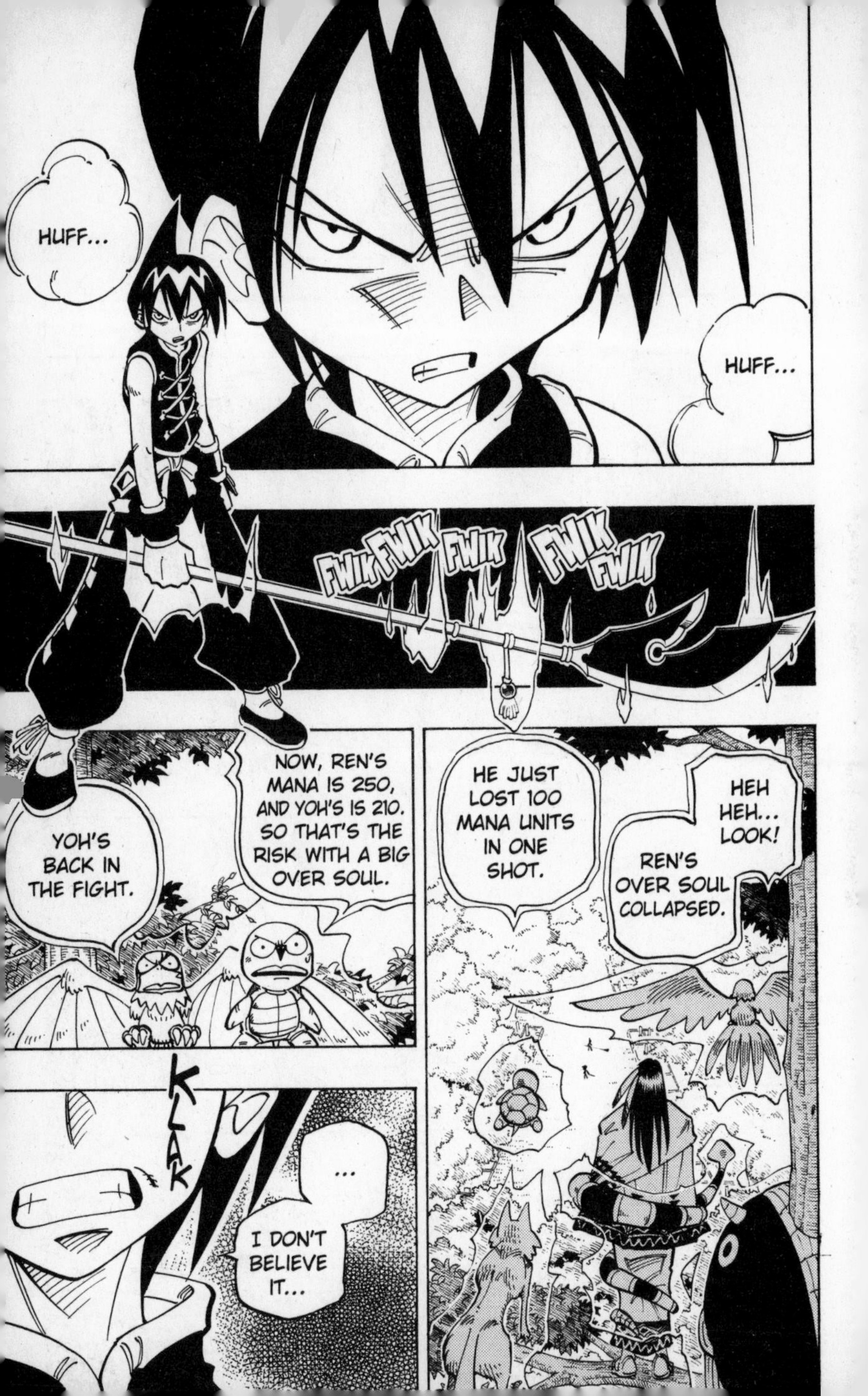
HUFF...
HUFF...
FWIK FWIK
FWIK
FWIK FWIK
HEH HEH... LOOK!
REN'S OVER SOUL COLLAPSED.
HE JUST LOST 100 MANA UNITS IN ONE SHOT.
NOW, REN'S MANA IS 250, AND YOH'S IS 210. SO THAT'S THE RISK WITH A BIG OVER SOUL.
YOH'S BACK IN THE FIGHT.
KLAK
...
I DON'T BELIEVE IT...

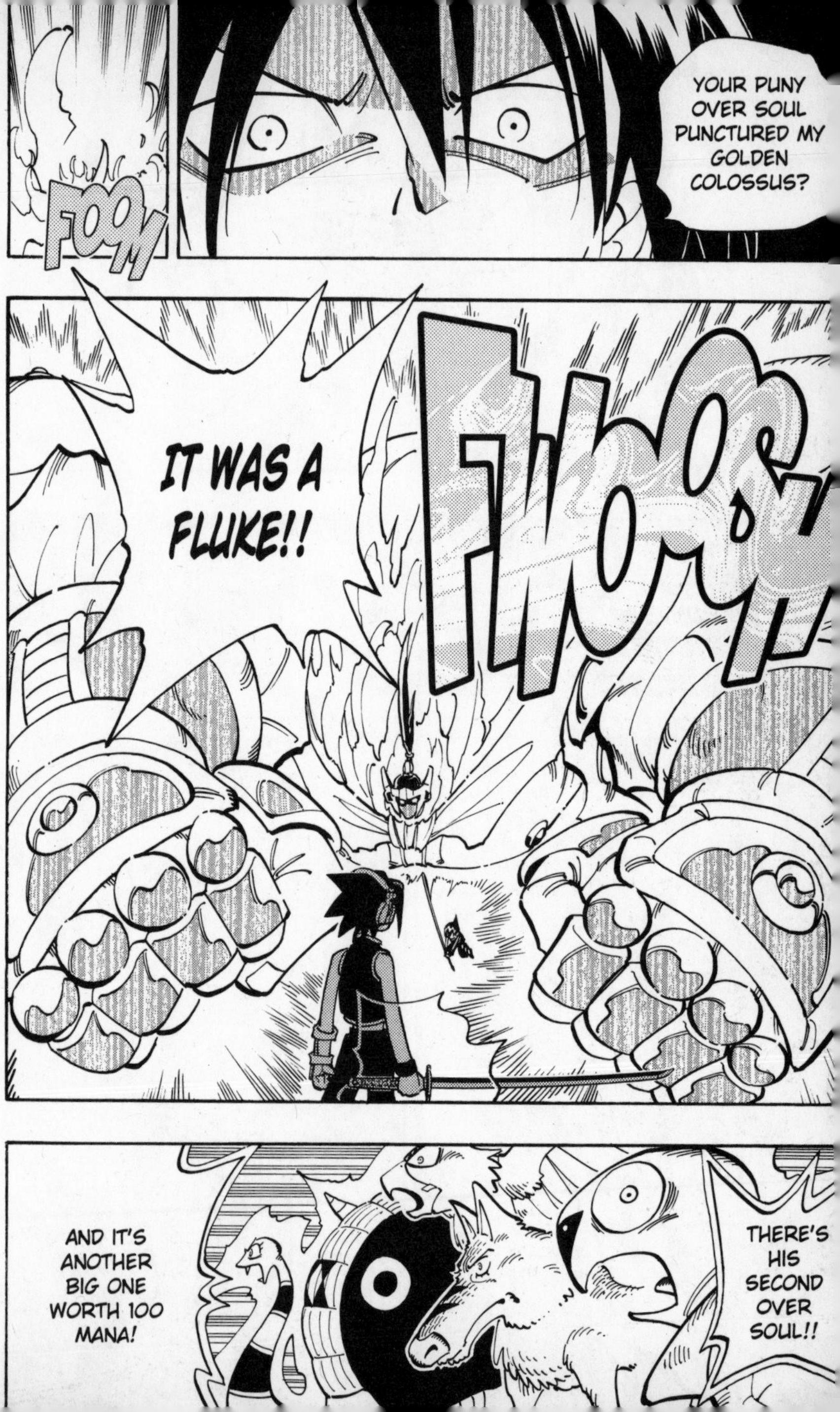
YOUR PUNY OVER SOUL PUNCTURED MY GOLDEN COLOSSUS?
FOOM
FWOOSH
IT WAS A FLUKE!!
THERE'S HIS SECOND OVER SOUL!!
AND IT'S ANOTHER BIG ONE WORTH 100 MANA!

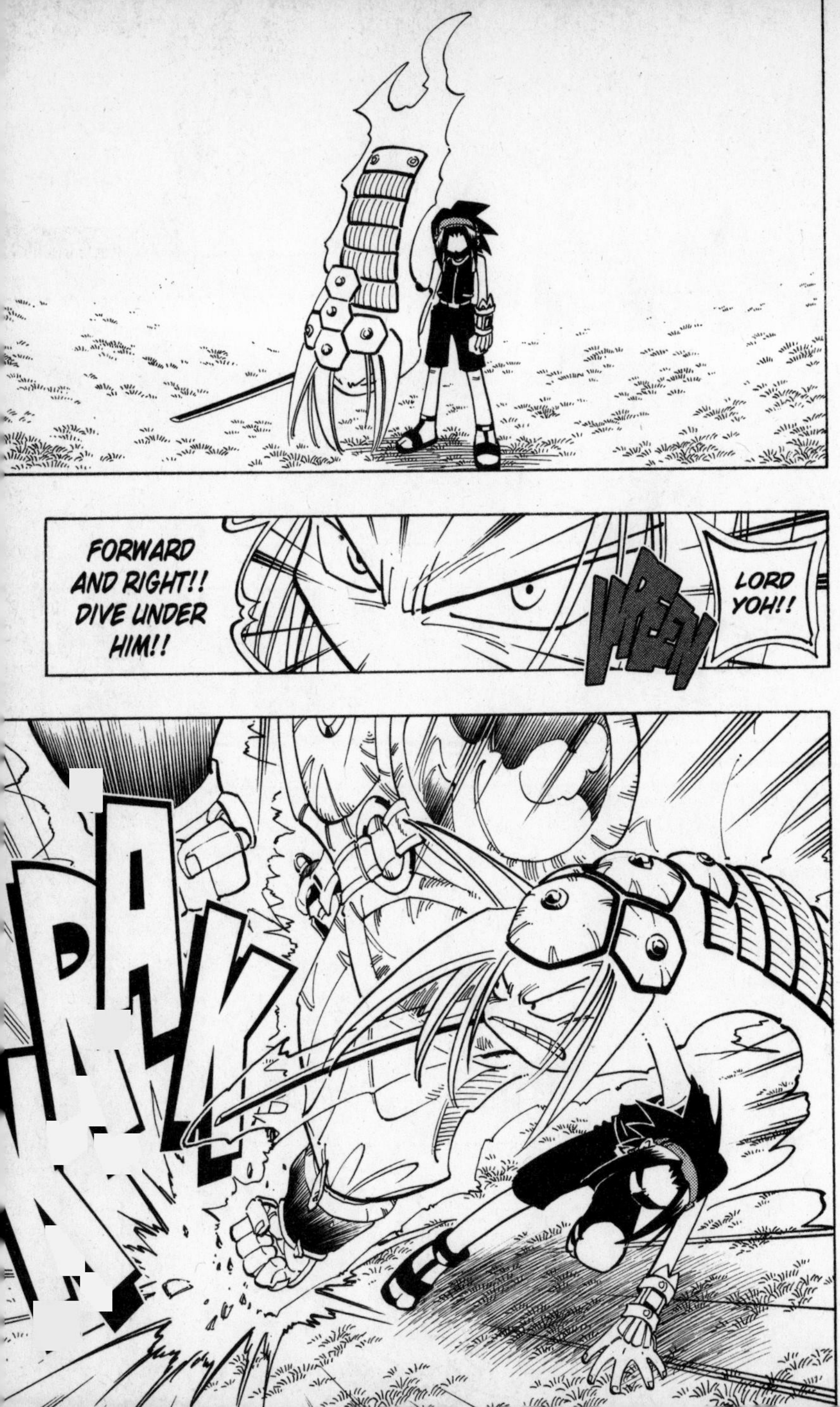
LORD YOH!!
VREEN
FORWARD AND RIGHT!! DIVE UNDER HIM!!

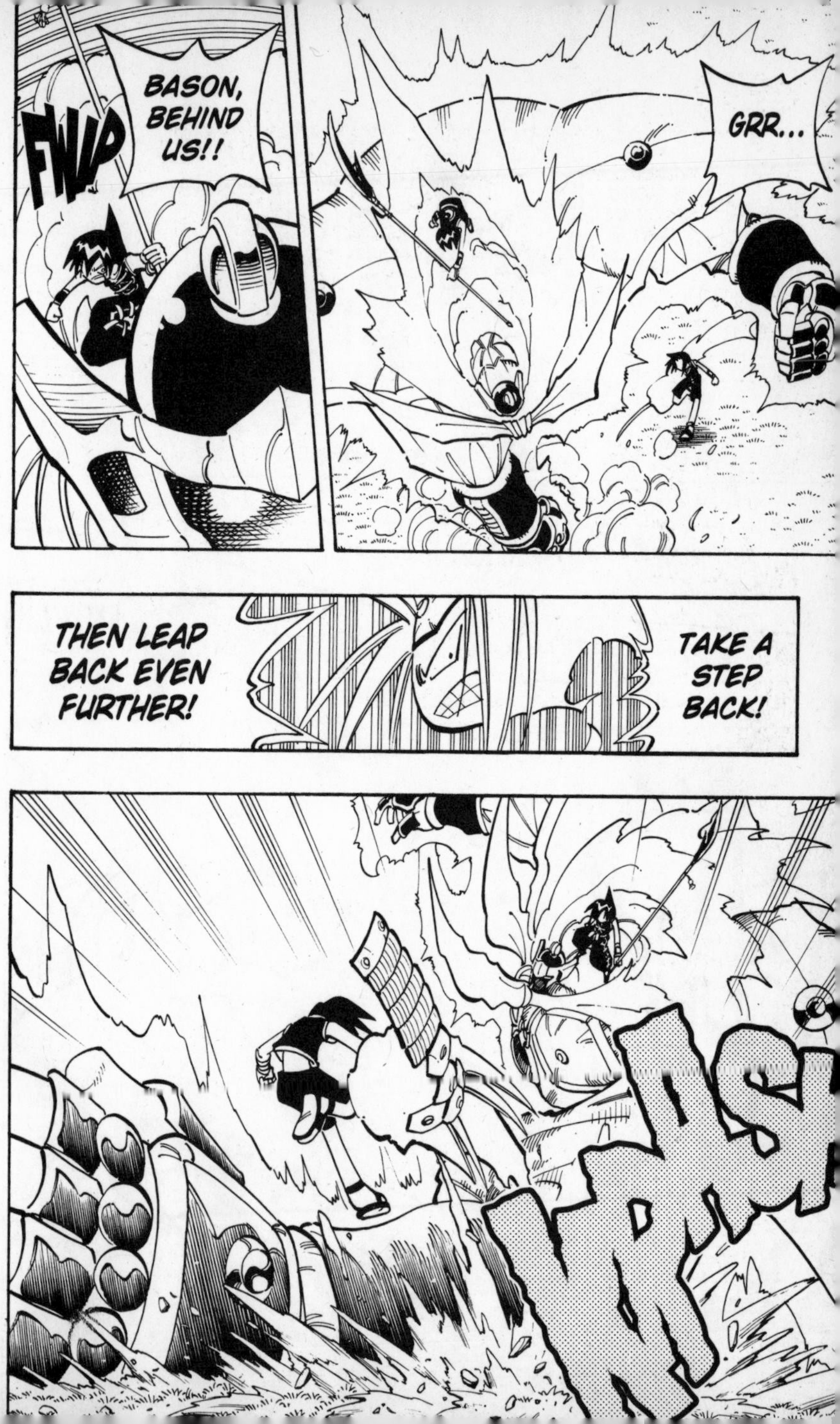
GRR...
BASON, BEHIND US!!
FWIP
TAKE A STEP BACK!
THEN LEAP BACK EVEN FURTHER!

READ THIS WAY

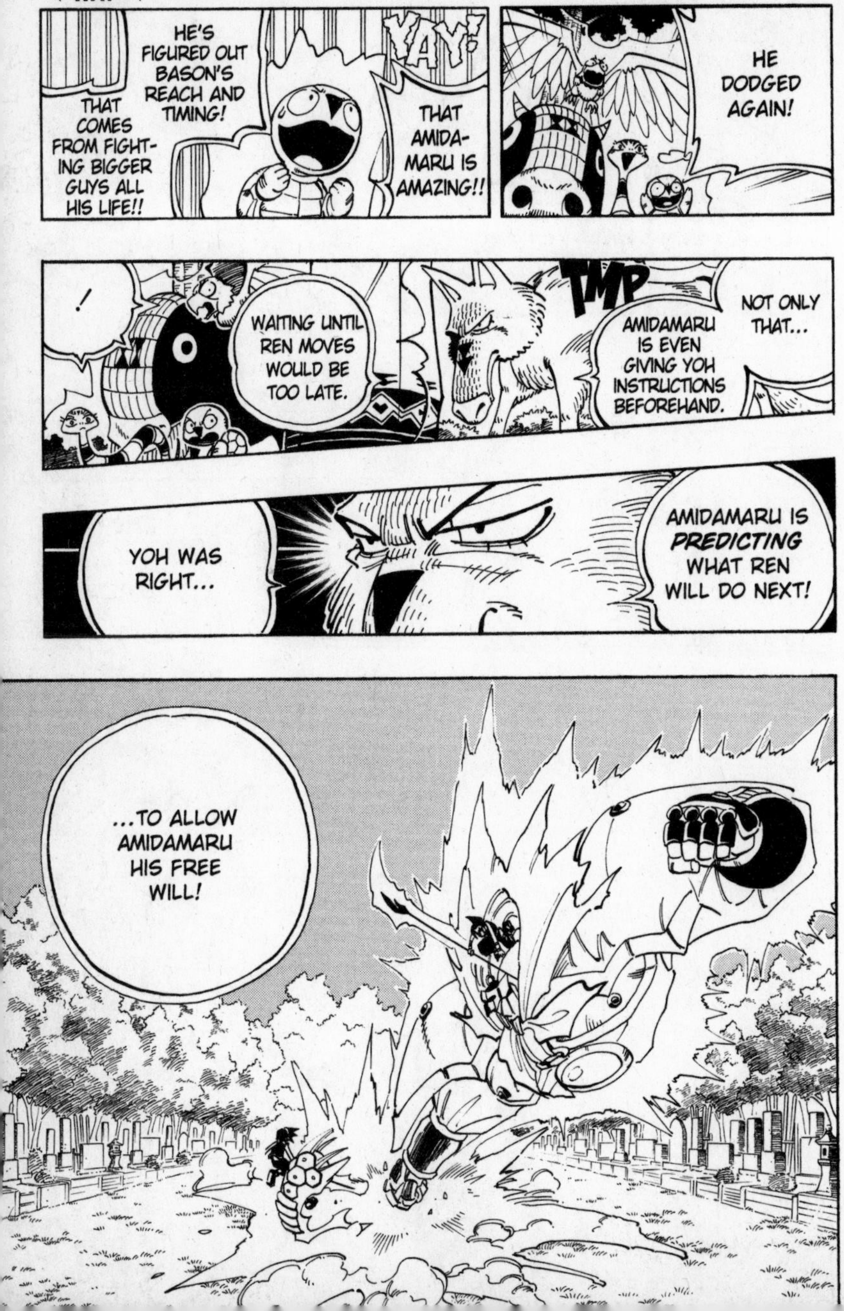

HE DODGED AGAIN!
YAY!
THAT AMIDAMARU IS AMAZING!!
HE'S FIGURED OUT BASON'S REACH AND TIMING!
THAT COMES FROM FIGHTING BIGGER GUYS ALL HIS LIFE!!
NOT ONLY THAT...
TMP
AMIDAMARU IS EVEN GIVING YOH INSTRUCTIONS BEFOREHAND.
WAITING UNTIL REN MOVES WOULD BE TOO LATE.
!
AMIDAMARU IS *PREDICTING* WHAT REN WILL DO NEXT!
YOH WAS RIGHT...
...TO ALLOW AMIDAMARU HIS FREE WILL!

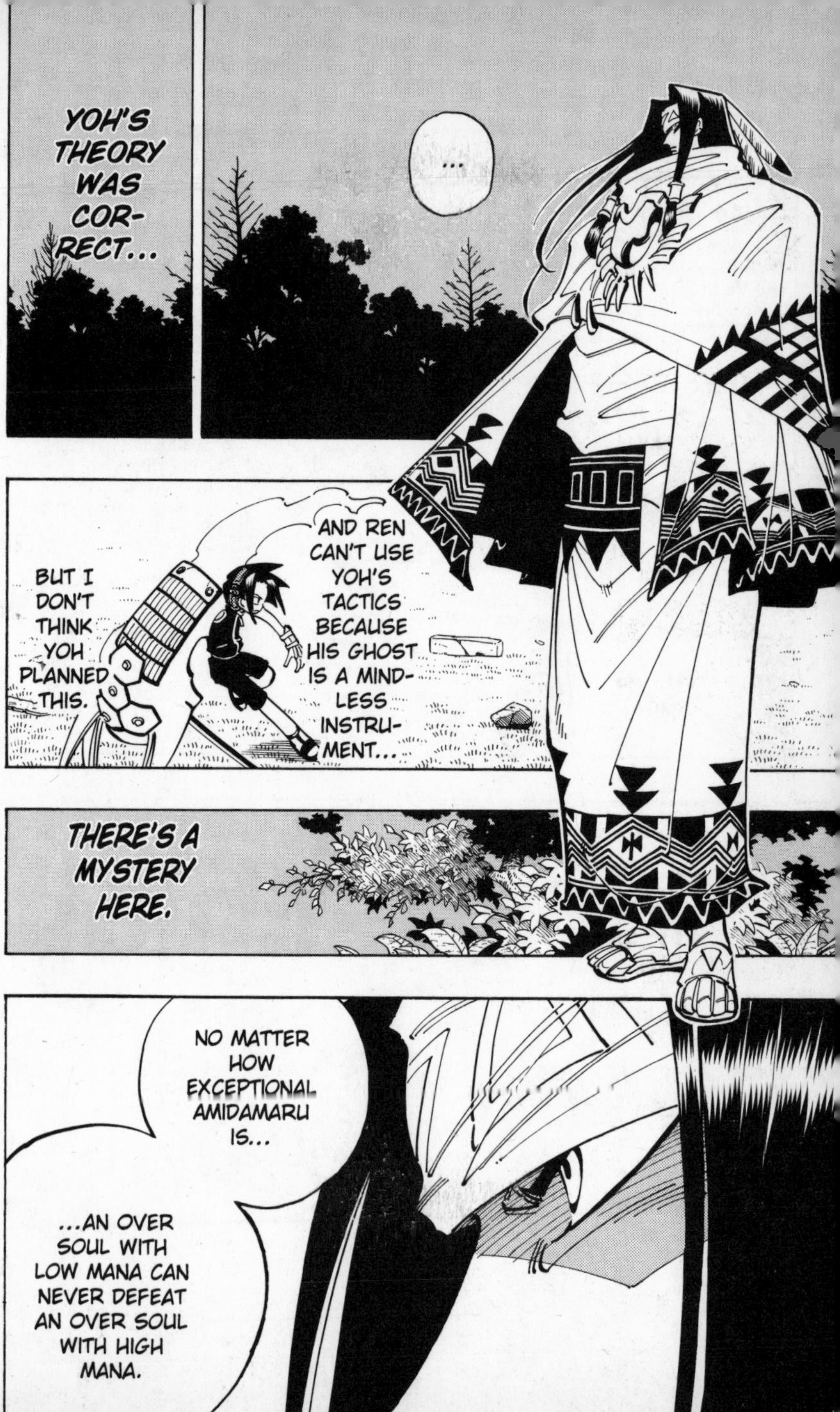
...
YOH'S THEORY WAS CORRECT...
AND REN CAN'T USE YOH'S TACTICS BECAUSE HIS GHOST IS A MINDLESS INSTRUMENT...
BUT I DON'T THINK YOH PLANNED THIS.
THERE'S A MYSTERY HERE.
NO MATTER HOW EXCEPTIONAL AMIDAMARU IS...
...AN OVER SOUL WITH LOW MANA CAN NEVER DEFEAT AN OVER SOUL WITH HIGH MANA.

READ THIS WAY

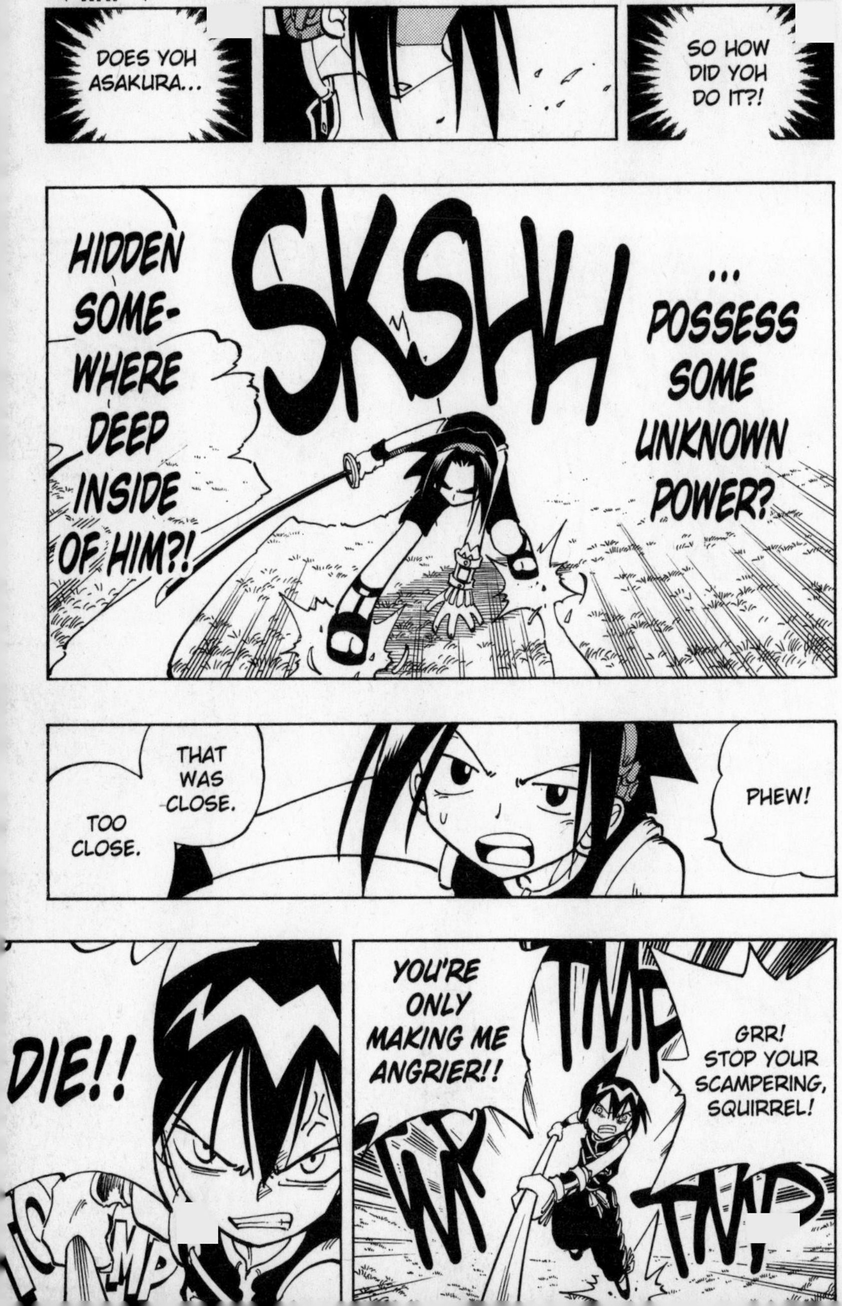
SO HOW DID YOH DO IT?!
DOES YOH ASAKURA...
... POSSESS SOME UNKNOWN POWER?
SKSHH
HIDDEN SOME-WHERE DEEP INSIDE OF HIM?!
PHEW!
THAT WAS CLOSE.
TOO CLOSE.
GRR! STOP YOUR SCAMPERING, SQUIRREL!
TMP
YOU'RE ONLY MAKING ME ANGRIER!!
DIE!!

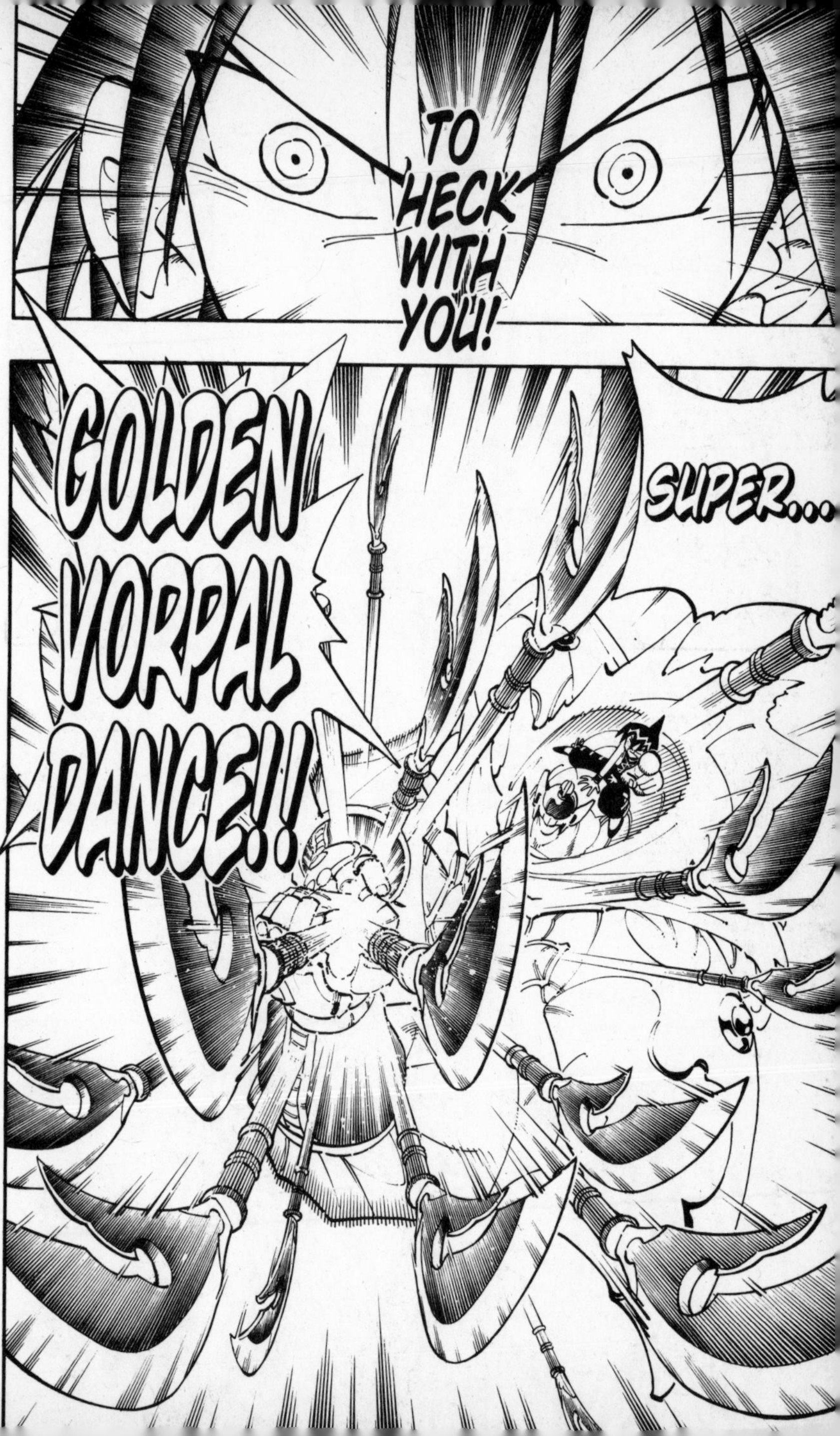
TO HECK WITH YOU!
SUPER...
GOLDEN VORPAL DANCE!!

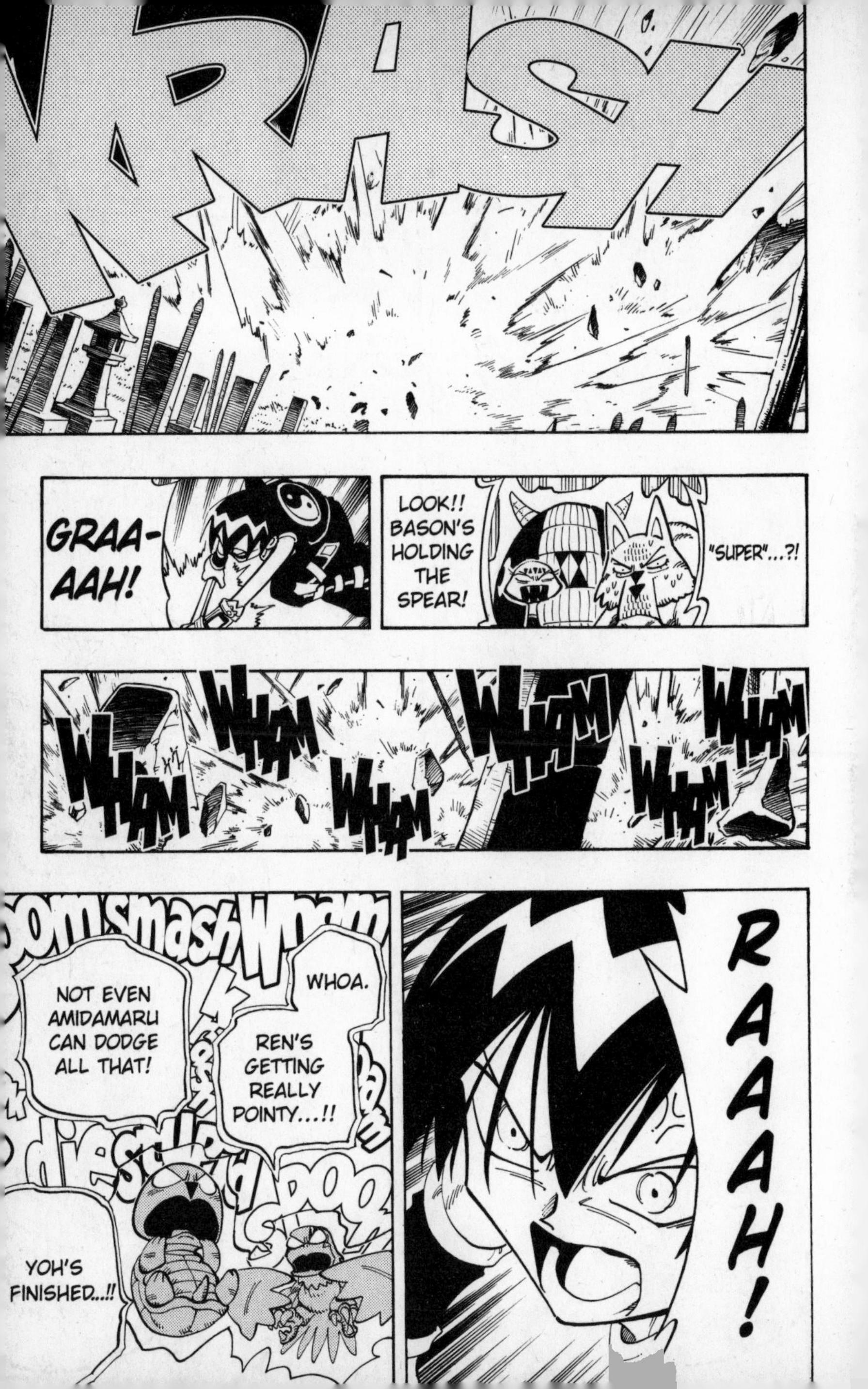

"SUPER"...?!
LOOK!! BASON'S HOLDING THE SPEAR!
GRAA-AAH!
WHAM
WHAM
WHAM
WHAM
WHAM
WHAM
RAAAAH!
smash
WHOA.
REN'S GETTING REALLY POINTY...!!
NOT EVEN AMIDAMARU CAN DODGE ALL THAT!
YOH'S FINISHED...!!

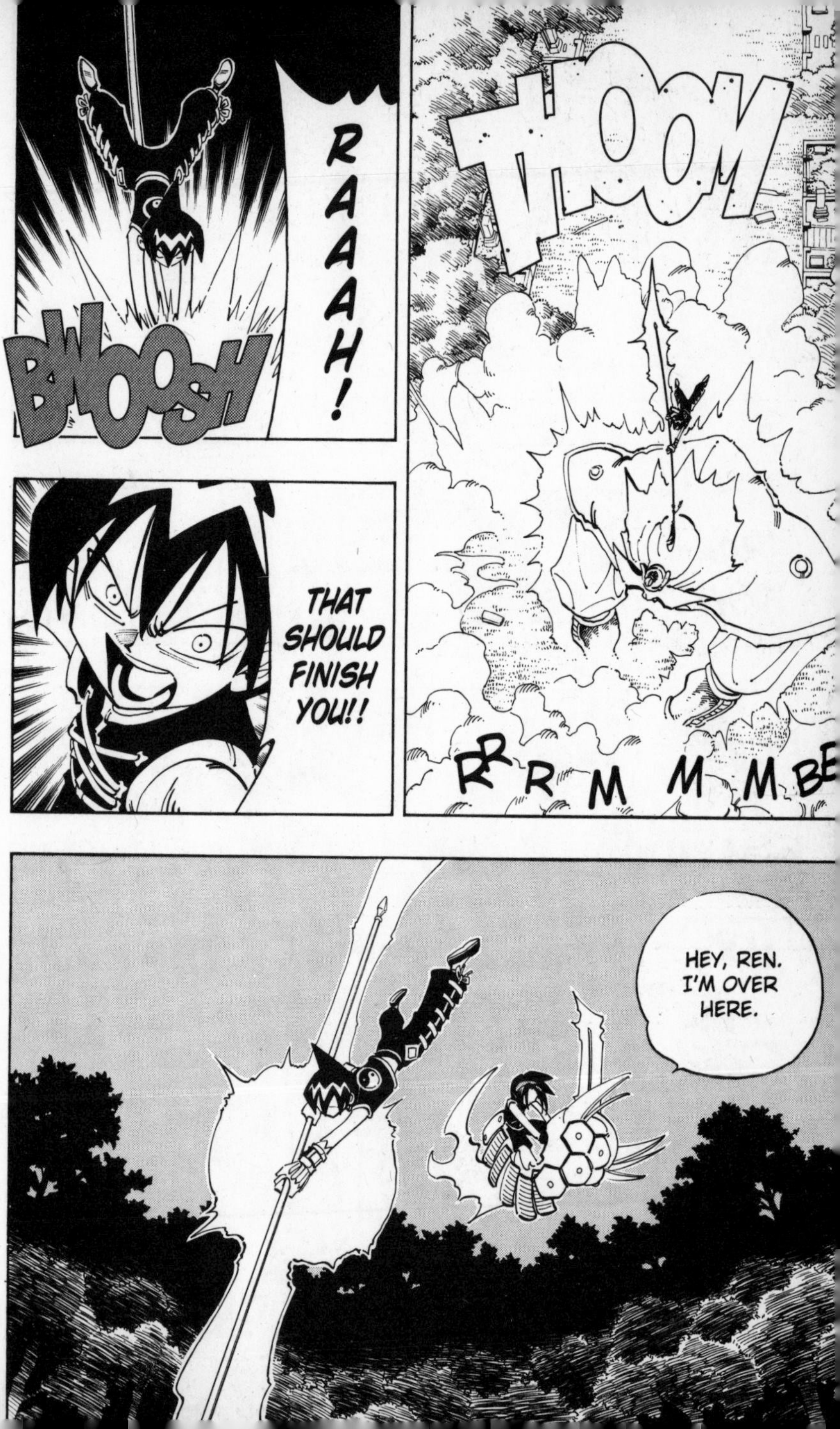
THOOM
RRRMMMBE
RAAAAH!
BWOOSH
THAT SHOULD FINISH YOU!!
HEY, REN. I'M OVER HERE.

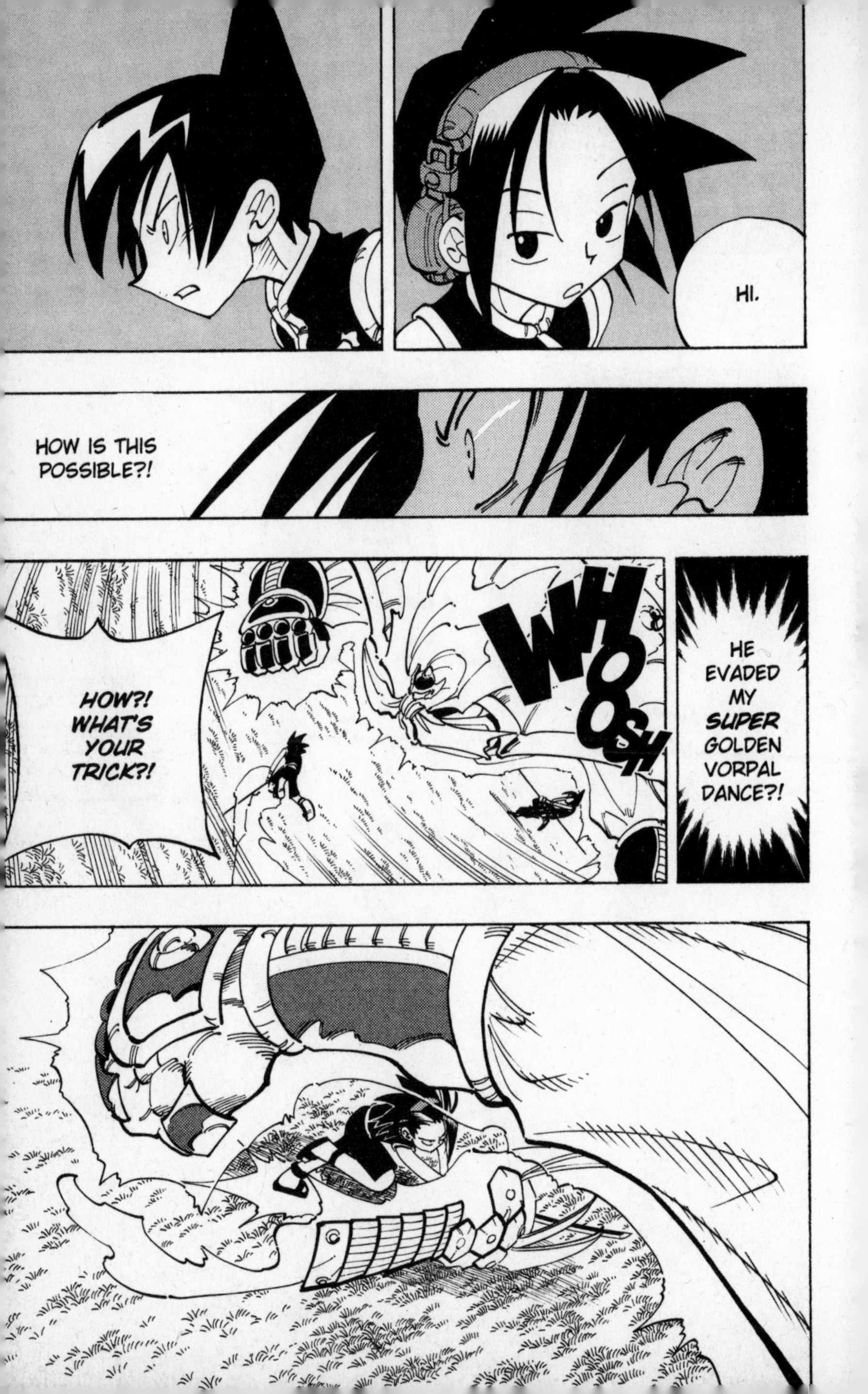
HI.
HOW IS THIS POSSIBLE?!
HE EVADED MY SUPER GOLDEN VORPAL DANCE?!
WHOOSH
HOW?! WHAT'S YOUR TRICK?!

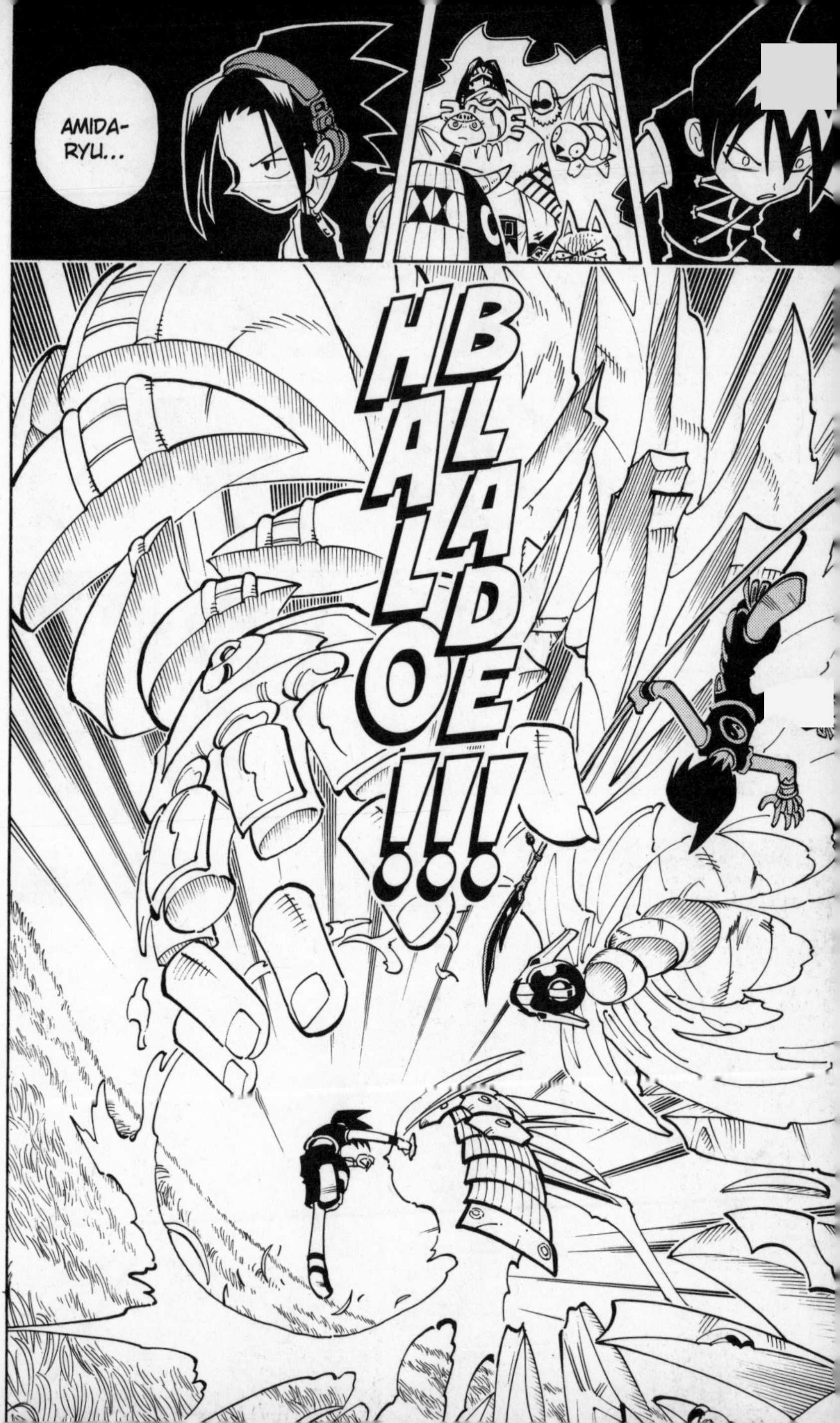
AMIDA-RYU...
HALLO BLADE!!!

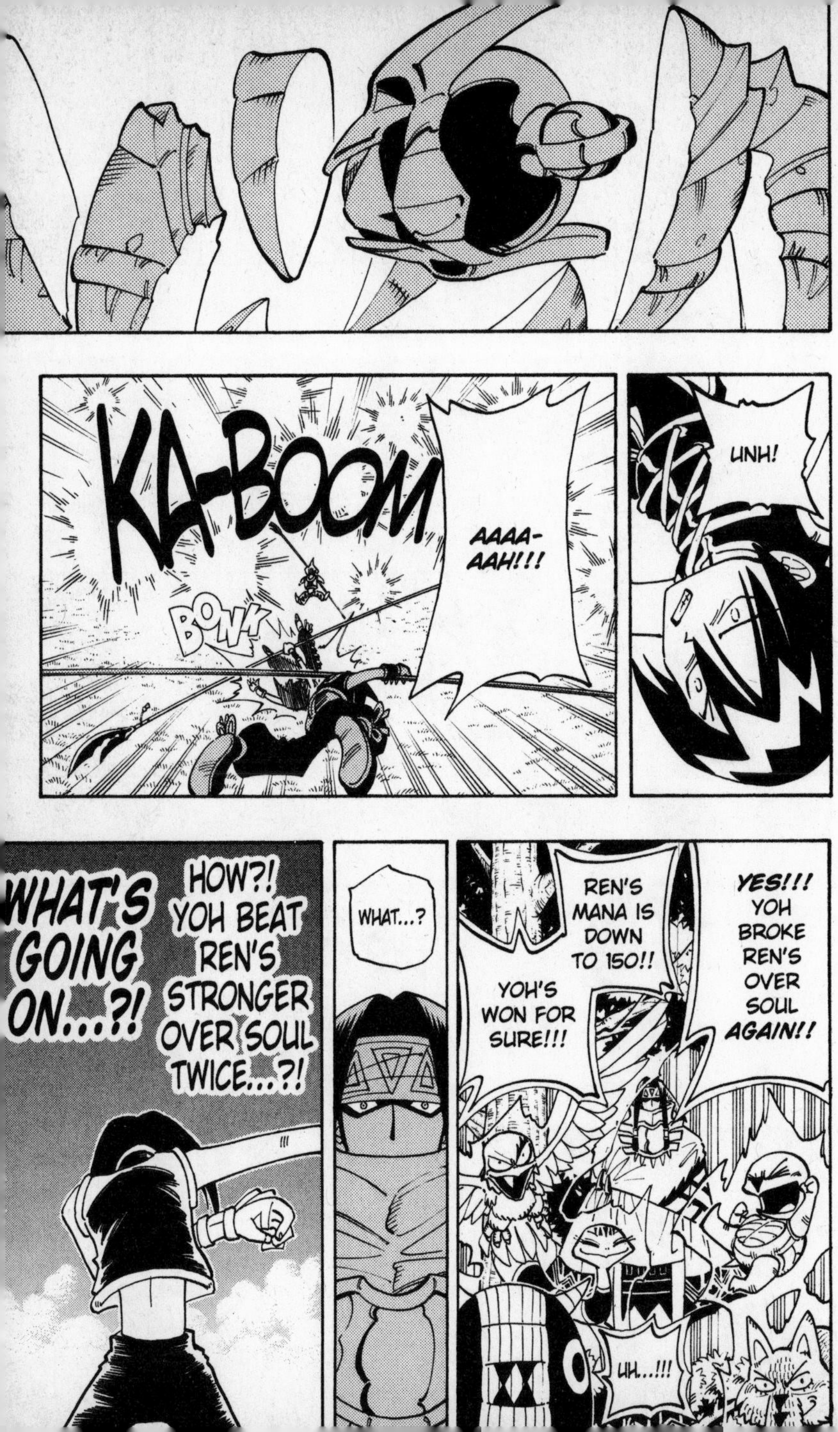
UNH!
AAAA-AAH!!!
KA-BOOM
BONK
YES!!! YOH BROKE REN'S OVER SOUL AGAIN!!
REN'S MANA IS DOWN TO 150!!
YOH'S WON FOR SURE!!!
UH...!!!
WHAT...?
HOW?! YOH BEAT REN'S STRONGER OVER SOUL TWICE...?!
WHAT'S GOING ON...?!

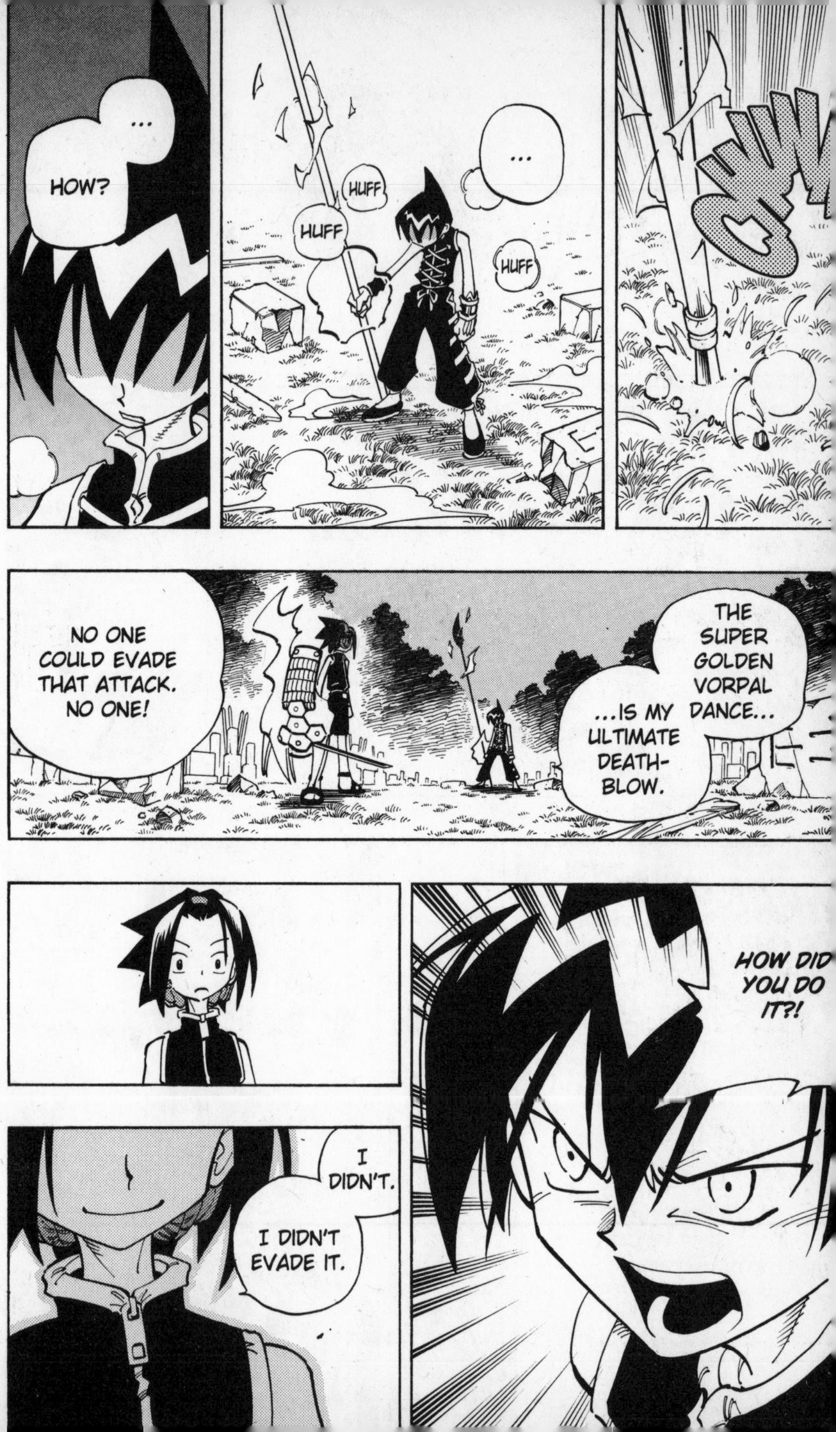
...
HUFF
HUFF
HUFF
...
HOW?
THE SUPER GOLDEN VORPAL DANCE...
...IS MY ULTIMATE DEATH-BLOW.
NO ONE COULD EVADE THAT ATTACK. NO ONE!
HOW DID YOU DO IT?!
I DIDN'T.
I DIDN'T EVADE IT.

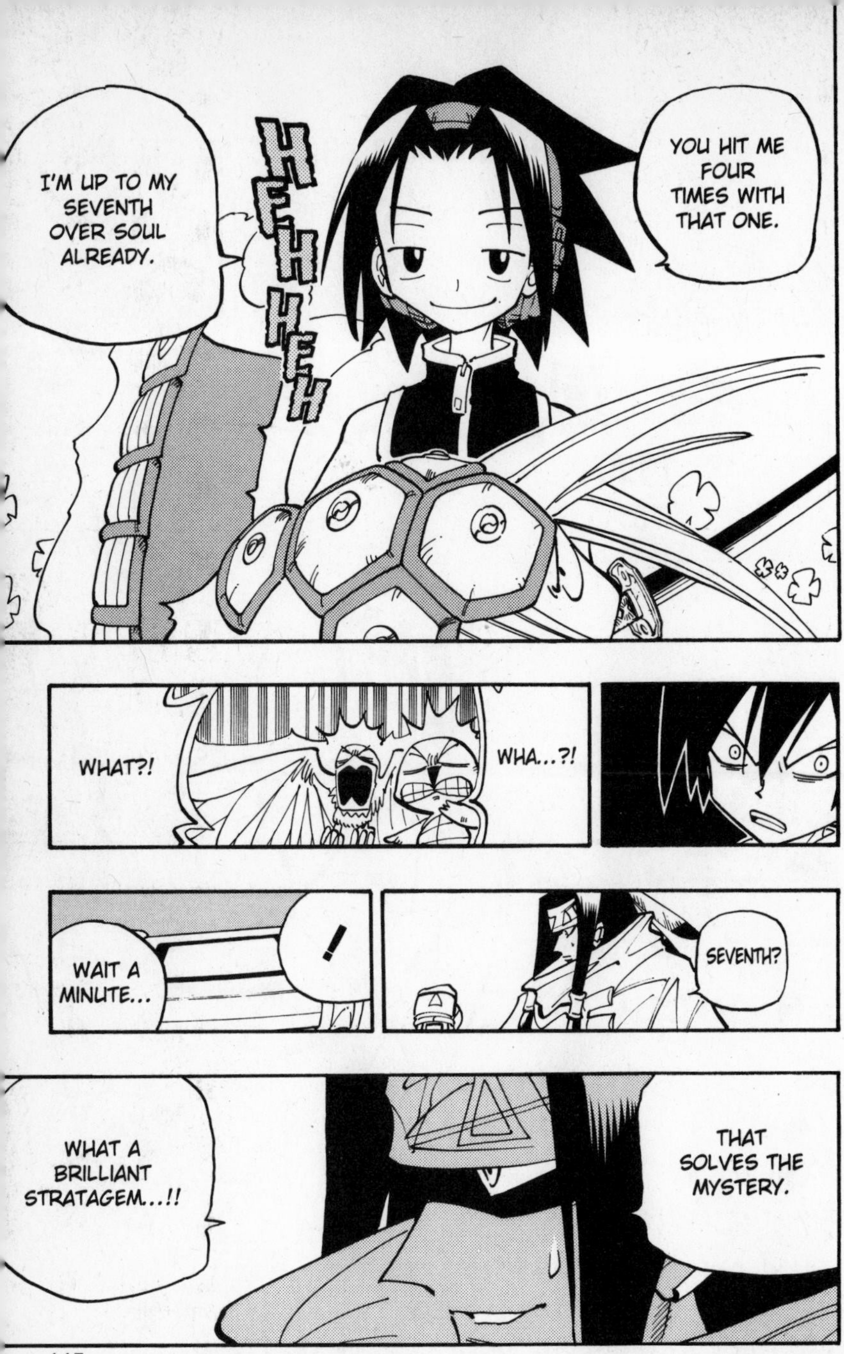
YOU HIT ME FOUR TIMES WITH THAT ONE.
HEH HEH HEH
I'M UP TO MY SEVENTH OVER SOUL ALREADY.
WHA...?!
WHAT?!
SEVENTH?
!
WAIT A MINUTE...
THAT SOLVES THE MYSTERY.
WHAT A BRILLIANT STRATAGEM...!!

SHAMAN KING CHARACTER FILE No.31

ハク　オー

白鳳

1999

(FEB)

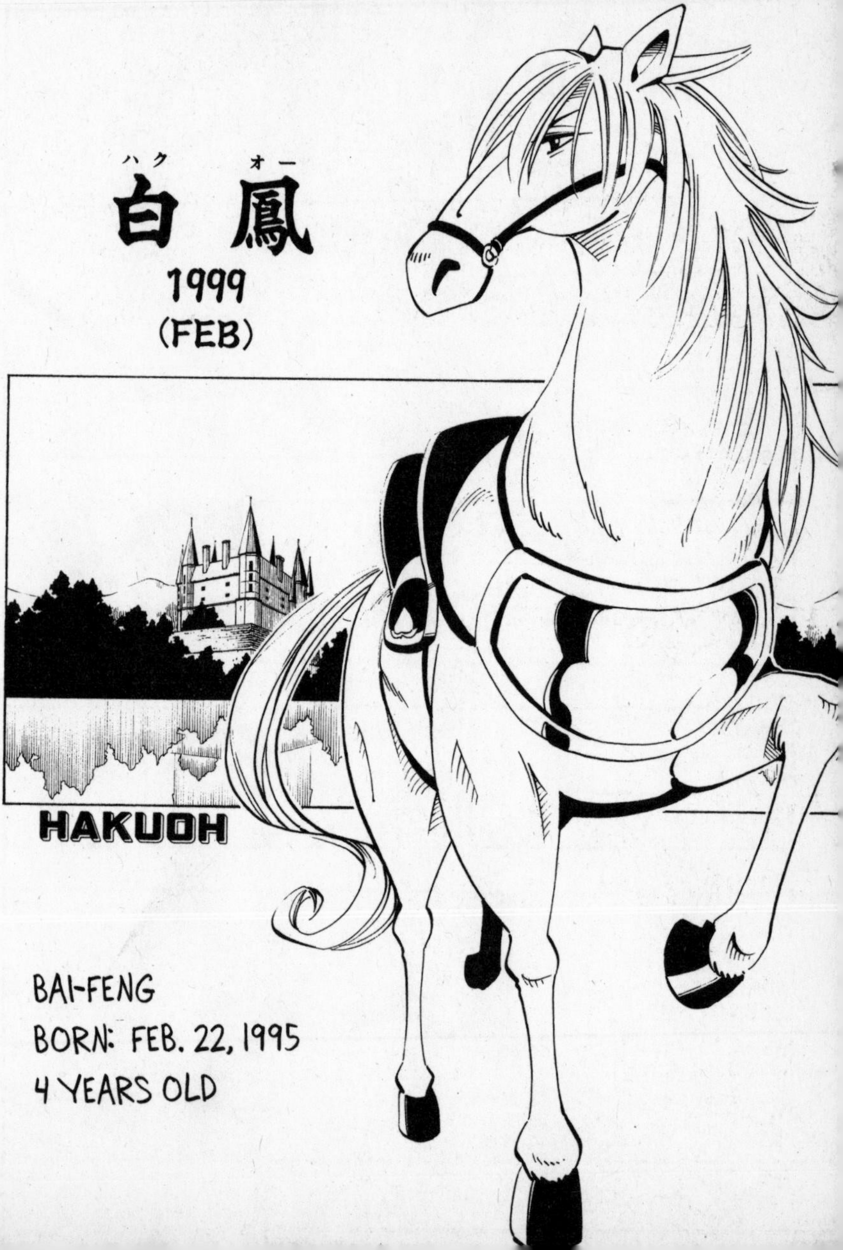

HAKUOH

BAI-FENG

BORN: FEB. 22, 1995

4 YEARS OLD

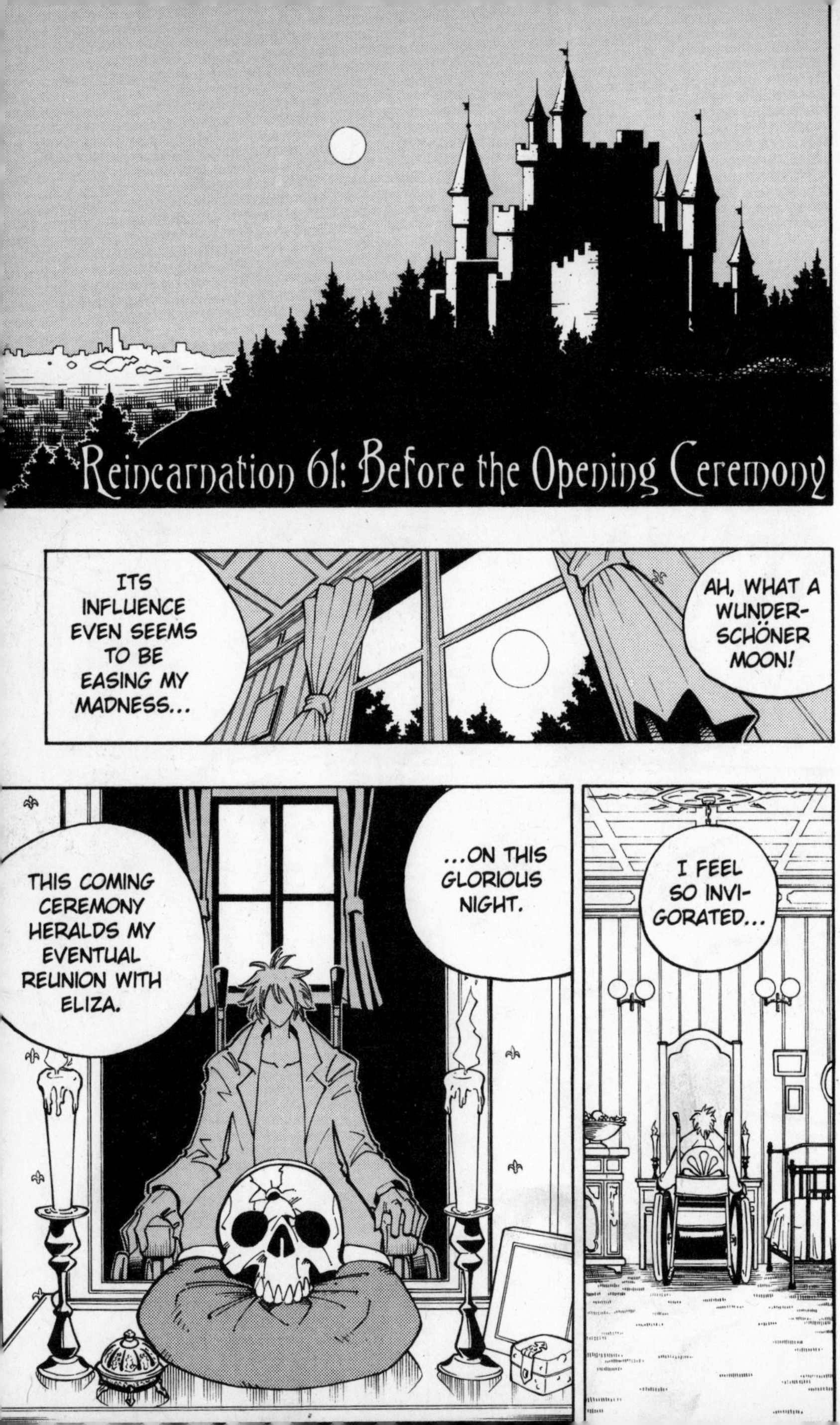
Reincarnation 61: Before the Opening Ceremony
AH, WHAT A WUNDER-SCHÖNER MOON!
ITS INFLUENCE EVEN SEEMS TO BE EASING MY MADNESS...
I FEEL SO INVI-GORATED...
...ON THIS GLORIOUS NIGHT.
THIS COMING CEREMONY HERALDS MY EVENTUAL REUNION WITH ELIZA.

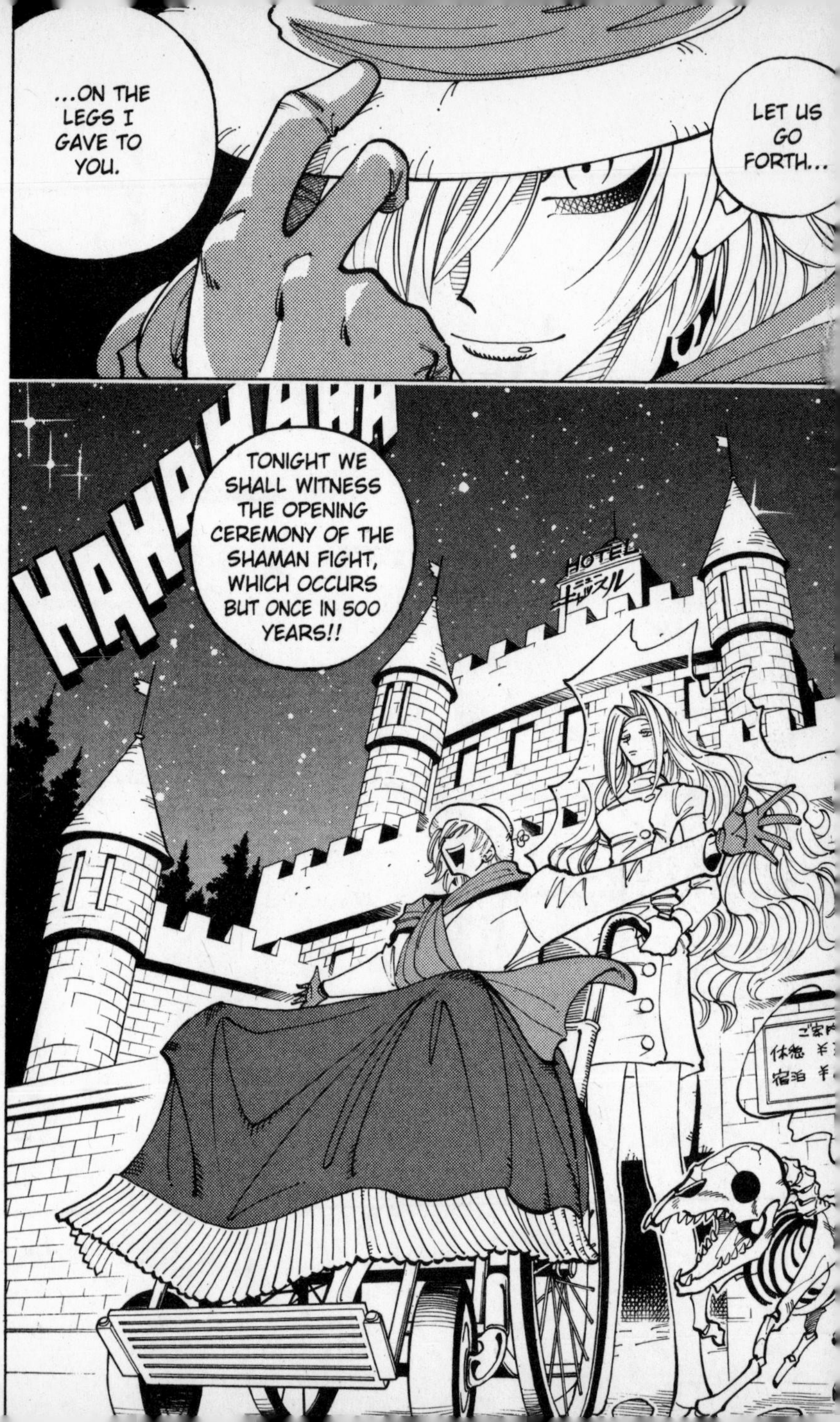
LET US GO FORTH...
...ON THE LEGS I GAVE TO YOU.
HAHAHAHAHA
TONIGHT WE SHALL WITNESS THE OPENING CEREMONY OF THE SHAMAN FIGHT, WHICH OCCURS BUT ONCE IN 500 YEARS!!
HOTEL
ニューキャッスル

Reincarnation 61:
Before the Opening Ceremony

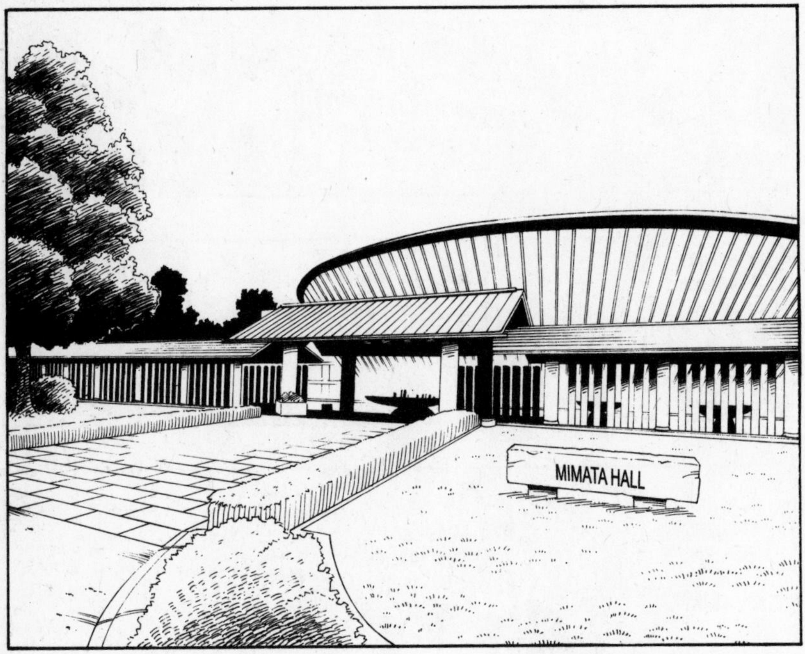
MIMATA HALL

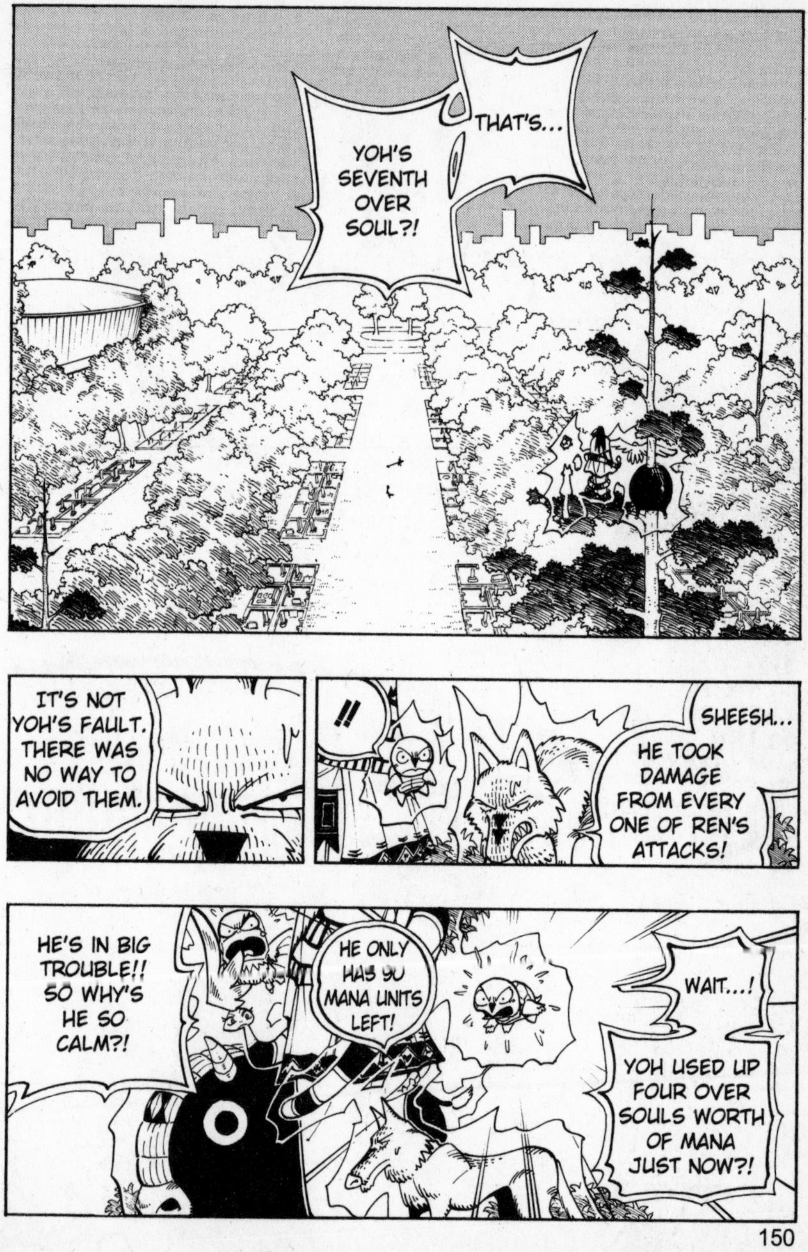
THAT'S...
YOH'S SEVENTH OVER SOUL?!
SHEESH...
HE TOOK DAMAGE FROM EVERY ONE OF REN'S ATTACKS!
!!
IT'S NOT YOH'S FAULT. THERE WAS NO WAY TO AVOID THEM.
WAIT...!
YOH USED UP FOUR OVER SOULS WORTH OF MANA JUST NOW?!
HE ONLY HAS 90 MANA UNITS LEFT!
HE'S IN BIG TROUBLE!! SO WHY'S HE SO CALM?!

READ THIS WAY

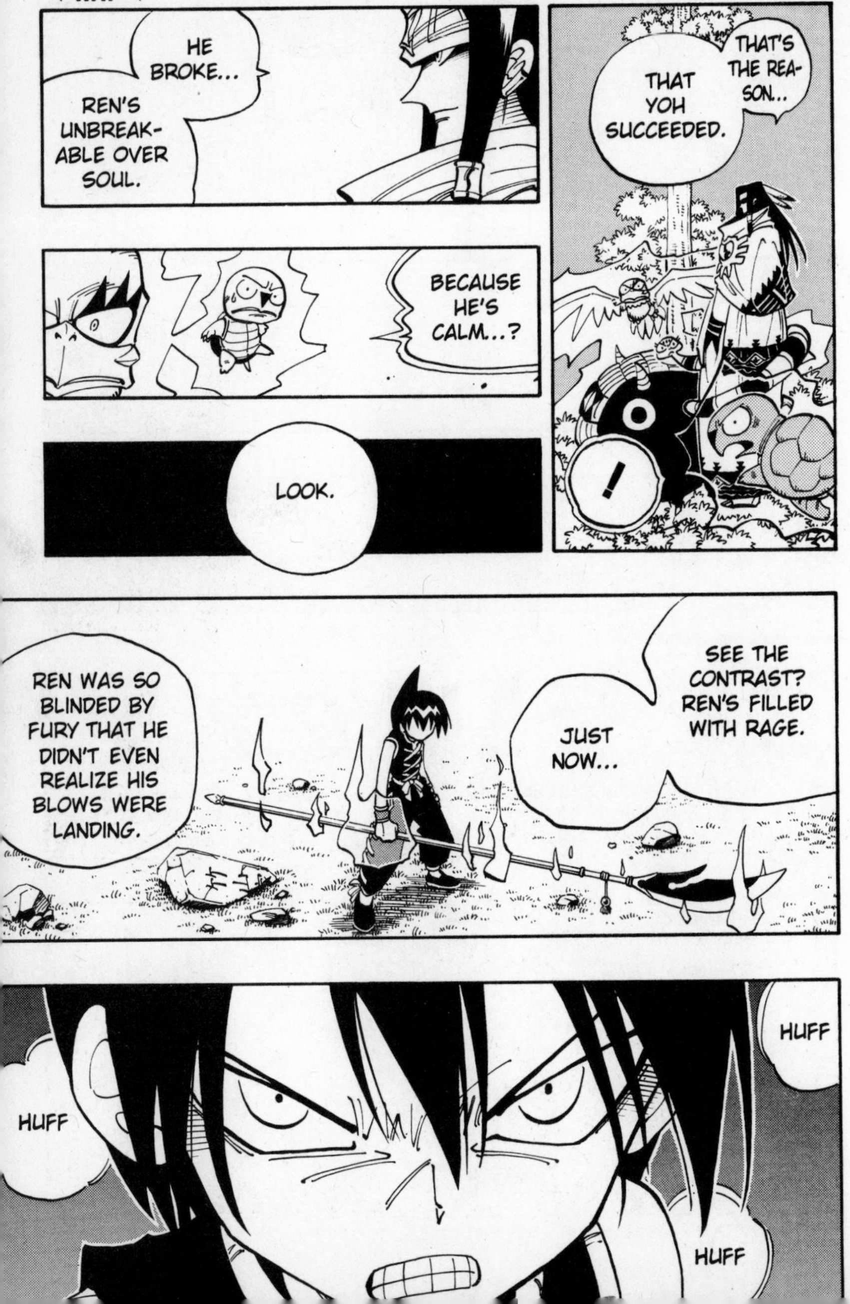
THAT'S THE REA-SON...
THAT YOH SUCCEEDED.
!
HE BROKE...
REN'S UNBREAK-ABLE OVER SOUL.
BECAUSE HE'S CALM...?
LOOK.
SEE THE CONTRAST? REN'S FILLED WITH RAGE.
JUST NOW...
REN WAS SO BLINDED BY FURY THAT HE DIDN'T EVEN REALIZE HIS BLOWS WERE LANDING.
HUFF
HUFF
HUFF

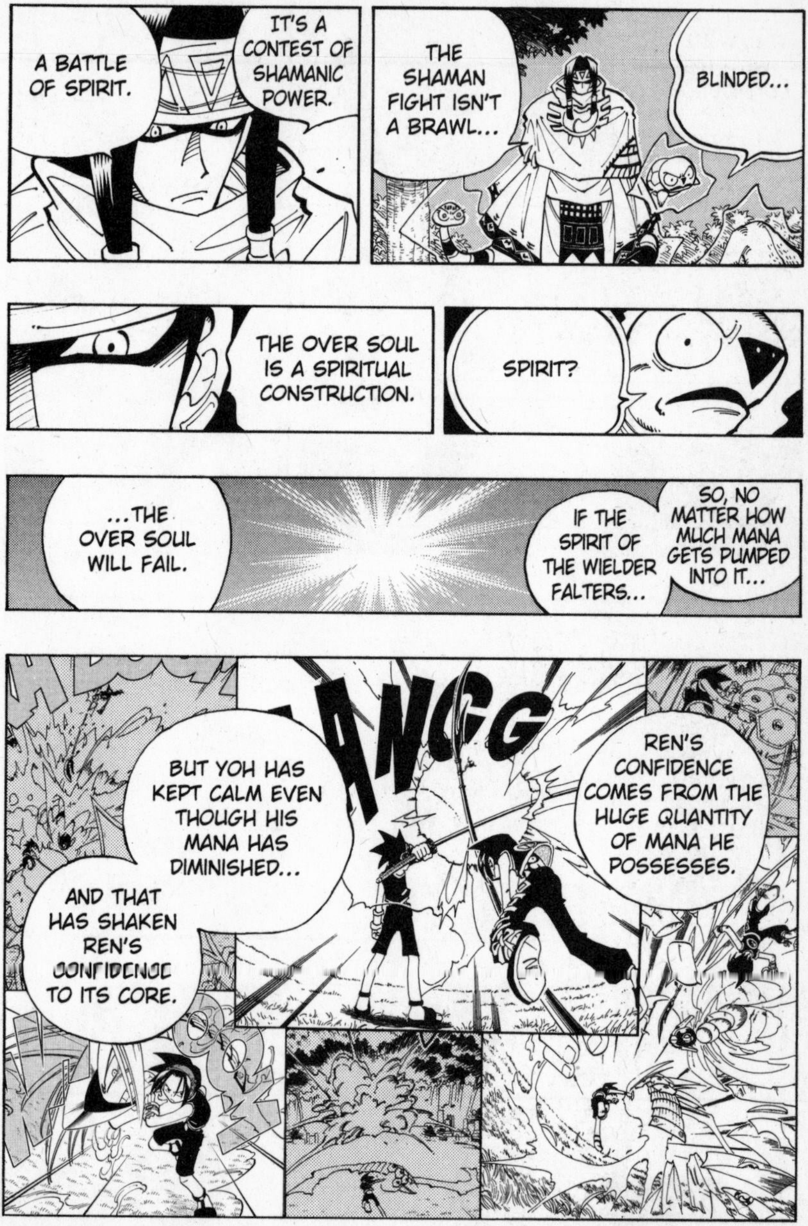
BLINDED...
THE SHAMAN FIGHT ISN'T A BRAWL...
IT'S A CONTEST OF SHAMANIC POWER.
A BATTLE OF SPIRIT.
SPIRIT?
THE OVER SOUL IS A SPIRITUAL CONSTRUCTION.
SO, NO MATTER HOW MUCH MANA GETS PUMPED INTO IT...
IF THE SPIRIT OF THE WIELDER FALTERS...
...THE OVER SOUL WILL FAIL.
REN'S CONFIDENCE COMES FROM THE HUGE QUANTITY OF MANA HE POSSESSES.
ANGG
BUT YOH HAS KEPT CALM EVEN THOUGH HIS MANA HAS DIMINISHED...
AND THAT HAS SHAKEN REN'S CONFIDENCE TO ITS CORE.

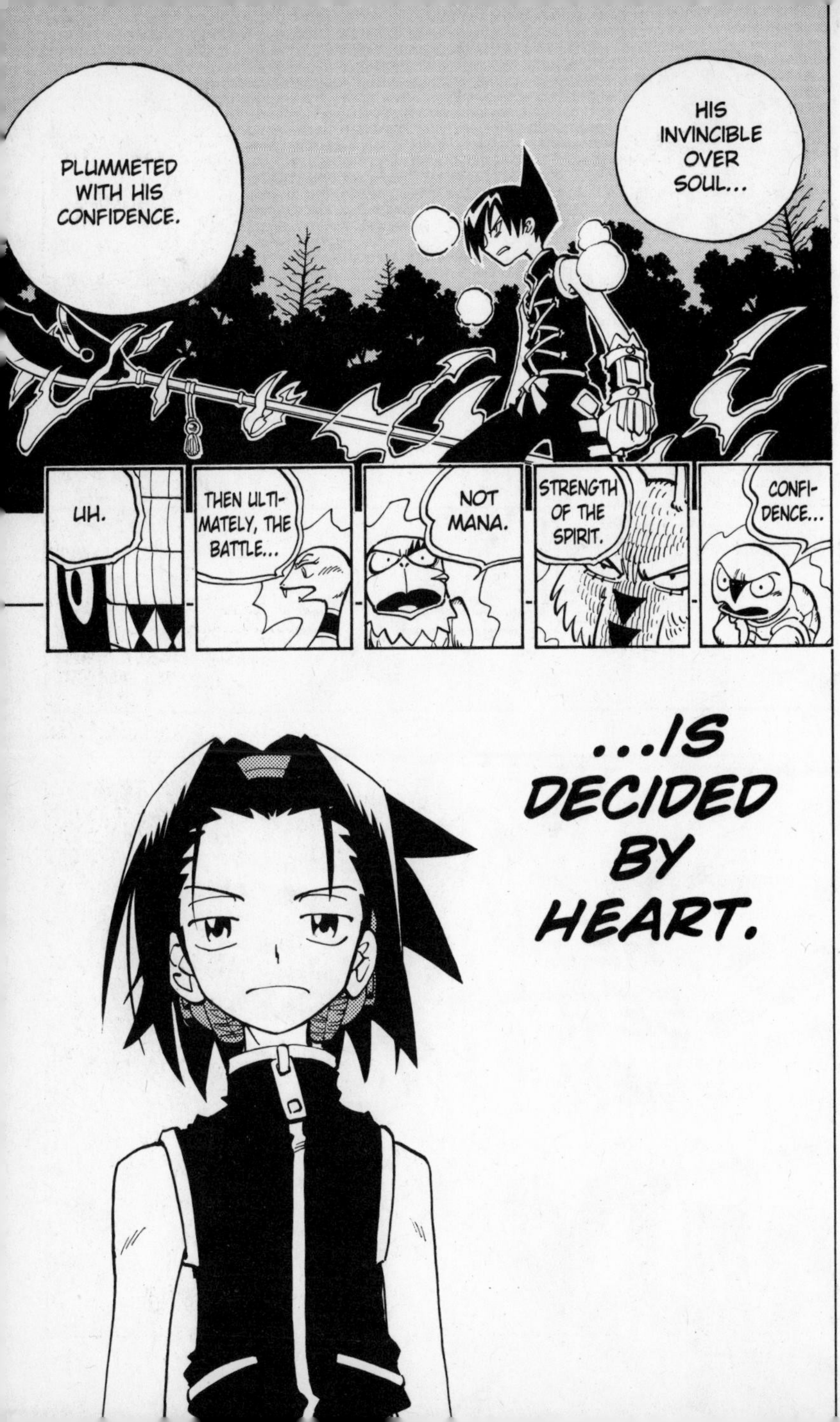
HIS INVINCIBLE OVER SOUL...
PLUMMETED WITH HIS CONFIDENCE.
CONFI-DENCE...
STRENGTH OF THE SPIRIT.
NOT MANA.
THEN ULTI-MATELY, THE BATTLE...
UH.
...IS DECIDED BY HEART.

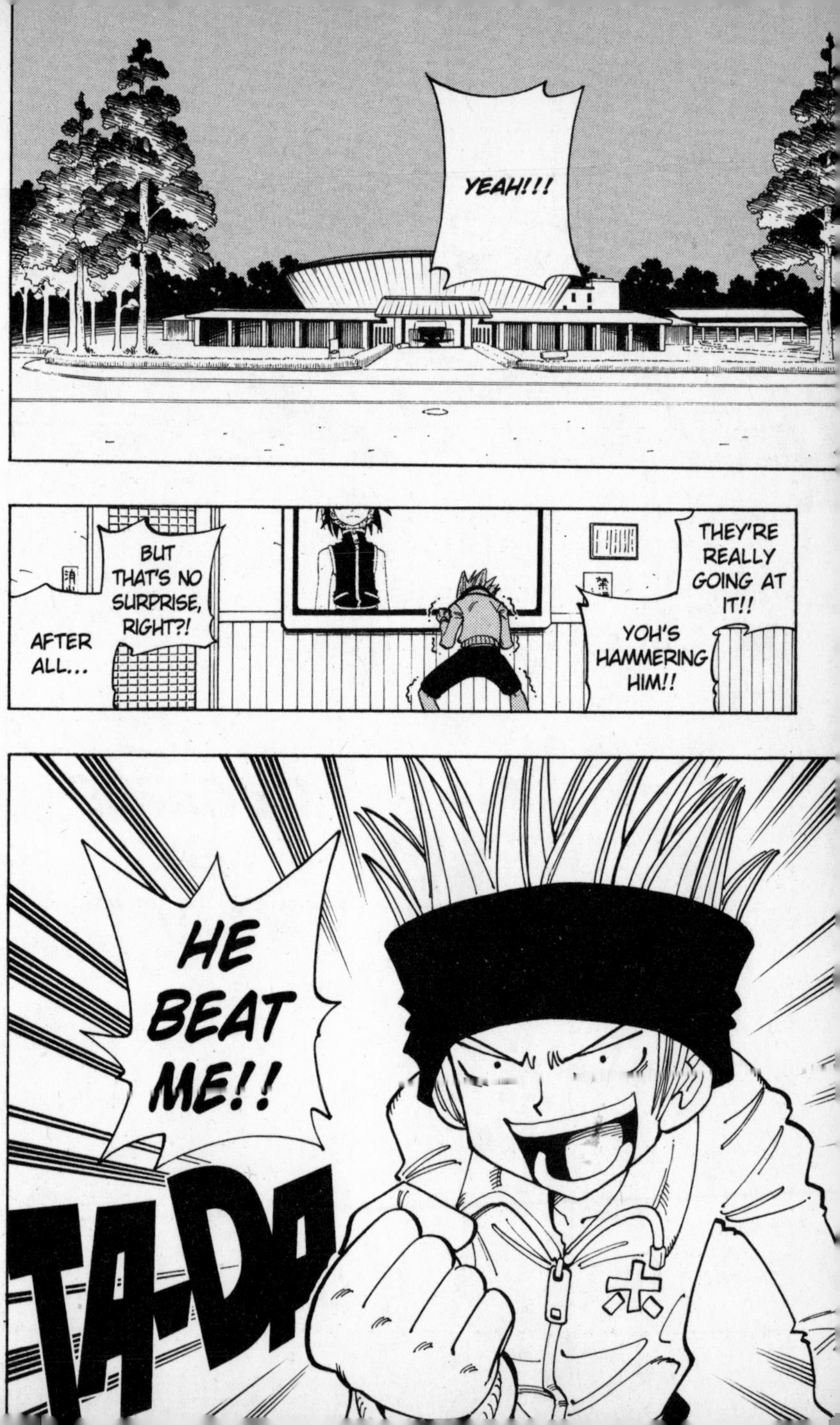
YEAH!!!
THEY'RE REALLY GOING AT IT!!
YOH'S HAMMERING HIM!!
BUT THAT'S NO SURPRISE, RIGHT?!
AFTER ALL...
HE BEAT ME!!
TA-DA

READ THIS WAY

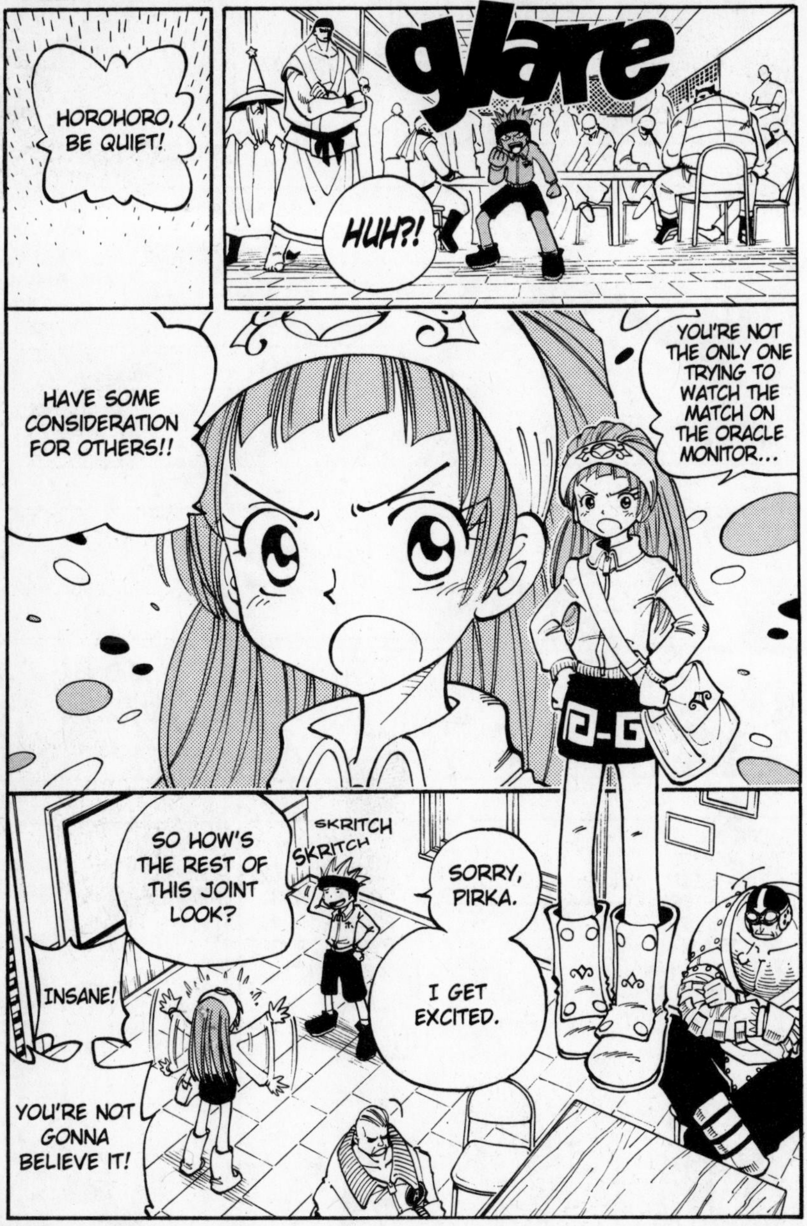
glare
HUH?!
HOROHORO, BE QUIET!
YOU'RE NOT THE ONLY ONE TRYING TO WATCH THE MATCH ON THE ORACLE MONITOR...
HAVE SOME CONSIDERATION FOR OTHERS!!
SORRY, PIRKA.
I GET EXCITED.
SKRITCH
SKRITCH
SO HOW'S THE REST OF THIS JOINT LOOK?
INSANE!
YOU'RE NOT GONNA BELIEVE IT!

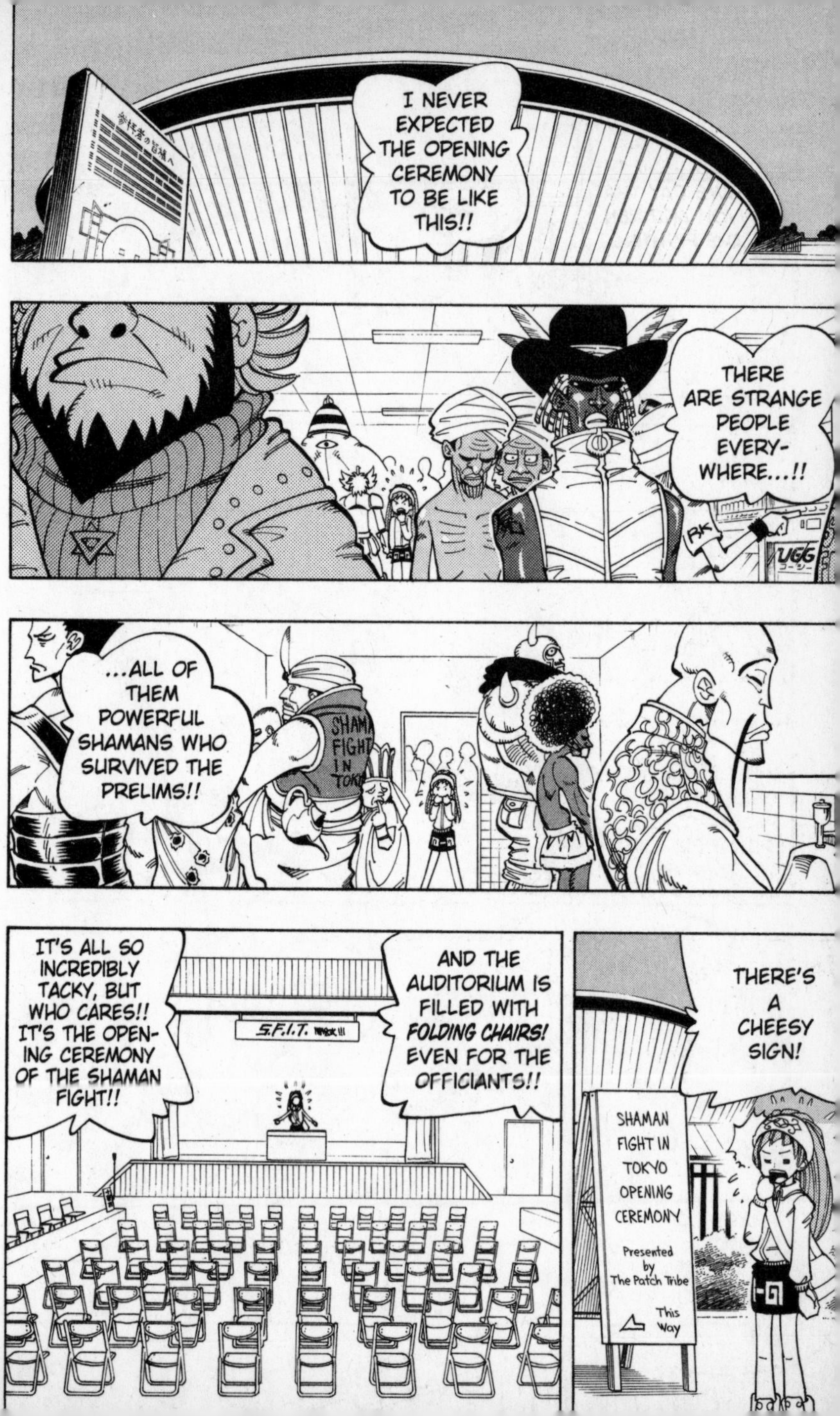

I NEVER EXPECTED THE OPENING CEREMONY TO BE LIKE THIS!!
THERE ARE STRANGE PEOPLE EVERY-WHERE...!!
...ALL OF THEM POWERFUL SHAMANS WHO SURVIVED THE PRELIMS!!
SHAMAN FIGHT IN TOKYO OPENING CEREMONY Presented by The Patch Tribe This Way
THERE'S A CHEESY SIGN!
AND THE AUDITORIUM IS FILLED WITH FOLDING CHAIRS! EVEN FOR THE OFFICIANTS!!
S.F.I.T.
IT'S ALL SO INCREDIBLY TACKY, BUT WHO CARES!! IT'S THE OPEN-ING CEREMONY OF THE SHAMAN FIGHT!!

READ THIS WAY

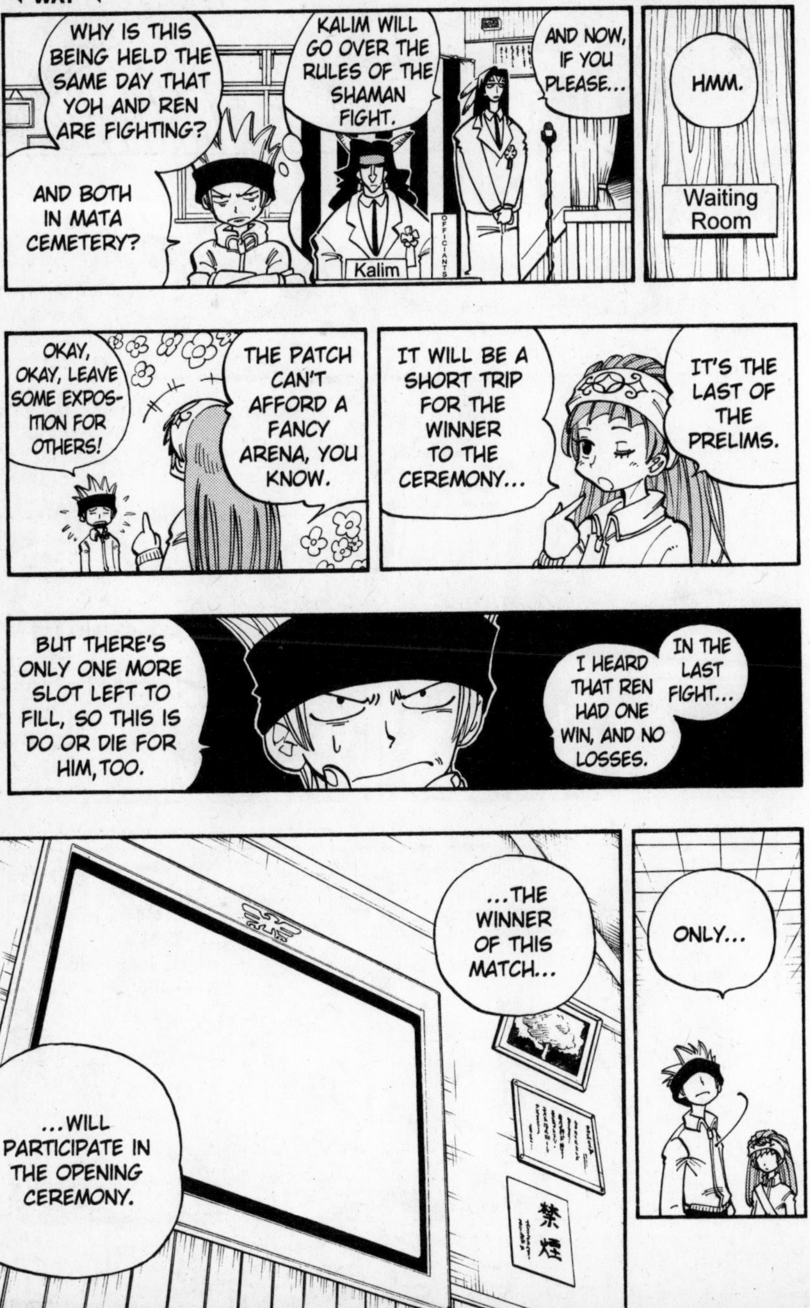
HMM.
Waiting Room
AND NOW, IF YOU PLEASE...
KALIM WILL GO OVER THE RULES OF THE SHAMAN FIGHT.
WHY IS THIS BEING HELD THE SAME DAY THAT YOH AND REN ARE FIGHTING?
AND BOTH IN MATA CEMETERY?
OFFICIANTS
Kalim
IT'S THE LAST OF THE PRELIMS.
IT WILL BE A SHORT TRIP FOR THE WINNER TO THE CEREMONY...
THE PATCH CAN'T AFFORD A FANCY ARENA, YOU KNOW.
OKAY, OKAY, LEAVE SOME EXPOSITION FOR OTHERS!
IN THE LAST FIGHT...
I HEARD THAT REN HAD ONE WIN, AND NO LOSSES.
BUT THERE'S ONLY ONE MORE SLOT LEFT TO FILL, SO THIS IS DO OR DIE FOR HIM, TOO.
ONLY...
...THE WINNER OF THIS MATCH...
...WILL PARTICIPATE IN THE OPENING CEREMONY.
禁煙

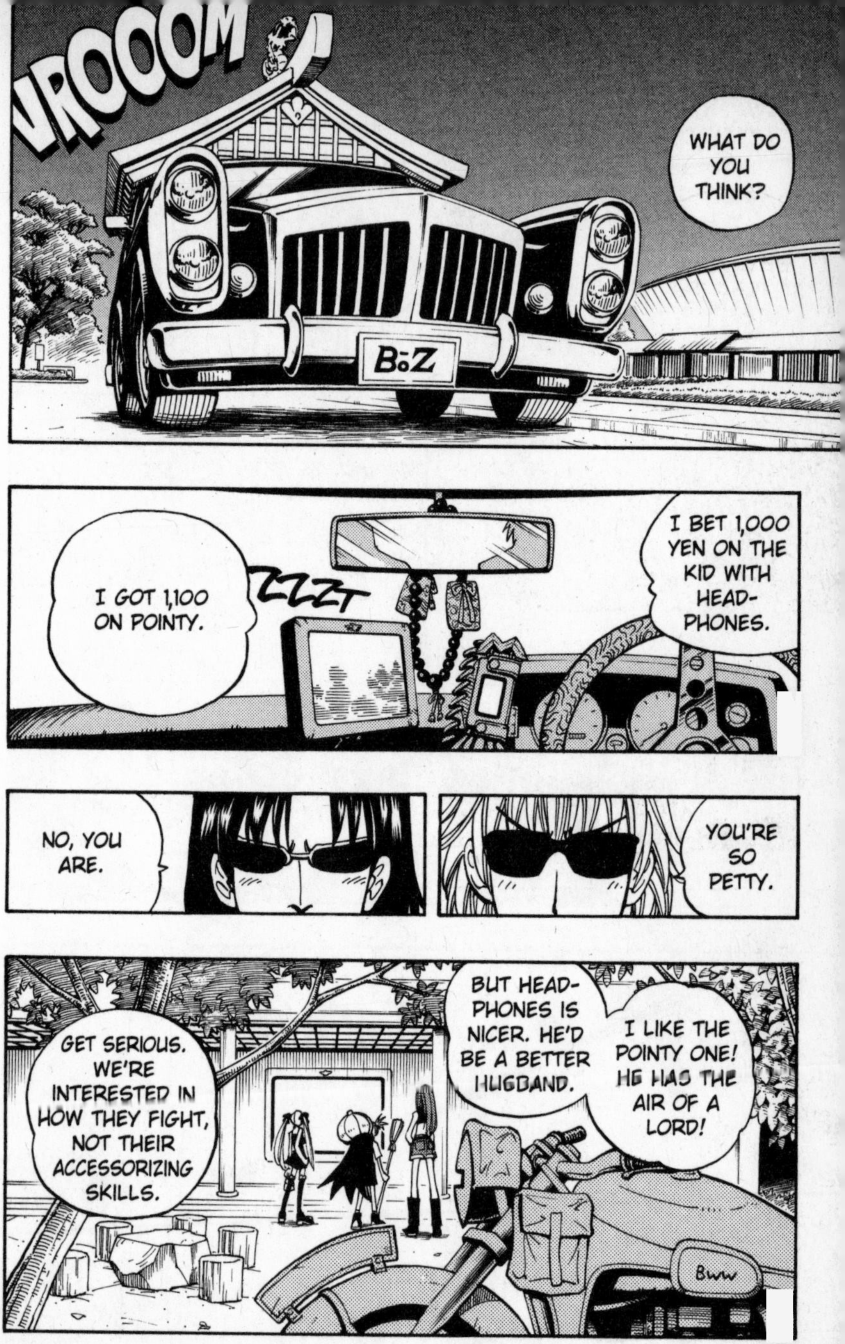
WHAT DO YOU THINK?
VROOOM
I BET 1,000 YEN ON THE KID WITH HEAD-PHONES.
ZZZZT
I GOT 1,100 ON POINTY.
YOU'RE SO PETTY.
NO, YOU ARE.
I LIKE THE POINTY ONE! HE HAS THE AIR OF A LORD!
BUT HEAD-PHONES IS NICER. HE'D BE A BETTER HUSBAND.
GET SERIOUS. WE'RE INTERESTED IN HOW THEY FIGHT, NOT THEIR ACCESSORIZING SKILLS.
Bww

READ THIS WAY

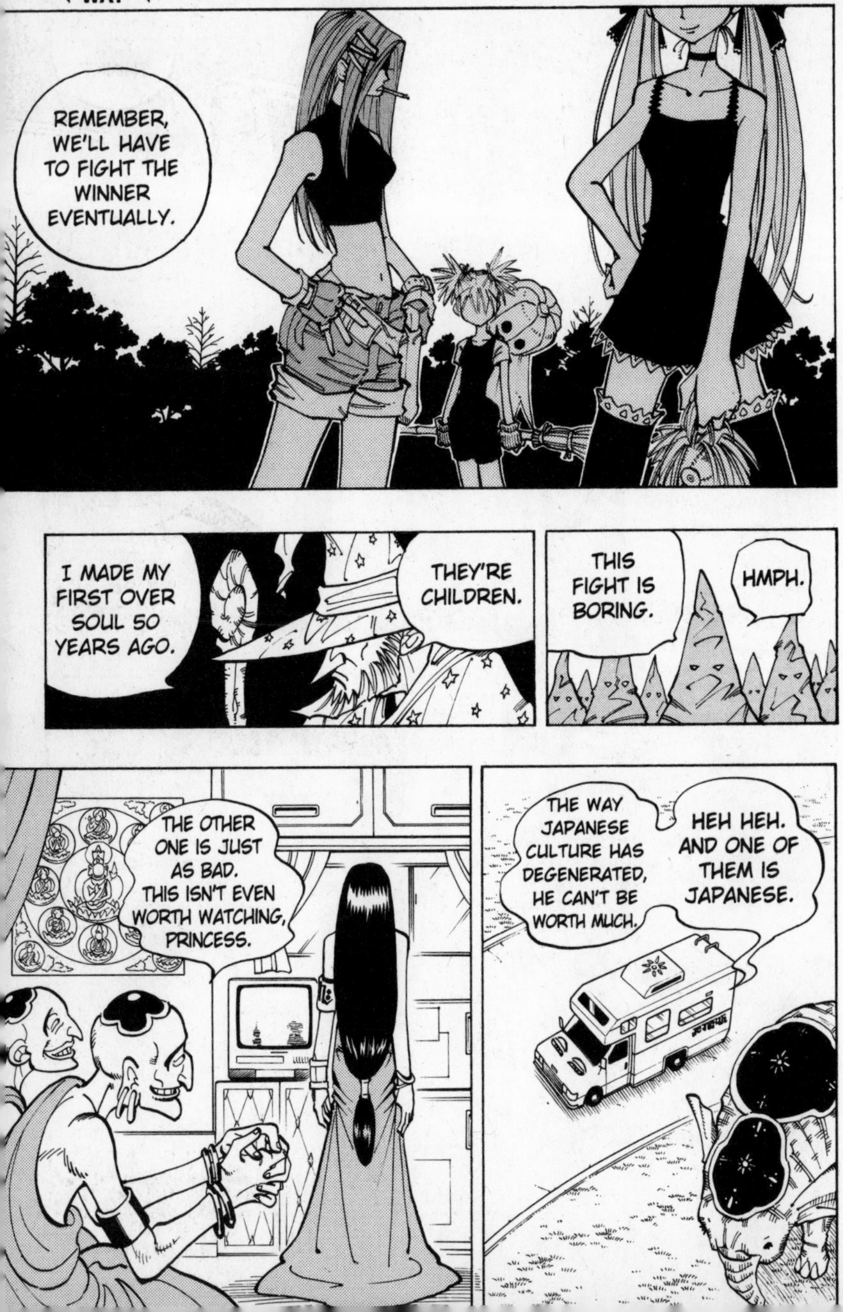
REMEMBER, WE'LL HAVE TO FIGHT THE WINNER EVENTUALLY.
HMPH.
THIS FIGHT IS BORING.
THEY'RE CHILDREN.
I MADE MY FIRST OVER SOUL 50 YEARS AGO.
HEH HEH. AND ONE OF THEM IS JAPANESE.
THE WAY JAPANESE CULTURE HAS DEGENERATED, HE CAN'T BE WORTH MUCH.
THE OTHER ONE IS JUST AS BAD. THIS ISN'T EVEN WORTH WATCHING, PRINCESS.

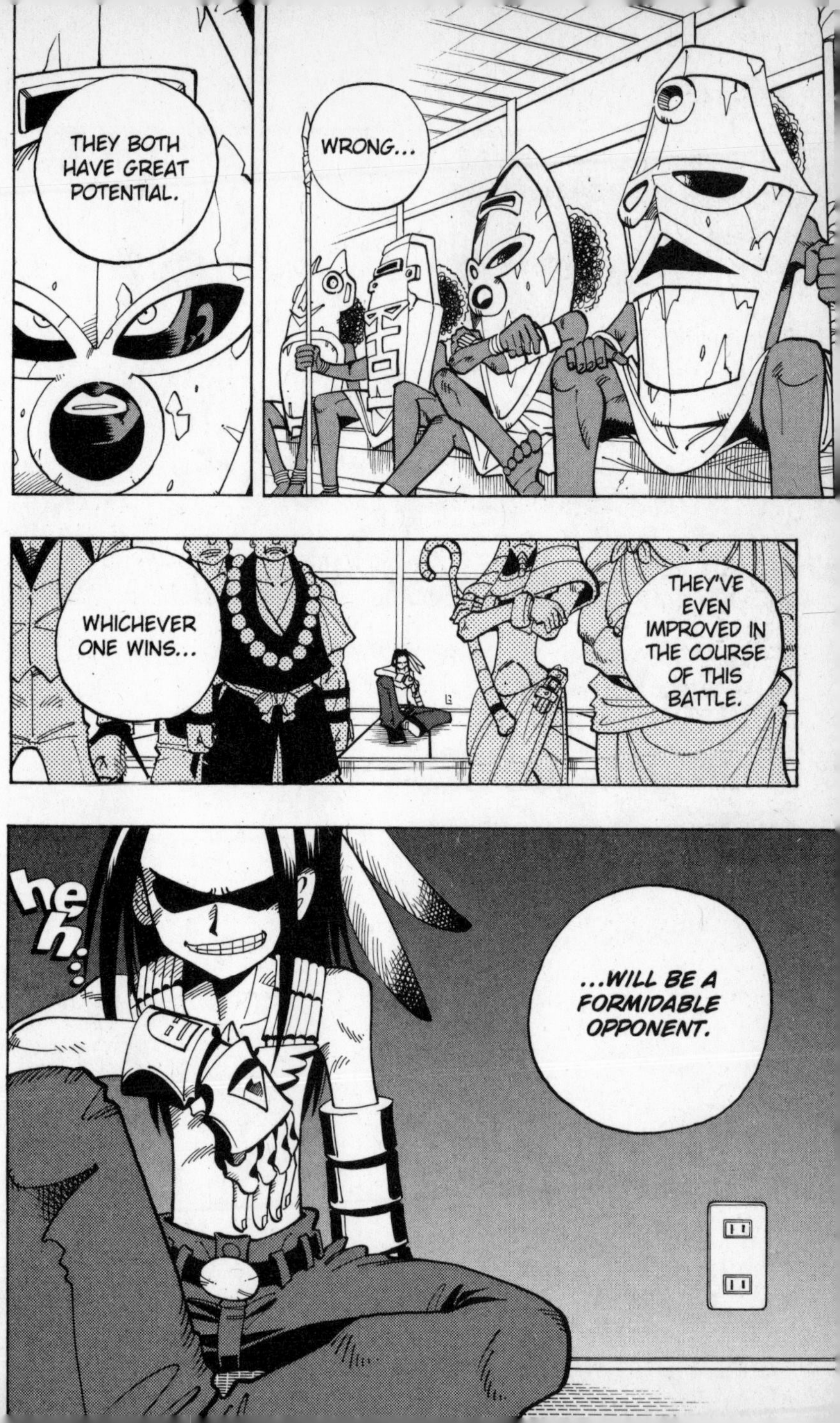
WRONG...
THEY BOTH HAVE GREAT POTENTIAL.
THEY'VE EVEN IMPROVED IN THE COURSE OF THIS BATTLE.
WHICHEVER ONE WINS...
...WILL BE A FORMIDABLE OPPONENT.
heh...

READ THIS WAY

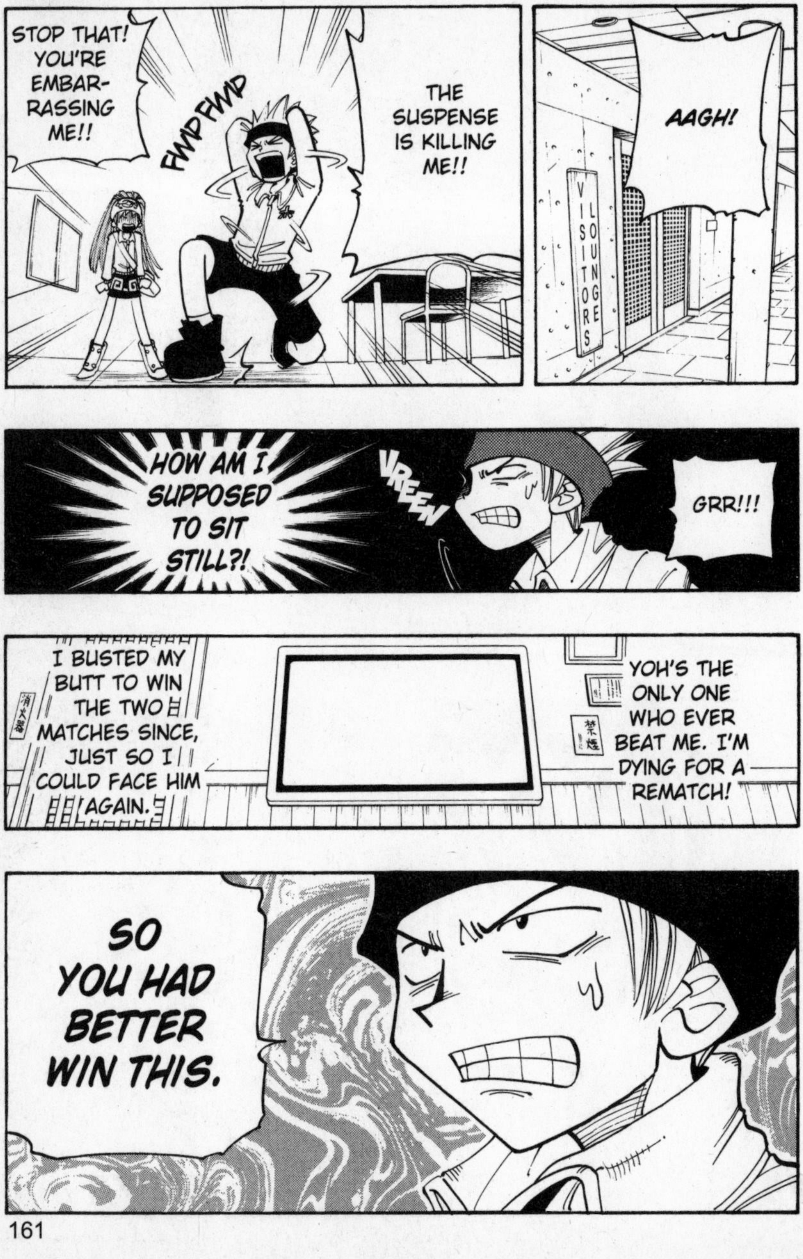
AAGH!
VISITORS LOUNGE
THE SUSPENSE IS KILLING ME!!
FWIP FWIP
STOP THAT! YOU'RE EMBARRASSING ME!!
GRR!!!
VREEN
HOW AM I SUPPOSED TO SIT STILL?!
YOH'S THE ONLY ONE WHO EVER BEAT ME. I'M DYING FOR A REMATCH!
禁煙
I BUSTED MY BUTT TO WIN THE TWO MATCHES SINCE, JUST SO I COULD FACE HIM AGAIN.
消火器
SO YOU HAD BETTER WIN THIS.

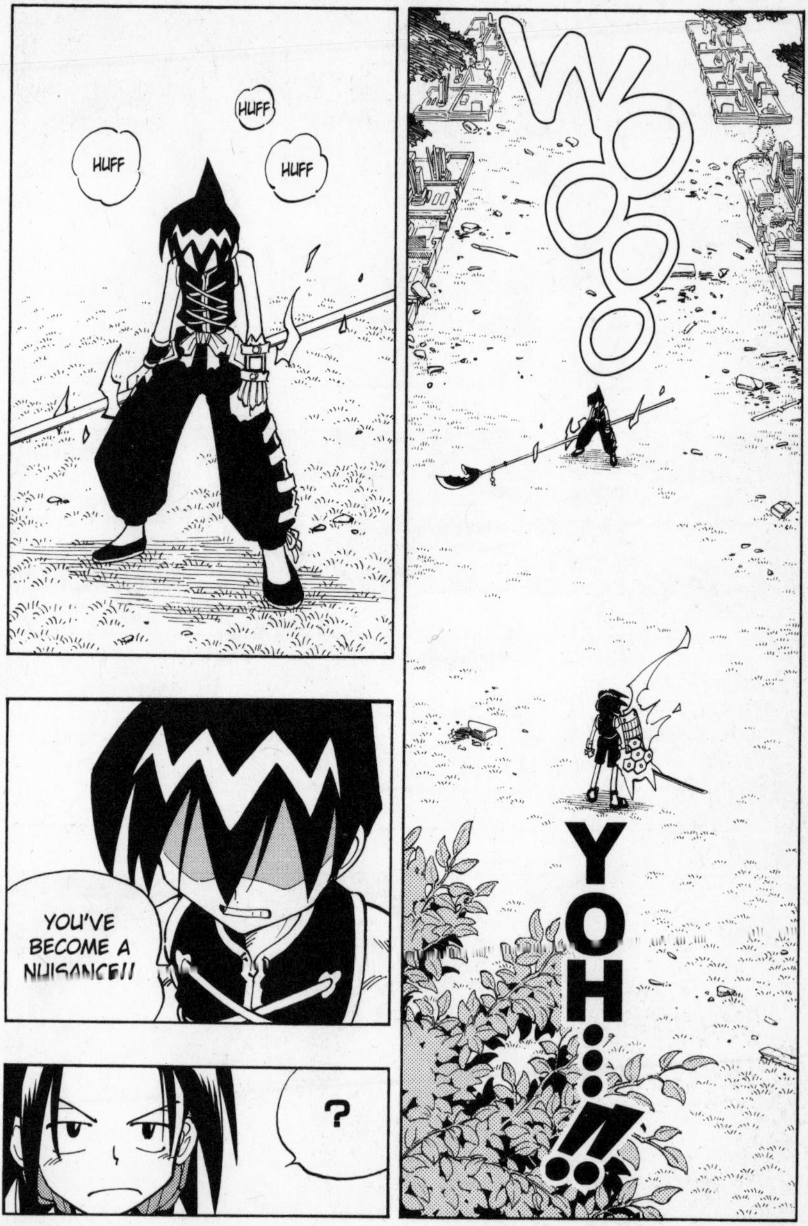
WOOOO
YOH...!!
HUFF
HUFF
HUFF
YOU'VE BECOME A NUISANCE!!
?

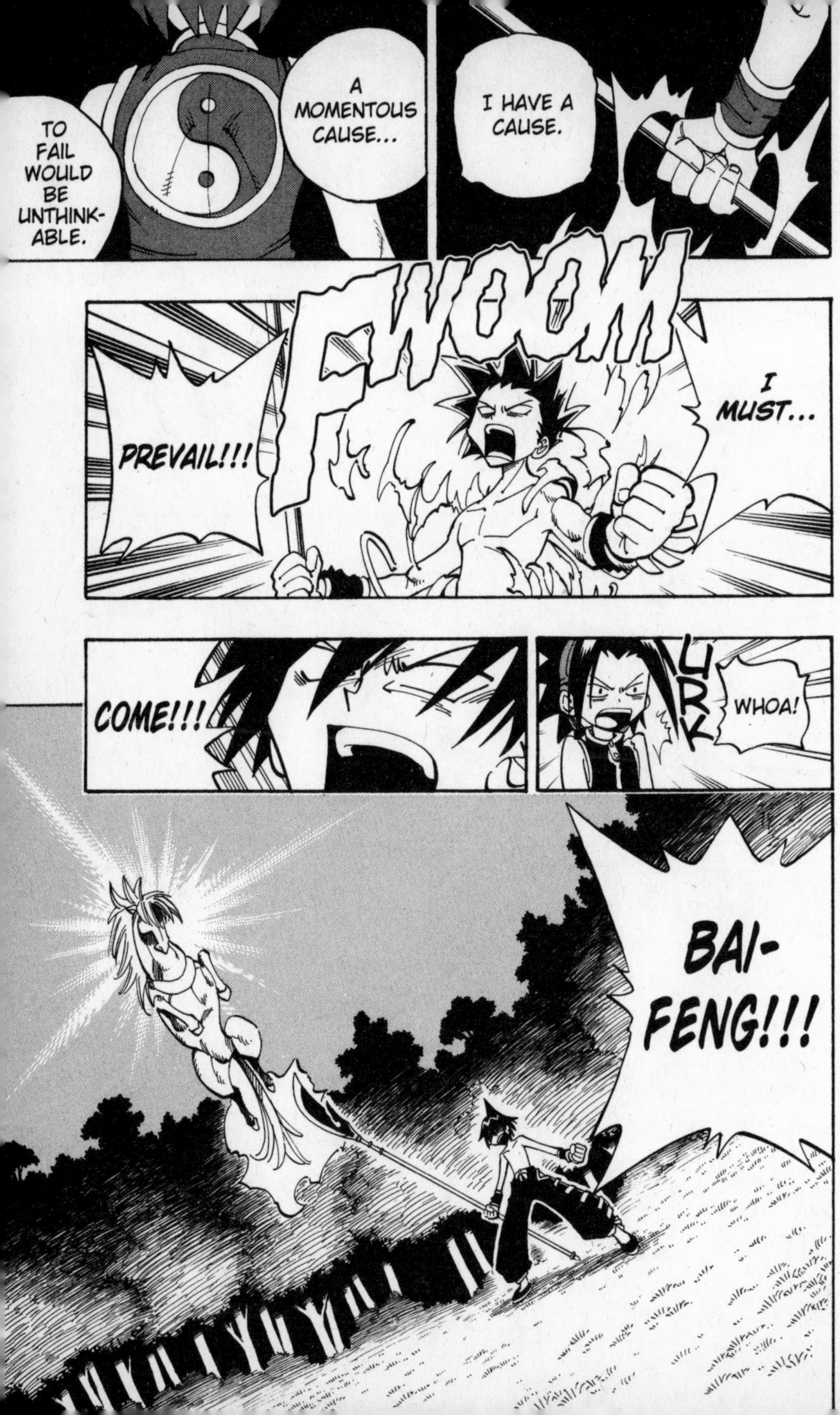
I HAVE A CAUSE.
A MOMENTOUS CAUSE...
TO FAIL WOULD BE UNTHINK-ABLE.
FWOOM
I MUST...
PREVAIL!!!
URK
WHOA!
COME!!!
BAI-FENG!!!

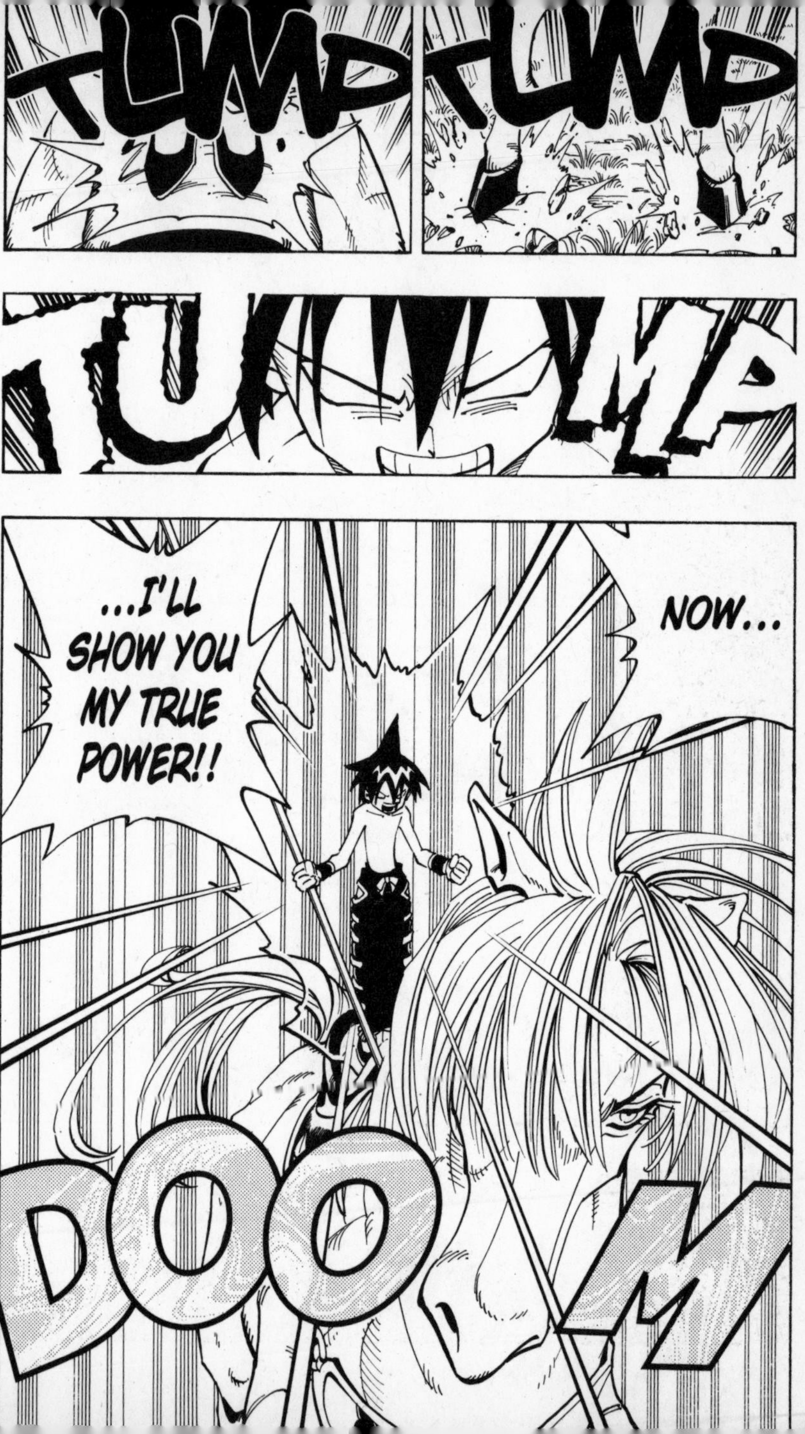
TUMP
TUMP
TUMP
NOW...
...I'LL SHOW YOU MY TRUE POWER!!
DOOM

Reincarnation 62: Ren's Past

...IS EVERYONE DEAD?

WHY...

WHY...

WHY DO YOU KILL EVERYONE?

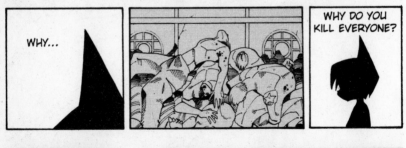

ARE PEOPLE SO ROTTEN?

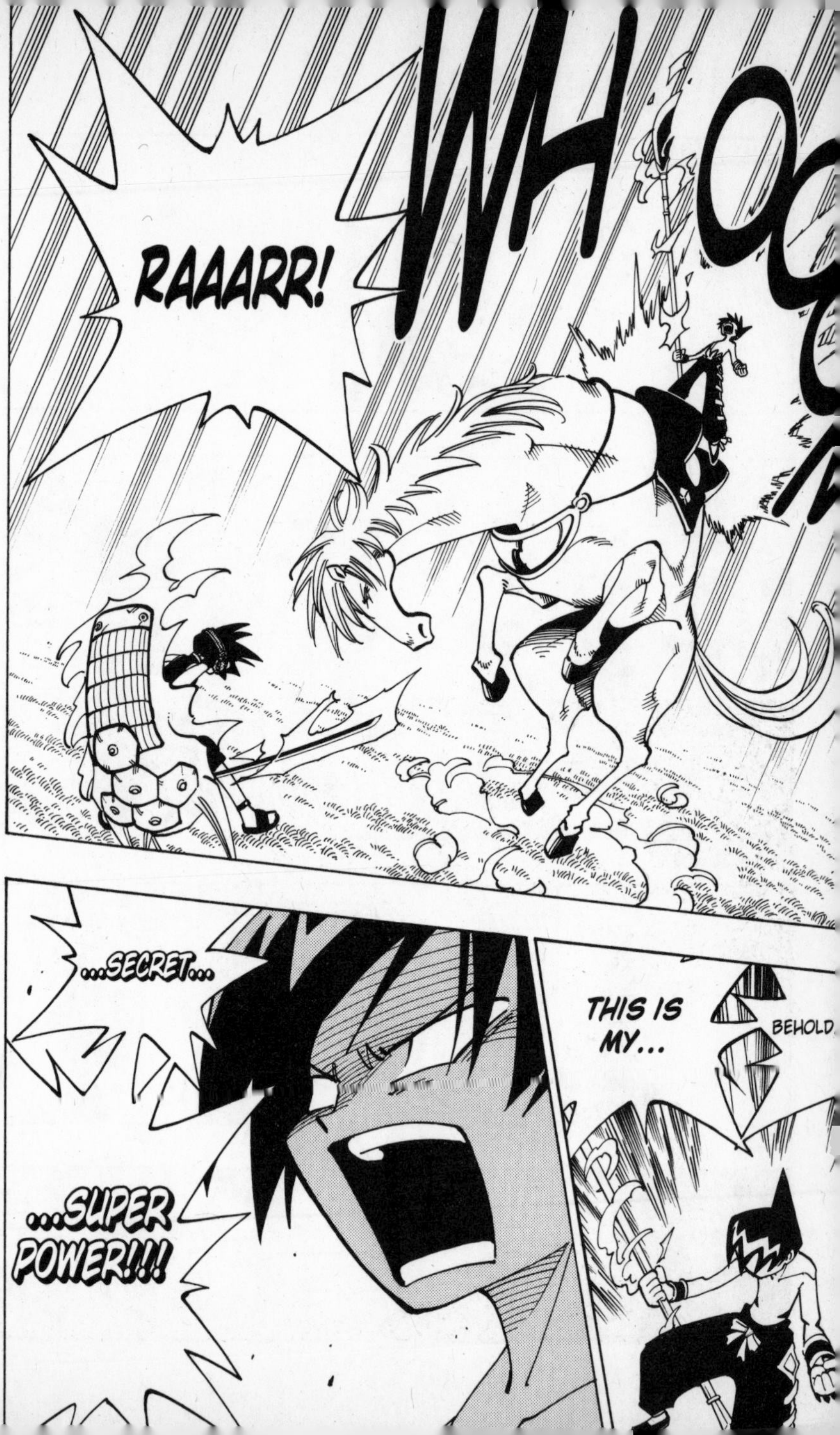
WHOO
RAAARR!
BEHOLD
THIS IS MY...
...SECRET...
...SUPER POWER!!!

Reincarnation 62: Ren's Past

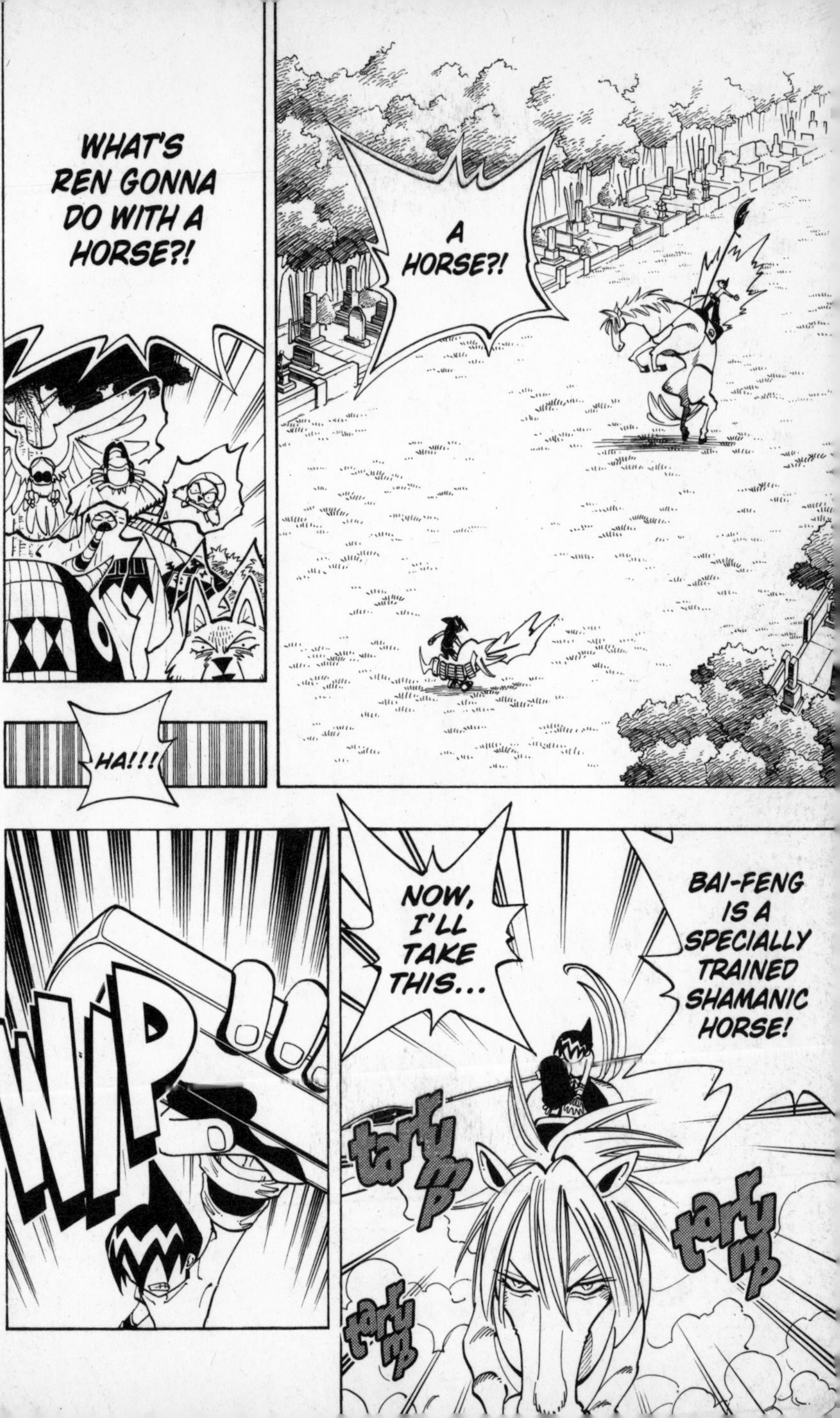
A HORSE?!
WHAT'S REN GONNA DO WITH A HORSE?!
HA!!!
BAI-FENG IS A SPECIALLY TRAINED SHAMANIC HORSE!
NOW, I'LL TAKE THIS...
WHIP

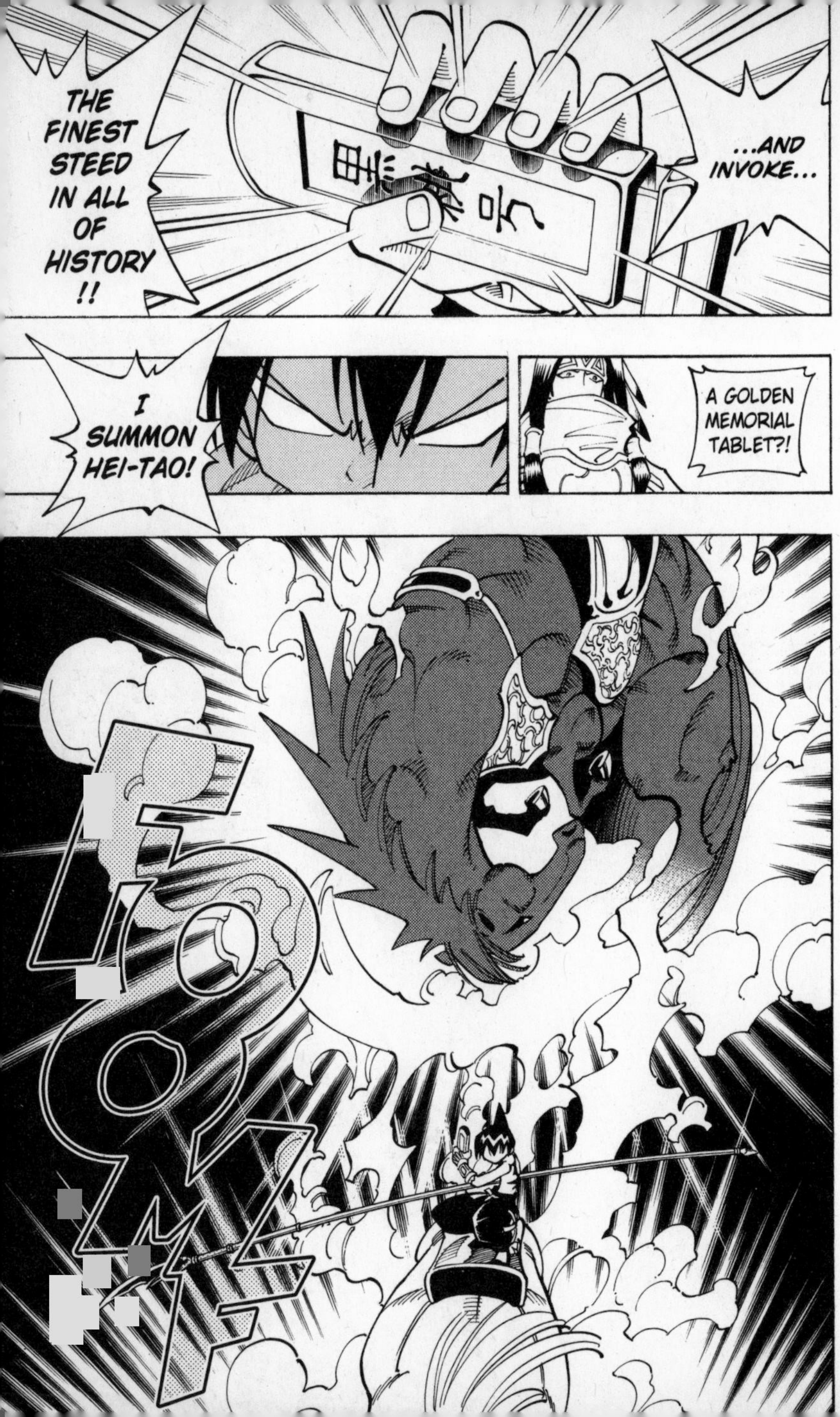
...AND INVOKE...
THE FINEST STEED IN ALL OF HISTORY!!
A GOLDEN MEMORIAL TABLET?!
I SUMMON HEI-TAO!

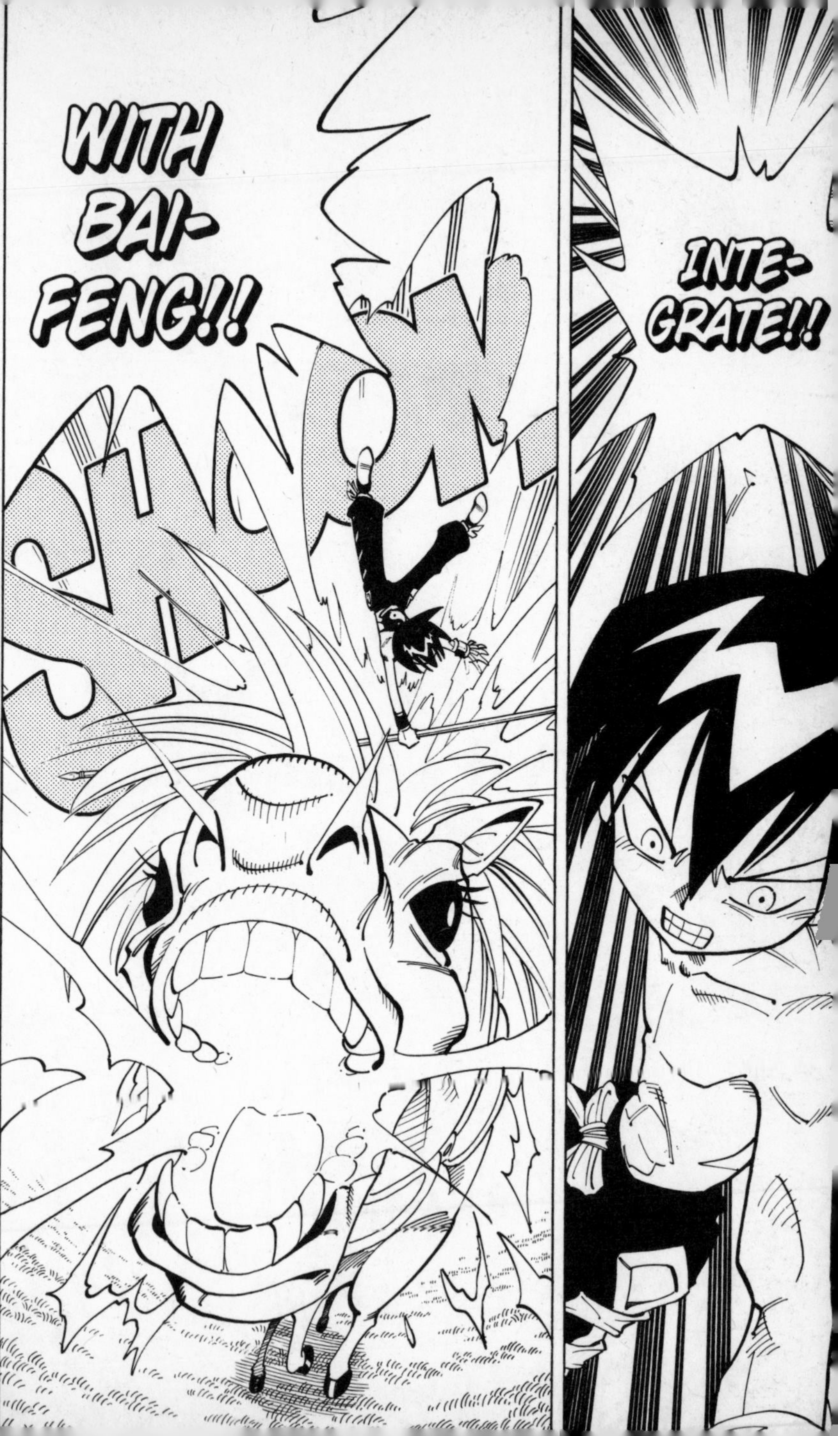
INTE-
GRATE!!
WITH
BAI-
FENG!!

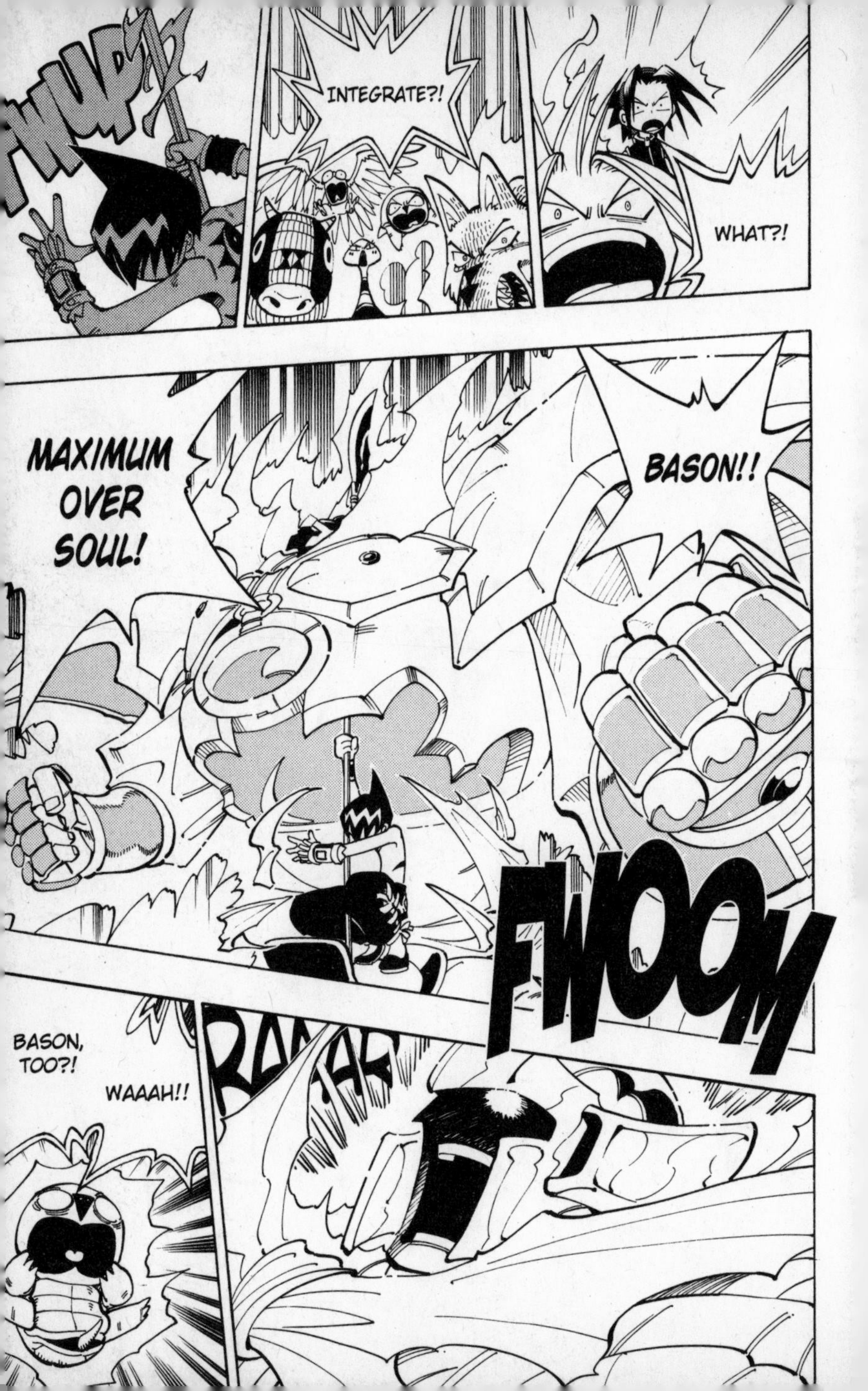
WHAT?!
INTEGRATE?!
THWUP
MAXIMUM OVER SOUL!
BASON!!
FWOOM
BASON, TOO?!
WAAAH!!

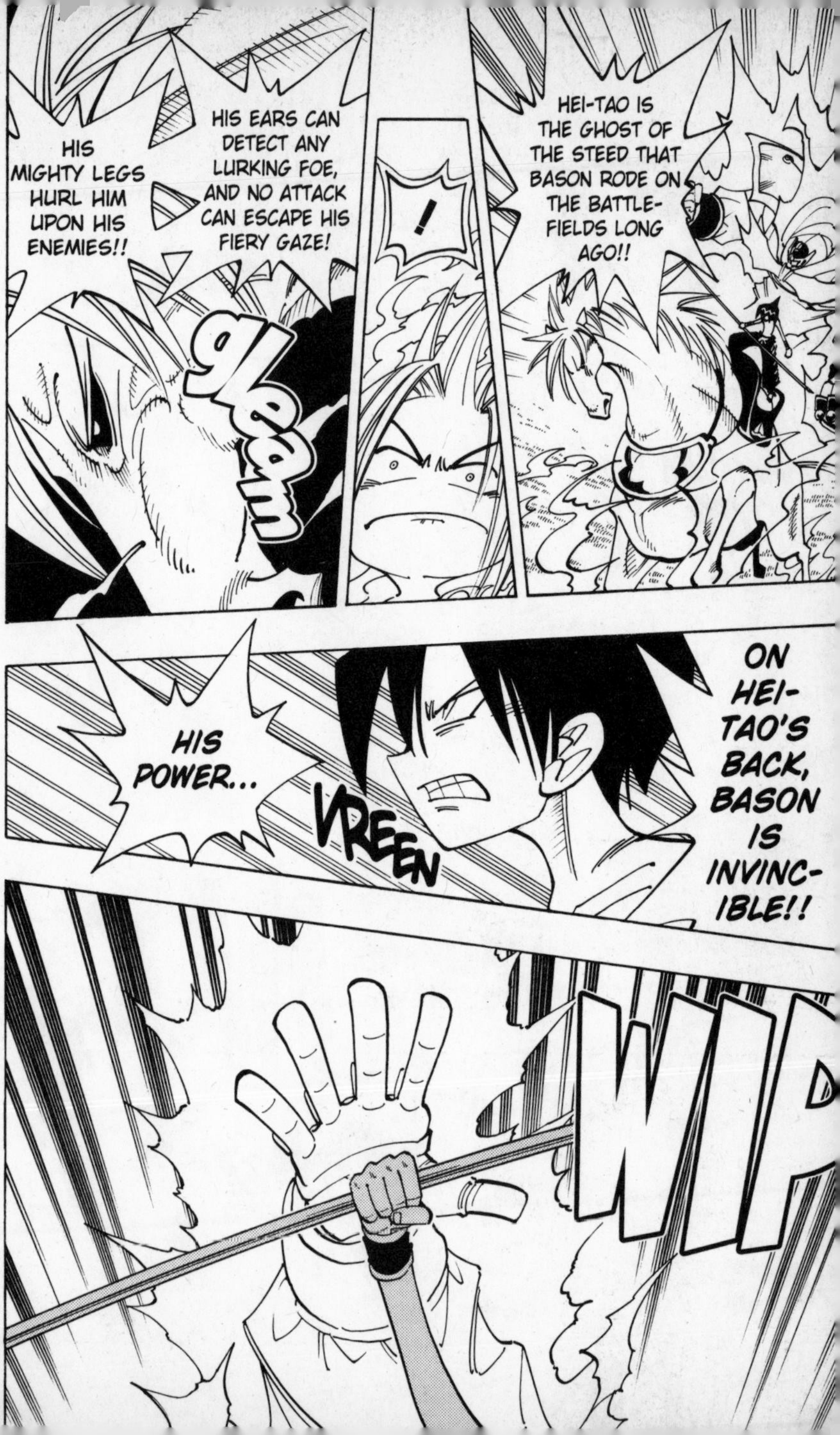
HEI-TAO IS THE GHOST OF THE STEED THAT BASON RODE ON THE BATTLE-FIELDS LONG AGO!!
!
HIS EARS CAN DETECT ANY LURKING FOE, AND NO ATTACK CAN ESCAPE HIS FIERY GAZE!
HIS MIGHTY LEGS HURL HIM UPON HIS ENEMIES!!
gleam
ON HEI-TAO'S BACK, BASON IS INVINC-IBLE!!
VREEN
HIS POWER...
WIP

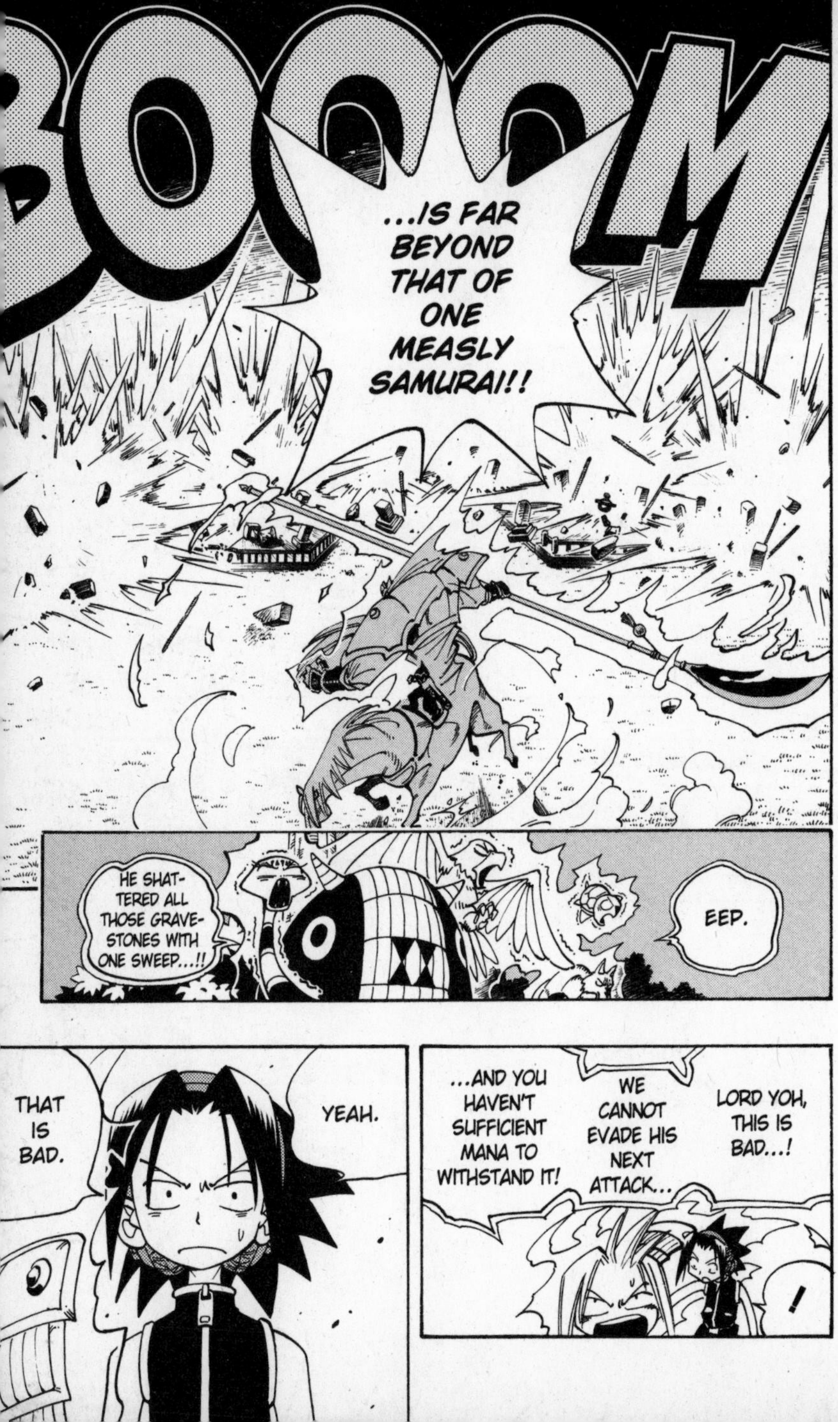
BOOOM
...IS FAR BEYOND THAT OF ONE MEASLY SAMURAI!!
EEP.
HE SHATTERED ALL THOSE GRAVESTONES WITH ONE SWEEP...!!
LORD YOH, THIS IS BAD...!
WE CANNOT EVADE HIS NEXT ATTACK...
...AND YOU HAVEN'T SUFFICIENT MANA TO WITHSTAND IT!
!
YEAH.
THAT IS BAD.

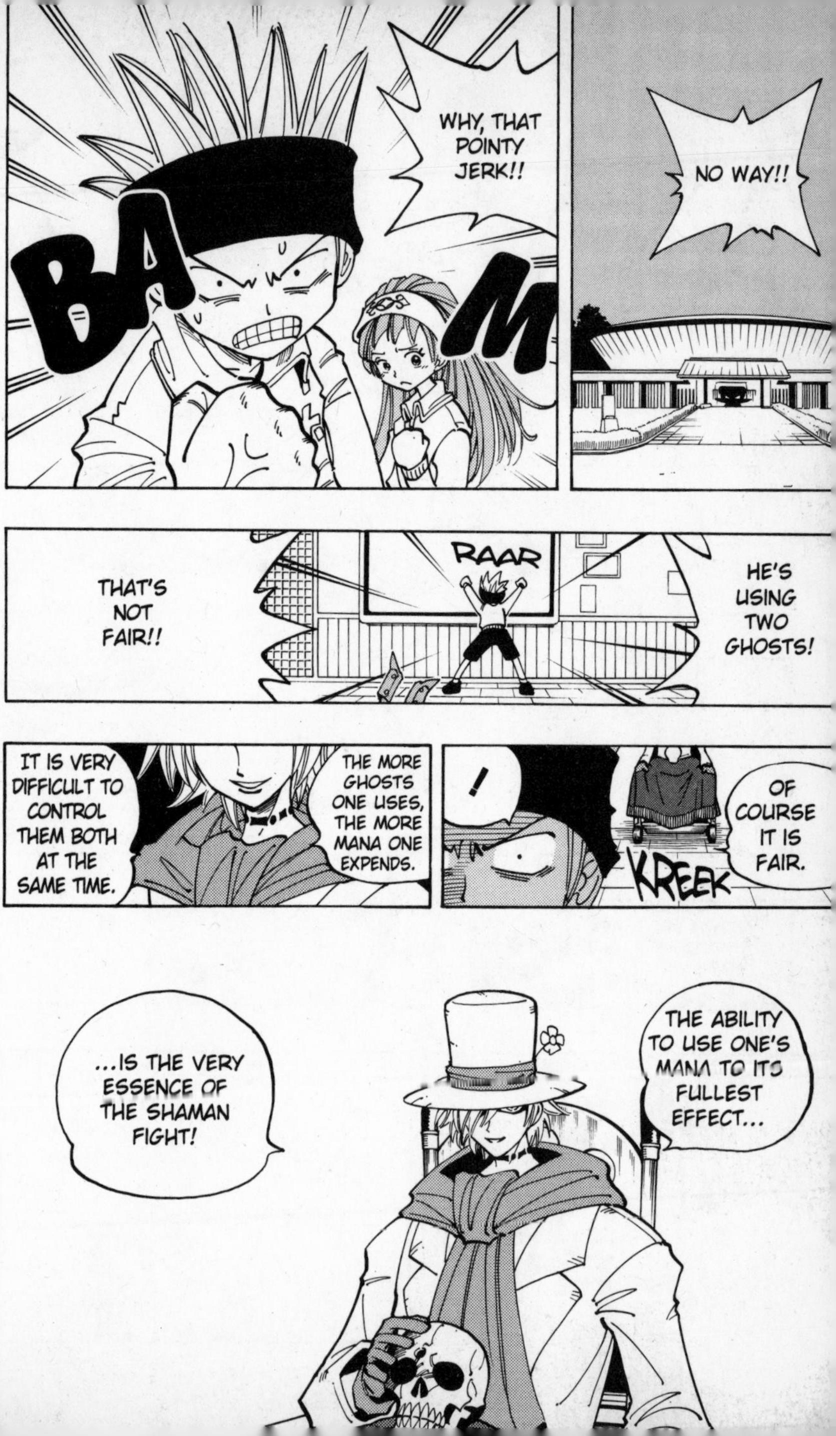
NO WAY!!
WHY, THAT POINTY JERK!!
BAM
HE'S USING TWO GHOSTS!
RAAR
THAT'S NOT FAIR!!
OF COURSE IT IS FAIR.
KREEK
!
THE MORE GHOSTS ONE USES, THE MORE MANA ONE EXPENDS.
IT IS VERY DIFFICULT TO CONTROL THEM BOTH AT THE SAME TIME.
THE ABILITY TO USE ONE'S MANA TO ITS FULLEST EFFECT...
...IS THE VERY ESSENCE OF THE SHAMAN FIGHT!

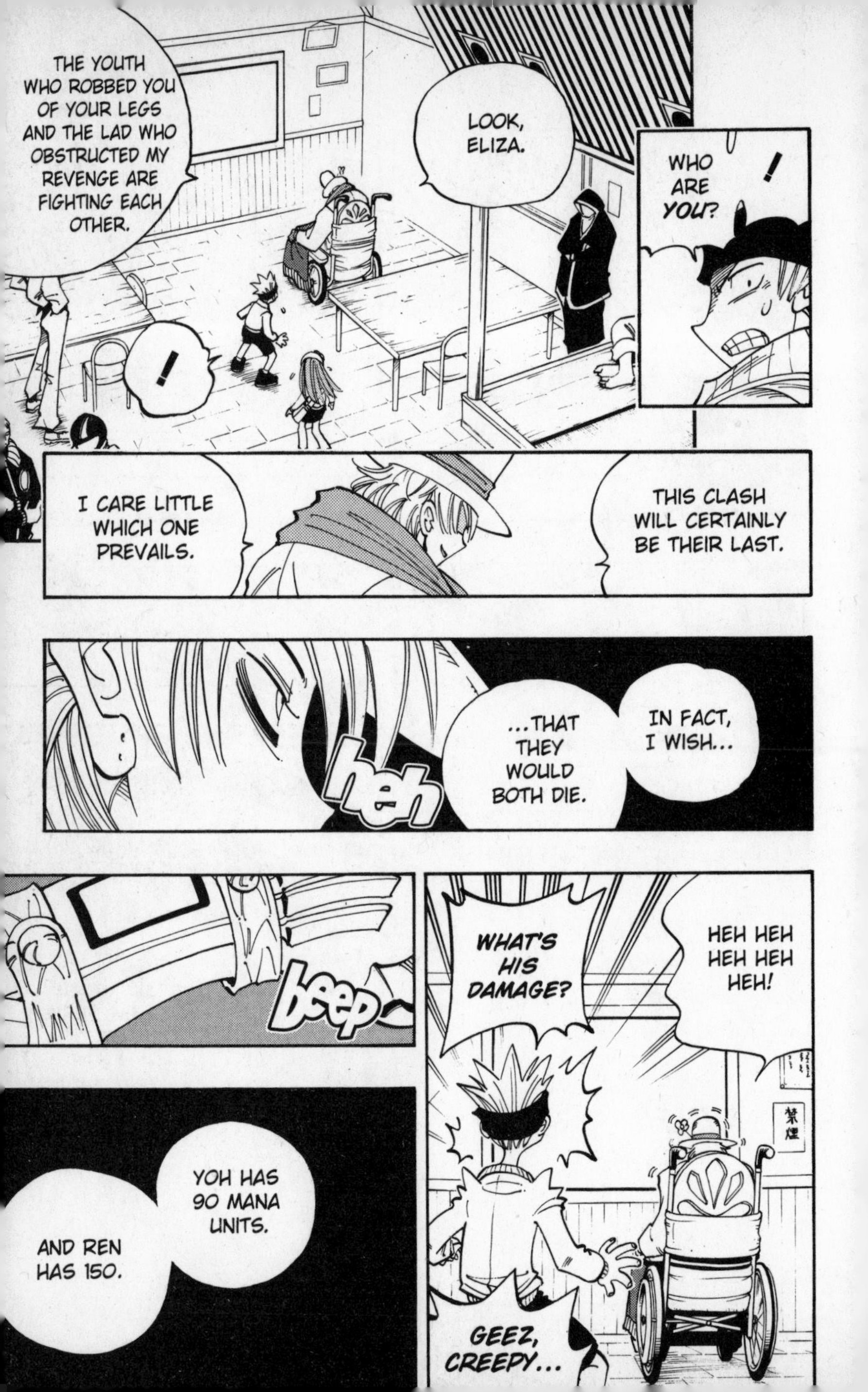
WHO ARE YOU?
!
LOOK, ELIZA.
THE YOUTH WHO ROBBED YOU OF YOUR LEGS AND THE LAD WHO OBSTRUCTED MY REVENGE ARE FIGHTING EACH OTHER.
!
THIS CLASH WILL CERTAINLY BE THEIR LAST.
I CARE LITTLE WHICH ONE PREVAILS.
IN FACT, I WISH...
...THAT THEY WOULD BOTH DIE.
heh
HEH HEH HEH HEH HEH!
WHAT'S HIS DAMAGE?
禁煙
GEEZ, CREEPY...
beep
YOH HAS 90 MANA UNITS.
AND REN HAS 150.

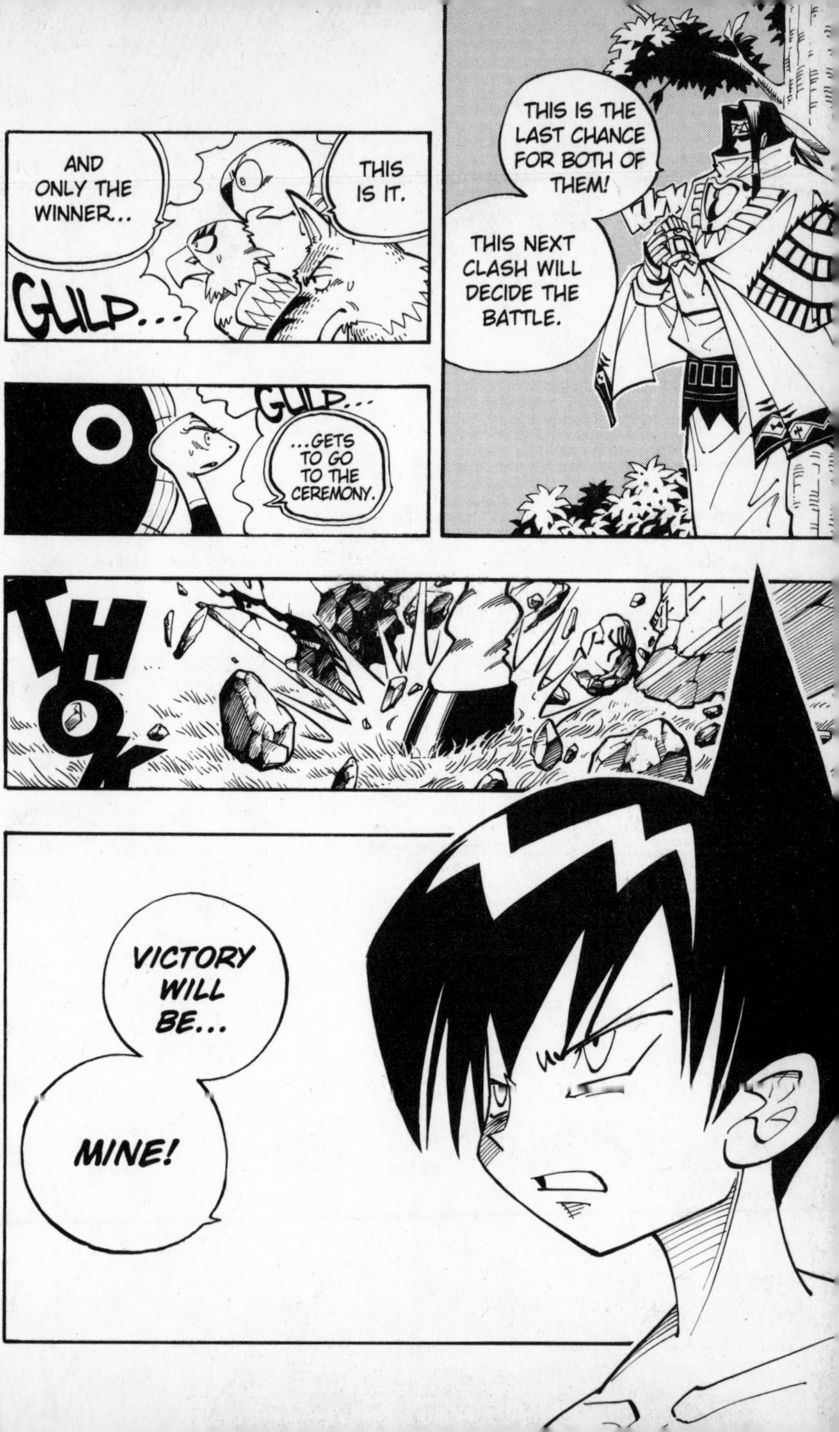
THIS IS THE LAST CHANCE FOR BOTH OF THEM!
THIS NEXT CLASH WILL DECIDE THE BATTLE.
THIS IS IT.
AND ONLY THE WINNER...
GULP...
GULP...
...GETS TO GO TO THE CEREMONY.
THOK
VICTORY WILL BE...
MINE!

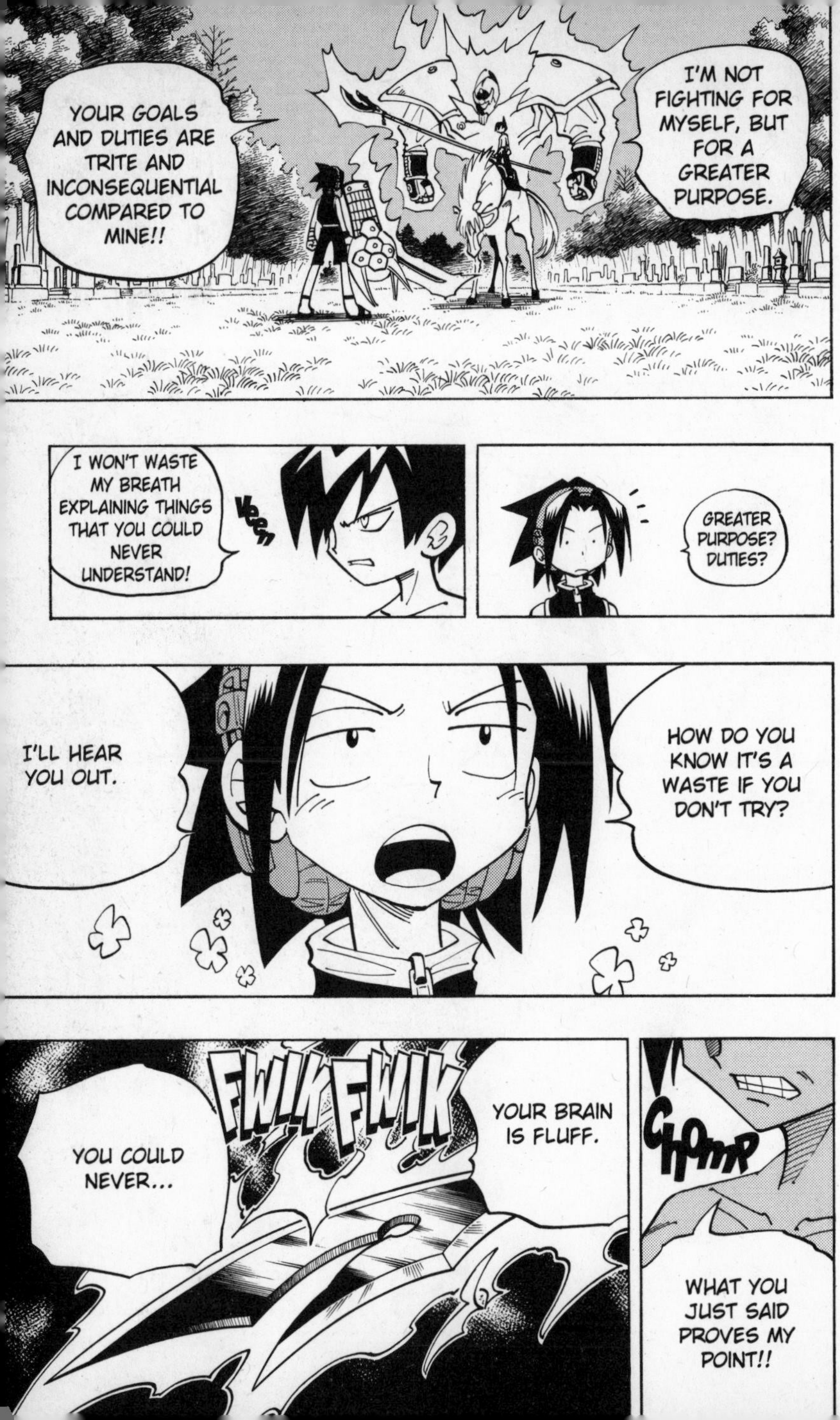
I'M NOT FIGHTING FOR MYSELF, BUT FOR A GREATER PURPOSE.
YOUR GOALS AND DUTIES ARE TRITE AND INCONSEQUENTIAL COMPARED TO MINE!!
GREATER PURPOSE? DUTIES?
I WON'T WASTE MY BREATH EXPLAINING THINGS THAT YOU COULD NEVER UNDERSTAND!
HOW DO YOU KNOW IT'S A WASTE IF YOU DON'T TRY?
I'LL HEAR YOU OUT.
CHOMP
WHAT YOU JUST SAID PROVES MY POINT!!
YOUR BRAIN IS FLUFF.
FWIK FWIK
YOU COULD NEVER...

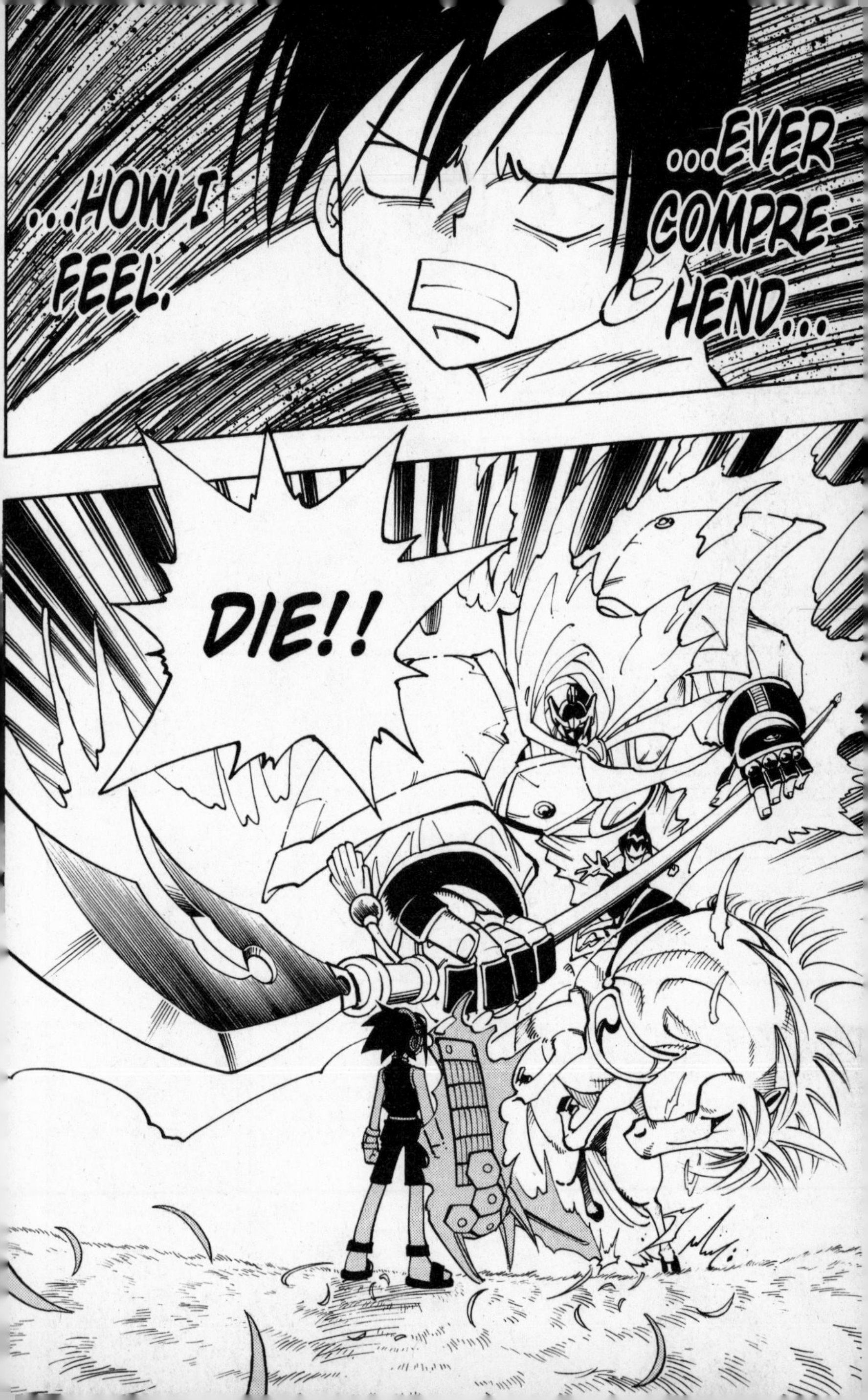
...EVER COMPRE-HEND...
...HOW I FEEL.
DIE!!

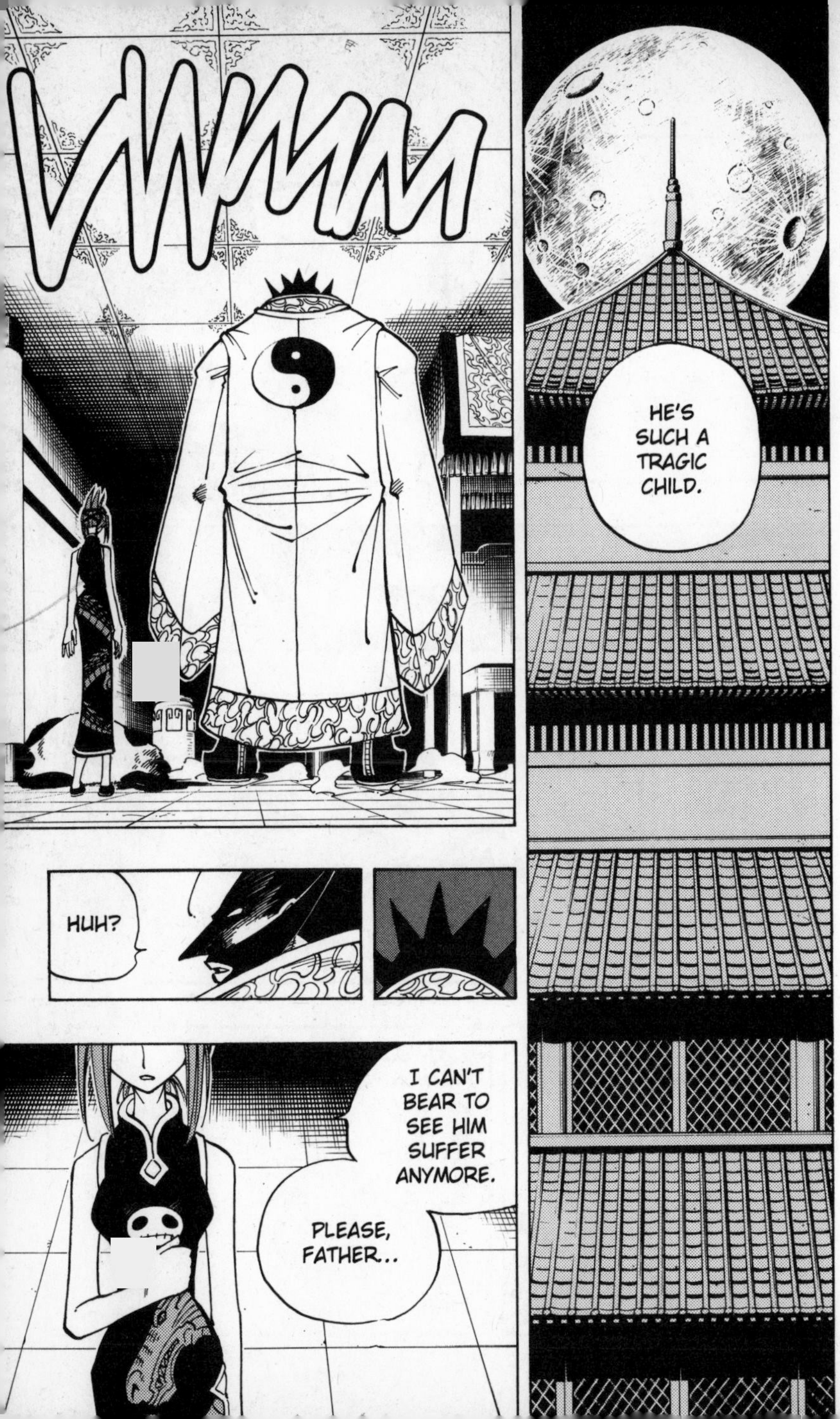
HE'S SUCH A TRAGIC CHILD.
VWMM
HUH?
I CAN'T BEAR TO SEE HIM SUFFER ANYMORE.
PLEASE, FATHER..

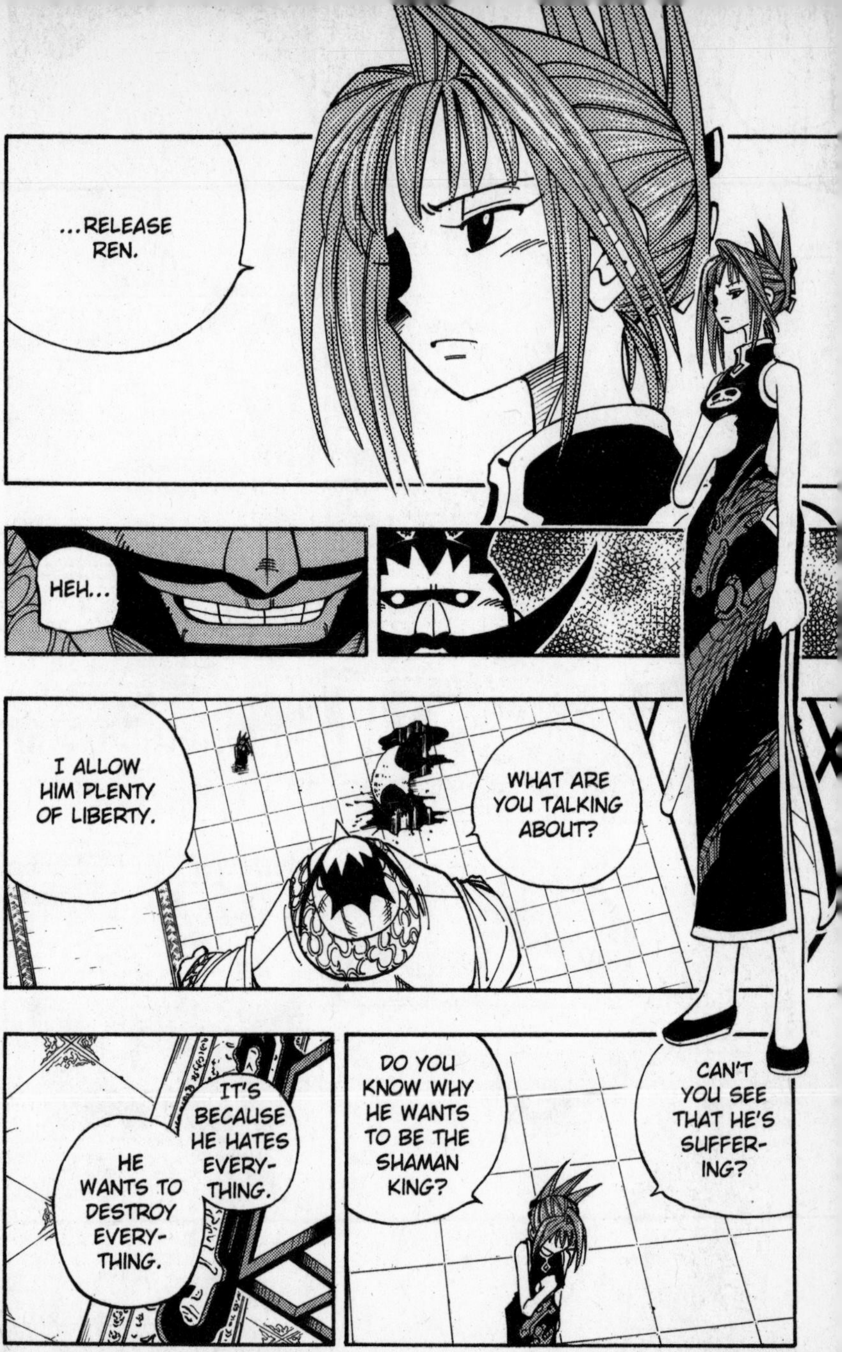
...RELEASE REN.
HEH...
WHAT ARE YOU TALKING ABOUT?
I ALLOW HIM PLENTY OF LIBERTY.
CAN'T YOU SEE THAT HE'S SUFFER-ING?
DO YOU KNOW WHY HE WANTS TO BE THE SHAMAN KING?
IT'S BECAUSE HE HATES EVERY-THING.
HE WANTS TO DESTROY EVERY-THING.

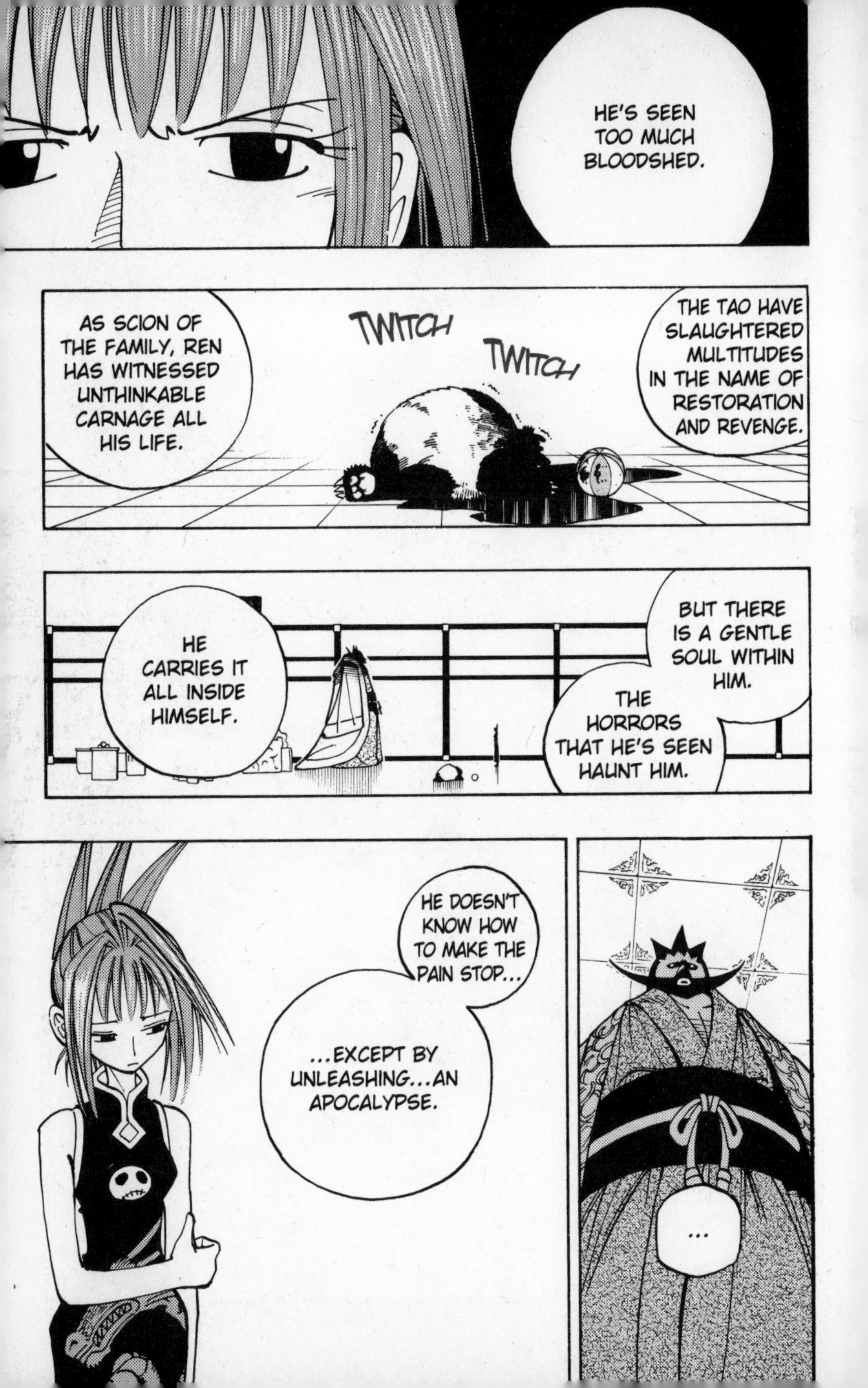
HE'S SEEN TOO MUCH BLOODSHED.
THE TAO HAVE SLAUGHTERED MULTITUDES IN THE NAME OF RESTORATION AND REVENGE.
TWITCH
TWITCH
AS SCION OF THE FAMILY, REN HAS WITNESSED UNTHINKABLE CARNAGE ALL HIS LIFE.
BUT THERE IS A GENTLE SOUL WITHIN HIM.
THE HORRORS THAT HE'S SEEN HAUNT HIM.
HE CARRIES IT ALL INSIDE HIMSELF.
...
HE DOESN'T KNOW HOW TO MAKE THE PAIN STOP...
...EXCEPT BY UNLEASHING...AN APOCALYPSE.

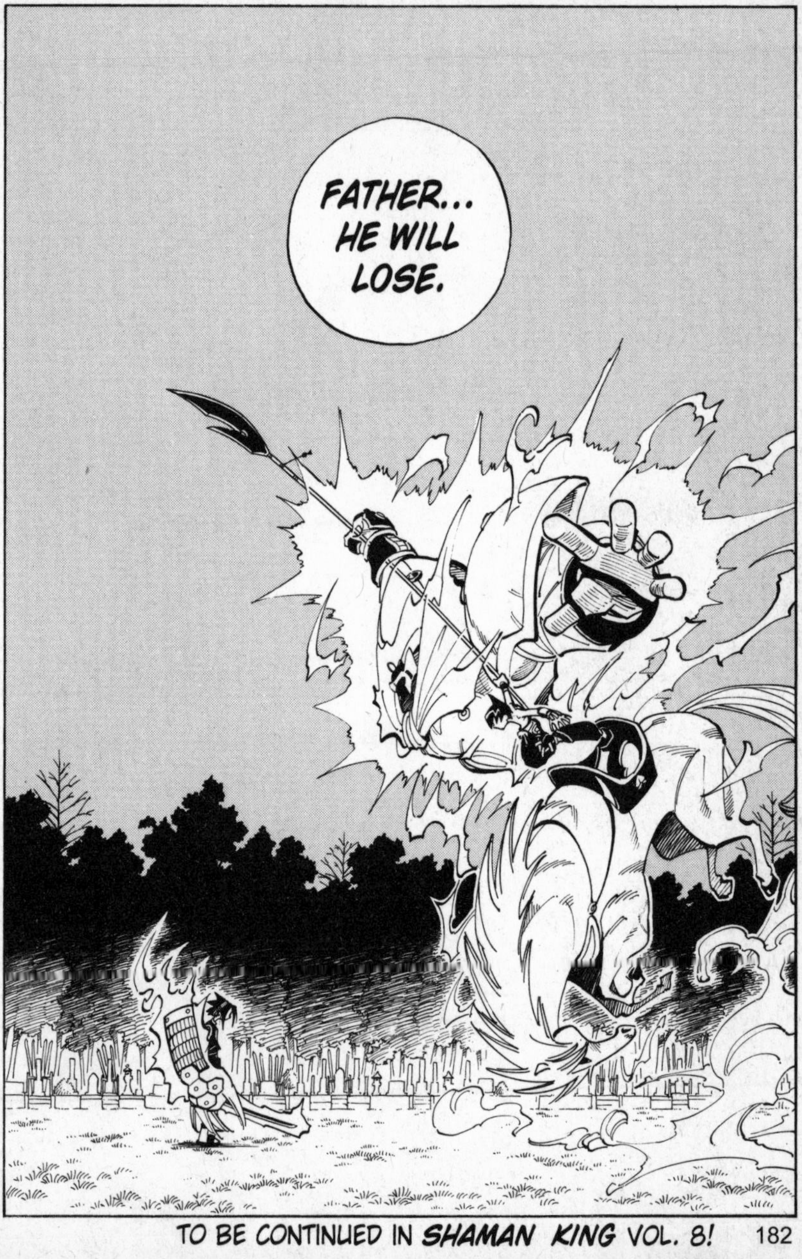
FATHER... HE WILL LOSE.

TO BE CONTINUED IN ***SHAMAN KING*** VOL. 8!

SHAMAN
KING
7

LAZY PANDA

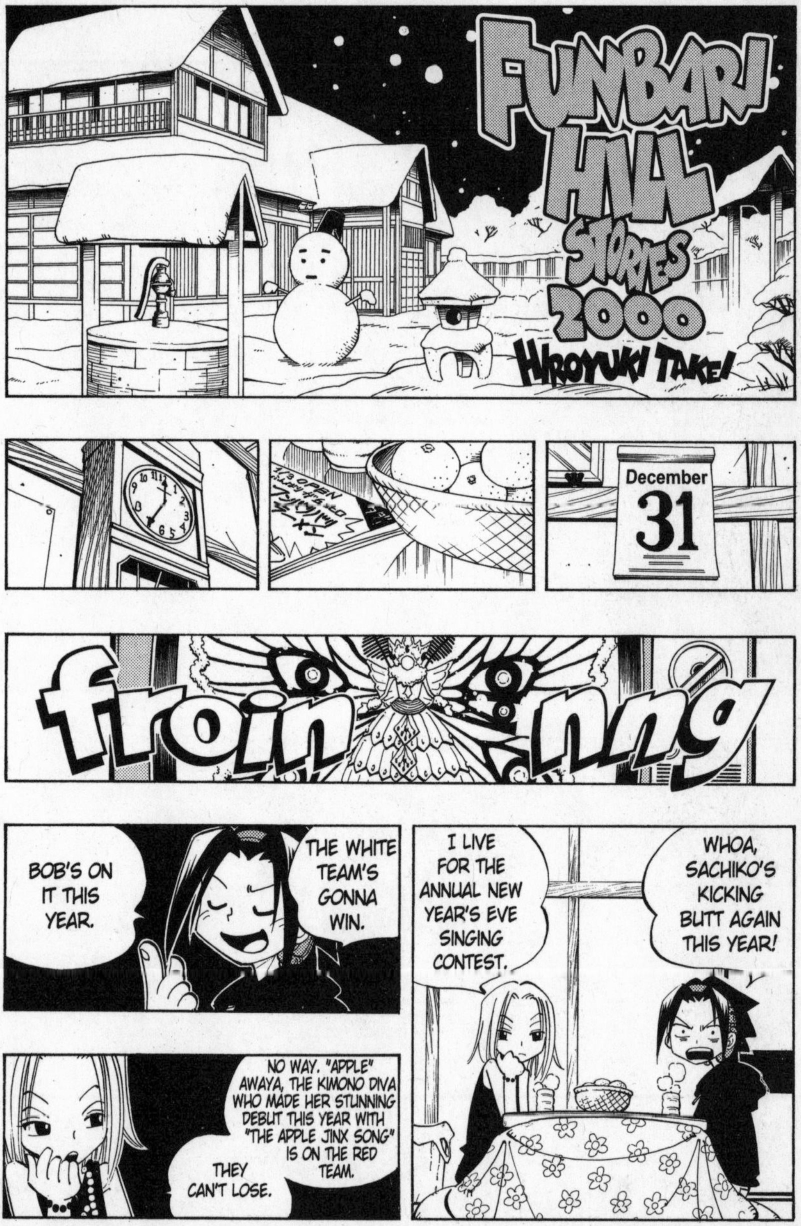
FUNBARI HILL STORIES 2000
HIROYUKI TAKEI
December
31
froin nng
WHOA, SACHIKO'S KICKING BUTT AGAIN THIS YEAR!
I LIVE FOR THE ANNUAL NEW YEAR'S EVE SINGING CONTEST.
THE WHITE TEAM'S GONNA WIN.
BOB'S ON IT THIS YEAR.
NO WAY. "APPLE" AWAYA, THE KIMONO DIVA WHO MADE HER STUNNING DEBUT THIS YEAR WITH "THE APPLE JINX SONG" IS ON THE RED TEAM.
THEY CAN'T LOSE.

READ THIS WAY

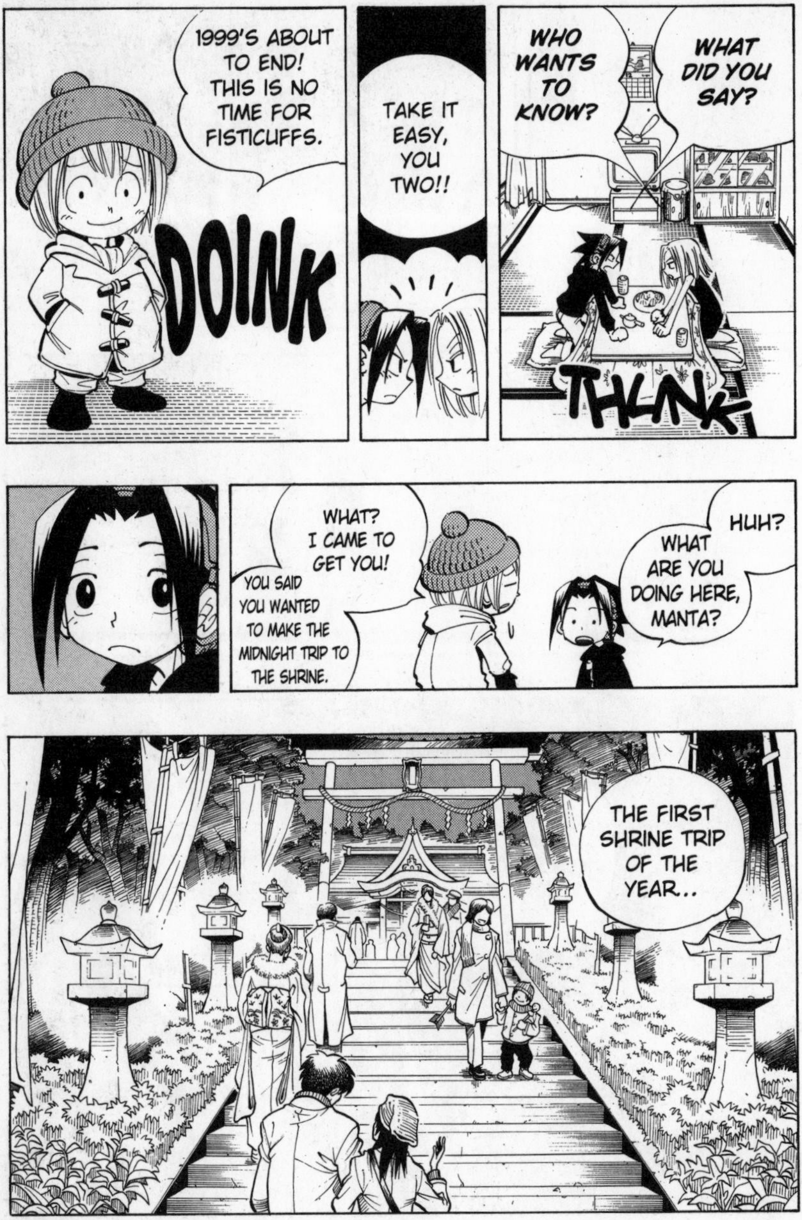

WHAT DID YOU SAY?
WHO WANTS TO KNOW?
THUNK
TAKE IT EASY, YOU TWO!!
1999'S ABOUT TO END! THIS IS NO TIME FOR FISTICUFFS.
DOINK
HUH?
WHAT ARE YOU DOING HERE, MANTA?
WHAT? I CAME TO GET YOU!
YOU SAID YOU WANTED TO MAKE THE MIDNIGHT TRIP TO THE SHRINE.
THE FIRST SHRINE TRIP OF THE YEAR...

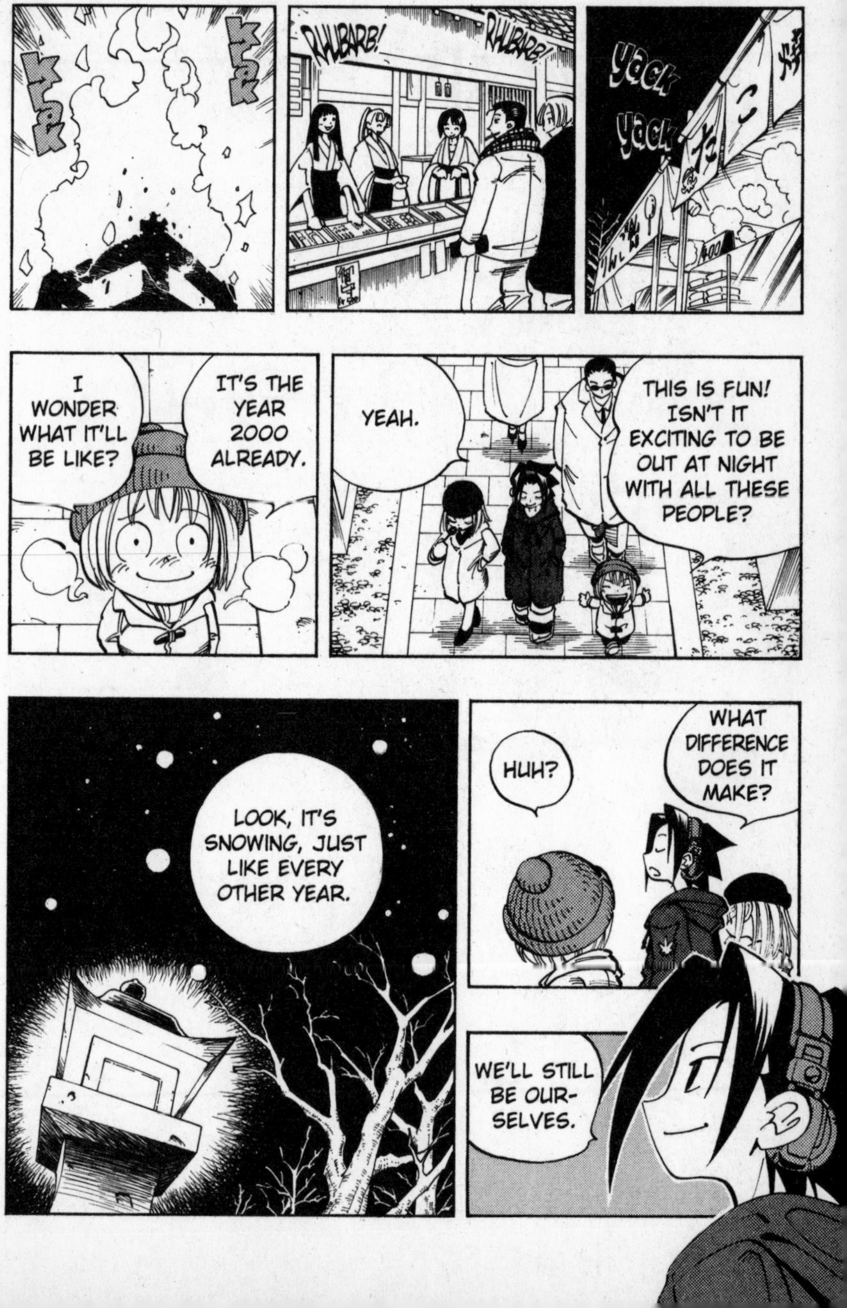
yack
yack
RHUBARB!
RHUBARB!
krak
krak
THIS IS FUN! ISN'T IT EXCITING TO BE OUT AT NIGHT WITH ALL THESE PEOPLE?
YEAH.
IT'S THE YEAR 2000 ALREADY.
I WONDER WHAT IT'LL BE LIKE?
WHAT DIFFERENCE DOES IT MAKE?
HUH?
WE'LL STILL BE OUR-SELVES.
LOOK, IT'S SNOWING, JUST LIKE EVERY OTHER YEAR.

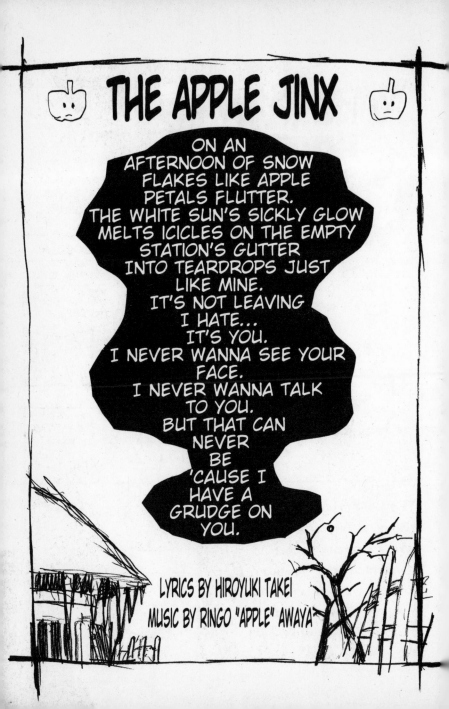

THE APPLE JINX

ON AN
AFTERNOON OF SNOW
FLAKES LIKE APPLE
PETALS FLUTTER.
THE WHITE SUN'S SICKLY GLOW
MELTS ICICLES ON THE EMPTY
STATION'S GUTTER
INTO TEARDROPS JUST
LIKE MINE.
IT'S NOT LEAVING
I HATE...
IT'S YOU.
I NEVER WANNA SEE YOUR
FACE.
I NEVER WANNA TALK
TO YOU.
BUT THAT CAN
NEVER
BE
'CAUSE I
HAVE A
GRUDGE ON
YOU.

LYRICS BY HIROYUKI TAKEI

MUSIC BY RINGO "APPLE" AWAYA

SHAMAN KING CHARACTER FILE No.32

amao: Kokkuri Angel CUPID

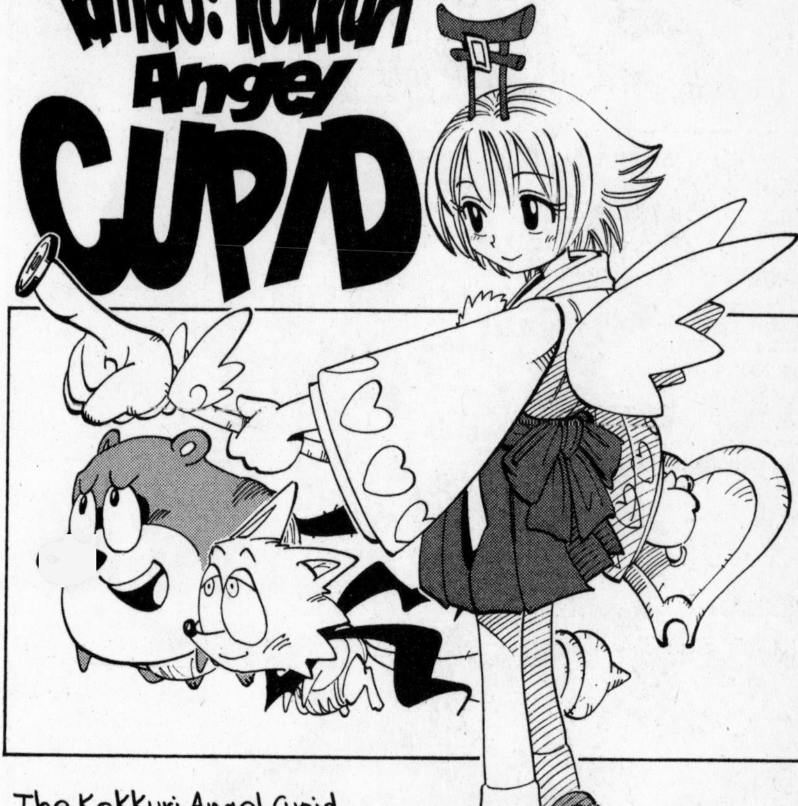

The Kokkuri Angel Cupid, the mysterious girl who controls those two adorable familiars with her super ascetic powers!! Things don't always go her way, but she won't tolerate evildoers (like "Wooden Sword" Ryu) who rampages through the world!!

BONUS MANGA

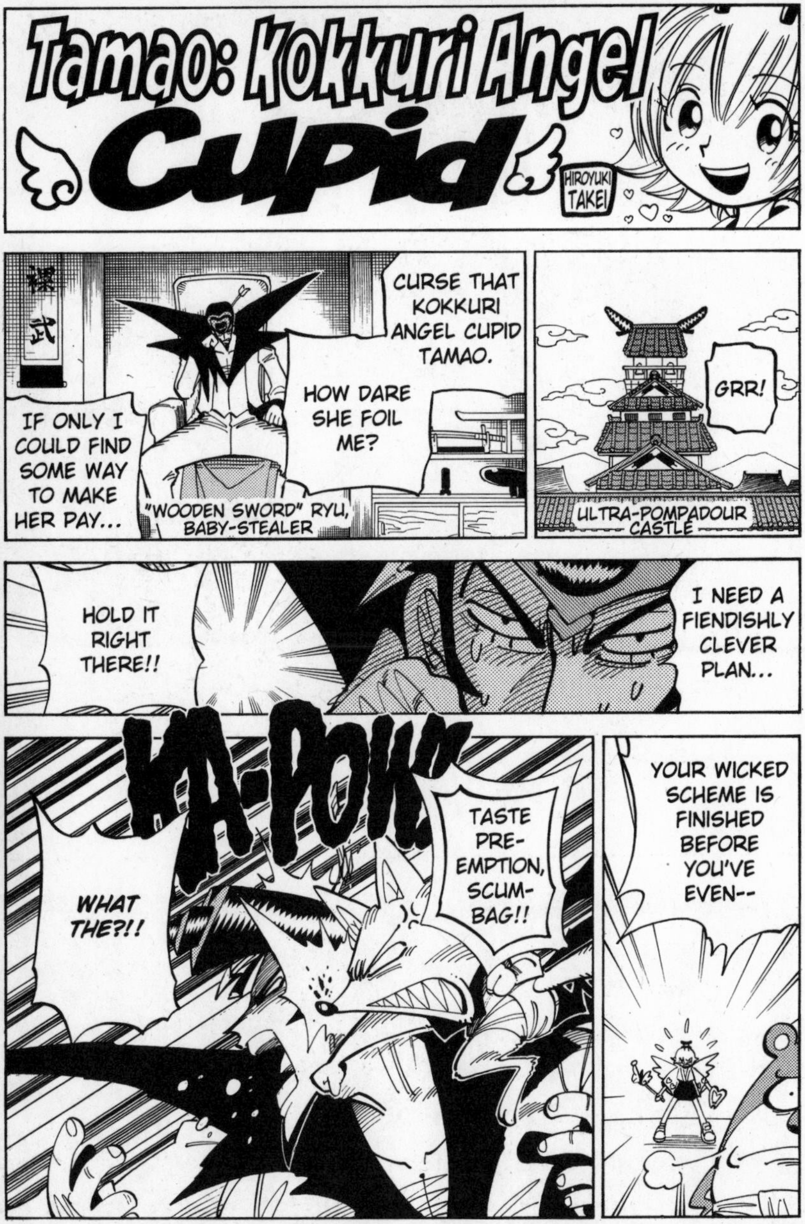
Tamao: Kokkuri Angel Cupid
HIROYUKI TAKEI
GRR!
ULTRA-POMPADOUR CASTLE
CURSE THAT KOKKURI ANGEL CUPID TAMAO.
HOW DARE SHE FOIL ME?
IF ONLY I COULD FIND SOME WAY TO MAKE HER PAY...
"WOODEN SWORD" RYU, BABY-STEALER
I NEED A FIENDISHLY CLEVER PLAN...
HOLD IT RIGHT THERE!!
YOUR WICKED SCHEME IS FINISHED BEFORE YOU'VE EVEN--
KA-POW!
TASTE PRE-EMPTION, SCUM-BAG!!
WHAT THE?!!

THE FAMILIARS HAVE DONE IT AGAIN!! BUT WHEN WILL WE GET TO SEE *TAMAO* DO SOMETHING?

← To Be Continued

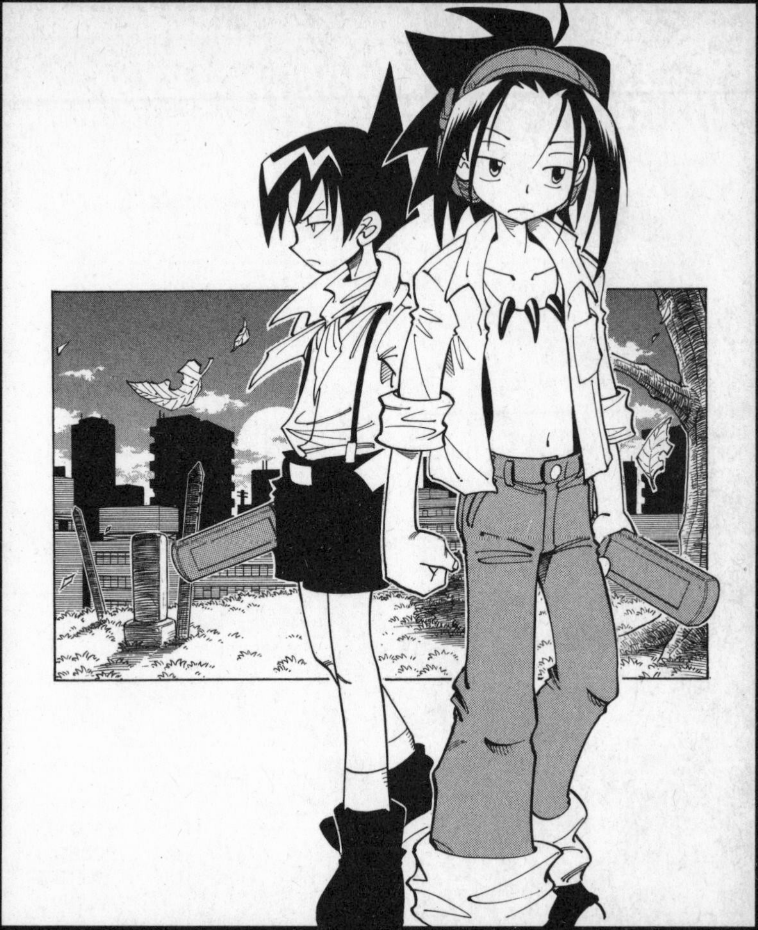

IN THE NEXT VOLUME...

In the end, Yoh takes to the hot springs to recover and Ren returns to home to China a changed shaman. After his experiences in Tokyo, Ren is determined to put an end to the Tao reign of terror. But to do so he must take down his father, the most feared shaman in China! When Ren's attack fails, it's up to Yoh to come to his enemy's rescue!

AVAILABLE JANUARY 2006!

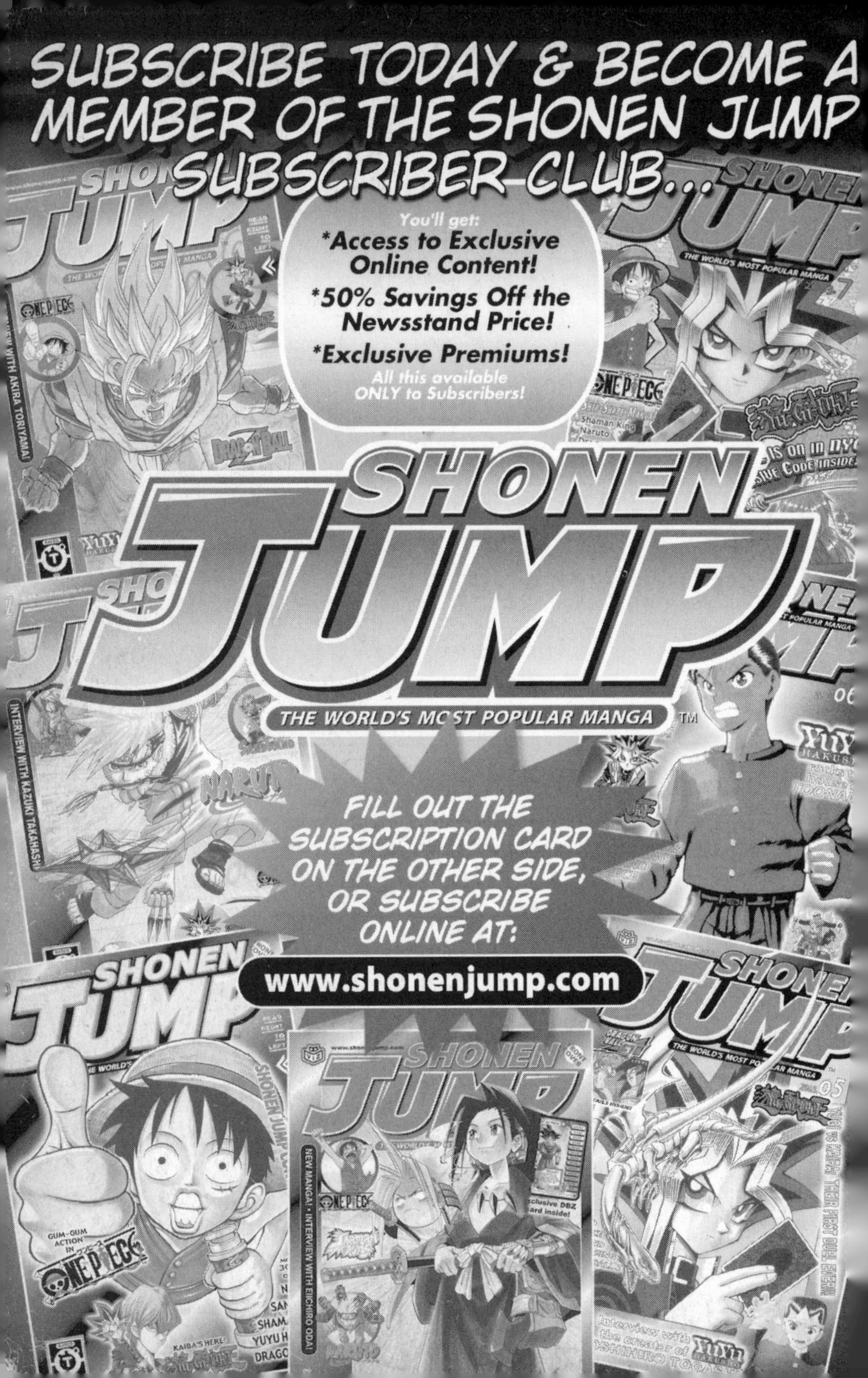

SUBSCRIBE TODAY & BECOME A MEMBER OF THE SHONEN JUMP SUBSCRIBER CLUB...
You'll get:
*Access to Exclusive Online Content!
*50% Savings Off the Newsstand Price!
*Exclusive Premiums!
All this available ONLY to Subscribers!
SHONEN JUMP
THE WORLD'S MOST POPULAR MANGA
TM
FILL OUT THE SUBSCRIPTION CARD ON THE OTHER SIDE, OR SUBSCRIBE ONLINE AT:
www.shonenjump.com